THE NEW YORK FOUNDLING HOSPITAL

An Index to Its Federal, State, and Local Census Records (1870–1925)

CAROLEE R. INSKEEP

CLEARFIELD

Printed for
Clearfield Company, Inc. by
Genealogical Publishing Co., Inc.
Baltimore, Maryland
1995

Reprinted for
Clearfield Company, Inc. by
Genealogical Publishing Co., Inc.
Baltimore, Maryland
1999, 2000, 2004

International Standard Book Number: 0-8063-4590-X

Made in the United States of America

For Steve

"In Thee my choice I do Rejoice"

CONTENTS

Introduction   i

Index to the 1870 Federal Census   1
Index to the 1880 Federal Census   4
Index to the 1890 New York City Police Census   47
Index to the 1900 Federal Census   58
Index to the 1905 New York State Census   112
Index to the 1910 Federal Census   167
Index to the 1915 New York State Census   235
Index to the 1920 Federal Census   259
Index to the 1925 New York State Census   308

INTRODUCTION

The names in this volume represent 13,000 children who lived in the New York Foundling Hospital, many of whom were sent to adoptive families in the West. They are more than statistics or lists; each name has a story to tell. The 1915 and 1920 enumerations include the name of Josephine Hefferman, who was taken to the Foundling Hospital as a baby and remained there until she was eight. In June of 1921, the Hospital placed her with an adoptive family in Wisconsin who called her Jeanette. Eventually, Josephine married and raised three daughters, but she always wanted to know who her natural parents were and whether she had siblings. She began a life-long search for information about them. Likewise, Giovanni Gerona's name appears in the 1910 enumeration. He was taken to the Foundling Hospital just a few days after his birth. At the age of two, Giovanni was sent to a childless family in North Dakota. They called him John. When he learned that he was adopted, he became bitter and angry. When Giovanni married in 1935, he turned to his new bride and told her, "For the first time in my life I have someone I can call my own and nobody can take that away." Still, questions about his biological parents dogged him.

The index begins with the 1870 Federal Enumeration of the Hospital (the first available census) and ends with the 1925 New York State Enumeration (the last available census). These census records tell us some of the story of the New York Foundling Hospital. The idea for a Roman Catholic Foundling Asylum had its inception with the Archbishop of New York, who noted that hardly a morning passed without newspapers reporting that an infant child had been found floating in the Hudson River, buried in an ash-barrel, or "flung into some lonely area." He also heard pleas for help from the Sisters of Charity of Saint Vincent de Paul, who often found infants abandoned at their mission houses or on the steps of their church. The Archbishop urged the Sisters to find a way to save neglected children.

In October of 1869, the Sisters of Charity founded their Asylum in a four-story brick house at 17 East Twelfth Street, New York City, under the leadership of Sister M. Irene. The Sisters hoped to shelter and protect infants who otherwise faced poverty, malnutrition, disease, child abuse, drugging, neglect, abandonment, and even infanticide. They hoped to help each child's mother, who was either poor, unwed, or a prostitute, to lead a life of virtue. They planned to offer her shelter and anonymity. They aspired to save her from disrepute, despair, and suicide. And when the child could not remain with its mother, the Sisters planned to place it in an adoptive home.

Opponents of the Asylum argued that such a facility would encourage parents to abandon their children or commit adultery. The Sisters believed that the need for an Asylum existed already and that the Asylum would prevent future crimes against children.

In fact, the need was so great that the Sisters of Charity began their child-saving work three months early. They planned to open the doors of the Foundling Asylum on January 1, 1870. But while they were making preparations, the first infant was abandoned at their door at dusk on October 11, 1869. The second arrived later that night, left upon the stoop during a torrential rainstorm. By the end of the month, the sisters sheltered 45 children. The first year in operation was not easy. Sister Irene remembered that the Asylum "commenced with two cups and saucers. The first morning we had to beg our breakfasts. We slept on straw on the floor...rolling the mattresses up during the day." Overcrowding, unsanitary conditions, and a high infant mortality rate finally forced the Sisters to relocate. During the Autumn of 1870, the Foundling Asylum moved to a rented four-story brick building at 3 Washington Square North. The new building was a great improvement upon the old location. It fronted Washington Square, allowing plenty of sunlight, fresh air, and access to the park.

Despite the initial difficulties, the Sisters cared for 2,560 infants in their first two years of operation, and soon the charity outgrew its accommodations. On November 1, 1873, the Foundling Asylum moved to a large, Upper East Side complex at 175 East 68th Street, filling the block bounded by Third and Lexington Avenues, and Sixty-eighth and Sixty-ninth Streets. Construction of this facility began in 1872 and continued for at least ten years. A May 1878 New York Times article describes the Asylum as consisting of a centrally located "administrative building, 99 by 60 feet, and five stories high, with a basement. In the basement are the kitchen, dining-rooms, and offices, and the cradles for the reception of infants, which, being under the archway of the high double stoop leading to the main story, are easily accessible from the street. The main story contains the chief offices, reception rooms and parlors for visitors, the community room, and an apartment for the resident physician. In the second story are the apartments for the Sisters, and the sewing and linen rooms. The third, fourth, and fifth stories contain dormitories, with an infirmary on the upper floor. The ward building, three stories high, is adjoining. It is in these elegant buildings of stone and red and white brick, that the foundlings are cared for." St. Ann's Maternity Hospital was added in 1880 and the Children's Hospital was added in 1882. The entire complex was fully wired for electricity by 1921. Just three blocks from Central Park, the Asylum featured a day nursery, kindergarten, chapel, and rooftop gardens.

The children also enjoyed a country branch at Sputen Duyvil, New York, a few miles north of the New York City border. During the 1893 National Conference of Charities and Correction, the Asylum reported that "the country branch is designed for delicate and convalescent children, and has accommodations for two hundred and fifty inmates." A second country branch was donated by the industrialist Charles M. Schwab in the summer of 1909. Located on the beach in Richmond Park, Long Island, this facility became known as the "Eurana Schwab Home" and as "St. Joseph's-by-the-Sea." During the summer months, about 500 children stayed there. The Sisters ordered construction of a school and chapel by 1925, and hoped that the construction of additional dormitories would allow them to send children to the shore year round.

The Foundling Asylum changed its name to the New York Foundling Hospital during the early 1890s. It remained at the East 68th Street location until 1958, after which the buildings were demolished and replaced by high-rise apartment buildings. The New York Foundling Hospital has since moved three times: to 1175 Third Avenue, 590 Avenue of the Americas, and, most recently, to 18 West 18th Street.

According its biennial reports, the Foundling Asylum received and cared for children in much the same way between 1869 and 1925. When a mother brought her child to the Asylum, she placed the baby in a cradle in the reception area. She gave the child's name, birthdate, and any other identifying information she wished to impart. On admission, the child was given a number, bathed, and clothed in a new outfit before being transferred to the reception room in the hospital building. The infant was then measured, weighed, and had its temperature taken. A medical examination of the head, chest, abdomen, bones, skin and blood followed. The child was immunized against diphtheria. Finally, the infant's condition was rated on a scale from one to ten: "one" meaning "very poor," and "ten" meaning "very good."

Sickly children, who could not be nursed, were spoon or bottle-fed a milk formula and remained in the Asylum. Children received in good condition were sent to be wet-nursed by women in the greater New York and New Jersey area. Representatives of the Foundling Asylum regularly inspected the living and physical condition of each child. Once a month, the wet nurse was required to bring her ward in for a physical examination. If the child was found to be in good condition, the wet nurse was paid a small sum for her trouble. Mothers coming into the institution from St. Ann's Maternity Hospital with their infants were immediately sent to the Asylum's nursery after a bath and change of clothing. These mothers remained in the Asylum at the Foundling's expense in exchange for nursing their own baby and one other infant. Mothers living in the institution to nurse babies are sometimes referred to in the census records as "Nurses," "Patients," and "Inmates."

Nursing infants between the ages of three and six months received a supplement of barley milk twice a day. Babies between the ages of six and twelve months received bread and milk twice a day, in addition to nursing. Bread, cereal, beef juice and whole milk were given to those between the ages of one and two. Those over the age of two were introduced to three meals a day. A typical menu included bread, oatmeal, and milk for breakfast; meat, potatoes, bread, a cooked vegetable, and milk for lunch; and for dinner, the children were served bread, milk and fruit. The older children took their meals in a large dining room, seated at long tables covered in oil-cloth, dining from tin cups and plates. Children who grew up in the Asylum also remember using good china and linen tablecloths on special occasions.

At the age of two, children who were nursed on the outside were placed back into the institution. In the 1881 Report of the Foundling Asylum, the Sisters reported that: "As the little ones advance in years, and approach and enter upon the age of reason, the Sisters impress upon their young minds the principles and necessity of truth, virtue, and obedience. The utmost pains are taken to accustom them to habits of order, neatness, and industry; while nothing is left undone to make the surroundings of their young lives cheerful and bright." Children who remained at the Asylum long enough also attended kindergarten and elementary classes. For recreation, the children went to Central

Park or entertained themselves at playground equipment located on the roof-top gardens. Generous patrons supplied the children with books, toys, ice cream, candy, and movies along with the necessities of food, clothing, and medical supplies. In 1923, donors included Kirkman's Soap Company (moving pictures), Bloomingdale Brothers (57 children's dresses), the Pupils of Hunter College (Christmas tree and toys), Junior Emergency Relief Society (1,000 gauze compresses), and Cushman & Company (two large trays of crullers and doughnuts every week of the year).

The Foundling Asylum's income came from several different sources. In 1923 the Asylum received $518,860.82 and supported 4,700 children (about $110.40 per child that year). Sixty-eight percent of this money came from the City of New York. The remaining thirty-two percent came from Westchester County, Nassau County, various Catholic charities, bequests, donations, investments, and fund-raising events. The primary expenditures that year went to provisions, salaries, and wet-nursing, while the remainder was generally spent on supplies. The Asylum spent over $22,000 on "Children's Traveling Expenses," the cost of sending children to families in the West. While the sources of funding and expenditure remained virtually the same between 1869 and 1925, the City of New York provided a greater proportion of the Asylum's funding in earlier years. In 1870, the City appropriated $100,000 for the Asylum on the condition that it be met with matching grants, but by 1880 the City no longer required the matching grants and supplied the Foundling with ninety-six percent of its income.

The question of what to do with the children once they had passed through infancy came up as the first foundlings reached the age of eight. New York City officials worried that the Asylum would require additional funds, while the institution itself was increasingly burdened with its growing number of residents. Following the example of the Children's Aid Society, the Foundling Asylum placed its children in permanent homes in the West and South. In the mid-1870s, the Foundling Asylum placed between two and three hundred abandoned children with families in the Maryland area. The Foundling's Silver Jubilee Report claims that by 1894, the Asylum had protected 25,697 infants and had placed ten thousand in adoptive homes (about 39%).

A look at the Foundling's 1881 Report suggests what happened to the children who never went to adoptive homes. In 1881, the Foundling Asylum supported 2,488 children. While only fourteen percent of them were placed with foster families, twenty-two percent had died, five percent were returned to their parents, and fifty-nine percent remained with the Sisters. Although the percentages change with the years, subsequent reports show that the fate of the children remained essentially the same.

For the children who were adopted by families in the West, answers to questions about the parents who left them at the Foundling Asylum are difficult to find. This quest has not only driven children like Josephine Hefferman and Giovanni Gerona, but also their descendants. Josephine began a search for her family that lasted sixty years. Not until three weeks before her death in 1994, did she learn that she was the daughter of Irish immigrants, and that she had at least three brothers. After her death, Josephine's daughters found the immigration records of their grandmother, as well as the name of the town where she came from. They planned to visit Ireland. Giovanni learned that his surname was actually "Gauna" and that his mother had him baptized at St. Anthony's Church before sending him to the Foundling Asylum. After his death in 1993, Giovanni's daughter continued the search. She has learned that the woman who sponsored her father's baptism was probably the mid-wife who delivered him. She has also learned that the name "Gauna" is endemic to Northern Italy.

Thousands of others are trying to answer similar questions. It is hoped that this volume will help them and their families.

Index to the
Federal Enumeration of the Inhabitants of

The Foundling Asylum

17 East 12th Street
New York, New York

July 2, 1870

Ward No. 15
Election District No. 10
Pages 50-52

Alfred Andrews,
Assistant Marshall and Enumerator

Guide to Column Headings

in the

1870 Federal Enumeration Index

Name   Name of each person whose usual place of abode was in this institution. Surname first, then the given name and middle initial.

R-G   Race and gender. "White" is designated by "W" and "Female" is designated by "F".

A   Age at last birthday.

Occupation   Work done by each person.

Note   Refer to the original census record for the birthplace of each adult and the birthplace of her parents. The enumerator did not make individual entries for children.

Name	R-G	A	Occupation
Chopin, Philomina	WF	32	Sister of Charity
Coolihan, Delia	WF	22	Servant
Derimple, Ewane	WF	17	Servant
Fitzgibbon, Catherine	WF	45	Sister of Charity
Gannon, Catharine	WF	17	Servant
Gerbach, Antinete	WF	40	Sister of Charity
Healy, Mary	WF	25	Servant
Hurdy, Mary	WF	22	Servant
Kingsley, Sarah	WF	35	Servant
Late, Ellen	WF	28	Servant
Lenahan, Mary	WF	21	Servant
Lynch, Bridget	WF	20	Servant
McCaffrey, May	WF	10	At School
McCristal, Jane	WF	27	Sister of Charity
McGrath, May	WF	45	Servant
Nesbit, Margaret	WF	25	Sister of Charity
O'Malley, Annie	WF	22	Servant
O'Neil, Ellen	WF	27	Servant
Oswald, Annie	WF	27	Servant
Riyes, Mary	WF	21	Servant
Rome, Eliza	WF	60	Servant
Taughan, Agnes	WF	20	Servant

34 White Female "Foundlings" born in New York
11 White Male "Foundlings" born in New York

Index to the
Federal Enumeration of the Inhabitants of

The Foundling Asylum

175 East 68th Street
New York, New York

June 1, 1880

Supervisor's District No. 1
Election District No. 594
Pages 41-74, 77-78

Thomas McManus, Enumerator

Guide to Column Headings

in the

1880 Federal Enumeration Index

Name   Name of each person whose usual place of abode was in this institution on June 1, 1880. Surname first, then the given name and middle initial.

R-G   Race and gender. White is designated by the letter "W", black by the letter "B" and Mulatto by the letters "Mu". Males are designated by the letter "M" and females are designated by the letter "F".

*   Notes that the enumerator may have listed the individual's name or gender incorrectly.

A   Age at last birthday prior to June 1, 1880. Designated in years, unless otherwise noted with an "m" for "months". Children who were less than one year old were described in terms of months.

MOB   If a child was born within the census year, the enumerator gave the month of birth.

Relation   Relationship of each person to the institution.

Note   All persons were listed as single. The birthplace of each child was listed as "New York" and birthplace of his parents was listed as "Unknown". Refer to the orginal census for the birthplace of adult occupants and their parents.

Name	R-G	A	MOB	Relation
Abbot, Charles	WM	4	-	Inmate
Abraham, Jacob	WM	7	-	Inmate
Adams, Mary A.	WF	5	-	Inmate
Addis, Thomas	WM	2	-	Inmate
Agnes, Annette	WF	1	-	Inmate
Agnes, Eloise	WF	1	-	Inmate
Agnes, Mary	WF	2	-	Inmate
Agnes, Rose	WF	1	-	Inmate
Agnes, Virginia	WF	1	-	Inmate
Agnese, James	WM	1	-	Inmate
Aid, Addie	WF	25	-	Nurse
Albert, Alfred	WM	1	-	Inmate
Alberts, Johanna	WF	18	-	Nurse
Alberts, Nellie	WF	1	-	Inmate
Albino, Louis	WM	2	-	Inmate
Aleds, William	WM	3	-	Inmate
Alexonde, Jerome	WM	5	-	Inmate
Alice, Maud	WF	1	-	Inmate
Allen, Grace	WF	2	-	Inmate
Allen, Louis	WM	10	-	Inmate
Allen, Minnie	WF	1	-	Inmate
Allen, Minnie	WF	2	-	Inmate
Allison, George	WM	1	-	Inmate
Allreston, Jon.	WM	1	-	Inmate
Allsworth, Alphonsius	WM	6	-	Inmate
Alward, Aloysius	WM	1	-	Inmate
Alward, Aloysius	WM	2	-	Inmate
Alward, Eugene	WM	1	May	Inmate
Alwood, Henry	WM	7	-	Inmate
Alword, Eugene	WM	1	-	Inmate
Ama, Phebe	WF	1	May	Inmate
Amand, Komanus	WM	1	-	Inmate
Ambriser, Sophie	WF	3	-	Inmate
Ambrose, Edward	WM	3	-	Inmate
Ambrose, Mary	WF	2	-	Inmate
Ambrose, Sophie	WF	1	-	Inmate
Anderson, Robert	WM	1	-	Inmate
Anderson, Robert	WM	2	-	Inmate
Andrew, Frank	WM	1	-	Inmate
Andrews, Anna	WF	1	-	Inmate

Andrews, Everett	WM	1	-	Inmate
Andrews, Fanny	WF	4	-	Inmate
Andrews, Louis	WM	1	-	Inmate
Angela, Anna	WF	1	-	Inmate
Angela, Anna	WF	3	-	Inmate
Angell, Electa	WF	4	-	Inmate
Angelo, Feresita	WF	2	-	Inmate
Angelo, Raphael	WM	2	-	Inmate
Anna, Phebe	WF	1	-	Inmate
Antoni, Agnatius	WM	3	-	Inmate
Anund, Romamio	WM	2	-	Inmate
Archibald, John	WM	3	-	Inmate
Arlington, Fannie	WF	2	-	Inmate
Armstrong, Elizabeth	WF	2	-	Inmate
Armstrong, Jessie	WF	2	-	Inmate
Arnold, James	WM	2	-	Inmate
Arnold, Laura	WF	18	-	Sister of Charity
Ascher, Ella Lyons	WF	3	-	Inmate
Assisium, Frank	MuM	1	-	Inmate
Asten, Edward	WM	1	-	Inmate
Astors, Fannie	WF	1	-	Inmate
Atherton, Clara	WF	4	-	Inmate
Atherton, Johnnie	WM	1	-	Inmate
Atkinson, Dryden	WM	1	-	Inmate
Aubrey, Stephen	WM	4	-	Inmate
Augusta, Agnes	WF	1	-	Inmate
Augusta, Josephine	WF	2	-	Inmate
Augusta, Sina	WF	1	May	Inmate
Augustus, Charles	WM	1	-	Inmate
Austin, Florence	MuF	2	-	Inmate
Austin, George	WM	1	-	Inmate
Austin, George	WM	3	-	Inmate
Austin, Laura	WF	1	-	Inmate
Austin, Margaret	WF	21	-	Seamstress
Avellino, Andrew	WM	2	-	Inmate
Averill, Agatha	MuF	7	-	Inmate
Aywas, Ainsetta	WF	2	-	Inmate
Baggim, Giovanina	WF	4	-	Inmate
Baggini, Alicia	WF	2	-	Inmate
Bagley, Edward	WM	4	-	Inmate
Bailey, George	WM	3	-	Inmate
Baily, Ellen	WF	18	-	Cook

Baker, Anges	WF	6m	-	Inmate
Baker, Annie	WF	6m	-	Inmate
Baker, Jane	WF	4m	Jan.	Inmate
Baldwin, Fannie	WF	1	-	Inmate
Banks, Anseton	WM	2m	Mar.	Inmate
Barker, Emma	WF	3	-	Inmate
Barker, Mary G.	WF	5	-	Inmate
Barrett, Alice	WF	1m	Apr.	Inmate
Barrett, Josephena	WF	6	-	Inmate
Barrett, Maggie	WF	18	-	Nurse
Barring, Elizabeth	WF	6m	-	Inmate
Barro, Josephine	WF	3m	Feb.	Inmate
Barter, Florence	WF	4m	Jan.	Inmate
Barton, Effie	WF	3	-	Inmate
Bartow, Joseph	WM	3	-	Inmate
Basso, John	WM	9m	-	Inmate
Baum, Lizzie	WF	4	-	Inmate
Beach, Charles	WM	2	-	Inmate
Beatrise, Angela	WF	3m	-	Inmate
Behal, Sophia	WF	22	-	Seamstress
Bell, Joseph	WM	2m	Mar.	Inmate
Bell, William	WM	2	-	Inmate
Bellamy, George	WM	1	-	Inmate
Bellows, Minnie	WF	7m	-	Inmate
Benite, Phillip	WM	2	-	Inmate
Bennara, Charles	WM	7m	-	Inmate
Bennett, Edward	WM	28	-	Laborer
Bennett, Ellen	WF	9m	-	Inmate
Bennett, William	MuM	2	-	Inmate
Benton, Benoni	WM	1	-	Inmate
Benton, Gertrude	WF	1	-	Inmate
Berconi, Joseph	WM	1	-	Inmate
Bergmann, Pauline	WF	3	-	Inmate
Bernard, Horitus	WM	2	-	Inmate
Bernardine, Cath.	WF	2	-	Inmate
Bertha, Agnes	WF	2m	Mar.	Inmate
Bertha, Celestine	WF	1m	Apr.	Inmate
Bertha, Mary	WF	6m	-	Inmate
Beudenberg, Mary W.	WF	4	-	Inmate
Beuson, Willie	WM	5	-	Inmate
Beyer, Alfred	WM	2	-	Inmate
Bield, Augusta	WF	4	-	Inmate

Binsi, Louis	WM	1m	Apr.	Inmate
Black, Dinah	MuF	2	-	Inmate
Black, Francis	WM	3m	Feb.	Inmate
Black, Terrance	WM	3	-	Inmate
Blake, Maggie	WF	10	-	Inmate
Blanche, Teresa	WF	1	-	Inmate
Blauchete, Jessie	WF	4	-	Inmate
Blender, Henry	WM	1	-	Inmate
Bloom, William	WM	3	-	Inmate
Bootham, Mary	WF	6	-	Inmate
Borden, Annie	WF	19	-	Nurse
Borden, William	WM	2	-	Inmate
Bossomby, Mary	WF	4	-	Inmate
Boucher, John	WM	3	-	Inmate
Bough, John Thomas	WM	3	-	Inmate
Bowder, Fannie	WF	1	-	Inmate
Bower, Allen	WM	1	-	Inmate
Boylan, John	WM	3	-	Inmate
Boyle, Annie	WF	1	-	Inmate
Boyle, Ella	WF	35	-	Sister of Charity
Boyle, Mary	WF	6m	-	Inmate
Boyle, Thomas	WM	3m	Mar.	Inmate
Bradford, Harry	WM	5	-	Inmate
Bradshaw, Margaret	WF	20	-	Nurse
Bradshaw, Matthew	WM	6m	-	Inmate
Bradshaw, Teresa	WF	1	-	Inmate
Brady, Joseph	WM	2	-	Inmate
Brady, Mary	WF	4	-	Inmate
Brady, Thomas	WM	5	-	Inmate
Brainigan, John	WM	9m	-	Inmate
Braudon, John	WM	4	-	Inmate
Bray, Anna	WF	5	-	Inmate
Breen, Thomas	WM	31	-	Carpenter
Breman, Rosie	WF	2m	Mar.	Inmate
Brennan, Ida	WF	3	-	Inmate
Brennan, Julia	WF	18	-	Nurse
Breslin, John T.	WM	8	-	Inmate
Breslin, Kate	WF	19	-	Nurse
Bressingham, Willie	WM	6	-	Inmate
Brice, Virginia	WF	3	-	Inmate
Brickman, Antonia	WM*	6	-	Inmate
Broderick, Richard	WM	4	-	Inmate

Bronze, Katie	WF	16	-	Nurse
Broody, Alonzo	WM	5	-	Inmate
Brookman, James	WM	2m	Mar.	Inmate
Brooks, Rosalie	MuF	3	-	Inmate
Broun, Delia	WF	16	-	Nurse
Brousean, Joseph	WM	1	-	Inmate
Brousen, Willie	WM	6	-	Inmate
Brousseau, Victoria	WF	19	-	Nurse
Brower, Annina	WF	4	-	Inmate
Brown, Agnes	WF	7	-	Inmate
Brown, Elizabeth	WF	17	-	Nurse
Brown, George	WM	9m	-	Inmate
Brown, Jacob	WM	4	-	Inmate
Brown, James	WM	1	-	Inmate
Brown, Lillie	WF	1	-	Inmate
Brown, Linda	WF	3	-	Inmate
Brown, Lizzie	WF	4	-	Inmate
Brown, Mary Jane	WF	6	-	Inmate
Brown, Mary	WF	1m	Apr.	Inmate
Brown, May C.	WF	3	-	Inmate
Brown, Minnie	WF	1	-	Inmate
Brown, Samuel	WM	2	-	Inmate
Browne, Carrie	WF	4	-	Inmate
Bruoer, John	WM	3	-	Inmate
Bryant, William	WM	3m	Feb.	Inmate
Bryson, Harold	WM	1	-	Inmate
Bryson, Mary Ellen	WF	3	-	Inmate
Buckly, Harry	WM	2	-	Inmate
Budd, Alexander	WM	1	-	Inmate
Bukett, Mary A.	WF	1	-	Inmate
Burke, John	WM	1	-	Inmate
Burke, Lizzie	WF	5	-	Inmate
Burke, Mary	WF	17	-	Nurse
Burke, Mary	WF	21	-	Nurse
Burke, Teresa	WF	18	-	Nurse
Burkel, Nettie	WF	3m	Feb.	Inmate
Burnell, Alfred	WM	3	-	Inmate
Burnes, Agnes	WF	2	-	Inmate
Burnes, Lizzie	WF	1	-	Inmate
Burno, Alpheus	WM	2m	Mar.	Inmate
Burrows, Rosa	WF	2	-	Inmate
Burton, George	WM	1	-	Inmate

Burton, Joseph	WM	2	-	Inmate
Burus, Sara	WF	3	-	Inmate
Bush, Elenora	WF	3	-	Inmate
Bush, Ellen	WF	26	-	Nurse
Busteed, Margaret	WF	18	-	Nurse
Bustiva, Mary	WF	6m	Feb.	Inmate
Butler, Annie	WF	1	-	Inmate
Butler, James	WM	1	-	Inmate
Butler, Richard	WM	6m	-	Inmate
Butler, Thomas	WM	1	-	Inmate
Butler, Willie	WM	4	-	Inmate
Butts, Augustin	WM	1	-	Inmate
Byrne, Annie	WF	4	-	Inmate
Byrne, Jane	WF	3	-	Inmate
Byron, Mary P.	WF	6	-	Inmate
Calahan, Jane	WF	2	-	Inmate
Callahan, Louis	WM	5	-	Inmate
Campbell, John	WM	9	-	Inmate
Campbell, Sarah	WF	20	-	Nurse
Cantelle, David	WM	-	Apr.	Inmate
Cantwell, Annie	WF	11m	-	Inmate
Cardale, Johnie	WM	1	-	Inmate
Carlin, Mary	WF	19	-	Nurse
Carlisle, Georgina	WF	5	-	Inmate
Carlton, Edwin	WM	1	-	Inmate
Carmichael, John	WM	-	Apr.	Inmate
Caroline, Mary	WF	1	-	Inmate
Caroline, Zeta	WF	-	Apr.	Inmate
Carpenter, Katie	WF	-	Apr.	Inmate
Carr, Annie	WF	1	-	Inmate
Carr, Mary E.	WF	2	-	Inmate
Carroll, Claudine	WF	1	-	Inmate
Carroll, John	WM	2	-	Inmate
Carroll, Rachel	WF	35	-	Sister of Charity
Carroll, Rose	WF	2	-	Inmate
Carter, Henry	WM	-	Mar.	Inmate
Cartur, Delia	WF	2	-	Inmate
Casey, Walter	WM	10m	-	Inmate
Casey, Willie	WM	1	-	Inmate
Cass, Mary	WF	1	-	Inmate
Cassidy, John	WM	5	-	Inmate
Casy, Richard	WM	11m	-	Inmate

Caulford, John	WM	2	-	Inmate
Cavanagh, Daniel	WM	1	-	Inmate
Cecilia, Alice	WF	-	Apr.	Inmate
Cecilia, Susan	WF	6m	-	Inmate
Cee, William	WM	4	-	Inmate
Cendin, Mary	WF	6m	-	Inmate
Chapman, John	WM	1	-	Inmate
Charity, Vincent	WM	6m	-	Inmate
Charles, David	WM	-	Mar.	Inmate
Charles, John	WM	6m	-	Inmate
Charles, John	WM	1	-	Inmate
Charleston, James	WM	5	-	Inmate
Chase, John	WM	1	-	Inmate
Chester, Bernard	WM	1	-	Inmate
Chiles, Margaret	WF	2	-	Inmate
Chillict, Thomas	WM	5	-	Inmate
Christi, Aloysius	WM	2	-	Inmate
Christie, Mary	WF	3	-	Inmate
Christopher, Pascoe	WM	10m	-	Inmate
Cinden, Annie	WF	-	Mar.	Inmate
Clarence, Joseph	WM	2	-	Inmate
Clarendon, Arthur	WM	2	-	Inmate
Clark, Alice	WF	2	-	Inmate
Clark, Anne	WF	-	Mar.	Inmate
Clark, Annie	WF	-	May	Inmate
Clark, Charles	WM	10m	-	Inmate
Clark, Ida	WF	6m	-	Inmate
Clark, Margaret	WF	22	-	Laundress
Clark, Robert	WM	4	-	Inmate
Clark, Willie	WM	1	-	Inmate
Cleary, Eddie	WM	2	-	Inmate
Cleary, Mary	WF	1	-	Inmate
Clement, John	WM	5	-	Inmate
Cliffont, Fannie	WF	-	Apr.	Inmate
Cliggert, Lizzie	WF	2	-	Inmate
Cline, Rose A.	WF	4	-	Inmate
Clinto, Joseph	WM	8	-	Inmate
Cobot, Sebastian	WM	11m	-	Inmate
Coffee, Mary	WF	22	-	Sister of Charity
Coffey, Alpheus	WM	2	-	Inmate
Cole, Harry	WM	2	-	Inmate
Cole, Jane	WF	6m	-	Inmate

Coleman, John	WM	-	Apr.	Inmate
Coleman, Joseph	WM	10	-	Inmate
Coleman, Mary	WF	2	-	Inmate
Coley, Mary	WF	4	-	Inmate
Colgan, Joseph	WM	1	-	Inmate
Collard, Edward	WM	4	-	Inmate
Collins, Charlie	WM	4	-	Inmate
Collins, Frances	WF	2	-	Inmate
Collins, James	WM	60	-	Watchman
Collins, Lizzie	WF	18	-	Nurse
Collins, Louise	WF	1	-	Inmate
Colon, John	WM	5	-	Inmate
Colter, Edith M.	WF	5	-	Inmate
Colver, Willie	WM	2	-	Inmate
Compton, Charles	WM	-	May	Inmate
Compton, Daisy	WF	17	-	Nurse
Concepto, Marie	WF	1	-	Inmate
Condy, Annie	WF	35	-	Sister of Charity
Condy, Mary	WF	21	-	Sister of Charity
Connolly, Edward	WM	4	-	Inmate
Connolly, Thomas	WM	11m	-	Inmate
Conrad, Emile	WM	4	-	Inmate
Conran, Alice	WF	2	-	Inmate
Constantius, Irene	WF	-	Feb.	Inmate
Conway, Loretto	WF	1	-	Inmate
Conway, Maria	WF	19	-	Nurse
Cook, George	WM	6	-	Inmate
Cook, Lizzie	WF	-	Mar.	Inmate
Cooney, John H.	WM	2	-	Inmate
Cooper, Allice	WF	4	-	Inmate
Corbet, Annie	WF	4	-	Inmate
Corbet, John	WM	-	Mar.	Inmate
Corciran, Jane	WF	11m	-	Inmate
Corcoran, Ellen	WF	18	-	Seamstress
Corcoran, Nellie	WF	1	-	Inmate
Cordin, Augustin	WM	5	-	Inmate
Cornell, Etta	WF	1	-	Inmate
Cornell, Frank	WM	1	-	Inmate
Cornell, Mary	WF	4	-	Inmate
Corrigan, Mary	WF	6	-	Inmate
Corsini, Andrew	WM	6	-	Inmate
Cosgrove, Delia	WF	25	-	Nurse

Cosgrove, Mary	WF	2	-	Inmate
Cosingor, Helena	WF	5	-	Inmate
Costa, John J.	WM	1	-	Inmate
Costel, James	WM	11m	-	Inmate
Costello, Edward	WM	4	-	Inmate
Costello, Maria	WF	21	-	Seamstress
Coulan, James	WM	1	-	Inmate
Cowan, Josephine	WF	11m	-	Inmate
Cowden, Mabel	WF	10m	-	Inmate
Cowden, Mary	WF	19	-	Nurse
Cox, Thomas	WM	5	-	Inmate
Coyle, Annie E.	WF	-	Mar.	Inmate
Coyle, May B.	WF	2	-	Inmate
Coyne, Christopher	WM	2	-	Inmate
Crawford, Willie	WM	-	May	Inmate
Credon, Maggie	WF	20	-	Nurse
Creighton, Maggie	WF	25	-	Sister of Charity
Croak, Mary	WF	23	-	Sister of Charity
Crop, Annie	WF	35	-	Sister of Charity
Crosby, Charles	WM	6m	-	Inmate
Cullin, James	WM	2	-	Inmate
Cunming, Mamie	WF	5	-	Inmate
Cunningham, Jane	WF	2	-	Inmate
Cunningham, Mary	WF	-	Feb.	Inmate
Curran, Katie	WF	1	-	Inmate
Curtis, Alma	WF	1	-	Inmate
Custello, Kate	WF	30	-	Nurse
Cutting, Mary	WF	2	-	Inmate
Dagan, Alice	WF	-	May	Inmate
Daley, John	WM	2	-	Inmate
Daley, Mary F.	WF	5	-	Inmate
Daley, Mary F.	WF	18	-	Seamstress
Daley, Rose	WF	22	-	Sister of Charity
Dalong, Agness	WF	3	-	Inmate
Dalrymple, Lizzie	WF	3	-	Inmate
Dalton, Chester	WM	3	-	Inmate
Dannigan, Annie	WF	3	-	Inmate
Davenport, Charles	WM	5	-	Inmate
Davie, Arn [illegible] d	WM	1	-	Inmate
Davis, Barbara	WF	1m	Apr.	Inmate
Davis, Bridget	WF	8	-	Inmate
Davis, Charlie	WM	4m	Feb.	Inmate

Davis, Stella	WF	10	-	Inmate
Deats, David	WM	3m	Mar.	Inmate
Decker, Flora M.	WF	5	-	Inmate
DeKaven, Lucy	WF	2	-	Inmate
Delany, Henry	WM	4	-	Inmate
Delfini, Francis	WM	3m	Mar.	Inmate
Delmar, Willie	WM	1	-	Inmate
Dennin, Sophia	WF	6	-	Inmate
Denville, Adele	WF	4	-	Inmate
Derby, Maud	WF	2	-	Inmate
Derwent, Maud	WF	2	-	Inmate
Derwin, George	WM	1	-	Inmate
Desmond, Lizzie	WF	5	-	Inmate
Develin, Joseph	WM	11m	-	Inmate
Devisey, Maria	WF	9m	-	Inmate
Devlin, Francis	WM	4	-	Inmate
Dickson, Maggie	WF	2	-	Inmate
Dinin, James	WM	5	-	Inmate
Dixon, George	BM	2	-	Inmate
Dodge, Edward	WM	9m	-	Inmate
Doherty, Mary	WF	18	-	Nurse
Dolan, Annie	WF	2	-	Inmate
Dolan, Joseph	WM	2	-	Inmate
Dolan, Mary	WF	2	-	Inmate
Dolen, Lizzie	WF	5	-	Inmate
Donaldson, Jane	WF	2	-	Inmate
Donavan, Joseph	WM	-	May	Inmate
Donlan, John J.	WM	3	-	Inmate
Donnelly, Mary	WF	2	-	Inmate
Donnin, Mary	WF	2	-	Inmate
Donnolly, Joseph	WM	4m	Feb.	Inmate
Donnolly, May	WF	6	-	Inmate
Donnolly, Peter	WM	1	-	Inmate
Donohue, Catharine	WF	2	-	Inmate
Doran, John	WM	3m	Mar.	Inmate
Dormally, Robert	WM	4	-	Inmate
Dorson, Willie	WM	5	-	Inmate
Dosseldorf, Ismina	WF	6	-	Inmate
Doughlass, Florense	WF	4	-	Inmate
Dover, Frances	WF	1	-	Inmate
Downey, Nellie	WF	11m	-	Inmate
Downing, James	WM	6	-	Inmate

Downs, Kate	WF	19	-	Nurse
Doyle, Cornelius	WM	5	-	Inmate
Doyle, Katie	WF	5	-	Inmate
Draper, Frank	WM	2	-	Inmate
Drew, Joseph	WM	1	-	Inmate
Drew, Joseph	WM	2	-	Inmate
Driscoll, Sarini	WF	4	-	Inmate
Druny, John	WM	4	-	Inmate
Dsumgold, George	WM	5	-	Inmate
Duff, John	WM	3	-	Inmate
Duffy, Annie	WF	20	-	Nurse
Duffy, Elmo	WM	2	-	Inmate
Duffy, Frank	WM	4	-	Inmate
Duffy, George	WM	11m	-	Inmate
Duffy, Katie	WF	2	-	Inmate
Duffy, Mary	WF	2m	Apr.	Inmate
Dugan, John	WM	2	-	Inmate
Dugan, Lucy	WF	9m	-	Inmate
Duggan, Kate	WF	20	-	Nurse
Dundass, Thomas	WM	2	-	Inmate
Dunmore, Annie	WF	1	-	Inmate
Dunmore, Hendry	WM	3	-	Inmate
Dunn, Anne	WF	26	-	Laundress
Dunn, Mary	WF	18	-	Nurse
Dunnigan, Maggie	WF	2	-	Inmate
Dunreath, Oscar	WM	2	-	Inmate
Dupuy, Robert	WM	4	-	Inmate
Dyer, Theodore	WM	11m	-	Inmate
Dykeman, Chester	WM	2	-	Inmate
Eagle, Harriet	WF	2	-	Inmate
Edle, Isabella	WF	18	-	Nurse
Edle, Richard	WM	1	-	Inmate
Edmond, John	WM	4m	-	Inmate
Edward, Germanus	WM	4	-	Inmate
Edward, Harry	WM	1	-	Inmate
Edwards, Alice	WF	6m	-	Inmate
Edwards, Charles	WM	2m	Apr.	Inmate
Edwards, Charles	WM	1	-	Inmate
Edwards, Clarence	WM	1	-	Inmate
Edwards, Frank	WM	1	-	Inmate
Edwards, Josephine	WF	2	-	Inmate
Edwards, Mary	WF	22	-	Nurse

Edwards, Patrick	WM	1	-	Inmate
Edwards, William	WM	2	-	Inmate
Eichler, Carl	WM	5m	Jan.	Inmate
Eilinger, Charles	WM	2	-	Inmate
Elizabeth, Annie	WF	4m	May	Inmate
Elizabeth, Fannie	WF	9m	-	Inmate
Elizabeth, Mary Jane	WF	6m	-	Inmate
Elliott, William	WM	2	-	Inmate
Elltard, Francis	WM	4	-	Inmate
Elroy, Eveline	WF	2	-	Inmate
Elton, Frank	WM	1	-	Inmate
Elton, Louisa	WF	2	-	Inmate
Elton, Madeleine	WF	1	-	Inmate
Ely, Mary	WF	2	-	Inmate
Ely, Smith B.	WM	2	-	Inmate
Emers, Clarissa	WF	4m	-	Inmate
Endiman, Sarah	WF	4	-	Inmate
England, Jennie	WF	1	-	Inmate
Enwright, Edward	WM	9m	-	Inmate
Enwright, Mary	WF	25	-	Nurse
Esson, Jerometa	WF	1	-	Inmate
Estelle, Marie	WF	1	-	Inmate
Eustace, Willie	WM	1	-	Inmate
Eva, Magdalena	WF	4m	-	Inmate
Eva, Vincentia	WF	11m	-	Inmate
Evans, Frank	WM	4	-	Inmate
Evans, Harry	WM	1	-	Inmate
Evans, Mary F.	WF	1	-	Inmate
Evens, Thomas	WM	5	-	Inmate
Evers, Elizabeth	WF	4	-	Inmate
Fagan, Mary	WF	6	-	Inmate
Fairchild, Eva	WF	35	-	Nurse
Fairchild, Eve. E.	MuF	-	Jan.	Inmate
Fairelly, Kate	WF	18	-	Nurse
Falkland, Ida F.	WF	4	-	Inmate
Farley, Elizabeth	WF	18	-	Seamstress
Farley, Mary E.	WF	7m	-	Inmate
Farning, Rose	WF	1	-	Inmate
Farrell, William	WM	4	-	Inmate
Farrelly, Thomas	WM	1	-	Inmate
Faster, Allice	WF	-	Jan.	Inmate
Fay, James	WM	-	Feb.	Inmate

Fay, Susan	WF	-	Apr.	Inmate
Felt, Johnnie	WM	3	-	Inmate
Fennerly, Thomas	WM	1	-	Inmate
Fern, Andrew	WM	-	Feb.	Inmate
Fernbach, Martha	WF	2	-	Inmate
Ferris, Mary	WF	-	Feb.	Inmate
Ferris, Sarah	WF	22	-	Seamstress
Ferris, Willie	WM	3	-	Inmate
Fisher, Nellie	WF	11m	-	Inmate
Fitz, Daniel	WM	4	-	Inmate
Fitzgibbon, Catharine	WF	50	-	Sister of Charity
Fitzhenry, Frank	WM	5	-	Inmate
Fitzpatrick, Ellie	WF	1	-	Inmate
Fitzpatrick, Julia	WF	21	-	Laundress
Fitzpatrick, Katie	WF	8	-	Inmate
Fitzpatrick, Mary	WF	6	-	Inmate
Fitzpatrick, Thomas	WM	2	-	Inmate
Fitzpatrick, William	WM	1	-	Inmate
Fletcher, Grace	WF	-	May	Inmate
Fletcher, Joseph	WM	4	-	Inmate
Fletcher, Maggie	WF	1	-	Inmate
Flood, John J.	WM	1	-	Inmate
Florence, Ethel	WF	4m	-	Inmate
Florence, Lizzie	WF	-	-	Inmate
Florens, Otto	WM	-	Mar.	Inmate
Flynn, Annie	WF	1	-	Inmate
Flynn, Ellen	WF	3	-	Inmate
Flynn, Frank	WM	4	-	Inmate
Flynn, Maggie	WF	4	-	Inmate
Flynn, Walworth	WM	2	-	Inmate
Foley, James	WM	5	-	Inmate
Foly, Ellen	WF	11m	-	Inmate
Foly, Mary	WF	11m	-	Inmate
Forbes, Sylvester	WM	-	Jan.	Inmate
Foreman, Lizzie	WF	4	-	Inmate
Forst, Annie	WF	2	-	Inmate
Fory, Irmini	WF	2	-	Inmate
Foster, Thomas	WM	2	-	Inmate
Frances, Aloysius	WM	1	-	Inmate
Frances, Augusta	WF	3	-	Inmate
Frances, Edith	WF	-	Apr.	Inmate
Frances, Edward	WM	1	-	Inmate

Frances, Harry E.	WM	4	-	Inmate
Frances, Mary	WF	-	Jan.	Inmate
Frances, Mary	WF	1	-	Inmate
Frances, Mary	WF	7m	-	Inmate
Francis, David	WM	11m	-	Inmate
Francis, Edward	WM	2	-	Inmate
Francis, George	WM	6	-	Inmate
Francis, Henry	WM	3	-	Inmate
Francis, John	WM	2	-	Inmate
Francis, Joseph	WM	-	Apr.	Inmate
Francis, Joseph	WM	7m	-	Inmate
Franklin, Edgar	WM	4m	-	Inmate
Franses, Cecilia	WF	7m	-	Inmate
Fraser, Samuel A.	MuM	1	-	Inmate
Freeman, Sarah	WF	11m	-	Inmate
Freemon, James	WM	2	-	Inmate
Friah, Elsie	WF	6	-	Inmate
Frurbier, Henrietta	WF	11m	-	Inmate
Fuller, Joseph	WM	-	May	Inmate
Fuller, Mary	WF	20	-	Nurse
Furgursen, John	WM	1	-	Inmate
Furlong, Eusebins	WM	4	-	Inmate
Fury, John	WM	4	-	Inmate
Gaffney, Catharine	WF	18	-	Nurse
Gaffney, Irene	WF	2	-	Inmate
Gaffney, John	WM	-	Jan.	Inmate
Gale, Emma	WF	2	-	Inmate
Gallagher, Lillie	WF	1	-	Inmate
Galoom, Kate	WF	20	-	Cook
Gardner, Freddie	WM	8m	-	Inmate
Garnar, Agnes	WF	2	-	Inmate
Garnar, Baptista	WF	2	-	Inmate
Gate, Paul	WM	7	-	Inmate
Gaunter, James	WM	8	-	Inmate
Geary, James	WM	6	-	Inmate
Gee, Rose Mary	WF	2	-	Inmate
George, Clement	WM	5m	-	Inmate
George, Fred	WM	2	-	Inmate
George, Gertrude	WF	8m	-	Inmate
George, John	WM	8m	-	Inmate
Georgina, Laura	WF	-	Apr.	Inmate
Germem, Kate	WF	-	Jan.	Inmate

Ghellian, Ida	WF	-	May	Inmate
Gill, Annie	WF	22	-	Sister of Charity
Gill, Mary	WF	23	-	Sister of Charity
Gillen, Willie	WM	5m	-	Inmate
Gillespie, John	WM	2	-	Inmate
Gilligan, Bridget	WF	20	-	Nurse
Gilligan, Hattie	WF	1	-	Inmate
Gilliland, Frank	WM	-	Apr.	Inmate
Gillmarks, Paul	WM	5m	-	Inmate
Gilmore, Thomas	WM	2	-	Inmate
Gilmorten, Winifred	WF	30	-	Laundress
Girard, Eugene	WM	5	-	Inmate
Glashoff, Hugo	WM	-	May	Inmate
Gleason, George	WM	4	-	Inmate
Goff, Agnes	WF	6	-	Inmate
Goldsmith, Edwin	WM	-	May	Inmate
Goldsmith, James	WM	11m	-	Inmate
Goldsmith, Marie	WF	4	-	Inmate
Goodman, Elizabeth	WF	3	-	Inmate
Goodwin, Lionel	WM	8m	-	Inmate
Gordon, Anna	WF	2	-	Inmate
Gorman, John	WM	11m	-	Inmate
Gourand, Thomas	WM	3	-	Inmate
Grace, Ada	WF	-	May	Inmate
Grace, Ada	WF	11m	-	Inmate
Grady, James	WM	1	-	Inmate
Graham, Isaac	WM	11m	-	Inmate
Graham, Robert	WM	5	-	Inmate
Graham, Willie	WM	4	-	Inmate
Gray, Charles	WM	4	-	Inmate
Gray, Louise	WF	5	-	Inmate
Gray, Mary	WF	4	-	Inmate
Green, Andrew	WM	1	-	Inmate
Green, Johnnie	WM	-	Feb.	Inmate
Greene, Mary	WF	19	-	Nurse
Greenragh, Dellia	WF	2	-	Inmate
Greenwood, Grase	WF	11m	-	Inmate
Grees, Marion	WF	-	Mar.	Inmate
Grevelle, Esther	WF	2	-	Inmate
Grey, James A.	WM	2	-	Inmate
Grey, Mary	WF	-	May	Inmate
Grey, Minnie	WF	8m	-	Inmate

Grey, Nellie	WF	8m	-	Inmate
Grey, Otto	WM	1	-	Inmate
Grey, Peter	WM	1	-	Inmate
Griffin, Margaret	WF	22	-	Sister of Charity
Griswold, Jasper	WM	11m	-	Inmate
Grossman, Pauline	WF	2	-	Inmate
Gruword, Augusta	WF	4	-	Inmate
Guilford, John	WM	2	-	Inmate
Guyer, Charles	WM	2	-	Inmate
Guyer, Jeanette	WF	2	-	Inmate
Haffner, Grace	WF	1	-	Inmate
Hairison, Andrew	WM	11m	-	Inmate
Hall, Gereldine	WF	1	-	Inmate
Hamil, Alexander	WM	3	-	Inmate
Hamil, Mary	WF	5	-	Inmate
Hamilton, Annie	WF	3	-	Inmate
Hamilton, Magdeline	WF	10m	-	Inmate
Hammell, Mary	WF	10	-	Inmate
Hanathan, Agnes	WF	1	-	Inmate
Hanley, Joseph	WM	5	-	Inmate
Hanly, Katie	WF	3	-	Inmate
Hannanay, Mary	WF	40	-	Sister of Charity
Hanrey, Daniel	WM	7m	-	Inmate
Harding, Joseph	WM	-	Apr.	Inmate
Harding, Kattie	WF	-	May	Inmate
Harold, Claude	WM	-	May	Inmate
Harriet, Agnes	WF	1	-	Inmate
Harris, Adel	WF	1	-	Inmate
Harris, David	WM	3	-	Inmate
Harris, Josephin	WF	2	-	Inmate
Harris, Mary	WF	8	-	Inmate
Harris, William	WM	1	-	Inmate
Harrision, Marie	WF	7m	-	Inmate
Harrison, Mary	WF	19	-	Nurse
Harvey, Charles	WM	1	-	Inmate
Hasrington, Mary	WF	1	-	Inmate
Hastings, Clarence	WM	-	Apr.	Inmate
Hastings, Martha	WF	1	-	Inmate
Haukel, Ernest	WM	-	Apr.	Inmate
Haurey, Mary Jane	WF	21	-	Sister of Charity
Haven, Mary	WF	4	-	Inmate
Haverlin, Alfred	WM	1	-	Inmate

Hawes, Ellen	WF	2	-	Inmate
Hawkins, Cora	WF	25	-	Sister of Charity
Hawkins, Louis	WM	1	-	Inmate
Hawthorne, William	WM	1	-	Inmate
Hayes, James	WM	1	-	Inmate
Hayes, Loretto	WF	1	-	Inmate
Hayes, Mary	WF	10m	-	Inmate
Hebron, Alicia	WF	2	-	Inmate
Heffert, John	WM	3	-	Inmate
Heft, Sarah	WF	1	-	Inmate
Heggest, John	WM	2	-	Inmate
Held, Christina	WF	4	-	Inmate
Helen, Joseph	WM	2	-	Inmate
Helen, Josephine	WF	5	-	Inmate
Hennessey, Joseph	WM	1	-	Inmate
Henrico, Joseph	WM	1	-	Inmate
Henry, Alfred	WM	-	Jan.	Inmate
Henry, Clarence	WM	1	-	Inmate
Henry, Eddie	WM	7m	-	Inmate
Henry, Francis	WM	3	-	Inmate
Henry, George	WM	-	Apr.	Inmate
Henry, George	WM	10m	-	Inmate
Henry, John	WM	1	-	Inmate
Henry, John	WM	3	-	Inmate
Henry, Joseph	WM	2	-	Inmate
Henry, Mary	WF	6m	-	Inmate
Henry, William	WM	-	Feb.	Inmate
Henry, William	BM	1	-	Inmate
Herman, Sarah	WF	18	-	Nurse
Herring, Francis	WM	2	-	Inmate
Hervie, Nellie	WF	5	-	Inmate
Hesly, Edward	WM	2	-	Inmate
Hickey, John	WM	9	-	Inmate
Hickey, Kittie	WF	-	Mar.	Inmate
Hicks, Arnelus	WM	1	-	Inmate
Higgins, Elizabeth	WF	1	-	Inmate
Higgins, Elizabeth	WF	2	-	Inmate
Higgins, Elizabeth	WF	40	-	Sister of Charity
Higgins, Joseph	WM	-	Mar.	Inmate
Hoey, Anna M.	WF	1	-	Inmate
Hoffman, Charlotte	WF	-	May	Inmate
Hoffman, Ellen	WF	16	-	Nurse

Name	Race/Sex	Age	Month	Role
Hoffman, Helen	WF	7m	-	Inmate
Hoffman, John	WM	-	Jan.	Inmate
Hoffman, Oscar	WM	1	-	Inmate
Hoffman, Walter	WM	1	-	Inmate
Hogan, Elizabeth	WF	-	Mar.	Inmate
Hogan, James	WM	2	-	Inmate
Holt, Basil	WM	3	-	Inmate
Holten, James	WM	-	May	Inmate
Homes, Willie	WM	1	-	Inmate
Hopkins, Margaret	WF	18	-	Nurse
Hopkins, Mary	WF	-	May	Inmate
Hopkins, Mary	WF	20	-	Nurse
Horton, Mary	WF	17	-	Nurse
Horton, William	WM	-	Feb.	Inmate
Hough, Eddie	WM	1	-	Inmate
Hovey, Nettie O.	WF	1	-	Inmate
Howard, Pauline	WF	11m	-	Inmate
Howe, Katie	WF	3	-	Inmate
Hoyt, Clarissa	WF	3	-	Inmate
Hughes, Edward	WM	4	-	Inmate
Hugons, Peter	WM	11m	-	Inmate
Hump, Angelita	WF	3	-	Inmate
Hunt, Edward	WM	3	-	Inmate
Hunter, Alma	WF	20	-	Sister of Charity
Hunter, Octaivi	WF	3	-	Inmate
Hurbert, Felix	WM	-	May	Inmate
Hurley, Mary	WF	40	-	Sister of Charity
Hurmon, Isidore	WM	2	-	Inmate
Hurnon, Clarissa	WF	1	-	Inmate
Hury, Clarence	WM	4	-	Inmate
Huser, Albert	WM	-	Feb.	Inmate
Huskline, Emily	WF	5	-	Inmate
Hust, James	WM	-	Apr.	Inmate
Hustia, Frank	WM	-	Apr.	Inmate
Hyde, Fanny	WF	26	-	Cook
Hyland, Mary	WF	21	-	Nurse
Hyler, William	WM	9m	-	Inmate
Ignatia, Lucy	WF	1	-	Inmate
Ingles, Cora	WF	2	-	Inmate
Ingles, Maggie	WF	1	-	Inmate
Ingles, Teresa	WF	3	-	Inmate
Irogirvis, Augusta	WF	2	-	Inmate

Irvan, Mary A.	WF	3	-	Inmate
Irving, Aloysius	WM	3	-	Inmate
Isabel, Daisy	WF	1	-	Inmate
Iseldorf, Miranda	WF	2	-	Inmate
Isle, Mary	WF	3	-	Inmate
Ison, Clotilda	WF	2	-	Inmate
Ives, Fannie	WF	2	-	Inmate
Ivison, Joseph	WM	3	-	Inmate
Jackson, Harry	WM	-	May	Inmate
Jackson, Katie	WF	1	-	Inmate
Jackson, Mary	WF	1	-	Inmate
James, Alexis	WM	9m	-	Inmate
James, Frank	WM	1	-	Inmate
James, Mable	WF	2	-	Inmate
James, Robert	WM	1	-	Inmate
James, Willie	WM	7m	-	Inmate
Jarvis, Samuel	WM	2	-	Inmate
Jegonitz, John	WM	3	-	Inmate
John, Joseph	WM	-	Mar.	Inmate
Johnsen, Clement	WM	6m	-	Inmate
Johnsen, Fannie	WF	-	Mar.	Inmate
Johnsen, Robert	WM	1	-	Inmate
Johnson, Agnes	WF	1	-	Inmate
Johnson, Claire	WF	30	-	Sister of Charity
Johnson, George	WM	11m	-	Inmate
Johnson, Hubert	WM	1	-	Inmate
Johnson, Jane	WF	35	-	Sister of Charity
Johnson, Maud	WF	1	-	Inmate
Johnson, Thomas	WM	1	-	Inmate
Johnson, [illeg.]fany	WF	1	-	Inmate
Joly, Joseph	WM	5	-	Inmate
Jones, Jennie	WF	3	-	Inmate
Jones, Leticia	WF	5	-	Inmate
Jones, Stephen	WM	7	-	Inmate
Jones, Willis	WM	9m	-	Inmate
Jonickie, Mary	WF	3	-	Inmate
Joseph, Angelo	WM	3	-	Inmate
Joseph, Bernard	WM	10m	-	Inmate
Joseph, Francis	WM	-	Jan.	Inmate
Joseph, Francis	WM	1	-	Inmate
Joseph, Hubert	WM	2	-	Inmate
Joseph, James	WM	-	Mar.	Inmate

Joseph, James	WM	1	-	Inmate
Joseph, John	WM	1	-	Inmate
Joseph, Leopold	WM	3	-	Inmate
Joseph, Maria	WF	3	-	Inmate
Joseph, Marietta	WF	2	-	Inmate
Joseph, Victor	WM	1	-	Inmate
Joseph, Willie	WM	1	-	Inmate
Josephine, Maria	WF	-	Jan.	Inmate
Josita, Annie	WF	1	-	Inmate
Julia, Emma	WF	7m	-	Inmate
June, Jennie	WF	8m	-	Inmate
Justine, Mercedes	WF	1	-	Inmate
Kahn, Mary Anne	WF	1	-	Inmate
Kalloran, Katie	WF	21	-	Sister of Charity
Kane, Annie	WF	2	-	Inmate
Kane, Camille	WF	2	-	Inmate
Kane, John	WM	8	-	Inmate
Kane, Margaret	WF	2	-	Inmate
Kasbrock, Christina	WF	1	-	Inmate
Kasselburg, John	WM	4	-	Inmate
Kavanagh, Sarah	WF	22	-	Laundress
Kearney, Angela	WF	1	-	Inmate
Kearney, Maggie	WF	18	-	Nurse
Keenan, Mary	WF	3	-	Inmate
Kehoe, Teresa	WF	21	-	Sister of Charity
Keller, Helena	WF	36	-	Sister of Charity
Keller, Lizzie	WF	5m	-	Inmate
Kelly, Charles	WM	1	-	Inmate
Kelly, Frank	WM	2	-	Inmate
Kelly, Kate	WF	1	-	Inmate
Kelly, Lilie	WF	1	-	Inmate
Kelly, Mary Agnes	WF	3	-	Inmate
Kelly, Mary	WF	2m	Apr.	Inmate
Kelly, Michael Joseph	WM	10	-	Inmate
Kelly, Thomas	WM	4m	Feb.	Inmate
Kelly, Thomas	WM	1	-	Inmate
Kelly, Thomas	WM	2	-	Inmate
Kemble, Emma	WF	18	-	Nurse
Kennally, Ellen	WF	1	-	Inmate
Kennedy, Georgianna	WF	1	-	Inmate
Kennedy, Joseph	WM	5m	-	Inmate
Kennedy, Maggie	WF	20	-	Nurse

Kennedy, Margaret	WF	21	-	Nurse
Kenny, Alice	WF	2	-	Inmate
Kenny, John	WM	1	-	Inmate
Kenny, Sylvester	WM	11m	-	Inmate
Keogh, Thomas	WM	3	-	Inmate
Keoghan, Thomas	WM	3m	Mar.	Inmate
Kernn, Effie	WF	1	-	Inmate
Kerrigan, Annie	WF	18	-	Nurse
Kerrigan, Eddie	WM	1m	May	Inmate
Kessler, Charlie	WM	1m	May	Inmate
Keyes, Minnie	WF	11m	-	Inmate
Kidd, Mary Alice	WF	3m	Mar.	Inmate
Kieffler, Frederick	WM	3	-	Inmate
Kiley, Amanda	WF	3m	Mar.	Inmate
Kimble, Robert	WM	1m	May	Inmate
King, Charlie	WM	1m	May	Inmate
King, Joseph	WM	5m	-	Inmate
King, Maud	WF	1	-	Inmate
King, Valentine	WM	3m	Mar.	Inmate
Kingman, Alice	WF	2	-	Inmate
Kinnear, Mary	WF	5m	-	Inmate
Kinny, Frank	WM	6	-	Inmate
Kinsella, George	WM	2	-	Inmate
Klaken, John	WM	1	-	Inmate
Kline, Annie	WF	6	-	Inmate
Kline, Jacob	WM	3m	Mar.	Inmate
Kline, Mary	WF	5	-	Inmate
Kline, Nellie	WF	1	-	Inmate
Knight, Augustus	WF*	4	-	Inmate
Knight, May	WF	1	-	Inmate
Knox, Joseph	WM	1	-	Inmate
Knox, William	WM	1	-	Inmate
Koehler, Emma	WF	3m	Mar.	Inmate
Kolman, Sylvester	WM	3	-	Inmate
Kolson, Augusta	WF	11m	-	Inmate
Korie, Annie	WF	2	-	Inmate
Krime, Henry G.	WM	5m	Jan.	Inmate
Krome, Margaret	WF	22	-	Nurse
Kurmen, Christine	WF	5m	-	Inmate
Kurtz, Chrysostorio	WM	5m	-	Inmate
Lacher, William	WM	2	-	Inmate
Lacock, Annie	WF	19	-	Nurse

Lacook, Joseph	WM	-	May	Inmate
Laird, Maria	WF	-	Jan.	Inmate
Laird, Mary	WF	20	-	Seamstress
Lander, margaret	WF	26	-	Seamstress
Lane, Joseph	WM	2	-	Inmate
Lane, Minetta	WF	2	-	Inmate
Lang, Delia	WF	20	-	Seamstress
Lang, George	WM	1	-	Inmate
Lang, Gertrude	WF	2	-	Inmate
Lang, John	WM	2	-	Inmate
Langdon, Richard	WM	3	-	Inmate
Lannigan, Bridget	WF	30	-	Nurse
Lanterie, James	WM	-	Mar.	Inmate
Large, Eliza	WF	9	-	Inmate
Largo, William	WM	5	-	Inmate
Larkin, Margaret	WF	20	-	Nurse
Larkin, Mary	WF	-	May	Inmate
Larkin, Thomas	WM	7m	-	Inmate
Laurence, Eddie	WM	-	Apr.	Inmate
Lawson, Eliza	WF	7	-	Inmate
Lazainie, Mary	WF	25	-	Sister of Charity
Leahy, Annie	WF	3	-	Inmate
Leahy, Hannah	WF	19	-	Nurse
Leander, Arthur	WM	2	-	Inmate
Leddy, Thomas H.	WM	2	-	Inmate
Lee, Beatrice	WF	1	-	Inmate
Lee, Blanche	WF	20	-	Seamstress
Lehman, Annie	WF	2	-	Inmate
Lemayne, Mineta	WF	2	-	Inmate
Lemosney, Christopher	WM	1	-	Inmate
Lennahan, Mary	WF	32	-	Sister of Charity
Lennox, Ignatius	WM	-	Feb.	Inmate
Leo, Rose	WF	2	-	Inmate
Leonard, Mary Anna	WF	2	-	Inmate
Leonard, Thomas	WM	1	-	Inmate
Leopold, Oswald	WM	10m	-	Inmate
Leppert, Mary	WF	18	-	Inmate
Leppert, Mary Eliza	WF	-	Apr.	Nurse
Leroy, James	WM	1	-	Inmate
Letellier, Edwin	WM	4	-	Inmate
Levi, Abraham	WM	4	-	Inmate
Levings, Walter Harry	WM	1	-	Inmate

Levy, Edward	WM	-	Mar.	Inmate
Levy, Leonard	WM	1	-	Inmate
Lewis, Florence	WF	18	-	Nurse
Lewis, Floyd	WM	-	Feb.	Inmate
Leyden, Loretto	WF	2	-	Inmate
Liebach, Ernest	WM	6m	-	Inmate
Lilly, Alexander	WM	-	Mar.	Inmate
Lilly, Mary	WF	1	-	Inmate
Linca, Lurebius	WF	6	-	Inmate
Lind, Lizzie	WF	2	-	Inmate
Linden, Ethel	WF	1	-	Inmate
Linden, Lilly Louise	WF	-	May	Inmate
Link, Eliza	WF	-	Feb.	Inmate
Linus, Sophia	WF	10m	-	Inmate
Little, Angelita	WF	-	Apr.	Inmate
Little, Jacob	WM	7m	-	Inmate
Little, Willie	WM	-	Feb.	Inmate
Livecy, John	WM	6	-	Inmate
Livingston, Alice	WF	-	Mar.	Inmate
Livingston, Charles	WM	1	-	Inmate
Lock, Andrew	WM	-	Feb.	Inmate
Lockwood, Annie	WF	18	-	Nurse
Lockwood, Frank	WM	-	Mar.	Inmate
Loeher, Christina	WF	2	-	Inmate
Logan, Bernard	WM	2	-	Inmate
Logan, Mary	WF	21	-	Laundress
Long, Jennie	WF	2	-	Inmate
Long, Louisa	WF	11m	-	Inmate
Loomis, Rose	WF	30	-	Sister of Charity
Loretto, Clara	WF	1	-	Inmate
Lotta, Cora	WF	2	-	Inmate
Louie, Lizzie	WF	1	-	Inmate
Louise, Clarissa	WF	2	-	Inmate
Louise, Geraldine	WF	11m	-	Inmate
Love, Alfred	WM	8	-	Inmate
Love, Andrew	WM	8m	-	Inmate
Lovel, Eugene	WM	7m	-	Inmate
Lozier, Henry	WM	1	-	Inmate
Lubeck, Agnes	WF	20	-	Nurse
Lucas, Henry	WM	8	-	Inmate
Lucy, Evangelista	WF	1	-	Inmate
Lully, Joseph W.	WM	6	-	Inmate

Lunenthal, Peter	WM	2	-	Inmate
Lyman, Rufus	WM	2	-	Inmate
Lynch, Edward	WM	-	Mar.	Inmate
Lynch, Katie	WF	-	Mar.	Inmate
Lynch, Lizzie	WF	3	-	Inmate
Lynch, Thomas	WM	3	-	Inmate
Lyons, Jeannette	WF	20	-	Nurse
Lyons, Maud Marie	WF	5	-	Inmate
Lyons, Thomas F.	WM	1	-	Inmate
Macauley, Mary Ann	WF	1	-	Inmate
Macbeth, Marian	WF	1	-	Inmate
Mack, Ellen	WF	1	-	Inmate
Mack, James	WM	1	-	Inmate
Mackey, Maggie	WF	1	-	Inmate
Mackin, Rose	WF	1	-	Inmate
Madison, Carmelita	WF	7	-	Inmate
Magdalena, Meyers	WM	1	-	Inmate
Magellon, Eugene	WM	2	-	Inmate
Mahon, Alice	WF	22	-	Nurse
Mahon, James	WM	1	-	Inmate
Mahon, John Thomas	WM	-	May	Inmate
Mahon, Mary	WF	18	-	Nurse
Mahon, Phoebe	WF	1	-	Inmate
Maitland, Zoe	WF	-	May	Inmate
Mallon, James	WM	1	-	Inmate
Maloge, Ellen	WF	2	-	Inmate
Manah, Victor	WM	-	Mar.	Inmate
Manin, James H.	WM	5	-	Inmate
Manns, Annie	WF	11m	-	Inmate
Mansfield, Clarence	WM	2	-	Inmate
Marcuell, Walter	WM	6	-	Inmate
Margaret, Julia	WF	1	-	Inmate
Maria, Annie	WF	1	-	Inmate
Maria, Dorothy	WF	1	-	Inmate
Maria, Gabriel	WM	1	-	Inmate
Maria, Grace	WF	6m	-	Inmate
Maria, Ruby	WF	-	Apr.	Inmate
Marie, Sylvania	WF	-	Apr.	Inmate
Marion, John	WM	2	-	Inmate
Marrin, Grace	WF	1	-	Inmate
Marsh, Maud	WF	-	Jan.	Inmate
Marshall Stephen	WM	1	-	Inmate

Marshall, Charlotte	WF	2	-	Inmate
Marshall, Hamilton	WM	2	-	Inmate
Marshall, John	WM	6m	-	Inmate
Marshall, Mary J.	WF	4	-	Inmate
Martel, Emma	WF	2	-	Inmate
Martin, Agnes	WF	11m	-	Inmate
Martin, Joseph	WM	6m	-	Inmate
Martin, Mary A.	WF	5	-	Inmate
Martin, Mary Agatha	WF	11m	-	Inmate
Martin, Oswald	WM	1	-	Inmate
Martin, Thomas	WM	-	Apr.	Inmate
Martina, Elizabeth	WF	2	-	Inmate
Marx, Joseph Odo	WM	-	Mar.	Inmate
Maskham, John	WM	-	May	Inmate
Mather, Julia	WF	40	-	Sister of Charity
Mathers, Lilly	WF	1	-	Inmate
Matthew, Harry	WM	2	-	Inmate
Matthews, John	WM	11m	-	Inmate
Maud, Alice	WF	-	Jan.	Inmate
Maud, Georgina	WF	-	May	Inmate
Maud, Gracie	WF	-	Jan.	Inmate
Maxwell, Mary A.	WF	2	-	Inmate
May, Annunciata	WF	-	Apr.	Inmate
May, Eva	WF	-	May	Inmate
May, Eva	WF	10m	-	Inmate
May, Florence Agnes	WF	3	-	Inmate
May, Justine	WM*	1	-	Inmate
May, Mabel	WF	-	May	Inmate
May, Magdalena	WF	-	Apr.	Inmate
May, Marie	WF	2	-	Inmate
May, Matilda	WF	1	-	Inmate
May, Rosie	WF	2	-	Inmate
May, Willie	WM	1	-	Inmate
McCabe, James J.	WM	3	-	Inmate
McCabe, Joseph	WM	-	Mar.	Inmate
McCabe, Katie	WF	20	-	Sister of Charity
McCann, Annie	WF	18	-	Nurse
McCarlty, Hannah	WF	18	-	Sister of Charity
McCarthy, Eddie	WM	5	-	Inmate
McCarthy, John	WM	-	Jan.	Inmate
McClean, Nora	WF	18	-	Sister of Charity
McCollum, Katie	WF	19	-	Nurse

McCook, Ida	WF	4	-	Inmate
McCormick, Jennie	WF	22	-	Sister of Charity
McCourt, William	WM	5	-	Inmate
McCreisty, Mary Margaret	WF	25	-	Nurse
McCrossen, Harry	WM	5	-	Inmate
McCrystal, Jane	WF	38	-	Sister of Charity
McDermott, Jane	WF	22	-	Seamstress
McDonald, Katie	WF	1	-	Inmate
McDonald, Maud	WF	-	Jan.	Inmate
McDonough, Rosanna	WF	-	Mar.	Inmate
McDougall, Jessie	WF	4	-	Inmate
McEelroy, Alice	WF	5	-	Inmate
McElroy, Joseph	WM	6	-	Inmate
McFadden, Mary	WF	19	-	Nurse
McFaden, Joseph	WM	3	-	Inmate
McGawan, Thomas	WM	1	-	Inmate
McGerrk, Mary	WF	1	-	Inmate
McGormerly, Mary	WF	19	-	Nurse
McGovern, May	WF	-	Mar.	Inmate
McGrath, John	WM	1	-	Inmate
McGuff, Annie	WF	4	-	Inmate
McGuire, Mary	WF	18	-	Nurse
McGurk, Matilda	WF	-	May	Inmate
McIntosh, Mary	WF	18	-	Nurse
McKeane, Catharine	WF	22	-	Sister of Charity
McKenna, Isabella	WF	1	-	Inmate
McKinley, Mary	WF	2	-	Inmate
McKvene, Jane	WF	-	May	Inmate
McLaughlin, Mary	WF	19	-	Nurse
McLaughlin, Thomas	WM	18	-	Laborer
McMahon, Annie	WF	3	-	Inmate
McMahon, Annie	WF	20	-	Sister of Charity
McManus, Margaret	WF	4	-	Inmate
McMartin, Bernard	WM	9m	-	Inmate
McNally, Kate	WF	17	-	Nurse
McNamara, Seraphine	WF	-	Jan.	Inmate
McNamee, Rose	WF	18	-	Nurse
McNeally, Margaret	WF	21	-	Sister of Charity
McQuellan, Annie	WF	1	-	Inmate
Meade, Andrew D.	WM	-	Feb.	Inmate
Meade, Sara	WF	17	-	Nurse
Mecker, Joseph	WM	-	Apr.	Inmate

Medlinh, Rudolph	WM	-	Mar.	Inmate
Meehan, John	WM	1	-	Inmate
Meek, Mary Almira	WF	2	-	Inmate
Meeker, Elizabeth	WF	18	-	Nurse
Meeker, Estella	WF	1	-	Inmate
Melia, Henry	WM	5	-	Inmate
Mellville, Angela	WF	5	-	Inmate
Mercent, Theresa	WF	6	-	Inmate
Mertel, William	WM	1	-	Inmate
Meyer, Elizabeth	WF	6	-	Inmate
Meyers, Edwin	WM	2	-	Inmate
Meyers, George	WM	11m	-	Inmate
Meyers, Johnnie	WM	2	-	Inmate
Meyers, Mary	WF	20	-	Sister of Charity
Meyers, Samuel	WM	1	-	Inmate
Meyers, Thomas	WM	-	Jan.	Inmate
Middleton, Harry	WM	1	-	Inmate
Miller, Annie	WF	-	Feb.	Inmate
Miller, Annie	WF	-	Mar.	Inmate
Miller, Edward	WM	1	-	Inmate
Miller, Gertrude	WF	6	-	Inmate
Miller, Kate	WF	17	-	Nurse
Miller, Mary	WF	20	-	Sister of Charity
Miller, William	WM	2	-	Inmate
Milton, Florence Mattie	WF	-	Feb.	Inmate
Minar, James	WM	2	-	Inmate
Miner, Maggie	WF	-	-	Inmate
Minna, Louise	WF	-	May	Inmate
Minyea, Joseph Thomas	WM	8	-	Inmate
Miranda, Genevieve	WF	1	-	Inmate
Mitchell, Gabriel	WM	3	-	Inmate
Mitchell, Maggie	MuF	4	-	Inmate
Mocquin, Mary A.	MuF	1	-	Inmate
Momey, Rose	WF	2	-	Inmate
Monahan, John	WM	2	-	Inmate
Monitor, John Joseph	WM	1	-	Inmate
Monroe, Nellie	WF	6	-	Inmate
Mooney, James	WM	2	-	Inmate
Moore, Flora	WF	4	-	Inmate
Moore, Rose	WF	2	-	Inmate
Moran, James	WM	2	-	Inmate
Moran, Joseph Thomas	WM	-	Jan.	Inmate

Moran, Mary	WF	19	-	Nurse
Morgan, Daniel J.	WM	-	Feb.	Inmate
Morgan, Maggie	WF	-	Apr.	Inmate
Morgan, Mary Anne	WF	1	-	Inmate
Morris, Catherine	WF	5	-	Inmate
Morris, James	WM	4	-	Inmate
Morris, John	WM	9	-	Inmate
Morrisey, John	WM	2	-	Inmate
Morse, Charles	WM	11m	-	Inmate
Mortimer, Grace	WF	2	-	Inmate
Moyers, Katie	WF	2	-	Inmate
Moylan, Nira	WF	3	-	Inmate
Muldouny, Bernard	WM	6	-	Inmate
Mullens, Willie	WM	10	-	Inmate
Mullins, Charles	WM	5	-	Inmate
Mullins, Elizabeth	WF	2	-	Inmate
Mumm, Adolph	WM	1	-	Inmate
Murphy, Annie	WF	5	-	Inmate
Murphy, Ellen	WF	1	-	Inmate
Murphy, Ellen	WF	24	-	Cook
Murphy, John	WM	11m	-	Inmate
Murphy, John	WM	6	-	Inmate
Murphy, Katie	WF	-	Mar.	Inmate
Murphy, Maggie	WF	1	-	Inmate
Murphy, Mary	WF	1	-	Inmate
Murphy, Mary	WF	17	-	Nurse
Murphy, Mary	WF	20	-	Nurse
Murphy, Willie	WM	-	Apr.	Inmate
Murphy, Willie	WM	-	Jan.	Inmate
Murray, Alice	WF	1	-	Inmate
Murray, Joseph	WM	-	Mar.	Inmate
Murray, Kate	WF	18	-	Nurse
Murray, Mary	WF	18	-	Sister of Charity
Murray, Sarah	WF	-	Feb.	Inmate
Murrell, Agnes	WF	6m	-	Inmate
Murrill, Charles	WM	1	-	Inmate
Murtah, Hugo	WM	1	-	Inmate
Murton, Victor	WM	6m	-	Inmate
Nally, Catharine	WF	1	-	Inmate
Naomi, Rowena	WF	-	Mar.	Inmate
Nash, Frank	WM	1	-	Inmate
Naze, John	WM	3	-	Inmate

Neal, Lucy	BF	2	-	Inmate
Neefus, Dolorita	WF	3	-	Inmate
Neekers, Paul	WM	2	-	Inmate
Nettol, Claude	WM	1	-	Inmate
Neuman, John	WM	-	May	Inmate
Neuman, Mary	WF	20	-	Nurse
Newburgh, Richard	WM	6m	-	Inmate
Newell, Frank	WM	1	-	Inmate
Newell, Germaine	WF	6	-	Inmate
Newton, Elizabeth	WF	1	-	Inmate
Newton, Katie	WF	4	-	Inmate
Niffin, Willie	WM	1	-	Inmate
Nile, Saborah	WF	27	-	Nurse
Nilsson, Eliza	WF	2	-	Inmate
Nixon, Mary	WF	3	-	Inmate
Noel, John	WM	6m	Jan.	Inmate
Noman, John	WM	2	-	Inmate
Noon, Robert John	WM	9	-	Inmate
Nordman, Paual	WM	3	-	Inmate
Norman, Cladius	WM	4	-	Inmate
Norman, William	WM	1	-	Inmate
Norral, Ella	WF	11m	-	Inmate
Norris, Agnes	WF	4	-	Inmate
North, Violet	WF	-	Jan.	Inmate
Norton, George	WM	4	-	Inmate
Nugent, Ethel	WF	10m	-	Inmate
Nulley, Mary L.	WF	4	-	Inmate
Oakley, Pauline	WF	3	-	Inmate
O'Brien, Annie	WF	-	May	Inmate
O'Brien, Lillie	WF	6	-	Inmate
O'Brien, Lizzie	WF	18	-	Nurse
O'Donnell, Mary	WF	18	-	Laundress
O'Keefe, Richard	WM	2	-	Inmate
Oldering, Katie	WF	6	-	Inmate
Oliver, Grace	WF	2	-	Inmate
Oliver, Mary	WF	2	-	Inmate
Ollins, Dominica	WF	10m	-	Inmate
Olney, Katie	WF	3	-	Inmate
Olney, Mary Ellen	WF	5	-	Inmate
O'Mara, Michael	WM	1	-	Inmate
O'Neill, Charles	WM	1	-	Inmate
O'Neill, Joseph	WM	1	-	Inmate

O'Neill, Kate	WF	22	-	Nurse
O'Neill, Mary	WF	9m	-	Inmate
Ore, Gabriella	WF	-	May	Inmate
Ormond, Ferdinand	WM	-	May	Inmate
Orr, James	WM	11m	-	Inmate
Osborne, Loretto	WF	2	-	Inmate
Osmand, Grace	WF	1	-	Inmate
O'Toole, Johnnie	WM	2	-	Inmate
Ottman, Gussie	WF	3	-	Inmate
Otts, George	WM	-	May	Inmate
Packer, Thomas	?M	6	-	Inmate
Palmer, Ada	WF	9m	-	Inmate
Park, Clarence	WM	8m	-	Inmate
Parker, Bernard	WM	1	-	Inmate
Parker, Eliza	WF	8	-	Inmate
Paterson, Mary E.	WF	6	-	Inmate
Patrick, Joseph	WM	8m	-	Inmate
Patton, Annie M.	WF	4m	-	Inmate
Paxton, Herbert	WM	2	-	Inmate
Pease, Charlie	WM	6m	-	Inmate
Pease, Emma	WF	3	-	Inmate
Pemberton, Ethel	WF	5m	-	Inmate
Pendleton, Charles	WM	4	-	Inmate
Perblum, Lena	WF	2m	-	Inmate
Perin, Raymond	WM	4	-	Inmate
Perkins, Lizzie	WF	6m	-	Inmate
Perley, Samuel	WM	1	-	Inmate
Permington, Mary	WF	6m	-	Inmate
Perry, Alice	WF	1	-	Inmate
Perry, Bridget	WF	9m	-	Inmate
Persoy, Mary Ellen	WF	4	-	Inmate
Peters, Margaret	WF	2	-	Inmate
Peters, Paul	WM	11m	-	Inmate
Peters, Rachel	WF	1m	-	Inmate
Peters, Raphael	WM	8m	-	Inmate
Peterson, Willie	WM	10m	-	Inmate
Pfaff, Emma	WF	3	-	Inmate
Philip, Andrew	WM	2	-	Inmate
Picarre, Charlie	WM	1	-	Inmate
Pietrez, John Henry	WM	4	-	Inmate
Pitcher, Augustin	WM	6	-	Inmate
Pitt, Rupert	WM	7	-	Inmate

Platz, Charles	WM	1m	-	Inmate
Poliznat, Henrich	WM	5	-	Inmate
Pollard, Alfred	WM	2m	-	Inmate
Pollard, Andrew	WM	1	-	Inmate
Pollard, Armenia	WF	2	-	Inmate
Pond, Frank Gaylord	WM	2	-	Inmate
Post, Lilly	WM*	11m	-	Inmate
Power, Joseph	WM	6m	-	Inmate
Powers, Amelia	WF	1	-	Inmate
Powers, John Ed.	WM	2	-	Inmate
Powers, Nellie	WF	9	-	Inmate
Pratt, Melinda	WF	2m	-	Inmate
Preston, Daisy	WF	4	-	Inmate
Price, Florence	WF	2	-	Inmate
Price, Josephine	WF	3m	-	Inmate
Proctor, Adelaide	WF	4m	-	Inmate
Purcel, Louise	WF	11m	-	Inmate
Purcel, Mary Eliz.	WF	1	-	Inmate
Purcell, Annie	WF	30	-	Sister of Charity
Putnam, Joseph	WM	11m	-	Inmate
Quack, Isabella	WF	6m	-	Inmate
Quidine, Frank	WM	3	-	Inmate
Quinlan, Mary	WF	8m	-	Inmate
Quinn, Annie	WF	1	-	Inmate
Quinn, Fannie	WF	1	-	Inmate
Quinn, Thomas	WM	50	-	Coachman
Quint, Louise	WF	1	-	Inmate
Rall, Pauline	WF	5m	-	Inmate
Randall, Harry	WM	7m	-	Inmate
Randolph, William	WM	?m	-	Inmate
Ravenel, Georgina	WF	3	-	Inmate
Ray, Ethel	WF	4m	-	Inmate
Rayes, Lizzie	WF	3	-	Inmate
Reardon, Mary Agnes	WF	3m	-	Inmate
Reddy, Charlie	WM	2	-	Inmate
Reding, Katie	WF	3	-	Inmate
Reedenback, Henrietta	WF	4m	-	Inmate
Reeves, Joseph [illeg.]	WM	2	-	Inmate
Reichardts, Thomas	WM	9m	-	Inmate
Reid, Charlie	WM	11m	-	Inmate
Reid, Willy	WM	7m	-	Inmate
Reilly, Francis	WM	11m	-	Inmate

Reilly, James	WM	2	-	Inmate
Reilly, John Francis	WM	1	-	Inmate
Reilly, Margaret	WF	1	-	Inmate
Reilly, Mary	WF	21	-	Nurse
Reilly, Maud Lizzie	WF	11m	-	Inmate
Reimer, Julia	WF	1m	-	Inmate
Reland, Jennie	WF	1	-	Inmate
Reynolds, Adeline	WF	2	-	Inmate
Reynolds, Amelia	WF	4	-	Inmate
Reynolds, Julia	WF	20	-	Sister of Charity
Reynolds, Susan	WF	1	-	Inmate
Reynolds, Thomas	WM	4	-	Inmate
Rhidine, Kate	WF	2m	-	Inmate
Rhodes, Charlotte	WF	1	-	Inmate
Richard, Joseph	WM	1m	-	Inmate
Richards, Joseph	WM	3	-	Inmate
Richmond, Robert	WM	7m	-	Inmate
Richter, Bruno	WM	1	-	Inmate
Riordan, John	WM	2m	-	Inmate
Roberts, Charles	WM	1m	-	Inmate
Roberts, Georgiana	WF	7	-	Inmate
Roberts, John	WM	1	-	Inmate
Roberts, Myrtilla	WF	2m	-	Inmate
Robinson, Charles	WM	1m	-	Inmate
Robinson, Frederick	WM	1m	-	Inmate
Robinson, Joseph	WM	3	-	Inmate
Roche, Eddie	WM	2m	-	Inmate
Roddam, William J.	WM	3m	-	Inmate
Rodgers, Mary	WF	3	-	Inmate
Roe, Joseph	WM	11m	-	Inmate
Rogers, Cora	WF	1m	-	Inmate
Roland, Katie	WF	19	-	Nurse
Roland, Zoe	WF	1	-	Inmate
Rollins, Emma	WF	11m	-	Inmate
Romanus, Oswald	WM	2	-	Inmate
Romey, John	WM	1m	-	Inmate
Romey, John	WM	2m	-	Inmate
Romlia, Carrie	WF	1m	-	Inmate
Rooney, Mary	WF	25	-	Seamstress
Roper, Thomas	WM	9m	-	Inmate
Rose, Amy	WF	11m	-	Inmate
Rose, Mary	WF	6	-	Inmate

Rose, Samuel	WM	8m	-	Inmate
Rose, Teresa	WF	4m	-	Inmate
Rosemond, Isidore	WF	1m	-	Inmate
Rosenburg, Emma	WF	2	-	Inmate
Rosenthal, Iman	WM	1m	-	Inmate
Rosetti, Frank	WM	4	-	Inmate
Ross, Joseph	WM	1	-	Inmate
Ross, Lizzie	WF	3m	-	Inmate
Ruble, Mary Josephine	WF	?m	-	Inmate
Rupert, John	WM	?m	-	Inmate
Rupert, Leander	WM	11m	-	Inmate
Rutledge, Frank	WM	8m	-	Inmate
Ryan, Annie	WF	?m	-	Inmate
Ryan, Bridget	WF	21	-	Sister of Charity
Ryan, Joseph	WM	2m	-	Inmate
Ryan, Joseph	WM	4m	-	Inmate
Ryan, Lizzie	WF	2m	-	Inmate
Ryan, Margaret	WF	11m	-	Inmate
Ryan, Nellie	WF	1m	-	Inmate
Ryan, Pauline	WF	25	-	Sister of Charity
Rytentin, Freddie	WM	2	-	Inmate
St. John, Mary E.	WF	1m	-	Inmate
Salvador, John	WM	6m	-	Inmate
Salvador, Mary A.	WF	1m	-	Inmate
Sampson, Katie	WF	11m	-	Inmate
Samuel, James	WM	2m	-	Inmate
Sanders, Frank	WM	-	Jan.	Inmate
Sanders, Minie	WF	1	-	Inmate
Sanderson, Mary	WF	2m	-	Inmate
Sanford, Nellie	WF	-	Apr.	Inmate
Santal, Nellie	WF	6m	-	Inmate
Schafer, Bertha	WF	-	Jan.	Inmate
Schafer, Otto	WM	1	-	Inmate
Schermmerhorn, Harry	WM	11m	-	Inmate
Schmidt, Louise	WF	3	-	Inmate
Schneider, Emile	WM	1	-	Inmate
Schnider, Celina	WF	7m	-	Inmate
Scott, Mary	WF	6	-	Inmate
Seaman, Emma	WF	5m	-	Inmate
Seward, Pauline	WF	11m	-	Inmate
Seymour, Agnes T.	WF	2	-	Inmate
Shain, Sylvester	WM	7m	-	Inmate

Shandly, John	WM	5m	-	Inmate
Shaw, Joseph	WM	6m	-	Inmate
Shea, Dennis	WM	11m	-	Inmate
Shea, Thomas	WM	2	-	Inmate
Sheehan, Edward	WM	2m	-	Inmate
Shenar, Frank	WM	3m	-	Inmate
Sheridan, Charles	WM	1	-	Inmate
Sheridan, Delia	WF	8m	-	Inmate
Shield, Maggie	WF	-	Mar.	Inmate
Shinn, Maurice	WM	-	Apr.	Inmate
Shofter, Louise	WF	11m	May	Inmate
Shroeder, Paul	WM	3m	-	Inmate
Simmons, Eddie	WM	-	Feb.	Inmate
Simpson, Cecilia	MuF	3m	-	Inmate
Simpson, Thomas	WM	1m	-	Inmate
Sinclair, Hattie	WF	-	May	Inmate
Singleton, Rupert	WF*	8m	-	Inmate
Siratz, Johnnie	WM	-	Mar.	Inmate
Slater, Grace	WF	18	-	Nurse
Slattery, John	WM	11m	-	Inmate
Smelt, John	WM	3	-	Inmate
Smith, Agnes	WF	6m	-	Inmate
Smith, Agnes	WF	2	-	Inmate
Smith, Albert	WM	1	-	Inmate
Smith, Alice	WF	3m	-	Inmate
Smith, Alice	WF	21	-	Nurse
Smith, Aloysius	WM	1	-	Inmate
Smith, Annie	WF	22	-	Laundress
Smith, Arthur	WM	-	Apr.	Inmate
Smith, Bernard	WM	7m	-	Inmate
Smith, Carrie	WF	11m	-	Inmate
Smith, Charlie	WM	1	-	Inmate
Smith, Clara Agnes	WF	11m	-	Inmate
Smith, Emma	WF	-	Mar.	Inmate
Smith, Esmerelda	WF	9m	-	Inmate
Smith, Frank	WM	-	Jan.	Inmate
Smith, Frank	WF*	7m	-.	Inmate
Smith, Freddie	WM	2	-	Inmate
Smith, Frederick	WM	1	-	Inmate
Smith, George	WM	8m	-	Inmate
Smith, George	WM	9m	-	Inmate
Smith, George	WM	2	-	Inmate

Smith, Harry E.	WM	-	May	Inmate
Smith, Henrietta	WF	2m	-	Inmate
Smith, Ira Michael	WM	1	-	Inmate
Smith, Isabella	WF	17	-	Seamstress
Smith, James	WM	2m	-	Inmate
Smith, James	WM	6m	-	Inmate
Smith, James	WM	1	-	Inmate
Smith, Jennie	WF	-	Mar.	Inmate
Smith, John W.	WM	9m	-	Inmate
Smith, John	WM	2m	-	Inmate
Smith, John	WM	3m	-	Inmate
Smith, John	WM	2	-	Inmate
Smith, Johnnie	WM	1	-	Inmate
Smith, Joseph	WM	2	-	Inmate
Smith, Katie	WF	-	Apr.	Inmate
Smith, Katie	WF	9m	-	Inmate
Smith, Mary	WF	-	Apr.	Inmate
Smith, Mary E.	WF	2m	-	Inmate
Smith, Patrick	WM	2	-	Inmate
Smith, Raymond	WM	4	-	Inmate
Smith, Sara	WF	24	-	Laundress
Smith, Stephen M.	WM	-	May	Inmate
Smith, Walter	WM	1	-	Inmate
Smith, Willis	WM	5m	-	Inmate
Snee, James	WM	-	Apr.	Inmate
Snitzer, Alma	WF	2m	-	Inmate
Snow, Ida	WF	5m	-	Inmate
Solnrali, John	WM	1	-	Inmate
Somers, Maggie	WF	-	Feb.	Inmate
Spathelf, Mary L.	WF	-	Apr.	Inmate
Staals, Charles	WM	10m	-	Inmate
Stanley, Arthur	WM	3m	-	Inmate
Stanley, Estella	WF	11m	-	Inmate
Stanton, Eva	WF	2m	-	Inmate
Stanton, Hannah	WF	20	-	Nurse
Stanton, Magdalena	WF	-	Mar.	Inmate
Starke, George	WM	1m	-	Inmate
Stegers, Maggie	WF	2	-	Inmate
Stephen, Francis	WM	1	-	Inmate
Sterling, Alexander	WM	4	-	Inmate
Stern, Myra	WF	1	-	Inmate
Sterne, Edward	WM	-	May	Inmate

Sterne, Kate	WF	19	-	Nurse
Stevens, Cath. Agnes	WF	11m	-	Inmate
Stevenson, Ernest	WM	1	-	Inmate
Stevenson, Willie	WM	1	-	Inmate
Steward, Thomas	WM	9m	-	Inmate
Stewart, Scott	WM	11m	-	Inmate
Stiner, Teresa	WF	7m	-	Inmate
Stocktin, Mary	WF	-	Feb.	Inmate
Storet, Tinetta	WF	1m	-	Inmate
Story, Edward	WM	2m	-	Inmate
Strodtman, John	WM	2	-	Inmate
Stuart, Annie	WF	38	-	Sister of Charity
Stunly, Eugene	WM	7m	-	Inmate
Sturart, Frank	WM	6m	-	Inmate
Sturges, Harry	WM	8m	-	Inmate
Stutters, Alice	WF	1	-	Inmate
Sullinger, Sara	WF	1	May	Inmate
Sullivan, Edward	WM	1	-	Inmate
Sullivan, Elizabeth	WF	3m	-	Inmate
Sullivan, Fannie	WF	8m	-	Inmate
Sullivan, Ida	WF	1	-	Inmate
Sullivan, Mary	WF	3m	-	Inmate
Sullivan, Mary	WF	2	-	Inmate
Sullivan, Mary	WF	24	-	Sister of Charity
Sullivan, Susan	WF	18	-	Nurse
Sutherland, Joseph	WM	-	May	Inmate
Sutherland, Katie	WF	21	-	Nurse
Sutherland, Robert	WM	-	May	Inmate
Sutton, Peter	WM	3	-	Inmate
Sutton, Sara	WF	10m	-	Inmate
Swahn, Margaret	WF	1m	-	Inmate
Sweeney, Annie	WF	2	-	Inmate
Sweeny, Frank	WM	-	Jan.	Inmate
Swift, John	WM	10m	-	Inmate
Sylvester, Fila	WF	-	Jan.	Inmate
Syron, Sara Elizabeth	WF	3	-	Inmate
Taggert, Henry	WM	3	-	Inmate
Talbot, Ernest	WM	-	Mar.	Inmate
Talbot, Sarah	WF	19	-	Nurse
Taylor, George S.	WM	1	-	Inmate
Taylor, Henrietta	WF	-	May	Inmate
Taylor, Joseph	WM	5m	-	Inmate

Taylor, Mary B.	WF	-	Apr.	Inmate
Taylor, Mary	WF	7	-	Inmate
Temple, Josita	WF	4	-	Inmate
Teresa, Annie	WF	1	-	Inmate
Terrebonnie, Cecelia	WF	22	-	Nurse
Thomas, Grace	WF	1	-	Inmate
Thomas, Henry	WM	6	-	Inmate
Thomas, John	WM	5m	-	Inmate
Thomas, Michael	WM	4	-	Inmate
Thomas, Richard	WM	2	-	Inmate
Thomas, Rufus	WM	2	-	Inmate
Thomas, William	WM	-	Feb.	Inmate
Thompson, Fannie	WF	3	-	Inmate
Thompson, Isadore	WM	-	Apr.	Inmate
Thompson, Joseph	WM	5m	-	Inmate
Tracy, Alice	WF	8	-	Inmate
Treadwell, Chauncy	WM	4	-	Inmate
Treiss, John	WM	1	-	Inmate
Trenton, Lizzie	WF	5m	-	Inmate
Trimble, Edward	WM	4	-	Inmate
Troy, Annie	WF	-	Jan.	Inmate
Trueman, Henry	WM	10	-	Inmate
Tudor, Lizzie	WF	5	-	Inmate
Tully, Mary	WF	22	-	Sister of Charity
Tyson, Henry	WM	6	-	Inmate
Uhl, Henry	WM	2	-	Inmate
Uhl, Lena	WF	20	-	Seamstress
Uniack, August	WF*	2	-	Inmate
Uniack, Georgetta	WF	2	-	Inmate
Upman, John	WM	1	-	Inmate
Upton, Frank	WM	5	-	Inmate
Valdoi, Fannie	WF	1	-	Inmate
Vale, Henry S.	WM	4	-	Inmate
Van Homan, William	WM	5	-	Inmate
Van Nostran, Edward	WM	2m	Apr.	Inmate
Van Shun, Harry	WM	-	May	Inmate
Vanburen, Minnie	WF	1	-	Inmate
Vaness, Marietta	WF	1	-	Inmate
Vant, Charlie	WM	1	-	Inmate
Varan, Jeanetta	WF	4	-	Inmate
Vass, Mary	WF	22	-	Sister of Charity
Vass, May	WF	2	-	Inmate

Verdun, Coletta	WF	6	-	Inmate
Verdun, Mary	WF	24	-	Sister of Charity
Verimica, Ella	WF	1	-	Inmate
Vernon, Linda	WF	4	-	Inmate
Vincent, Eddie	WM	1	-	Inmate
Vincent, Emmeline	WF	2	-	Inmate
Vincent, Eugene	WF*	2	-	Inmate
Vincent, Francis	WM	2	-	Inmate
Vincent, Harry	WM	1	-	Inmate
Viola, Edward	WM	1	-	Inmate
Vogler, Martha	WF	2	-	Inmate
Voncassal, Alfred	WM	1	-	Inmate
Voughan, Clara	WF	1	-	Inmate
Vradon, Honorine	WF	2	-	Inmate
Wabberton, Lizzie	WF	1	-	Inmate
Wadsworth, Harry	WM	4	-	Inmate
Wagner, Willie	WM	4	-	Inmate
Waldron, Katie	WF	2	-	Inmate
Waldron, Walter	WM	2	-	Inmate
Wallace, Blanche	WF	-	Feb.	Inmate
Wallace, Gertrude	WF	3	-	Inmate
Wallace, Henry	WM	6m	-	Inmate
Wallum, John	WM	2	-	Inmate
Walsh, Mary J.	WF	2	-	Inmate
Walsh, Willie	WM	1	-	Inmate
Walson, John	WM	4	-	Inmate
Walter, Williams	WM	5m	-	Inmate
Walton, Helena	WF	5	-	Inmate
Ward, George	WM	2	-	Inmate
Ward, Henry	WM	2	-	Inmate
Ward, John	WM	2	-	Inmate
Ward, Nellie	WF	2	-	Inmate
Ward, William	WM	1	-	Inmate
Ward, Willie	WM	1	-	Inmate
Ware, Harry	WM	5	-	Inmate
Warner, Edwin A.	WM	3	-	Inmate
Warner, James	WM	4	-	Inmate
Washington, George	WM	-	Feb.	Inmate
Washington, George	BM	1	-	Inmate
Washington, George	WM	5	-	Inmate
Washington, Martha	WF	2	-	Inmate
Waters, C.	WF	3	-	Inmate

Waters, Horace	WM	4	-	Inmate
Waters, Teresa	WF	2	-	Inmate
Watkins, Mary B.	WF	-	Apr.	Inmate
Watson, Lucy	WF	7m	-	Inmate
Webler, George	WM	2	-	Inmate
Webster, Maud	WF	-	Apr.	Inmate
Weed, Fraser	WM	3	-	Inmate
Weinder, Victor	WM	5	-	Inmate
Welsh, Alexander	WM	-	Jan.	Inmate
Welsh, Delia	WF	6m	-	Inmate
Welsh, Frank	WM	-	Jan.	Inmate
Welsh, Jennie	WF	2	-	Inmate
Welsh, Jennie	WF	25	-	Sister of Charity
Wetter, Lizzie	WF	1	-	Inmate
Whain, Edward	WM	1	-	Inmate
Wheeler, Martha	WF	1	-	Inmate
Whelan, John	WM	5	-	Inmate
Whelen, May	WF	4	-	Inmate
While, Emma	WF	1	-	Inmate
While, Mary F.	WF	1	-	Inmate
White, Bertha	WF	6m	-	Inmate
White, Elizabeth	WF	6m	-	Inmate
White, Elizabeth	WF	18	-	Seamstress
White, Henry	WM	-	Jan.	Inmate
White, John	WM	-	Mar.	Inmate
White, Josephine	WF	18	-	Seamstress
White, Willi	WM	4	-	Inmate
Whitney, Frank	WM	7m	-	Inmate
Whittemore, Edward	WM	4m	-	Inmate
Wilard, Emma	WF	4	-	Inmate
Wilis, Walter	WM	6	-	Inmate
William, Joseph	WM	1	-	Inmate
Williams, Hilda	WF	5	-	Inmate
Williams, James	WM	2	-	Inmate
Williams, John	WM	2	-	Inmate
Williams, Joseph A.	WM	2	-	Inmate
Williams, Willie	WM	1	-	Inmate
Williamson, Eddie	WM	4	-	Inmate
Williamson, Irene	WF	5	-	Inmate
Willis, Minnie	WF	1	-	Inmate
Willis, Willie	WM	1	-	Inmate
Willoughby, Francis W.	WM	2	-	Inmate

Wilson, Alexander	WM	7	-	Inmate
Wilson, Alice	WF	8m	-	Inmate
Wilson, Charles	WM	1	-	Inmate
Wilson, Clotilda	WF	7m	-	Inmate
Wilson, Edith	WF	2	-	Inmate
Wilson, Edward	WM	1	-	Inmate
Wilson, Edward	WM	4	-	Inmate
Wilson, Florence	WF	8m	-	Inmate
Wilson, Francisco	WM	1	-	Inmate
Wilson, Fred	WM	-	Feb.	Inmate
Wilson, Joseph	WM	-	Jan.	Inmate
Wilson, Joseph	WM	9m	-	Inmate
Wilson, Lizzie	WF	18	-	Nurse
Wilson, Mary F.	WF	8	-	Inmate
Wilson, William	WM	1	-	Inmate
Wilton, Anthony	WM	4	-	Inmate
Winona, Emma	WF	4	-	Inmate
Winters, Mary Ann	WF	4	-	Inmate
Wiseman, Mary	WF	2	-	Inmate
Witroski, James	WM	1	-	Inmate
Witz, Eddie	WM	-	Mar.	Inmate
Wogaty, Flora	WF	6m	-	Inmate
Wolf, Sara	WF	1	-	Inmate
Wood, John	WM	-	Feb.	Inmate
Woods, Joseph	WM	1	-	Inmate
Woods, Mary	WF	16	-	Nurse
Woods, Willie	WM	-	Mar.	Inmate
Woolridge, Julia A.	WF	2	-	Inmate
Word, Joseph	WM	6	-	Inmate
Worth, John	WM	4	-	Inmate
Wright, Clarence	WM	1	-	Inmate
Wright, Ida E.	WF	2	-	Inmate
Wright, Thomas	WM	-	Mar.	Inmate
Wylde, Charles F.	WM	3	-	Inmate
Wyman, Christina	WF	5	-	Inmate
Wynn, Ellen	WF	18	-	Nurse
Wyrm, Marie	WF	-	Feb.	Inmate
Yore, Loretto	WF*	7	-	Inmate
Yost, Jennie	WF	4	-	Inmate
Young, Maud A.	WF	4	-	Inmate
Young, Teresa	WF	14	-	Seamstress
Young, Veronica	WF	3	-	Inmate

Zimmerman, Agneta   WF   1   -   Inmate

Index to the
The New York City Police Enumeration
of the Inhabitants of

The Foundling Asylum

175 East 68th Street
New York, New York

On or About
October 6, 1890

Police Precinct No. 25
Assembly District No. 22
Election District No. 2
Book No. 752

John Ballester,
Patrolman and Enumerator

Guide to Column Headings

in the

1890 New York City Police Enumeration Index

Name   Name of each person whose usual place of abode was in this institution. Surname first, then the given name and middle initial.

S   Gender.

A   Age. Designated in years, unless otherwise noted with a "d" for "days", "w" for "weeks", or "m" for "month".

Note   No other information was given.

Name	S	A
Ackerman, Albert	M	3m
Ackerman, Lizzie	F	23
Addison, Mary	F	31
Adler, Ruth	F	5
Albro, Mercedes	F	1m
Alcroft, Alfred	M	5
Aldamo, Mannela	F	3
Alice, Ada	F	4
Allen, Angelita	F	15
Allen, Frank	M	3m
Allen, Linis	M	20
Allen, Rebecca	F	20
Alnjsius, Francis	M	6
Alsop, Lena	F	3
Alton, Rose	F	2m
Anderson, Ada	F	4m
Anderson, Agnes	F	6m
Anderson, Mary	F	20
Andrews, Wm.	M	5
Angel, Rudolph	M	3
Ann, Mary	F	2m
Anna, Tessie	F	3
Arellino, Arnette	F	14
Armen, Madeline	F	4
Arronius, Giovanni	M	5
Babtista, Marie	F	3
Bartier, Jules	M	3
Basset, Albert	M	7m
Basson, Edgar	M	4
Bell, Minnie	F	2
Bell, Peter	M	4
Bender, Mary	F	21
Bender, Mary E.	F	27
Benson, Lena	F	26
Benson, Teresa	F	3
Bergen, Alice	F	3
Bergh, Marie	F	3m
Bergh, Marie	F	21
Beryne, Gertie	F	3
Binke, Lizzie	F	3

Black, May	F	7m
Blair, Anna	F	37
Blakel, Monica	F	3
Blum, Pauline	F	3
Blumer, Mary	F	2
Bogardus, Angela	F	27
Bohen, Ellen	F	34
Boucher, Jennie	F	19
Bowen, Cathrine	F	27
Bowers, Wm.	M	3m
Bradley, Jos.	M	5m
Bradley, Mary	F	27
Bradly, Stephen	M	4
Brady, Kate	F	27
Brady, Minnie	F	2m
Brady, Rose	F	21
Bragen, Maggie	F	3w
Brennan, John	M	9
Brennan, Mary	F	1
Brennan, Mary	F	25
Bright, Arthur	M	2
Broderick, Martin	M	5
Brown, Cathrine	F	39
Brown, Joseph	M	6
Brugan, Jennie	F	29
Budding, Grace May	F	7
Bundeson, Dore	F	22
Burke, John	M	11
Burke, Nellie	F	3w
Burke, Nora	F	24
Burns, Anna	F	19
Burtsell, Adele	F	4
Byrne, Chas.	M	6
Byrnes, Mary	F	3
Cahill, Alice	F	34
Cahill, Elizabeth	F	25
Camion, Julia	F	4
Campbell, Louis	M	3
Campbell, Maria	F	24
Campbell, Mary	F	14
Carlin, Vilma	F	2w
Carling, Arank	F	27

Carpenter, Arthur	M	3	Corbett, Teresa	F	20
Carr, Cathrine	F	23	Corcoran, Mary	F	18
Carren, Mary	F	24	Corrigan, Mary	F	25
Carroll, Alice	F	2	Cosey, Mary	F	28
Carroll, Bridget	F	25	Costello, Kate	F	37
Carroll, Edward	M	3	Coughlin, Mamie	F	5m
Carroll, James	M	4	Coughlin, Mary	F	26
Carroll, Julia	F	2	Craig, Annie	F	3
Carroll, Mary	F	21	Cramer, Benjamin	M	5
Carter, Jennie	F	4	Creighton, Marguerite	F	40
Casey, Nora	F	16	Cronin, Hannah	F	22
Chapman, Etta	F	5	Cronin, Mary	F	3m
Chopman, Julia	F	3	Cronin, Mary	F	28
Clare, Eddie	M	4	Crosby, John	M	2m
Clare, Mary	F	25	Cross, Jesse	F	40
Clark, Catharine	F	24	Cullen, Sarah	F	31
Clark, Mary	F	10	Cunningham, Agnes	F	24
Clayton, Francis	M	3	Curran, Richd.	M	3
Cleary, Anna	F	5	Curtin, Delia	F	18
Clemens, Clementina	F	10	Curtis, Kate	F	27
Clement, Esther	F	5	Curtis, Reginald	M	6m
Cmwy, Ella	F	2	Cushman, Grace	F	2
Code, Josephine	F	3	Cwnay, Delia	F	26
Coffey, Margaret	F	32	Daley, Julia	F	23
Cohen, Chas.	M	9m	Daley, Katie	F	17
Cole, Bessie	F	1w	Daley, Maria	F	3m
Cole, Ima	F	23	Davenport, Cyril	M	4w
Collett, Rosalia	F	1m	Davenport, Fanny	F	3
Colton, Thos.	-	5m	Davis, Minnie	F	6m
Colvay, Marguerite	F	3	Day, Walter	M	6m
Comstock, Addie	F	5	Deane, Marion	F	7m
Condy, Miss	F	53	Deitch, Marie	F	33
Conghla, Mary	F	3m	Delvoie, Inez	F	3
Connay, Alice	F	20	DeRitz, Edward	M	3
Connel, Estelle	F	3m	Derjo, Mamie	F	4
Conner, Maggie	F	22	DeSoto, Emilita	F	5
Conners, Joseph	M	4	Devalle, Cecilia	F	2
Connolly, James	M	4	Dinger, Annie	F	22
Connors, Maggie	F	30	Dinjer, Mamie	F	6w
Conroy, Mary A.	F	35	Dodge, Josephine	F	3
Conway, Julia	F	24	Dolan, Anna	F	5
Cook, Maggie	F	19	Donaties, Carlo	M	4

Donavan, Margaret	F	23	Eyler, Mamie	F	3
Donnelly, Bridget	F	35	Fagan, John	M	5w
Donnelly, Martin	M	2	Falk, Fanny	F	3w
Donney, Julia	F	23	Fall, Teresa	F	20
Donohue, Honora	F	32	Farrell, Anthony	M	3
Dougherty, Alice	F	43	Faucett, Deborah	F	24
Dougherty, Matilda	F	22	Fay, Wm.	M	6
Douney, Margaret	F	16	Fenton, Levinia	F	23
Doyle, Annie	F	40	Ferrari, Rosa	F	3
Doyle, Josephine	F	34	Fitzgibbon, Cathrine	F	67
Doyle, May	F	33	Flagg, Eliza	F	14m
Doyle, Rose	F	3	Flagg, Eliza	F	39
Driscoll, Celia	F	2	Flagg, Katie	F	32
Drumnet, John	M	11m	Flattery, Mary	F	32
Duane, John	M	3	Fleize, Annie	F	21
Duffy, Agnes	F	30	Fleming [Blank]	F	7m
Duffy, Rose	F	20	Fleming, John	M	5m
Duncan, Mary	F	17	Flezer, Lena	F	25
Dunn, Mary	F	22	Flynn, Lizzie	F	26
Dunn, Mary	F	29	Ford, Ada	F	25
Dunn, Mary	F	32	Forrester, Dollie	F	19
Dunnigan, Annie	F	5w	Francesco, Marie	F	5m
Dunreath, Oscar	M	12	Francis, John	M	2
Dutko, Mary	F	30	Frazer, Mary	F	33
Ecker, Otto	M	3	Freeman, Henry	M	2m
Edgar, Pauline	F	2	Freeman, Mary	F	23
Egan, John	M	28	Fulton, Kitty	F	4m
Eichler, Esther	F	4	Furley, Mary	F	20
Eicken, Emma	F	6m	Fury, Mary	F	27
Eiler, Louis	M	3	Galhoun, Annie	F	6
Einzel, Victoria	F	3	Gallagher, Mary	F	37
Elberon, Esther	F	4	Gannon, Mary	F	28
Elizabeth, Mary	F	4	Gannon, Robert	M	6
Epps, Henry	M	2w	Garagons, Marie	F	4
Erhman, Ernest	M	4	Gasser, Lizzie	F	4
Erwin, Joseph	M	9	Gassner, Frieda	F	19
Eskel, Marion	F	3	Gaston, Ada	F	5
Este, August	M	6m	Gay, Ella	F	3
Ettiner, Sarah	F	3	George, Ed Clark	M	27
Eustace, James	M	4	George, Henrietta	F	6
Evans, Francis	M	4	George, John	M	5m
Evans, Justin	M	5m	Gerald, Evelyn	F	5

Gerrity, Mary	F	4	Higgins, Elizabeth	F	50
Gibney, Mary	F	24	Higgins, Sarah	F	48
Gibs, Susie	F	-	Hill, Bernard	M	2m
Gibson, Katie	F	26	Hill, James	M	5
Gillman, Ed.	M	1m	Hill, Sara	F	24
Giroux, Anna	F	29	Hillary, Maggie	F	3
Givis, Mary	F	3	Hoffler, Theodore	M	4
Glassner, Josephine	F	5m	Hoffman, Joseph	M	3
Gleason, Agatha	F	8m	Hogan, Ellen	F	21
Glogan, Helen	F	3m	Holly, Mary	F	24
Goggin, Norah	F	27	Home, Mary	F	32
Graham, Mary	F	22	Hope, Eddie	M	5
Graham, Nellie	F	5	Hopkins, Johanna	F	40
Gray, Anna	F	4	Horgan, Margaret	F	71
Green, Oscar	M	4	Horne, Henry	M	40
Grenner, May	F	6	Horner, Ida	F	3
Griffin, Lizzie	F	34	Horton, Rachel	F	5
Groffol, Lizzie	F	2	Hughes, Elizabeth	F	26
Gross, Gregory	M	3	Hughes, Joseph	M	8m
Guthrie, Anna	F	32	Hughton, Mary	F	23
Haffy, Mary	F	3	Humboldt, Marion	F	3
Haines, Bertha	F	3	Hunter, George	M	3
Halbag, Raphael	M	3	Hurley, Annie	F	29
Hall, Anna	F	35	Hurley, Mary	F	49
Hamlin, Marie	F	3	Hyde, Fanny	F	25
Hanly, Mary A.	F	17	Hyland, Peter	M	8
Hannanay, Bridget	F	50	Ives, Loretta	F	3
Hannebury, Mary	F	26	Jackson, Sylvia	F	6
Hanrahan, Oliver	M	6m	James, Louise	F	25
Harper, Helen	F	3	Janeway, Rose	F	3
Harrison, Anna	F	25	Jarvis, Cecilia	F	18
Harrison, Eleanor	F	6	Jerome, Paul	M	3d
Hastings, Jos.	M	4	Jewell, Josephine	F	1
Hathaway, James	M	6m	Jinbert, Annette	F	4
Hatton, Heneretta	F	3	Joescrak, Annie	F	28
Hayes, Joseph	M	4	Jo[e]scrak, Rudolph	M	5m
Helsel, Clara	F	5	Johnson, Bessie	F	3m
Hennebury, Annie	F	4m	Johnson, Chas.	M	5m
Hennessy, Agnes	F	3	Johnson, Christina	F	3
Henning, Michael	M	4	Johnson, Grace	F	6
Henry, May	F	5	Johnson, Isabel	F	3
Herbert, Henrietta	F	3m	Johnson, Jane	F	47

Johnson, Jos.	M	5m	Lacey, Cataline	F	4m
Johnson, Mark	M	10d	Lacey, Wm.	M	2w
Jones, John	M	3	Laight, Addie	F	3
Jordan, Maria	F	1m	Lally, Annie	F	36
Joseph, Harold	M	2w	Lally, Ellen	F	22
Jugs, Teresa	F	5	Lambert, Regina	F	2
Kahn, John	M	2	Lanchez, Rita	F	4
Kane, Mamie	F	2	Lanes, Frank	M	10m
Kannarron, Mary	F	2w	Lardner, Margaret	F	36
Katie, Kelly	F	1w	Large, Eliza	F	19
Kearney, Bridget	F	48	Larkin, Elizabeth	F	38
Kelleher, James	M	5m	Larkin, Genevieve	F	19
Keller, Helena	F	38	Larkin, Maggie	F	31
Kelly, Charlotte	F	23	Larkin, Margaret	F	30
Kelly, Jane	F	4	Latimer, Eunice	F	4
Kelly, Joseph	-	6m	Laurence, Maud	F	3
Kelly, Katie	F	20	Lawson, Annie	F	3
Kelly, Maria	F	28	Lawson, William	M	3
Kelly, Mary	F	21	LeBlanc, Louise	F	30
Kennedy, Mary	F	22	Lee, Katie	F	19
Kennefick, Irene	F	3m	Lee, Laura	F	3w
Kenny, Ellen	F	43	Lee, Willie	M	4m
Kenny, Frank	M	17	Lennon, Thos.	M	4
Kent, Edgar	M	5m	Lenohan, Mary	F	40
Kent, Warren	F*	2	Lesser, Katie	F	3
Kerns, Frank	M	5m	LeStrange, Ann	F	53
Kert, Raymona	F	2	Levenand, Caroline	F	26
Kiely, Aloysius	M	4m	Lewis, Martha	F	2
Kiely, Cataline	F	2	Liszt, Ogreta	F	3
Kilburn, Elsie	F	3	Livingston, Grace	F	4m
King, Chester	M	5	Livingston, Mary	F	3
King, Geo.	M	8m	Lonvaier, William	M	4
King, Jennita	F	6	Loomis, Minnie	F	11m
Kinsella, Blanche	F	20	Loughlin, Julia	F	22
Kinsella, Cathrine	F	16	Louis, Anthony	M	5
Klepp, Bertha	F	5m	Lowe, Bessie	F	4
Klinck, Bessie	F	4	Lowell, Percy	M	4
Knight, Bridget	F	28	Loyola, Marguerite	F	4
Knight, Norman	M	10m	Lubin, Charles	M	4
Koll, Henrietta	F	21	Ludwig, Joseph	M	3
Konirran, Annie	F	22	Lynch, Annie	F	19
Krauss, Annie	F	24	Lynch, Susan	F	30

Lyons, Kate	F	30	McKenna, Maggie	F	2
Mack, Katie	F	23	McKeon, Ellen	F	35
Maderia, Helen	F	4	McKeon, Maggie	F	22
Maderia, Mary	F	28	McLoughlin, Jennie	F	2
Mahar, Margaret	F	28	McLoughlin, Mary	F	2
Mahon, John	M	38	McNulty, Margery	F	31
Mahon, Katie	F	7	McVay, John	M	3
Maitiga, Mary	F	1	Meehan, Francis	M	5
Maitigo, Mary	F	20	Mentor, Louis	M	4
Malden, Lizzie	F	25	Mereu, Angela	F	3
Malory, Annie	F	5m	Merritt, John	M	4m
Manresa, Ignatius	M	3m	Merritt, Mary	F	3
Marcllae, Louise	F	4	Miller, Cecilia	F	3
Marco, Marie	F	3	Miller, Mary	F	3
Markham, Mary	F	19	Minton, Henry	M	19
Marshall, Lottie	F	6	Mitchell, Emily	F	3m
Martin, Mary	F	29	Mitchell, Lizzie	F	25
Mason, Francis	F	7	Mohowkran, Annie	F	19
Maury, Grace	F	3	Mole, Eulalia	F	3
May, Dolores	F	3	Mooney, Margaret	F	43
May, Grace	F	6	Mooney, Rachel	F	45
May, Maggie	F	3	Moore, Emma	F	26
McCann, Bridget	F	24	Moore, Maggie	F	6
McCarthy, Adelaide	F	3	Moran, Anna	F	26
McCarthy, Mary	F	3w	Morgan, Joseph	M	5m
McCarthy, Nora	F	31	Morris, Annie	F	3m
McCarthy, Thos.	M	4m	Morris, Joseph	M	4
McConville, Alice	F	31	Morris, Kate	F	44
McCrystal, Jane	F	48	Morrison, Harry	M	5
McCue, Robert	M	5m	Morse, Annie	F	45
McDermott, Jennie	F	38	Mortel, Louise	F	2
McDonald, Maggie	F	22	Morton, Charles	M	6
McDonough, L.	M	7	Morton, Mary	F	3
McEarhearn, Mary	F	29	Mulcahy, Ellen	F	64
McGovern, Annie	F	3	Muller, Madge	F	4
McGrath, Carrie	F	17	Mullin, Margaret	F	21
McGrath, Mary	F	2	Munger, Joseph	M	3
McGrath, Mary	F	28	Murphey, Cathrine	F	22
McGueria, Evelyn	F	3	Murphy, Ella	F	23
McGuire, Cathrine	F	25	Murphy, Frank	M	28
McIntyre, Fanny	F	42	Murphy, Mamie	F	4
McIntyre, Julia	F	38	Murphy, Mary	F	25

Murray, Angela	F	2	Pella, Victorine	F	3
Murray, Frank	M	6w	Percival, Emma	F	3
Murray, Hattie	F	6m	Percival, Geo.	M	4m
Murray, Julia	F	21	Percival, Maurilla	F	17
Murter, Agnes	F	3	Perrine, Marie	F	3
Nagle, Abbie	F	21	Perry, Gertrude	F	3
Nally, Cathrine	F	24	Peters, Elizabeth	F	27
Nelson, Adelaide	F	4m	Pierce, Annie	F	3
Neri, Philip	M	3	Plunkett, Rose	F	2w
Newton, Charles	M	5	Pmkman, Sara	F	22
Newton, Irene	F	5	Prescott, Effie	F	5
Newton, Raymond	M	3	Preston, Leonard	M	3
Nicholas, Ellen	F	24	Price, Mary	F	25
Nicholl, Cathrine	F	27	Prinder, Margaret	F	20
Nolan, Rose	F	4	Proulz, Flora	F	28
Noon, Harry	M	4	Purcell, Annie	F	42
Nugent, Bridget	F	19	Quintard, Fred	M	3
Nugent, Mamie	F	1m	Rankin, Genevieve	F	4m
Nugent, Thomas	M	19	Raymond, Louis	M	3
O'Brien, Edwin	M	3m	Ready, Annie	F	30
O'Brien, Kate	F	23	Redder, Elizabeth	F	17
O'Brien, Mary	F	22	Reeder, Esther	F	3
O'Connell, John	M	28	Regan, Chas.	M	3
O'Connor, Willie	M	5m	Regan, Henrietta	F	28
O'Donnell, Margaret	F	29	Regan, Joseph	M	6
O'Donnell, Mary	F	19	Regan, Peter	M	25
O'Neil, Maggie	F	18	Regis, Mercedes	F	3
O'Neil, Mary	F	3m	Reid, Regina	F	5
O'Neil, Terence	M	4	Remsen, Hattie	F	3
O'Neill, Margaret	F	20	Rennell, Anna	F	4
O'Rourke, John	M	1m	Reynolds, Mary	F	26
O'Sullivan, Maurice	M	50	Rice, Carrie	F	10m
Oaks, Mary	F	3	Rice, Mary	F	25
Oaths, Oscar	M	5m	Richards, Joseph	M	11
Olier, Leon	M	3	Rierdan, James	M	3
Osmond, Mary	F	21	Rigney, Patrick	M	27
Otis, Lambert	M	3	Riordan, Mary	F	30
Parker, Anna	F	36	Rogers, Lizzie	F	6m
Parsons, Benjamin	M	3	Roi, Marguerite	F	3
Patton, John	M	3	Rooney, John	M	15
Paul, Eva	F	3	Rooney, Mary	F	39
Paul, Wilhemina	F	6	Rosecrans, Anthony	M	4

Rosmore, Howard	-	6m	Smith, Lilly	F	5w
Roso, John	M	9m	Smith, Louis	M	1
Rossiter, Mary	F	5	Smith, Mamie	F	3w
Rufino, Mary	F	3m	Smith, Mary	F	21
Rush, Eustace	M	2	Smith, Minnie	F	4
Russell, Tillie	F	10	Soles, Veronica	F	3
Ryan, Catherine	F	22	Spiegel, Henry	M	1m
Ryan, Lilly	F	4	Stehison, Alfred	M	4
Ryan, Mary	F	3m	Stevens, Annie	F	5
Ryan, Mary	F	20	Stevens, Mary	F	28
Sack, Margaret	F	2	String, Josephus	M	3
Sadlier, Teresa	F	34	Stuart, Henry	M	3w
Sales, Veronica	F	3m	Sullivan, Eddie	M	6m
Sanderson, Annie	F	24	Sullivan, John	M	4m
Sanger, Marguirete	F	3	Sullivan, Julia	F	23
Sarvey, Sophia	F	34	Sullivan, Mamie	F	17
Savage, Mary	F	3	Sullivan, Mary	F	34
Scally, Margaret	F	26	Sullivan, Nora	F	21
Scanlon, Mary E.	F	40	Sutton, Gilbert	M	4
Schimlar, Annie	F	2	Sweeny, Jerry	M	9m
Schmidkauer, Louis	M	2	Sweeny, Sarah	F	27
Schneider, Agnes	F	2m	Sylvester, Mary	F	1m
Schneider, Nellie	F	6m	Tayarneth, Adrian	M	3
Schrader, August	M	7m	Taylor, Justin	M	5m
Schwartz, Bessie	F	1	Temple, Josita	F	12
Schwartz, Mary	F	25	Thilin, Chas.	M	8m
Scribner, Mary	F	3	Thompson, Agnes	F	3m
Selvin, Agnes	F	3	Thompson, Edie	M	5
Seyler, Minnie	F	3	Thompson, Jos.	M	9m
Shay, Maggie	F	2	Thorndall, Anna	F	26
Sheehan, Agnes	F	25	Thurston, Henry	M	4
Sheehan, Kate	F	24	Thurston, Rita	F	6m
Sheehan, Willie	M	6m	Tierney, Tillie	F	22
Sherman, Wm.	M	4	Tinssant, Helen	F	3
Shiridan, Marguerite	F	4	Townsend, Evelyn	F	4m
Simpson, Arthur	M	6	Tracy, Loretto	F	21
Skivington, Annie	F	20	Trasher, George	M	6
Skivington, Mamie	F	4	Travers, Louis	M	3w
Smith, Annie	F	33	Travis, Clotilda	F	2m
Smith, Edith	F	3	Tressel, Rose	F	3m
Smith, Katie	F	5	Turner, Laurence	M	4
Smith, Lena	F	23	Valzeir, Robert	M	3

Vaughan, Katie	F	3	Wilson, Harry	M	8m
Veitch, Maude	F	18	Wilson, Lottie	F	18
Vergne, Pauline	F	4	Wilson, Mary Frances	F	17
Vermilye, Viola	F	26	Wilson, Miriam	F	5
Verrier, Leon	M	9m	Windsor, Raphael	M	3
Verrier, Marie	F	36	Winkle, Cora	F	2
Vincent, Helen	F	3	Winthrop, Ellen	F	3
Vincent, Marie	F	3	Woodruff, John	M	3
Wagner, Harry	M	4	Wooster, George	M	4
Waite, Joseph	M	3	Wrilward, James	M	4
Walker, Bertha	F	1m	Wueman, Mary	F	6
Wall, Alice	F	23	Wyman, Anita	F	4
Wallace, Benjamin	M	3	Young, Mamie	F	21
Wallace, Maggie	F	23	Zeller, Marie	F	4
Wallace, Oswald	M	4			
Walsh, John	M	5m			
Walsh, John	M	30			
Walsh, Mary	F	25			
Walsh, Patrick	M	26			
Walters, Wm.	M	3			
Walworth, Otto	M	3m			
Ward, Emma	F	28			
Wareham, Hilda	F	3			
Warren, Elma	F	4			
Warren, Sydney	M	4			
Waters, Annie	F	18			
Waters, Rose	F	18			
Watkins, Thos.	M	5m			
Weeks, Annie	F	3			
Weir, Otto	M	3			
Weiser, Louis	M	3			
Wells, Agnes	F	4			
Werley, Mary	F	26			
West, Matilda	F	3			
Weston, Wm.	M	4m			
White, Agnes	F	4			
White, Louis	M	4			
White, Rose	F	4			
Whittier, Theodore	M	3			
William, Francis	M	3			
Williams, Mamie	F	6m			
Willis, Mary	F	2			

Index to the
Federal Enumeration of the Inhabitants of

The New York Foundling Hospital

175 East 68th Street
New York, New York

June 1, 1900

Supervisor's District No. 1
Election District No. 699
Pages 15A - 36A

Joseph Vesey, Enumerator

Guide to Column Headings

in the

1900 Federal Enumeration Index

Name
Name of each person whose usual place of abode was in the institution on June 1, 1900. The census includes the name of every person living on June 1, 1900. Children born since June 1, 1900 were omitted. The surname is listed first, then the given name and middle initial.

R-G
Race and gender. White is designated by the letter "W", black by the letter "B", and Mulatto by the letters "Mu". Males are designated by the letter "M" and females are designated by the letter "F".

*
Notes that the enumerator may have reported the name or gender incorrectly.

M
Month of birth.

Y
Year of birth.

A
Age at last birthday. Designated in years, unless otherwise noted with an "m" for "months". Generally, children who were less than one year old were described in terms of months.

Relation
Relationship of each person to the institution.

Continued...

Note   All persons were listed as "Single". The birth-
        place of each child and his parents were listed as
        "Unknown". Refer to the orginal census for the
        birthplace of each adult occupant and her parents.
        An adult inmate whose relationship is listed as
        "St. Ann's" resided at St. Ann's Maternity Hospi-
        tal, a division of the New York Foundling Asy-
        lum. Although the building itself occupied the
        same grounds as the Foundling Asylum, the main
        entrance for St. Ann's faced East 69th Street. The
        enumerator included St. Ann's residents with those
        of the Asylum, but noted their separate entrance.

Name	R-G	M	Y	A	Relation
Abel, Annetta	WF	Nov.	1897	2	Inmate
Aberussi, Fred	WM	Nov.	1896	3	Inmate
Ackerman, Harold	WM	Nov.	1899	0	Inmate
Adams, Francis	WM	May	1897	3	Inmate
Adams, Jennie	WF	Nov.	1897	2	Inmate
Adams, John	WM	May	1897	3	Inmate
Adams, Joseph	WM	Nov.	1897	2	Inmate
Adams, Joseph	WM	Oct.	1897	2	Inmate
Adams, Mary	WF	July	1896	3	Inmate
Adamson, Louisa	WF	Feb.	1877	23	St. Ann's
Adee, Walter	WM	Dec.	1893	6	Inmate
Agnel, Joseph	WM	Jan.	1896	4	Inmate
Agnew, L. Joseph	WM	May	1893	7	Inmate
Ahern, Francis	WM	Nov.	1899	0	Inmate
Albright, Alice	WF	Sept.	1899	0	Inmate
Albright, Lizzie	WF	May	1880	20	Inmate
Alexander, Joseph	WM	Sept.	1897	2	Inmate
Alexander, Mary	WF	Mar.	1899	1	Inmate
Allen, Agnes	WF	Mar.	1900	0	Inmate
Allen, Ellen	WF	Mar.	1873	27	Inmate
Allen, Gertrude	WF	Nov.	1899	0	Inmate
Allen, Margaret	WF	Jan.	1898	2	Inmate
Allen, Mary	WF	June	1896	4	Inmate
Allison, Agnes	WF	Jan.	1899	1	Inmate
Almer, Ida	WF	Aug.	1897	2	Inmate
Alms, Edward	WM	Aug.	1899	0	Inmate
Aloysius, John	WM	May	1898	2	Inmate
Alphonsus, Joseph	WM	Feb.	1900	0	Inmate
Alvetti, Marie	WF	Aug.	1897	2	Inmate
Ambler, James	WM	Apr.	1898	2	Inmate
Amet, Joseph	WM	Jan.	1896	4	Inmate
Anderson, Carl	WM	Sept.	1899	0	Inmate
Anderson, Charles	WM	Mar.	1898	2	Inmate
Anderson, Christine	WF	Mar.	1898	2	Inmate
Anderson, Thomas	WM	Nov.	1899	0	Inmate
Anderson, Willie	WM	Nov.	1897	2	Inmate
Andrew, Edward	WM	Sept.	1899	0	Inmate
Andrew, Edward	WM	Apr.	1899	1	Inmate
Andrews, Louise	WF	Jan.	1900	0	Inmate
Aner, Joseph	WM	May	1896	4	Inmate
Anogart, Josephine	WF	Mar.	1899	1	Inmate
Anthony, Vincent	WM	Feb.	1900	0	Inmate

Appelton, Edith	WF	Feb.	1876	24	St. Ann's
Appleton, Adam	WM	May	1890	10	Inmate
Appotti, Joseph	WM	Sept.	1899	0	Inmate
Archer, Nellie	WF	Dec.	1874	25	Inmate
Armstrong, Alberto	WM	Aug.	1897	2	Inmate
Armstrong, Mary	WF	July	1898	1	Inmate
Arnold, Alice	WF	Sept.	1897	2	Inmate
Atinstei, John	WM	Jun.	1897	2	Inmate
Atkinson, Catherine	WF	Sept.	1896	3	Inmate
Aubrey, Gaston	WM	Oct.	1897	2	Inmate
Audley, Wm.	WM	Dec.	1899	0	Inmate
Auslander, Sonif	WF	Mar.	1897	3	Inmate
Austin, Oliver	WM	July	1899	0	Inmate
Avenson, Jacob	WM	Dec.	1897	2	Inmate
Bailley, Sidney	WM	May	1899	1	Inmate
Baker, Francis	WM	Feb.	1893	6	Inmate
Baker, John	WM	Jan.	1898	2	Inmate
Baker, Josita	WF	Mar.	1900	0	Inmate
Baker, Rose	WF	Apr.	1897	3	Inmate
Baldwin, Luca	WF	Oct.	1897	2	Inmate
Baldwin, Regina	WM	July	1899	0	Inmate
Bappaceno, Gerard	WM	May	1898	2	Inmate
Baptist, John	WM	June	1898	1	Inmate
Barber, Horace	WM	May	1899	1	Inmate
Barey, Herbert	WM	Feb.	1899	1	Inmate
Bargebuhr, Maude	WF	Mar.	1898	2	Inmate
Barlow, Alfred	WM	Dec.	1897	2	Inmate
Barn, Peter	WM	Apr.	1900	0	Inmate
Barnes, Edna	WF	Mar.	1900	0	Inmate
Barocki, Mary	WF	Oct.	1897	2	Inmate
Barr, Edward	WM	Feb.	1897	3	Inmate
Barr, George	WM	July	1898	1	Inmate
Barra, Ida	WF	Apr.	1898	2	Inmate
Barrett, Raymond	WM	Feb.	1900	0	Inmate
Barri, Annie	WF	Mar.	1880	20	Inmate
Barron, Patricia	WM	Mar.	1899	1	Inmate
Barry, Delia	WF	Dec.	1873	26	Inmate
Barry, Hannah	WF	Mar.	1874	26	Sister
Barry, Lizzie	WF	June	1897	2	Inmate
Barry, Margaret	WF	Dec.	1898	1	Inmate
Barry, Mary	WF	Mar.	1897	3	Inmate
Barry, Thomas	WM	Dec.	1899	0	Inmate

Bartlett, Theresa	WF	Apr.	1869	31	St. Ann's
Bartom, Wm.	WM	July	1899	0	Inmate
Baunstein, Francis	WM	Apr.	1895	5	Inmate
Beckenorf, Chas.	WM	Oct.	1897	2	Inmate
Becker, George	WM	Apr.	1898	2	Inmate
Becker, Madeline	WF	May	1900	0	Inmate
Becker, Minnie	WF	Feb.	1884	16	St. Ann's
Beckman, Bertha	WF	Mar.	1899	1	Inmate
Becraft, Jeanette	WF	May	1897	3	Inmate
Beerbaum, Dan.	WM	Jan.	1898	2	Inmate
Beffi, John	WM	Oct.	1898	1	Inmate
Beiner, Fannie	WF	Nov.	1899	0	Inmate
Belevedere, Meli	WF	Sept.	1896	3	Inmate
Bell, Anna	Wf	Nov.	1899	0	Inmate
Bell, Joseph	WM	Aug.	1897	2	Inmate
Bell, Lillie	WF	May	1900	0	Inmate
Bell, Mary	WF	July	1897	2	Inmate
Bell, William	WM	Nov.	1897	2	Inmate
Bellin, Marie	WF	Dec.	1897	2	Inmate
Belvin, Mary	WF	Mr.	1900	0	Inmate
Beng, William	WM	Jan.	1897	3	Inmate
Benheimer, Wm.	WM	May	1899	1	Inmate
Bennett, Edward	WM	Aug.	1898	1	Inmate
Benning, Mary	WF	Aug.	1899	0	Inmate
Benson, Richard	WM	May	1898	2	Inmate
Bergen, Clara	WF	Oct.	1899	0	Inmate
Bergen, Julia	WF	Apr.	1900	0	Inmate
Bernard, Agatha	WF	Mar.	1898	2	Inmate
Bernard, George	WM	Apr.	1894	6	Inmate
Bernhardt, Thelma	WF	Dec.	1897	2	Inmate
Bertrand, Willie	WM	Jun	1896	4	Inmate
Best, Rose	WF	Mar.	1898	2	Inmate
Beyer, Constance	WF	Feb.	1882	18	St. Ann's
Biebian, Mary	WF	Aug.	1898	1	Inmate
Biggins, Joseph	WM	July	1899	0	Inmate
Biggins, Mary	WF	Mar.	1864	36	Inmate
Bird, Helen	WF	July	1899	0	Inmate
Black, Elizabeth	WF	May	1874	26	Inmate
Black, Irene	WF	Sept.	1896	3	Inmate
Blanchard, Anita	WF	Sept.	1897	2	Inmate
Blaschki, Cath.	WF	Nov.	1898	1	Inmate
Blind, Joseph	WM	Jan.	1896	4	Inmate

Block, Albert	WM	Feb.	1895	5	Inmate
Block, Sara	WF	Aug.	1898	1	Inmate
Bocenlini, David	WM	Nov.	1899	0	Inmate
Boger, Agnes	WF	Mar.	1881	19	Inmate
Boken, Annie	WF	Oct.	1899	0	Inmate
Bolger, Michael	WM	Mar.	1900	0	Inmate
Bono, Joseph	WM	Nov.	1897	2	Inmate
Booth, Fredrick	WM	Nov.	1897	2	Inmate
Booth, John	WM	Mar.	1900	0	Inmate
Bosbata, Marie	WF	Dec.	1897	2	Inmate
Bostle, Thomas	WM	Mar.	1900	0	Inmate
Bowen, Catherine	WF	Aug.	1863	36	Sister
Bowen, John	WM	Jan.	1899	1	Inmate
Bower, Alma	WM	Jan.	1898	2	Inmate
Bower, Marie	WF	Mar.	1900	0	Inmate
Bowker, George	WM	June	1896	4	Inmate
Boylan, Joseph	WM	Jan.	1899	1	Inmate
Bradley, Francis	WM	Dec.	1896	3	Inmate
Bradley, James	WM	Aug.	1898	1	Inmate
Bradley, Joseph	WM	Jan.	1893	7	Inmate
Bradley, Mary	WF	Mar.	1898	2	Inmate
Bradshaw, John	WM	June	1898	2	Inmate
Brady, Adeline	WF	Apr.	1898	2	Inmate
Brady, Henry	WM	Feb.	1898	2	Inmate
Brady, Mary	WF	May	1862	38	Inmate
Brain, Annie	WF	Jan.	1898	2	Inmate
Bransley, Fred	WM	July	1897	2	Inmate
Brant, Joseph	WM	Apr.	1900	0	Inmate
Brant, Margaret	WF	May	1900	0	Inmate
Braun, Louis	WM	Sept.	1897	2	Inmate
Bray, Thomas	WM	May	1897	3	Inmate
Brecht, Margaret	WF	July	1895	4	Inmate
Bremanshire, Paul	WM	Aug.	1897	2	Inmate
Bremka, Maria	WF	Dec.	1876	23	Inmate
Bremka, Richard	WM	Apr.	1900	0	Inmate
Brennan, Ambrose	WM	Dec.	1896	3	Inmate
Brennan, Gertrude	WF	Dec.	1897	2	Inmate
Brennan, Mary	WF	Jan.	1900	0	Inmate
Brennan, Veronica	WF	Nov.	1898	1	Inmate
Brevario, Nelson	WM	May	1899	1	Inmate
Bridges, Edward	WM	Aug	1897	2	Inmate
Brindisi, Rosina	WF	Aug.	1898	1	Inmate

Britt, Ernest	WM	Apr.	1900	0	Inmate
Brock, Rose	WF	May	1898	2	Inmate
Brogan, Francis	WM	Aug.	1898	1	Inmate
Brogan, Joseph	WM	Jan.	1900	0	Inmate
Brogan, Rose	WF	July	1878	21	Inmate
Bron, Joseph	WM	Aug.	1898	1	Inmate
Bronet, Mary	WF	Nov.	1897	2	Inmate
Bronson, John	WM	July	1896	3	Inmate
Brophy, Harry	WM	May	1895	5	Inmate
Brosge, Gertrude	WF	Jan.	1899	1	Inmate
Brown, Catherine	WF	Dec.	1898	1	Inmate
Brown, Chas.	WM	Aug.	1898	1	Inmate
Brown, Edith	WF	June	1897	2	Inmate
Brown, Edwin	WM	Aug.	1896	3	Inmate
Brown, Florence	WF	Jan.	1899	1	Inmate
Brown, Francis	WM	Dec.	1898	1	Inmate
Brown, Francis	WM	May	1896	4	Inmate
Brown, Hannah	WF	June	1897	2	Inmate
Brown, John	WM	June	1898	2	Inmate
Brown, Josephine	WF	Apr.	1895	6	Inmate
Brown, Lillian	WF	Mar.	1898	2	Inmate
Brown, Lizzie	WF	Aug.	1892	7	Inmate
Brown, Mamie	WF	Jan.	1897	3	Inmate
Brown, Margaret	WF	Aug.	1896	3	Inmate
Brown, Mary	WF	Jan.	1899	1	Inmate
Brown, Mary	WF	Sept.	1897	2	Inmate
Brown, Mary	WF	May	1893	7	Inmate
Brown, Mary	WF	May	1885	15	St. Ann's
Brown, Michall	WM	Mar	1895	5	Inmate
Brown, Raymond	WM	Jan.	1898	2	Inmate
Brown, Sara	WF	Nov.	1899	0	Inmate
Brown, Tessie	WF	July	1898	1	Inmate
Brown, Walter	WM	Oct.	1896	3	Inmate
Browning, Edna	WF	Feb.	1899	1	Inmate
Brum, James	WM	June	1899	0	Inmate
Brume, Rose	WF	Nov.	1896	3	Inmate
Bruno, Annie	WF	Nov.	1897	2	Inmate
Bruno, Bertha	WF	Aug.	1899	0	Inmate
Bruno, Mary	WF	Feb.	1899	1	Inmate
Brunski, Lena	WF	July	1899	0	Inmate
Bryan, Alfred	WM	Apr.	1895	5	Inmate
Bryne, Mary	WF	Mar.	1897	3	Inmate

Buff, Lorretto	WF	Feb.	1899	1	Inmate
Buffi, Louisa	WF	July	1897	2	Inmate
Bulger, Maurice	WM	Apr.	1899	1	Inmate
Buller, William	WM	June	1898	2	Inmate
Bumer, Michael	WM	Nov.	1896	3	Inmate
Bunting, Helen	WF	Oct.	1899	0	Inmate
Burgmyer, Leo	WM	Apr.	1899	1	Inmate
Burk, Charles	WM	Sept.	1897	2	Inmate
Burk, Frances	WF	Nov.	1899	0	Inmate
Burke, Anna	WF	May	1900	0	Inmate
Burke, Cora	WF	Mar.	1882	18	Inmate
Burke, Florence	WF	Oct.	1897	2	Inmate
Burke, Gerard	WM	Oct.	1899	0	Inmate
Burke, Gertrude	WF	May	1899	1	Inmate
Burke, John	WM	Mar.	1900	0	Inmate
Burke, Julia	WF	Mar.	1880	20	Inmate
Burke, Kate	WF	Sept.	1894	5	Inmate
Burne, Antonetta	WF	June	1898	2	Inmate
Burns, Anastasia	WF	Mar.	1877	23	Inmate
Burns, Anna	WF	Nov.	1884	15	Inmate
Burns, Catherine	WF	Apr.	1838	62	Sister
Burns, Edward	WM	May	1898	2	Inmate
Burns, Ellen	WF	Jan.	1896	4	Inmate
Burns, Gertrude	WF	Feb.	1898	2	Inmate
Burns, James	WM	Oct.	1899	0	Inmate
Burns, John	WM	July	1894	5	Inmate
Burns, Joseph	WM	June	1899	0	Inmate
Burns, Mary	WF	Feb.	1900	0	Inmate
Burns, Mary	WF	Nov.	1878	21	Inmate
Burns, Philip	WM	Feb.	1900	0	Inmate
Burns, Veronica	WF	Jan.	1900	0	Inmate
Burns, William	WM	Feb.	1900	0	Inmate
Butler, Francis	WM	Dec.	1895	4	Inmate
Butt, Mary	WF	Aug.	1897	2	Inmate
Butterfield, Julia	WF	Oct.	1899	0	Inmate
Cadiz, Mary	WF	Apr.	1900	0	Inmate
Caffery, Julia	WF	Jan.	1900	0	Inmate
Cahill, Edward	WF*	Apr.	1898	2	Inmate
Cahill, Elizabed	WF	Mar.	1864	36	St. Ann's
Cain, William	WM	May	1898	2	Inmate
Callahan, Elizabeth	WF	Apr.	1898	2	Inmate
Calvin, William	WM	Mar.	1900	0	Inmate

Campbell, Anthony	WM	June	1897	2	Inmate
Canavan, Teresa	WF	Oct.	1896	3	Inmate
Canning, Mary	WF	Sept.	1899	0	Inmate
Cannon, Teresa	WF	Feb.	1899	1	Inmate
Capsra, John	WM	Apr.	1900	0	Inmate
Carey, Henry	WM	June	1899	1	Inmate
Carl, Augusta	WM*	Aug.	1899	0	Inmate
Carlson, Ethel	WF	May	1898	2	Inmate
Carolton, Katie	WF	Nov.	1898	1	Inmate
Carpenter, Wm.	WM	Dec.	1899	0	Inmate
Carr, Beatrice	WF	Mar.	1899	1	Inmate
Carr, Mary	WF	Feb.	1882	18	St. Ann's
Carroll, Eliza	WF	Feb.	1899	1	Inmate
Carroll, Katie	WF	Mar.	1898	2	Inmate
Carroll, Marie	WF	Dec.	1898	1	Inmate
Carroll, Mary	WF	Feb.	1899	1	Inmate
Carson, Margaret	WF	Aug.	1897	2	Inmate
Carter, Herbert	WM	Dec.	1895	4	Inmate
Casey, John	WF*	Feb.	1900	0	Inmate
Casey, Joseph	WM	July	1897	2	Inmate
Cassalo, Louise	WF	Jan.	1899	0	Inmate
Cassidy, Agatha	WF	Oct.	1899	0	Inmate
Cassidy, Henry	WM	June	1899	1	Inmate
Cassidy, John	WM	Nov.	1899	0	Inmate
Cassidy, Mary	WF	Nov.	1896	3	Inmate
Cassidy, Pauline	WF	Sept.	1897	2	Inmate
Caumi, Anna	WF	May	1899	1	Inmate
Cavalvetz, Joseph	WM	Sept.	1899	0	Inmate
Cayton, Annie	WF	Feb.	1897	3	Inmate
Chadini, Frank	WM	Nov.	1899	0	Inmate
Chambers, Mary	WF	Jan.	1900	0	Inmate
Chambers, Mary	WF	Nov.	1879	20	Inmate
Charles, Lillie	WF	Sept.	1897	2	Inmate
Charters, Daisy	WF	Oct.	1897	2	Inmate
Chatham, Oscar	WM	June	1898	1	Inmate
Chessman, Francis	WM	Apr.	1900	0	Inmate
Chizola, Louise	WF	May	1900	0	Inmate
Christ, Christopher	WM	Jan.	1895	5	Inmate
Christian, Edward	WM	July	1898	1	Inmate
Christiansen, Fred	WM	Aug.	1898	1	Inmate
Church, Vincent	WM	May	1898	2	Inmate
Claire, John	WM	Apr.	1895	5	Inmate

Clancy, Mary	WF	June	1899	1	Inmate
Clanton, Evelyn	WF	Feb.	1900	0	Inmate
Clark, Augustus	WM	June	1896	3	Inmate
Clark, Edward	WM	Aug.	1899	0	Inmate
Clark, Fred	WM	May	1899	1	Inmate
Clark, Helen	WF	Feb.	1899	1	Inmate
Clark, Herbert	WM	July	1898	1	Inmate
Clark, Jerome	WM	Oct.	1897	2	Inmate
Clark, John	WM	Jan.	1900	0	Inmate
Clark, Marion	WF	Mar.	1882	18	St. Ann's
Clark, Mary	WF	Apr.	1900	0	Inmate
Clark, Mary	WF	Aug.	1898	1	Inmate
Clark, Mary	WF	May	1877	23	St. Ann's
Clark, Matthew	WM	Dec.	1898	1	Inmate
Clark, Nellie	WF	Nov.	1898	1	Inmate
Clark, Rose	WF	Feb.	1880	20	Inmate
Clark, Thomas	WM	Feb.	1892	8	Inmate
Clark, William	WM	May	1899	1	Inmate
Clarkson, Wm.	WM	Jan.	1899	1	Inmate
Clenent, John	WM	June	1896	3	Inmate
Clinton, Frank	WM	Apr.	1898	2	Inmate
Cludet, Louis	WM	Apr.	1898	2	Inmate
Codge, Ernest	WM	Apr.	1900	0	Inmate
Codye, Emma	WF	Feb.	1875	25	Inmate
Coe, Rose	WF	Mar.	1899	1	Inmate
Coffer, John	WM	Nov.	1899	0	Inmate
Coger, George	WM	Mar.	1893	7	Inmate
Cogley, Lillian	WF	May	1900	0	Inmate
Cohen, Bertha	WF	May	1897	3	Inmate
Cohen, Bessie	WF	May	1899	1	Inmate
Cohen, Edward	WM	Aug.	1897	2	Inmate
Cohen, Esther	WF	Aug.	1897	2	Inmate
Cohen, Joseph	WM	Mar.	1900	0	Inmate
Cohen, Julian	WM	Nov.	1895	4	Inmate
Cohen, Lester	WM	Oct.	1898	1	Inmate
Cohen, Ludwig	WM	Aug.	1896	3	Inmate
Cohn, Lillian	WF	Jan.	1897	3	Inmate
Cole, Joseph	WM	Apr.	1897	3	Inmate
Coleman, Cath.	WF	Nov.	1899	1	Inmate
Coleman, Jennie	WF	Oct.	1898	1	Inmate
Colley, Joseph	WM	Dec.	1897	2	Inmate
Collier, John	WM	Nov.	1895	4	Inmate

Collins, Annie	WF	Jan.	1900	0	Inmate
Collins, Annie	WF	Feb.	1899	1	Inmate
Collins, Dorothy	WF	Feb.	1899	1	Inmate
Collins, George	WM	Dec.	1897	2	Inmate
Collins, Henry	WM	Oct.	1895	4	Inmate
Collins, Mary	WF	Sept.	1899	0	Inmate
Collins, Walter	WM	Sept.	1897	2	Inmate
Collins, William	WM	July	1896	3	Inmate
Colman, John	WM	Mar.	1893	7	Inmate
Colman, Mark	WM	Oct.	1898	1	Inmate
Colon, Harry	WM	Sept.	1898	1	Inmate
Comell, Mary	WF	Feb.	1896	4	Inmate
Commerce, Edna	WF	Jan.	1896	4	Inmate
Commesky, Ed.	WM	Apr.	1900	0	Inmate
Committo, Antonio	WM	Feb.	1899	1	Inmate
Condy, Mary	WF	May	1855	45	Inmate
Conkling, Daisy	WF	Mar.	1899	1	Inmate
Conlon, Lillian	WF	Jan.	1896	4	Inmate
Conlon, Margaret	WF	Dec.	1896	3	Inmate
Connelly, Delia	WF	Jan.	1879	21	St. Ann's
Connerron, Joseph	WM	Apr.	1897	3	Inmate
Conners, Kate	WF	May	1881	19	St. Ann's
Connolly, George	WM	Apr.	1898	2	Inmate
Connolly, Joseph	WM	Sept.	1899	0	Inmate
Connolly, Mary	WF	Mar.	1898	2	Inmate
Connolly, Rose	WF	Nov.	1899	0	Inmate
Connor, Mary	WF	Nov.	1880	19	Inmate
Connor, Thomas	WM	Apr.	1900	0	Inmate
Connors, Alma	WF	June	1899	1	Inmate
Connors, Joseph	WM	Aug.	1899	0	Inmate
Conologue, Jos.	WM	Mar.	1899	1	Inmate
Conroy, Catherine	WF	May	1871	29	Inmate
Conroy, Irene	WF	Apr.	1900	0	Inmate
Conroy, Mary	WF	July	1898	1	Inmate
Conway, Burt	WM	July	1897	2	Inmate
Cook, John	WM	July	1897	2	Inmate
Cook, Mary	WF	Jan.	1900	0	Inmate
Cooke, Mary	WF	Nov.	1879	20	Inmate
Coon, Florence	WF	July	1899	0	Inmate
Cooney, Frederick	WM	Mar.	1897	3	Inmate
Cooper, Francis	WM	May	1900	0	Inmate
Cooper, Louisa	WF	Aug.	1898	1	Inmate

Corbett, Anthony	WM	Jan.	1893	7	Inmate
Corbett, Joseph	WM	Apr.	1900	0	Inmate
Corbett, Walter	WM	Apr.	1895	5	Inmate
Corcoran, Lillian	WF	Nov.	1898	1	Inmate
Corrigan, Florence	WF	May	1899	1	Inmate
Cortelyou, Beatrice	WF	Nov.	1898	1	Inmate
Cosgrove, Agnes	WF	Sept.	1897	2	Inmate
Cosgrove, Joseph	WM	Apr.	1898	2	Inmate
Costello, Augustine	WM	Apr.	1898	2	Inmate
Costello, Wm.	WM	Aug.	1899	0	Inmate
Coughlin, Kate	WF	Mar.	1896	4	Inmate
Coughlin, Wm.	WM	July	1897	2	Inmate
Coulter, Philip	WM	May	1900	0	Inmate
Cowley, Helen	WF	Oct.	1898	1	Inmate
Cowley, Joseph	WM	Sept.	1898	1	Inmate
Cox, Mary	WF	Feb.	1898	2	Inmate
Cox, William	WM	Mar.	1898	2	Inmate
Craig, Irma	WM*	July	1898	1	Inmate
Crane, James	WM	July	1896	3	Inmate
Crans, Ruth	WF	Dec.	1899	0	Inmate
Craus, Katie	WF	Apr.	1898	2	Inmate
Cresky, Florence	WF	Oct.	1897	2	Inmate
Crieghton, Mary	WF	July	1850	49	St. Ann's
Croff, Egfie	WF	July	1898	1	Inmate
Cronin, Mary	WF	Sept.	1898	1	Inmate
Crooks, Aloysius	WM	Oct.	1896	3	Inmate
Crosby, Genevieve	WM	Dec.	1897	2	Inmate
Crosby, James	WM	Sept.	1897	2	Inmate
Cross, John	WM	Nov.	1899	0	Inmate
Crudder, Adelaid	WF	Feb.	1899	1	Inmate
Cuddihy, Richard	WM	Sept.	1898	1	Inmate
Cummings, Athor	WM	Apr.	1897	3	Inmate
Cunningham, John	WM	June	1897	2	Inmate
Cunningham, Jos.	WM	Sept.	1898	1	Inmate
Cunningham, Marg't.	WF	June	1873	27	Inmate
Cunningham, Mary	WF	May	1900	0	Inmate
Curey, Alexander	WM	Feb.	1898	2	Inmate
Curn, Marion	WF	Mar.	1900	0	Inmate
Curry, Mary	WF	July	1897	2	Inmate
Curtin, Margaret	WF	Nov.	1899	0	Inmate
Curtin, Terrance	WM	Oct.	1896	3	Inmate
Curtis, Joseph	WM	Nov.	1893	6	Inmate

Cusack, Alice	WF	Oct.	1898	1	Inmate
Cushinski, Ida	WF	Aug.	1898	1	Inmate
Daley, Francis	WM	Apr.	1899	1	Inmate
Dalry, James	WM	Dec.	1897	2	Inmate
Dalton, Hugh	WM	Dec.	1898	1	Inmate
Dalton, Veronica	WF	Oct.	1899	0	Inmate
Damas, Chas.	WM	Dec.	1898	1	Inmate
Davenport, Frances	WF	Oct.	1899	0	Inmate
Davis, Gertrude	WF	Feb.	1899	1	Inmate
Davis, James	WM	June	1899	1	Inmate
Davis, Mary	WF	Sept.	1897	2	Inmate
Davis, Vincent	WM	May	1899	1	Inmate
De Paul, Joseph	WM	Aug.	1892	7	Inmate
Deale, Agnes	WF	June	1898	1	Inmate
Dealy, Joseph	WM	May	1892	8	Inmate
Dean, Harriet	WF	Apr.	1900	0	Inmate
Dean, Marion	WF	July	1898	1	Inmate
Deasey, Augustine	WF	Feb.	1897	3	Inmate
Debardu, Mandeline	WF	June	1897	2	Inmate
Dejannnie, Mary	WF	June	1897	2	Inmate
Delaney, Alice	WF	Mar.	1875	25	St. Ann's
Demeres, Aloy	WF	Feb.	1899	1	Inmate
Demmers, Alms	WM	Feb.	1899	1	Inmate
Dempsey, Eliza	WF	June	1898	1	Inmate
Denk, Peter	WM	Oct.	1899	0	Inmate
Denning, Bernard	WM	Nov.	1898	1	Inmate
Dennis, Salone	WM	Apr.	1898	2	Inmate
Denny, Joseph	WM	Dec.	1899	0	Inmate
Derne, Sarah	WF	Feb.	1900	0	Inmate
Derr, William	WM	Mar.	1899	1	Inmate
Derrido, Antoin	WM	Nov.	1898	1	Inmate
Desmond, Francis	WM	Oct.	1897	2	Inmate
Destler, Emanuel	WM	Dec.	1899	0	Inmate
Deverix, Mary	WF	Feb.	1865	35	Inmate
Deverix, Wm.	WM	Oct.	1899	0	Inmate
Devine, John	WM	Oct.	1899	0	Inmate
Devins, Wilham	WM	Nov.	1899	0	Inmate
Devlin, Agnes	WF	Dec.	1895	4	Inmate
Devlin, Mary	WF	Oct.	1899	0	Inmate
Devlin, Mary	WF	Dec.	1863	36	Inmate
Dewey, Margaret	WF	Apr.	1841	59	Sister
Dey, Lumma	WF	Oct.	1896	3	Inmate

Dietz, Frederic	WM	July	1899	0	Inmate
Dijunki, Harold	WM	June	1897	2	Inmate
Dilchist, John	WM	Nov.	1898	1	Inmate
Dillon, Frank	WM	Sept.	1897	2	Inmate
Dion, Marie	WF	June	1898	1	Inmate
Disarli, Maria	WF	May	1900	0	Inmate
Disbrow, Irving	WM	May	1897	3	Inmate
Ditmar, Helen	WF	Jan.	1898	2	Inmate
Ditmar, John	WM	Jan.	1900	0	Inmate
Dixon, Agnes	WF	Aug.	1899	0	Inmate
Dixon, John	WM	Dec.	1897	2	Inmate
Dixon, John	WM	June	1897	2	Inmate
Doan, Mary	WF	July	1897	2	Inmate
Dobettle, Joseph	WM	Feb.	1897	3	Inmate
Dodge, Kate	WF	Dec.	1878	21	St. Ann's
Doey, Louis	WM	Mar.	1899	1	Inmate
Dolan, John	WM	Aug.	1892	7	Inmate
Dolan, Nellie	WF	Jan.	1898	2	Inmate
Dolon, Catherine	WF	July	1897	2	Inmate
Dolorosa, Mary	WF	Mar.	1897	3	Inmate
Donahoe, Thomas	WM	Nov.	1899	0	Inmate
Donnelly, Louise	WF	Sept.	1895	4	Inmate
Donnovan, John	WM	Nov.	1899	0	Inmate
Donohoe, Agnes	WF	Dec.	1899	0	Inmate
Donohue, Kate	WF	Mar.	1875	25	Inmate
Donovan, Daniel	WM	Dec.	1897	2	Inmate
Doohan, Chas.	WM	Dec.	1898	1	Inmate
Dooley, James	WM	Oct.	1899	0	Inmate
Doran, Anthony	WM	July	1898	1	Inmate
Dougherty, Edward	WM	Dec.	1899	0	Inmate
Douhan, Paul	WM	Dec.	1898	1	Inmate
Dowd, Francis	WM	Mar.	1899	1	Inmate
Dowd, Irene	WF	Feb.	1899	1	Inmate
Dowd, James	WM	Nov.	1899	0	Inmate
Downey, Raymond	WM	Aug.	1895	4	Inmate
Downs, Albert	WM	May	1897	3	Inmate
Downs, Raymond	WM	Jan.	1900	0	Inmate
Doyle, Anna	WF	Jan.	1900	0	Inmate
Doyle, Annie	WF	May	1899	1	Inmate
Doyle, Francis	WM	July	1896	3	Inmate
Doyle, Joseph	WM	Oct.	1897	2	Inmate
Doyle, Josephine	WF	Oct.	1857	42	Sister

Doyle, Thomas	WM	July	1897	2	Inmate
Drebel, Charles	WM	Apr.	1900	0	Inmate
Dresler, Charles	WM	Jan.	1900	0	Inmate
Driscoll, Annie	WF	Oct.	1898	1	Inmate
Driscoll, Mary	WF	Dec.	1894	5	Inmate
Drummond, Helen	WF	Apr.	1899	1	Inmate
Duane, Bernard	WM	July	1899	0	Inmate
Dubor, Ella	WF	Jan.	1900	0	Inmate
Dudley, Horace	WM	Oct.	1899	0	Inmate
Dudley, John	WM	Dec.	1896	3	Inmate
Duffy, Andrew	WM	Mar.	1900	0	Inmate
Duffy, Charles	WM	Nov.	1899	0	Inmate
Duffy, John	WM	May	1899	1	Inmate
Duffy, Joseph	WM	Oct.	1899	0	Inmate
Duffy, Magaret	WF	Apr.	1900	0	Inmate
Duffy, Margaret	WF	Mar.	1874	26	Inmate
Duffy, Victor	WM	Dec.	1898	1	Inmate
Dugan, Annie	WF	Jan.	1898	2	Inmate
Dugan, Anthony	WM	Jan.	1898	2	Inmate
Dugan, Ethel	WF	Oct.	1895	4	Inmate
Dugan, Thomas	WM	Oct.	1896	3	Inmate
Duggan, Peter	WM	Mar.	1900	0	Inmate
Dume, Ellen J.	WF	May	1858	42	Sister
Duncan, Joseph	WM	July	1895	4	Inmate
Dunman, Arthura	WF	May	1898	2	Inmate
Dunn, Clementine	WF	June	1898	1	Inmate
Dunn, Hannah	WF	Nov.	1863	36	Inmate
Dunn, Josephine	WF	Mar.	1900	0	Inmate
Dunn, Madeline	WF	Oct.	1898	1	Inmate
Dunn, Timothy	WM	Oct.	1899	0	Inmate
Durning, Annie	WF	Nov.	1896	3	Inmate
Dwyer, Archie	WM	Aug.	1888	11	Inmate
Dyas, Mary	WF	May	1883	17	St. Ann's
Dyer, Elizabeth	WF	Jan.	1898	2	Inmate
Dyner, John	WM	July	1899	0	Inmate
Eames, Leonard	WM	Nov.	1895	4	Inmate
Eastward, Irene	WF	July	1896	3	Inmate
Eckers, Henry	WM	July	1898	1	Inmate
Edenburgh, Rudolph	WM	June	1899	1	Inmate
Edith, Sarah	WF	-	1869	30	Sister
Edlington, Lucinan	WF	Dec.	1897	2	Inmate
Edmundson, James	WM	Feb.	1898	2	Inmate

Edward, Ellen	WF	Mar.	1876	24	Inmate
Edwards, Agnes	WF	Jan.	1900	0	Inmate
Edwards, Antonia	WM*	Jan.	1900	0	Inmate
Edwards, Chas.	WM	Mar.	1896	4	Inmate
Edwards, Eliza	WF	Jan.	1900	0	Inmate
Edwards, Francis	WM	Jan.	1898	2	Inmate
Edwards, John	WM	Feb.	1900	0	Inmate
Edwards, Teresa	WF	Oct.	1898	1	Inmate
Egan, Joseph	WM	June	1895	5	Inmate
Egan, Mary	WF	Mar.	1900	0	Inmate
Egan, Mary M.	WF	Mar.	1900	0	Inmate
Ehrichson, Jennie	WF	Mar.	1883	17	St. Ann's
Ehrick, Thomas	WM	Oct.	1894	5	Inmate
Eisen, Annie	WF	May	1899	1	Inmate
Elbert, Harold	WM	Nov.	1899	0	Inmate
Eldesarn, Lucy	WF	May	1897	3	Inmate
Ellcourt, Leo.	WM	Aug.	1896	3	Inmate
Elliott, Eliza	WF	Aug.	1899	1	Inmate
Ellis, Bridget	WF	Mar.	1896	4	Inmate
Ellis, Madeline	WF	Dec.	1899	0	Inmate
Elmer, Edward	WM	Jan.	1900	0	Inmate
Elsen, Joseph	WM	Sept.	1899	0	Inmate
Elstein, Blanche	WF	Dec.	1899	0	Inmate
Elton, Stella	WF	Nov.	1899	0	Inmate
Embree, Joseph	WM	Jan.	1897	3	Inmate
Emerson, Gertrude	WF	July	1898	1	Inmate
Emerson, Vincent	WM	Apr.	1900	0	Inmate
Emons, Rose	WF	Dec.	1897	2	Inmate
English, Alice	WF	Nov.	1897	2	Inmate
Enny, Josephine	WF	Dec.	1898	1	Inmate
Ensign, Charles	WM	Jan.	1899	1	Inmate
Enton, Louis	WM	Jan.	1897	3	Inmate
Eppstein, Joseph	WM	Mar.	1895	5	Inmate
Eustace, Joseph	WM	Sept.	1898	1	Inmate
Eustace, Lucy	WF	Aug.	1899	0	Inmate
Euvis, Lucy	WF	Apr.	1895	5	Inmate
Evans, Edward	WM	July	1897	2	Inmate
Evans, Ella	WF	May	1899	1	Inmate
Everard, Emma	WF	Nov.	1899	0	Inmate
Faber, John	WM	Feb.	1900	0	Inmate
Fabian, Mary	WF	June	1894	6	Inmate
Fagan, Annie	WF	Apr.	1898	2	Inmate

Fagan, Mary	WF	Jan.	1870	30	Inmate
Fahenback, Howard	WM	Dec.	1898	1	Inmate
Faille, Annie	WF	Nov.	1896	3	Inmate
Fairchild, Wm.	WM	Dec.	1897	2	Inmate
Falling, Florence	WF	Feb.	1900	0	Inmate
Fallon, James	WM	Feb.	1900	0	Inmate
Falls, Madeline	WF	Dec.	1898	1	Inmate
Fantalli, Mary	WF	Dec.	1899	0	Inmate
Farley, Anna	WF	June	1876	23	Inmate
Farley, Maragret	WF	Mar.	1898	2	Inmate
Farley, Maria	WF	May	1900	0	Inmate
Farley, William	WM	Oct.	1896	3	Inmate
Farrell, Margaret	WF	Mar.	1894	6	Inmate
Fasano, Joseph	WM	Oct.	1897	2	Inmate
Faulkner, Wm.	WM	Jan.	1897	3	Inmate
Fay, Anthony	WM	Nov.	1899	0	Inmate
Fay, Elizabeth	WF	Aug.	1899	0	Inmate
Fay, Margaret	WF	Jan.	1878	22	Inmate
Feeney, Frederick	WM	May	1896	4	Inmate
Feiler, Joseph	WM	Jan.	1899	1	Inmate
Fein, Rose	WF	Nov.	1897	2	Inmate
Feldman, Annie	WF	Dec.	1899	0	Inmate
Felice, Mary	WF	Oct.	1897	2	Inmate
Felly, Elizabeth	WF	July	1872	27	Sister
Fenton, Edward	WM	Apr.	1899	1	Inmate
Fenton, Mary	WF	May	1896	4	Inmate
Feraro, Anthony	WM	Dec.	1898	1	Inmate
Ferdinand, Jos.	WM	Dec.	1899	0	Inmate
Fergerson, Agnes	WF	July	1899	0	Inmate
Ferguson, Mary	WF	Mar.	1898	2	Inmate
Ferrari, Marie	WM	Apr.	1899	1	Inmate
Ferris, Eliza	WF	July	1899	0	Inmate
Ferris, Rose	WF	Jan.	1900	0	Inmate
Field, Eliza	WF	May	1877	23	St. Ann's
Field, Harold	WM	Jan.	1897	3	Inmate
Filde, Rachel	WF	Mar.	1899	1	Inmate
Finalli, Louise	WF	May	1896	4	Inmate
Finn, Mary	WF	Feb.	1900	0	Inmate
Fischer, Frederick	WM	Feb.	1898	2	Inmate
Fischer, Grace	WF	June	1892	8	Inmate
Fitz, Irene	WF	Sept.	1896	3	Inmate
Fitzgerald, Henry	WM	Feb.	1896	4	Inmate

Fitzgerald, Julia	WF	Nov.	1898	1	Inmate
Fitzgerald, Marg.	WF	Nov.	1899	0	Inmate
Fitzgerald, Mary	WF	Jan.	1899	1	Inmate
Fitzgerald, Paul	WM	Nov.	1898	1	Inmate
Fitzhenry, Angela	WF	Aug.	1899	0	Inmate
Fitzhenry, Nellie	WF	May	1885	15	Inmate
Fitzpatrick, William	WM	Dec.	1897	2	Inmate
Fitzsimmons, Cecellia	WF	May	1899	1	Inmate
Fitzsimmons, Frank	WM	Mar.	1900	0	Inmate
Fitzsimons, Gertrude	WF	Feb.	1897	3	Inmate
Flanagan, Jessie	WF	May	1898	2	Inmate
Flanigan, Susie	WF	Oct.	1899	0	Inmate
Flannigan, Harry	WM	May	1897	3	Inmate
Fleming, Geo.	WM	Dec.	1898	1	Inmate
Fleming, Margaret	WF	Dec.	1898	1	Inmate
Florenti, Clara	WF	Aug.	1898	1	Inmate
Floris, Albert	WM	Oct.	1898	1	Inmate
Flury, Geraldine	WF	Feb.	1900	0	Inmate
Flyme, Annie	WF	Dec.	1874	25	Inmate
Flynn, Agatha	WF	Feb.	1900	0	Inmate
Flynn, Ethel	WF	Sept.	1897	2	Inmate
Flynn, John	WM	Mar.	1897	3	Inmate
Flynn, Katie	WF	May	1882	18	St. Ann's
Flynn, Mary	WF	Aug.	1899	0	Inmate
Flynn, Mary	WF	May	1875	25	Inmate
Foley, Mary	WF	Feb.	1900	0	Inmate
Foley, Mary	WF	Dec.	1874	25	Inmate
Foley, Sarah	WF	Sept.	1872	27	Sister
Ford, Agnes	WF	Feb.	1898	2	Inmate
Ford, Mercedes	WF	July	1899	0	Inmate
Fortana, Amelia	WF	May	1898	2	Inmate
Foster, Andrew	WM	Mar.	1899	1	Inmate
Foster, James	WM	Dec.	1897	2	Inmate
Foster, John	WM	June	1898	1	Inmate
Foster, Ruth	WF	May	1899	1	Inmate
Founder, George	WM	Nov.	1894	5	Inmate
Fowler, Bertrand	WF	Aug.	1895	4	Inmate
Fowler, Stephen	WM	Dec.	1897	2	Inmate
Fox, Annie	WF	Jan.	1898	2	Inmate
Foy, James	WM	June	1896	4	Inmate
Francis, Louise	WF	Nov.	1898	1	Inmate
Frazer, George	WM	Feb.	1898	2	Inmate

Fredinger, John	WM	Mar.	1900	0	Inmate
Fredinger, Mary	WF	Jan.	1875	25	Inmate
Fredricks, Wm.	WM	Aug.	1898	1	Inmate
Freeman, William	WM	Feb.	1898	2	Inmate
Freidman, James	WM	Mar.	1900	0	Inmate
French, Francis	WM	Feb.	1898	2	Inmate
Frenchman, Helen	WF	Aug.	1898	1	Inmate
Friedman, Jennie	WF	Apr.	1900	0	Inmate
From, Minnie	WF	May	1899	1	Inmate
Frost, Carl	WM	Feb.	1900	0	Inmate
Fryer, Harry	WM	May	1898	2	Inmate
Fuller, Norman	WM	Nov.	1897	2	Inmate
Funn, Lillian	WF	Dec.	1898	1	Inmate
Furman, Lucy	WF	Mar.	1877	23	St. Ann's
Gabbei, Rose	WF	Feb.	1899	1	Inmate
Gabotten, Sam	WM	Dec.	1896	3	Inmate
Gains, Julius	WM	Nov.	1895	4	Inmate
Gale, Gladys	WF	Dec.	1897	2	Inmate
Gallagher, Guy	WM	Nov.	1897	2	Inmate
Gallagher, Mary	WF	Feb.	1858	42	Inmate
Gamble, John	WM	Jan.	1899	1	Inmate
Ganaver, Frances	WF	June	1899	1	Inmate
Gardner, Oscar	WM	Nov.	1895	4	Inmate
Garrison, Marry	WF	Dec.	1897	2	Inmate
Garvey, Esthel	WF	Feb.	1899	1	Inmate
Gates, Alice	WF	Dec.	1871	28	St. Ann's
Gauger, Caroline	WF	Dec.	1897	2	Inmate
Gaughan, Mary	WF	Dec.	1896	3	Inmate
Gavan, Mary	WF	Apr.	1900	0	Inmate
Gear, Lester	WM	Apr.	1900	0	Inmate
Gennie, Augustine	WF	Feb.	1898	2	Inmate
Geralding, Mary	WF	July	1899	0	Inmate
Germain, Joseph	WM	June	1896	4	Inmate
Gerrity, Eugene	WM	May	1898	2	Inmate
Gerrity, John	WM	Aug.	1898	1	Inmate
Gerrity, Paul	WM	June	1989	2	Inmate
Geyser, Victoria	WF	May	1898	2	Inmate
Gibbin, Irene	WF	Nov.	1895	4	Inmate
Gibbs, Rosalind	WF	Oct.	1899	0	Inmate
Giblin, William	WM	Jan.	1897	3	Inmate
Gibson, Nellie	WF	Nov.	1878	21	St. Ann's
Giem, Joseph	WM	Nov.	1898	1	Inmate

Gilbert, Mary	WF	July.	1898	1	Inmate
Gill, Ellen	WF	Apr.	1899	1	Inmate
Gillon, Michael	WM	July	1899	0	Inmate
Gilmartin, Mary	WF	July	1896	3	Inmate
Giroux, Marianna	WF	Aug.	1860	39	Sister
Gleason, Elizabeth	WF	Mar.	1860	40	Inmate
Gleason, Ida	WF	Dec.	1898	1	Inmate
Gleason, Teresa	WF	Sept.	1898	1	Inmate
Glenn, Gerald	WM	Apr.	1899	1	Inmate
Glennon, Violette	WF	July	1897	2	Inmate
Glunz, Edward	WM	June	1895	5	Inmate
Goggin, Nora	WF	Aug.	1860	39	Sister
Gohrring, Maria	WF	Dec.	1864	35	Inmate
Gohrring, Mercedes	WF	Sept.	1899	0	Inmate
Gold, Joseph	WM	Oct	1896	3	Inmate
Goldback, Julia	WF	June	1898	2	Inmate
Goldberg, Adrian	WM	June	1899	1	Inmate
Golden, Esther	WF	Jan.	1899	1	Inmate
Goldsmith, Eva	WF	June	1899	1	Inmate
Goldstein, Clara	WF	Aug.	1898	1	Inmate
Goldstein, Henry	WM	Sept.	1895	4	Inmate
Goldstein, Katie	WF	Sept.	1895	4	Inmate
Goldstein, Minnie	WF	Jan.	1898	2	Inmate
Goodwin, Anthony	WM	Jan.	1900	0	Inmate
Goodwin, Margaret	WF	June	1877	22	Inmate
Goodwin, Marion	WF	Feb.	1877	23	St. Ann's
Gordon, Anna	WF	Oct.	1899	0	Inmate
Gordon, Anna	WF	Dec.	1871	28	Inmate
Gordon, Elizabeth	WF	Nov.	1896	3	Inmate
Gordon, Martin	WM	Jan.	1899	1	Inmate
Gorman, James	WM	Nov.	1897	2	Inmate
Gotthre, George	WM	July	1897	2	Inmate
Gould, John	WM	May	1896	4	Inmate
Grace, Joseph	WM	Sept.	1896	3	Inmate
Grage, Winifred	WF	Jan.	1899	1	Inmate
Graham, Catherine	WF	Nov.	1899	0	Inmate
Graham, Fannie	WF	June	1875	25	Inmate
Gramps, Mary	WF	Feb.	1900	0	Inmate
Granger, Marie	WF	June	1899	1	Inmate
Grant, Philip	WM	May	1898	2	Inmate
Graves, Frances	WF	Nov.	1899	0	Inmate
Graves, Luther	WF*	Oct.	1896	3	Inmate

Gray, Elnora	WF	Dec.	1898	1	Inmate
Gray, Frank	WM	Aug.	1898	2	Inmate
Gray, George	WM	May	1895	5	Inmate
Gray, Mary	WF	Mar.	1877	23	St. Ann's
Gray, Sylvia	WF	Dec.	1899	0	Inmate
Grazia, John	WM	July	1899	0	Inmate
Green, Annie	WF	June	1899	1	Inmate
Green, Louis	WF*	Oct.	1896	3	Inmate
Green, Mary	WF	Jan.	1900	0	Inmate
Green, Minnie	WF	Jan.	1872	28	Inmate
Greenback, Faurey	WF	Sept.	1899	0	Inmate
Greene, Mary	WF	Mar.	1899	1	Inmate
Greene, Robert	WM	July	1898	1	Inmate
Greenspar, J.	WM	Aug.	1898	1	Inmate
Gregorg, Cecilia	WF	Nov.	1899	0	Inmate
Grellet, Anna	WF	Oct.	1898	1	Inmate
Grey, Milfred	WF*	Jan.	1899	1	Inmate
Greye, Joseph	WM	Feb.	1900	0	Inmate
Grieber, Eliz.	WF	May	1896	4	Inmate
Griffin, Adelaide	WF	Nov.	1898	1	Inmate
Griffin, Beatrice	WF	Dec.	1898	1	Inmate
Griffin, John	WM	Feb.	1900	0	Inmate
Griffin, Mary	WM*	Oct.	1897	2	Inmate
Gross, Lena	WF	Sept.	1898	1	Inmate
Gross, Matilda	WF	Dec.	1899	0	Inmate
Gross, Oscar	WM	May	1895	5	Inmate
Grove, Agnes	WF	June	1898	2	Inmate
Gruinell, Harry	WM	Jan.	1897	3	Inmate
Gueren, James	WM	Dec.	1897	2	Inmate
Gulsky, John	WM	Nov.	1897	2	Inmate
Gunnirey, Lillie	WF	May	1900	0	Inmate
Gutherie, John	WM	July	1897	2	Inmate
Haberthur, Elma	WM*	Sept.	1895	4	Inmate
Hackett, Jennie	WF	Jan.	1897	3	Inmate
Hackett, Susan	WF	Jan.	1897	3	Inmate
Haffle, Albertine	WM*	Jan.	1893	7	Inmate
Haggerty, Marg't.	WF	June	1899	1	Inmate
Hahn, Rose	WF	Sept.	1898	1	Inmate
Hale, Clarence	WF*	Aug.	1898	1	Inmate
Halladay, Rose	WF	Sept.	1899	0	Inmate
Halleck, Joseph	WM	Jan.	1898	2	Inmate
Halleck, Mary	WF	Sept.	1898	1	Inmate

Halwoth, John	WM	June	1898	1	Inmate
Hamerman, Albert	WM	July	1898	1	Inmate
Hamilton, Ida	WF	Jan.	1898	2	Inmate
Hammany, Bridget	WF	Mar.	1865	65	Sister
Hand, Joseph	WM	Dec.	1899	0	Inmate
Handley, Francis	WM	June	1898	1	Inmate
Hanfner, Annie	WF	Nov.	1898	1	Inmate
Hanley, Mildred	WM	Aug	1897	2	Inmate
Hanlon, Delia	WF	Mar.	1900	0	Inmate
Hannigan, Benj.	WM	Jan.	1899	1	Inmate
Hannigan, John	WM	Mar.	1899	1	Inmate
Hannon, Wm.	WM	Dec.	1899	0	Inmate
Hanrahan, Thomas	WM	May	1900	0	Inmate
Harden, James	WM	Feb.	1897	3	Inmate
Harison, Augustave	WM	June	1897	2	Inmate
Harmon, William	WM	Sept.	1893	6	Inmate
Harmony, Annie	WF	Nov.	1897	2	Inmate
Harrigan, Sherman	WM	Dec.	1895	4	Inmate
Harrington, Harry	WM	Sept.	1898	1	Inmate
Harrington, Martin	WM	Nov.	1899	0	Inmate
Harris, Agatha	WF	Dec.	1899	0	Inmate
Harris, Agatha	WF	Dec.	1881	18	Inmate
Harris, Carrolyn	WF	Nov.	1899	0	Inmate
Harris, Gladwell	WF	Mar.	1898	2	Inmate
Harris, Sarah	WF	Apr.	1874	26	St. Ann's
Harris, Teresa	WF	Jan.	1900	0	Inmate
Harrison, Frances	WF	Dec.	1899	0	Inmate
Hart, Camilla	WF	Nov.	1899	0	Inmate
Hart, Sylvester	WM	Dec.	1899	0	Inmate
Hart, William	WM	Sept.	1896	3	Inmate
Hartman, Cath.	WF	Apr.	1900	0	Inmate
Haskell, Bernard	WM	July	1899	0	Inmate
Hass, Margaret	WF	Apr.	1899	1	Inmate
Hatch, Bessie	WF	June	1899	1	Inmate
Hatfield, Joseph	WM	Apr.	1899	1	Inmate
Hauser, Mary	WF	Nov.	1897	2	Inmate
Haust, Eliza	WF	May	1896	4	Inmate
Havican, Mary	WF	Oct.	1899	0	Inmate
Hawke, Lawrence	WM	Sept.	1899	0	Inmate
Hawthorne, Mary	WF	Oct.	1899	0	Inmate
Hayes, Alexander	WM	Mar.	1900	0	Inmate
Hayes, Cecil	WF	Oct.	1897	2	Inmate

Hayes, Mary	WF	Feb.	1900	0	Inmate
Hayes, Mary	WF	Apr.	1897	3	Inmate
Hayes, Raymond	WM	Jan.	1899	1	Inmate
Hayes, Robert	WM	July	1897	2	Inmate
Hayes, Valentine	WM	Jan.	1899	1	Inmate
Hays, Joseph	WM	July	1896	3	Inmate
Heal, Albert	WM	Nov.	1898	1	Inmate
Healey, Bernard	WM	Mar.	1900	0	Inmate
Healey, Constance	WF	Feb.	1900	0	Inmate
Healey, Francis	WM	Dec.	1899	0	Inmate
Hearn, Agnes	WF	Jan.	1898	2	Inmate
Hearn, Mary	WF	Jan.	1870	30	St. Ann's
Hegal, Edward	WM	Oct.	1899	0	Inmate
Hellem, Joseph	WM	July	1899	0	Inmate
Henderson, Mary	WF	Apr.	1899	1	Inmate
Henderson, Stephen	WM	Jan.	1897	3	Inmate
Hennessy, Geo.	WM	July	1897	2	Inmate
Henry, John	WM	June	1898	1	Inmate
Henry, Mary	WF	June	1872	27	St. Ann's
Hensley, Henry	WM	Apr.	1900	0	Inmate
Herbert, Wm.	WM	Aug.	1899	0	Inmate
Herdling, Joseph	WM	July	1899	0	Inmate
Herke, Annie	WF	June	1898	2	Inmate
Herman, Augustine	WF	Apr.	1900	0	Inmate
Herman, Chas.	WM	Apr.	1899	1	Inmate
Herman, Wm.	WM	Apr.	1899	1	Inmate
Hersh, Carrie	WF	Feb.	1879	21	St. Ann's
Hetchan, Sadie	WF	Nov.	1880	19	Inmate
Hetherton, John	WM	Aug.	1897	2	Inmate
Hickey, Josephine	WF	Mar.	1896	4	Inmate
Higgins, Charles	WM	May	1900	0	Inmate
Higgins, Harold	WM	Jan.	1900	0	Inmate
Higgins, John	WM	June	1899	1	Inmate
Hill, Catherine	WF	Nov.	1899	0	Inmate
Hill, Joseph	WM	Mar.	1899	1	Inmate
Hirsch, Eliza	WF	Feb.	1897	3	Inmate
Hodac, Andrew	WM	Feb.	1895	5	Inmate
Hode, John	WM	Jan.	1897	3	Inmate
Hoff, Augustine	WF	June	1898	1	Inmate
Hoffman, Jos.	WM	Jan.	1899	1	Inmate
Hoffman, Mary	WF	Apr.	1900	0	Inmate
Hoffman, Mary	WF	Nov.	1873	26	Inmate

Hoffman, Nora	WF	Nov.	1898	1	Inmate
Hoffman, Wihelmina	WF	June	1899	0	Inmate
Hoffman, Wm.	WM	Feb.	1899	1	Inmate
Hogan, John	WM	Jan.	1896	4	Inmate
Hogan, Louis	WM	July	1897	2	Inmate
Holenback, Harvy	WM	Sept.	1896	3	Inmate
Holmes, Eliza	WF	Mar.	1900	0	Inmate
Holster, Charles	WM	Nov.	1899	0	Inmate
Holziger, Reginald	WF*	Feb.	1900	0	Inmate
Holzka, Blanche	WF	Feb.	1900	0	Inmate
Holzman, Alex	WM	July	1898	1	Inmate
Hooper, Rusilla	WF	Feb.	1899	1	Inmate
Hopson, Leonard	WM	Jan.	1900	0	Inmate
Hosey, Joseph	WM	Mar.	1897	3	Inmate
Houghton, Mary	WF	Mar.	1884	16	Inmate
Houghton, Vincent	WM	Apr.	1900	0	Inmate
Howard, Harry	WM	Jan.	1899	1	Inmate
Howard, Margaret	WF	Nov.	1898	1	Inmate
Howe, Mary	WF	June	1898	1	Inmate
Howe, Mary	WF	Sept.	1896	3	Inmate
Howe, Priscilla	WF	May	1898	2	Inmate
Howell, Fred	WM	Feb.	1897	3	Inmate
Hoyan, Charles	WM	Aug.	1898	1	Inmate
Hoyt, Catherine	WF	Mar.	1899	1	Inmate
Hughe, Horace	WM	Nov.	1895	4	Inmate
Hughes, Joseph	WM	July	1898	1	Inmate
Hughes, Mary	WF	May	1897	3	Inmate
Hughes, Pauline	WF	June	1899	1	Inmate
Humphrey, Eliza	WM*	Apr.	1900	0	Inmate
Hunt, Genevieve	WF	Sept.	1899	0	Inmate
Hurley, Anna	WF	Feb.	1863	37	Sister
Hurley, Mary	WF	Jan.	1850	50	Inmate
Hurran, Ellen	WF	July	1899	0	Inmate
Hutton, Joseph	WM	Jan.	1900	0	Inmate
Huyler, Jeanette	WF	Mar.	1900	0	Inmate
Huyler, Mary	WF	Feb.	1900	0	Inmate
Hyles, Ida	WF	Mar.	1899	1	Inmate
Hyman, Rose	WF	Apr.	1900	0	Inmate
Hymes, Lawrence	WM	Dec.	1899	0	Inmate
Hynes, Alice	WF	July	1864	35	Sister
Hynes, Josephine	WF	June	1898	1	Inmate
Hynes, Margaret	WF	Nov.	1877	22	Inmate

Hynes, Mary	WF	Dec.	1877	22	Inmate
Ignatius, Alphonsus	WM	July	1890	9	Inmate
Ingrahm, Lucy	WF	Feb.	1897	3	Inmate
Intyre, Joseph	WM	June	1899	1	Inmate
Ippolito, Michael	WM	Mar.	1899	1	Inmate
Irving, Albert	WM	Feb.	1899	1	Inmate
Issm, Florence	WF	Feb.	1899	1	Inmate
Iverson, Paul	WM	Jan.	1898	2	Inmate
Jackson, Frances	WF	Feb.	1900	0	Inmate
Jackson, Minnie	WF	Apr.	1897	3	Inmate
Jackson, Robert	WM	Mar.	1900	0	Inmate
Jackson, Wm.	WM	Oct.	1895	4	Inmate
Jacobs, Ward	WM	Feb.	1900	0	Inmate
Jaick, Mary	WF	June	1880	20	Inmate
Janak, Joseph	WM	Jan.	1899	1	Inmate
Jardet, Sylvester	WM	Apr.	1898	2	Inmate
Jastzenboski, Stanley	WM	July	1898	1	Inmate
Jeffery, Margaret	WF	Mar.	1879	21	Inmate
Jenkins, Lucian	WF	Apr.	1898	2	Inmate
Jennings, Bridget	WF	Jan.	1899	1	Inmate
John, Dennis	WM	Dec.	1899	0	Inmate
Johns, Elizabeth	WF	Feb.	1893	7	Inmate
Johnson, Alice	WF	Dec.	1895	4	Inmate
Johnson, Anna	WF	Apr.	1899	1	Inmate
Johnson, Cora	WF	Jan.	1894	6	Inmate
Johnson, Edward	WM	Nov.	1899	0	Inmate
Johnson, Emma	WF	Mar.	1900	0	Inmate
Johnson, Ernest	WM	Mar.	1899	1	Inmate
Johnson, Frederic	WM	Apr.	1900	0	Inmate
Johnson, Henry	WM	Dec.	1892	7	Inmate
Johnson, Jennie	WF	May	1899	1	Inmate
Johnson, John	WM	Feb.	1900	0	Inmate
Johnson, John	WM	Jan.	1900	0	Inmate
Johnson, Joseph	WM	June	1898	1	Inmate
Johnson, Lillian	WF	Oct.	1895	4	Inmate
Johnson, Lizzie	WF	Apr.	1900	0	Inmate
Johnson, Loriane	WF	Oct.	1899	0	Inmate
Johnson, Mary	WF	Apr.	1899	1	Inmate
Johnson, May	WF	Dec.	1897	2	Inmate
Johnson, William	WM	June	1897	2	Inmate
Johnston, Edith	WF	Feb.	1898	2	Inmate
Jones, Angela	WF	Apjr.	1899	1	Inmate

Jones, Bessie	WF	Mar.	1890	10	Inmate
Jones, Edna	WF	Jan.	1899	1	Inmate
Jones, Helen	WF	Aug.	1898	1	Inmate
Jones, Lillian	WF	Jan.	1900	0	Inmate
Jones, Louise	WF	May	1896	3	Inmate
Jones, Veronica	WF	Jan.	1900	0	Inmate
Jones, Walter	WF	Feb.	1896	4	Inmate
Jordan, Anna	WF	Apr.	1899	1	Inmate
Jordan, Fidellis	WF	Sept.	1899	0	Inmate
Jordan, Marie	WF	Mar.	1898	2	Inmate
Jordan, Ursula	WF	May	1898	2	Inmate
Joseph, Anthony	WM	Mar.	1900	0	Inmate
Joseph, Francis	WM	Aug.	1899	0	Inmate
Joseph, Joseph	WM	June	1898	1	Inmate
Jossi, Josephine	WF	Mar.	1898	2	Inmate
Jotsky, Joseph	WM	June	1899	1	Inmate
Joyce, Anna	WF	May	1876	24	Inmate
Joyce, John	WM	Feb.	1900	0	Inmate
Joyce, Marie	WF	Sept.	1899	0	Inmate
Julian, Mildred	WF	Feb.	1900	0	Inmate
Jund, Alice	WF	June	1898	1	Inmate
Kabbert, Paul	WM	June	1897	2	Inmate
Kahn, Esther	WF	Nov.	1899	0	Inmate
Kaiser, Guilare	WM	Nov.	1897	2	Inmate
Kalbera, Chas.	WM	Mar.	1899	1	Inmate
Kalvotz, Joseph	WM	Aug.	1896	3	Inmate
Kane, Edward	WM	Oct.	1896	3	Inmate
Kane, Elizabeth	WF	Apr.	1899	1	Inmate
Kane, Francis	WM	Nov.	1899	0	Inmate
Kane, George	WM	Apr.	1898	2	Inmate
Kane, John	WM	Jan.	1899	1	Inmate
Kane, Lawrence	WM	Apr.	1900	0	Inmate
Kane, Raymond	WM	Apr.	1899	1	Inmate
Kans, Anna	WF	Oct.	1897	2	Inmate
Karbe, Edith	WF	May	1900	0	Inmate
Karpi, Joseph	WM	Nov.	1899	0	Inmate
Katovitch, Esther	WF	July	1899	0	Inmate
Katz, Nellie	WF	Dec.	1880	19	St. Ann's
Kavanagh, Mary	WF	Dec.	1896	3	Inmate
Kearns, Ambrose	WM	Mar.	1900	0	Inmate
Keefe, Daniel	WM	Dec.	1896	3	Inmate
Keeffer, Joseph	WM	Oct.	1899	0	Inmate

Keensu, James	WM	July	1897	2	Inmate
Kehoe, Katie	WF	Apr.	1900	0	Inmate
Keht, Edward	WM	Nov.	1899	0	Inmate
Keller, Helena	WF	July	1845	54	Sister
Kelly, Agnes	WF	Apr.	1900	0	Inmate
Kelly, Andrew	WM	Mar.	1899	1	Inmate
Kelly, Annie	WF	Oct.	1899	0	Inmate
Kelly, Catherine	WF	May	1897	3	Inmate
Kelly, Catherine	WF	Mar.	1897	3	Inmate
Kelly, Elizabeth	WF	Mar.	1899	1	Inmate
Kelly, Francis	WM	July	1894	5	Inmate
Kelly, Frank	WM	Nov.	1899	0	Inmate
Kelly, George	WM	July	1899	0	Inmate
Kelly, Jeromita	WM*	Jan.	1900	0	Inmate
Kelly, John	WM	Jan.	1900	0	Inmate
Kelly, Joseph	WM	June	1898	2	Inmate
Kelly, Joseph	WM	Jan.	1898	2	Inmate
Kelly, Julia	WF	Apr.	1900	0	Inmate
Kelly, Lillian	WF	July	1898	1	Inmate
Kelly, Paul	WM	Nov.	1897	2	Inmate
Kelly, Sara	WF	Aug.	1898	1	Inmate
Kelly, Sarah	WF	Dec.	1879	20	Inmate
Kencall, Mary	WF	June	1894	5	Inmate
Kennedy, Agnes	WF	Nov.	1899	0	Inmate
Kennedy, Alver	WF	Dec.	1897	2	Inmate
Kennedy, James	WM	Apr.	1900	0	Inmate
Kennedy, Mary	WF	Sept.	1897	2	Inmate
Kennedy, Mary	WF	Jan.	1891	9	Inmate
Kennedy, Raymond	WM	May	1900	0	Inmate
Kennedy, Walter	WM	Feb.	1900	0	Inmate
Kennedy, William	WM	Apr.	1893	7	Inmate
Kennry, Mary	WF	July	1861	38	St. Ann's
Kenny, Ellen	WF	Feb.	1855	45	Inmate
Kenny, Francis	WM	July	1899	0	Inmate
Kenny, William	WM	Oct.	1898	1	Inmate
Kerby, John	WM	Feb.	1899	1	Inmate
Kerby, Mary	WF	Jan.	1899	1	Inmate
Kern, Annie	WF	Jan.	1899	1	Inmate
Kettler, Edwin	WM	Oct.	1897	2	Inmate
Keyes, Joseph	WM	Apr.	1900	0	Inmate
Keyser, Charles	WM	Mar.	1898	2	Inmate
Kierns, Joseph	WM	Feb.	1896	4	Inmate

Kimmen, Frances	WF	Feb.	1874	26	Inmate
Kimmen, Stanislaus	WM	Feb.	1900	0	Inmate
King, Annie	WF	Apr.	1898	2	Inmate
King, George	WM	July	1898	1	Inmate
King, Harry	WM	Dec.	1899	0	Inmate
King, Henrietta	WF	Mar.	1899	1	Inmate
King, Joseph	WM	June	1899	0	Inmate
King, Mary	WF	Apr.	1894	6	Inmate
King, Nellie	WF	Oct.	1877	22	St. Ann's
King, Peter	WM	Mar.	1899	1	Inmate
King, Sarah	WF	Dec.	1896	3	Inmate
Kingston, Thomas	WM	May	1900	0	Inmate
Kirk, Madeline	WF	May	1897	3	Inmate
Klavea, William	WM	Oct.	1898	1	Inmate
Klein, Aloysius	WM	July	1899	0	Inmate
Klein, Edward	WM	July	1899	0	Inmate
Klenholt, Louis	WM	June	1898	2	Inmate
Klindt, George	WM	July	1897	2	Inmate
Kline, John	WM	Apr.	1897	3	Inmate
Kline, Joseph	WM	Aug.	1896	3	Inmate
Kloping, Fred	WM	May	1898	2	Inmate
Knobble, Joseph	WM	Aug.	1898	1	Inmate
Knowlton, Marg't.	WF	June	1898	2	Inmate
Koch, Henry	WM	Dec.	1899	0	Inmate
Koch, Michael	WM	Dec.	1899	0	Inmate
Koebler, Rudolph	WM	Apr.	1897	3	Inmate
Koeing, Paul	WM	Jan.	1894	6	Inmate
Kohler, Harry	WM	Oct.	1899	0	Inmate
Kopler, Wm.	WM	Jan.	1899	1	Inmate
Koplovitch, Louis	WM	Jan.	1898	2	Inmate
Kornstein, Jennie	WF	Dec.	1899	0	Inmate
Koslik, Frank	WM	Feb.	1897	3	Inmate
Koster, Gertrude	WF	May	1894	6	Inmate
Kotz, Ada	WF	Oct.	1897	2	Inmate
Krantz, Yetta	WF	July	1899	0	Inmate
Kreiger, Maurice	WM	July	1897	2	Inmate
Kruer, Wm.	WM	Nov.	1894	5	Inmate
Kudoic, Paul	WM	Sept.	1899	0	Inmate
Kuhn, Christine	WF	Mar.	1878	22	St. Ann's
Kultilacky, Sophie	WF	Dec.	1897	2	Inmate
Kuppler, David	WM	Oct.	1896	5	Inmate
LaFarge, Marie	WF	May	1897	3	Inmate

Lafferty, Katie	WF	Nov.	1899	0	Inmate
Laird, Mary	WF	Oct.	1899	0	Inmate
Landgridge, Harry	WM	Nov.	1898	1	Inmate
Landi, Dora	WF	June	1899	1	Inmate
Landis, Joseph	WM	Nov.	1898	1	Inmate
Landrigan, Joseph	WM	Mar.	1900	0	Inmate
Lane, Florence	WF	Nov.	1898	1	Inmate
Lane, William	WM	Aug.	1897	2	Inmate
Lang, Benjiman	WM	Apr.	1897	3	Inmate
Lang, Bernard	WM	Dec.	1893	6	Inmate
Lang, Thomas	WM	Dec.	1898	1	Inmate
Lappont, Willie	WM	Oct	1898	1	Inmate
Lardner, Marg't.	WF	Jan.	1865	35	Inmate
Larkin, Elizabeth	WF	May	1852	48	Sister
Larkin, Maggie	WF	Mar.	1873	27	Inmate
Lavelli, Lucy	WF	Apr.	1898	2	Inmate
Laveriese, Orrie	WM	Apr.	1900	0	Inmate
Laville, John	WM	Dec.	1899	0	Inmate
Lavin, Ellen	WF	Dec.	1876	23	Inmate
Lavin, William	WM	May	1900	0	Inmate
Lavine, Maggie	WF	May	1880	20	St. Ann's
Law, Rudolph	WM	Nov.	1897	2	Inmate
Lawlor, Mary	WF	Mar.	1896	4	Inmate
Lawrence, Florence	WF	July	1897	2	Inmate
Lawrence, Wilfred	WM	Oct.	1893	6	Inmate
Lawrey, Winifred	WF	Oct.	1896	3	Inmate
Lawton, Fred	WM	Mar.	1897	3	Inmate
Layton, Augustine	WF	Jan.	1899	1	Inmate
Leander, Esther	WF	Mar.	1899	1	Inmate
Leary, Joseph	WM	Mar.	1900	0	Inmate
Leary, William	WM	Dec.	1899	0	Inmate
LeDue, Clare	WF	Dec.	1898	1	Inmate
Lee, Frencis	WM	Dec.	1897	2	Inmate
Lee, Genevieve	WF	Apr.	1898	2	Inmate
Lee, Helen	WF	May	1876	24	St. Ann's
Lee, Henrietta	WF	Nov.	1896	3	Inmate
Lee, Lucinda	WF	Oct.	1899	0	Inmate
Leech, John	WM	Sept.	1893	6	Inmate
Leitner, Annie	WF	Apr.	1899	1	Inmate
Lemardi, Frances	WF	Jan.	1896	4	Inmate
Lenahan, Gerald	WM	Mar.	1900	0	Inmate
Lenahan, Mary	WF	Dec.	1846	53	Sister

Lenhardt, Edward	WM	Jan.	1899	1	Inmate
Lennet, John	WM	Jan.	1898	2	Inmate
Lennon, John	WM	Mar.	1900	0	Inmate
Lennon, Mary	WF	Jan.	1899	1	Inmate
Lenock, Mary	WF	July	1899	0	Inmate
Lenshan, Laura	WF	May	1899	1	Inmate
Leo, Alphonsus	WM	Sept.	1896	3	Inmate
Leo, Henry	WM	Feb.	1899	1	Inmate
Leonard, Catherine	WF	Nov.	1898	1	Inmate
Leonard, George	WM	Dec.	1898	1	Inmate
Leonard, Laura	WF	Feb.	1878	22	Inmate
Leonard, Mary	WF	July	1898	1	Inmate
Leroy, Eugene	WM	Mar.	1898	2	Inmate
Lesky, Bertha	WF	Jan.	1900	0	Inmate
Lesser, Martha	WF	Apr.	1898	2	Inmate
Lester, Bernard	WM	Apr.	1898	2	Inmate
Lester, Irving	WM	Mar.	1900	0	Inmate
Levet, Helen	WF	Mar.	1899	1	Inmate
Levine, Joseph	WM	Dec.	1893	6	Inmate
Levy, Anna	WF	May	1872	23	Inmate
Levy, Joseph	WM	May	1900	0	Inmate
Levy, Ronald	WM	Nov.	1899	0	Inmate
Lewis, Fanny	WF	June	1895	5	Inmate
Lewis, Henry	WM	Nov.	1895	4	Inmate
Lewis, Mary	WF	Jan.	1899	1	Inmate
Liddy, Catherine	WF	Jan.	1882	18	St. Ann's
Liffuss, Wm.	WM	Nov.	1899	0	Inmate
Likaner, Wm.	WM	Sept.	1898	1	Inmate
Lindie, Katie	WF	Jan.	1898	2	Inmate
Lindner, Tillie	WF	Feb.	1898	2	Inmate
Linshaw, Dennis	WM	Sept.	1896	3	Inmate
Linton, George	WM	Feb.	1898	2	Inmate
Linwood, Ernest	WM	Sept.	1897	2	Inmate
Lippinan, John	WM	Oct.	1899	0	Inmate
Liquidice, Frecesco	WM	Nov.	1897	2	Inmate
Little, Alice	WF	Jan.	1899	1	Inmate
Littlewood, Wm.	WM	July	1898	1	Inmate
Locke, Joseph	WM	July	1897	2	Inmate
Lockwood, Ellen	WF	May	1874	26	Inmate
Lockwood, Wm.	WM	Aug.	1899	0	Inmate
Lococo, Annie	WF	Sept.	1899	0	Inmate
Loep, Carrie	WF	Sept.	1891	9	Inmate

Logan, Henry	WM	Jan.	1899	1	Inmate
Long, Beatrice	WF	Oct.	1897	2	Inmate
Longo, Raphael	WM	Feb.	1899	1	Inmate
Looney, John	WM	June	1899	1	Inmate
Looney, Mary	WF	Mar.	1875	25	Inmate
Lopez, James	WM	Oct.	1895	4	Inmate
Lord, Helen	WF	Feb.	1900	0	Inmate
Lott, Mary	WF	June	1899	1	Inmate
Louger, Arthur	WM	June	1899	1	Inmate
Louger, George	WM	Apr.	1896	4	Inmate
Louger, William	WM	Feb.	1900	0	Inmate
Loughran, Cora	WF	Jan.	1899	1	Inmate
Louis, Harold	WM	Aug.	1896	3	Inmate
Lova, Isabella	WF	May	1896	4	Inmate
Lovatt, Benjamin	WM	Oct.	1899	0	Inmate
Lucaex, Regina	WF	Feb.	1899	1	Inmate
Luco, Marie	WF	Dec.	1898	1	Inmate
Ludeman, Clara	WF	Nov.	1899	0	Inmate
Ludeman, Lena	WF	Nov.	1899	0	Inmate
Lunch, Anastasia	WF	Dec.	1898	1	Inmate
Lustra, Anthony	WM	Apr.	1899	1	Inmate
Lyle, Adaline	WF	June	1899	1	Inmate
Lynch, Bernard	WM	Apr.	1900	0	Inmate
Lynch, Celestia	WF	May	1900	0	Inmate
Lynch, Ernest	WM	Dec.	1898	1	Inmate
Lynch, Joseph	WM	June	1897	2	Inmate
Lynch, Katie	WF	July	1897	2	Inmate
Lynch, Margaret	WF	July	1896	3	Inmate
Lynch, Mary	WF	Oct.	1895	4	Inmate
Lynch, Mary	WF	Sept.	1878	21	Inmate
Lynch, Winifred	WF	Sept.	1898	1	Inmate
Lyons, Agnes	WF	Aug.	1899	0	Inmate
Lyons, Catherine	WF	Jan.	1858	42	Sister
Lyons, Henry	WM	Dec.	1891	9	Inmate
Lyons, William	WM	Mar.	1898	2	Inmate
Mackey, Adeline	WF	Jan.	1899	1	Inmate
Mackey, Maragret	WF	Oct.	1894	5	Inmate
Madden, Adeline	WF	Oct.	1896	3	Inmate
Madden, Mary	WF	Jan.	1898	2	Inmate
Maddson, Joseph	WM	Nov.	1899	0	Inmate
Madigan, Maurice	WM	Sept.	1897	2	Inmate
Magher, Joseph	WM	May	1898	2	Inmate

Maguire, Agnes	WF	May	1897	3	Inmate
Maguire, Thomas	WM	Jan.	1900	0	Inmate
Mahan, Richard	WM	Oct.	1899	0	Inmate
Maher, Mary	WF	Nov.	1898	1	Inmate
Mahon, Justina	WM*	July	1899	0	Inmate
Mahoney, Eliza	WF	Jan.	1898	2	Inmate
Mahoney, Mary	WF	Jan.	1898	2	Inmate
Mairrer, Marie	WF	Nov.	1897	2	Inmate
Mallow, Robert	WM	Oct.	1899	0	Inmate
Malloy, George	WM	Nov.	1897	2	Inmate
Mally, Walter	WM	Feb.	1899	1	Inmate
Maloney, Joseph	WM	Aug.	1899	0	Inmate
Maloney, Maggie	WF	June	1880	20	St. Ann's
Manchester, Mary	WF	Jan.	1895	5	Inmate
Mangan, Mary	WF	Feb.	1899	1	Inmate
Manley, Cecellia	WF	Feb.	1898	2	Inmate
Mann, Rosetta	WF	Oct.	1896	3	Inmate
Manning, Arthur	WM	Nov.	1899	0	Inmate
Manning, Loretto	WF	May	1888	12	St. Ann's
Manofaki, Lizzie	WF	Mar.	1898	2	Inmate
Mantz, William	WM	Apr.	1896	4	Inmate
Manville, Emily	WF	Apr.	1900	0	Inmate
Mare, Blanche	WF	June	1899	1	Inmate
Margi, Harold	WM	Nov.	1899	0	Inmate
Marieki, Vincent	WM	Jan.	1900	0	Inmate
Marion, Mary	WF	Jan.	1898	2	Inmate
Mark, Julia	WF	Apr.	1899	1	Inmate
Marks, Epold	WF	Jan.	1898	2	Inmate
Marlo, Marie	WF	July	1899	0	Inmate
Marlow, Anthony	WM	Jan.	1900	0	Inmate
Marquis, Charles	WM	May	1898	2	Inmate
Mars, Diana	WF	Nov.	1899	0	Inmate
Marshall, Alfred	WM	Jan.	1898	2	Inmate
Martin, Alfred	WM	Feb.	1897	3	Inmate
Martin, Bernard	WM	May	1899	1	Inmate
Martin, Cecilla	WF	July	1899	0	Inmate
Martin, John	WM	Sept.	1897	2	Inmate
Martin, Joseph	WM	Dec.	1899	6m	Inmate
Martin, Margaret	WF	Apr.	1874	26	Inmate
Martin, Marie	WF	Feb.	1899	1	Inmate
Martin, Mark	WM	Dec.	1899	0	Inmate
Martin, Mary	WF	July	1899	0	Inmate

Martin, Mary	WF	Mar.	1899	1	Inmate
Martin, Mary	WF	Feb.	1898	2	Inmate
Martin, Mary	WF	Dec.	1863	36	Inmate
Martin, Rose	WF	Mar.	1899	1	Inmate
Martin, Thomas	WM	Mar.	1899	1	Inmate
Marzi, Irene	WF	Feb.	1899	1	Inmate
Marzo, Joseph	WM	Mar.	1898	2	Inmate
Mass, Francis	WM	Mar.	1899	1	Inmate
Masters, Emeline	WF	Mar.	1899	1	Inmate
Mathews, Josephine	WF	Mar.	1900	0	Inmate
Matthews, Marie	WF	Mar.	1900	0	Inmate
Mauer, Augustine	WF	Feb.	1900	0	Inmate
Maur, Rose	WF	Jan.	1900	0	Inmate
Maurice, Mary	WF	June	1898	1	Inmate
May, Bernardo	WM	Apr.	1900	0	Inmate
May, Charles	WM	May	1900	0	Inmate
May, Charles	WM	May	1898	2	Inmate
May, Lillian	WF	Nov.	1898	2	Inmate
May, Matilda	WF	Mar.	1900	0	Inmate
Mayer, Irene	WF	Apr.	1900	0	Inmate
Mazarti, John	WM	Dec.	1899	0	Inmate
McAlke, Jane	WF	Aug.	1867	32	Sister
McArthur, Raphael	WM	Nov.	1899	0	Inmate
McAvoy, Charles	WM	Sept.	1899	0	Inmate
McAvoy, Mary	WF	Nov.	1878	21	Inmate
McBride, Edna	WF	Dec.	1899	0	Inmate
McCabe, Edward	WM	Sept.	1899	0	Inmate
McCabe, Hugh	WM	Dec.	1899	0	Inmate
McCabe, James	WM	Oct.	1899	0	Inmate
McCabe, Kate	WF	Apr.	1876	24	St. Ann's
McCabe, Madeline	WF	Sept.	1899	0	Inmate
McCaffery, Bernard	WM	Aug.	1897	2	Inmate
McCaffery, Florence	WF	Dec.	1899	0	Inmate
McCaffery, Teresa	WF	Jan.	1900	0	Inmate
McCaffery, Teresa	WF	Mar.	1870	20	Inmate
McCandlers, Cath.	WF	Apr.	1900	0	Inmate
McCandlers, Mary	WF	May	1879	21	Inmate
McCann, Cath.	WF	Jan.	1899	1	Inmate
McCann, Elizabeth	WF	Mar.	1900	0	Inmate
McCann, Julia	WF	Jan.	1899	1	Inmate
McCann, Minnie	WF	Mar.	1880	20	Inmate
McCarthy, Arthur	WM	Dec.	1896	3	Inmate

McCarthy, Bella	WF	Sept.	1899	0	Inmate
McCarthy, John	WM	Dec.	1897	2	Inmate
McCarthy, Mary	WF	Oct.	1899	0	Inmate
McCarthy, Mary	WF	Jan.	1899	1	Inmate
McCarthy, Monican	WM	Nov.	1894	5	Inmate
McCarthy, Thomas	WM	Apr.	1897	3	Inmate
McClain, Florence	WF	Dec.	1899	0	Inmate
McCloskey, Thomas	WM	Apr.	1897	3	Inmate
McCollough, Edward	WM	Apr.	1897	3	Inmate
McCormack, Anna	WF	July	1869	30	Sister
McCormack, Henry	WM	July	1897	2	Inmate
McCormack, James	WM	Jan.	1899	1	Inmate
McCoy, Henry	WM	Apr.	1900	0	Inmate
McCrystal, Jane	WF	July	1842	57	Sister
McCullen, Chas.	WM	Dec.	1899	0	Inmate
McCullough, John	WM	Apr.	1900	0	Inmate
McCur, James	WM	Apr.	1900	0	Inmate
McDavitt, Irene	WF	Sept.	1899	0	Inmate
McDonald, Andrew	WM	Feb.	1900	0	Inmate
McDonald, Anna	WF	Apr.	1900	0	Inmate
McDonald, Edward	WM	Apr.	1897	3	Inmate
McDonald, Joseph	WM	June	1897	2	Inmate
McDonald, Marie	WF	Oct.	1897	2	Inmate
McDonald, Mary	WF	Jan.	1900	0	Inmate
McDonald, Mary	WF	Oct.	1896	3	Inmate
McDonald, Thomas	WM	Mar.	1898	2	Inmate
McDonnell, James	WM	May	1899	1	Inmate
McDowell, George	WM	Nov.	1899	0	Inmate
McEntyre, Mildred	WF	June	1898	1	Inmate
McFadden, Teresa	WM*	Mar.	1898	2	Inmate
McGavan, James	WM	Jan.	1896	4	Inmate
McGee, Ellen	WF	Apr.	1860	40	Inmate
McGirr, Delia	WF	Mar.	1868	32	Inmate
McGovern, James	WM	Sept.	1897	2	Inmate
McGovern, John	WM	Nov.	1899	0	Inmate
McGowan, Catherine	WF	May	1876	24	Inmate
McGowan, Mary	WF	Mar.	1900	0	Inmate
McGrath, Agueline	WF	June	1898	2	Inmate
McGrath, Jeanetta	WF	Oct.	1899	0	Inmate
McGrath, Nellie	WF	Mar.	1876	24	Inmate
McGratten, Annie	WF	Apr.	1899	1	Inmate
McGreevy, James	WM	Mar.	1898	2	Inmate

McGuire, Alice	WF	Feb.	1899	1	Inmate
McGuire, Arthur	WM	May	1900	0	Inmate
McGuire, Ralph	WM	Sept.	1897	2	Inmate
McGur, Mary	WF	Apr.	1900	0	Inmate
McKelvey, Annie	WF	June	1878	22	Inmate
McKenna, Catherine	WF	July	1860	39	Sister
McKenna, Dora	WF	Apr.	1897	3	Inmate
McKenna, Martin	WM	Dec.	1899	0	Inmate
McKewey, Mary	WF	Oct.	1899	0	Inmate
McLaughlin, Anita	WF	Dec.	1899	0	Inmate
McLaughlin, Helen	WF	Aug.	1897	2	Inmate
McManus, John	WM	Jan.	1896	4	Inmate
McMullin, Mary	WF	Feb.	1875	25	Inmate
McMurrough, Mary	WF	Apr.	1900	0	Inmate
McNulty, Margery	WF	Aug.	1859	40	Sister
McSherry, Maggie	WF	Oct.	1899	0	Inmate
McTigue, Joseph	WM	Oct.	1899	0	Inmate
McTigue, Joseph	WM	Oct.	1895	4	Inmate
McTummey, Annie	WF	Feb.	1899	1	Inmate
Meade, John	WM	Jan.	1898	2	Inmate
Mealey, Wm.	WM	June	1899	1	Inmate
Meeder, James	WM	Feb.	1899	1	Inmate
Meehan, John	WM	Aug.	1899	0	Inmate
Meehan, Katie	WF	Jan.	1894	6	Inmate
Meiser, Martha	WF	Aug.	1899	0	Inmate
Melia, Joseph	WM	May	1900	0	Inmate
Melley, James	WM	Mar.	1899	1	Inmate
Mendell, Thelma	WF	Nov.	1899	0	Inmate
Mentha, Joseph	WM	Jan.	1897	3	Inmate
Merchant, Henry	WM	July	1897	2	Inmate
Merrall, Joseph	WM	July	1896	3	Inmate
Merrill, Grace	WF	Nov.	1899	0	Inmate
Merrishe, Margaret	WF	Nov.	1896	3	Inmate
Merrit, Isabella	WF	Mar.	1899	1	Inmate
Methrodene, Hannah	WF	Sept.	1899	0	Inmate
Metz, Isidore	WM	Apr.	1899	1	Inmate
Meyer, Annie	WF	Mar.	1900	0	Inmate
Meyer, George	WM	Oct.	1896	3	Inmate
Meyer, Laura	WF	Dec.	1896	3	Inmate
Meyers, Eddie	WF*	Mar.	1898	2	Inmate
Meyers, John	WM	Feb.	1898	2	Inmate
Millard, Ralph	WM	Oct.	1899	0	Inmate

Miller, Chas.	WM	Dec.	1891	9	Inmate
Miller, Edna	WF	Aug.	1899	0	Inmate
Miller, Emma	WF	Dec.	1896	3	Inmate
Miller, Joseph	WM	Feb.	1898	2	Inmate
Miller, Louis	WM	Feb.	1898	2	Inmate
Miller, Louisa	WF	Dec.	1897	2	Inmate
Miller, Marie	WF	Aug.	1899	1	Inmate
Mills, Albert	WM	July	1899	0	Inmate
Mills, Albert	WM	May	1899	1	Inmate
Mills, Elizabeth	WF	Dec.	1897	2	Inmate
Mills, Harold	WM	Dec.	1899	0	Inmate
Mills, Mary	WF	Apr.	1900	0	Inmate
Mills, Mary	WF	May	1898	2	Inmate
Millstein, Harry	WM	Oct.	1896	3	Inmate
Mitchell, Mary	WF	May	1897	3	Inmate
Mitton, Ellen	WF	Apr.	1897	3	Inmate
Mizell, Harold	WM	Aug.	1894	5	Inmate
Mizert, John	WM	Oct.	1899	0	Inmate
Monahan, Francis	WM	Jan.	1898	2	Inmate
Mongenont, Frances	WF	Feb.	1900	0	Inmate
Monroe, Margaret	WF	Dec.	1896	3	Inmate
Monze, Tessie	WF	Sept.	1899	0	Inmate
Mooney, Rachel	WF	Feb.	1844	56	Sister
Moore, Grace	WF	Jan.	1898	2	Inmate
Moore, Maude	WF	June	1898	1	Inmate
Moore, Sadie	WF	Mar.	1897	3	Inmate
Moran, Anna	WF	Aug.	1863	36	Sister
Moran, Annie	WF	Dec.	1871	28	Inmate
Moran, Edward	WM	July	1897	2	Inmate
Moran, Joseph	WM	June	1899	1	Inmate
Moran, Ruth	WF	Nov.	1898	1	Inmate
Moran, Victoria	WF	Mar.	1900	0	Inmate
Morgan, Mary	WF	Mar.	1898	2	Inmate
Morgan, Mary	WF	Dec.	1897	2	Inmate
Morgenstein, Kate	WF	Jan.	1879	21	Inmate
Morgenstein, Rose	WF	May	1900	0	Inmate
Morrel, Florence	WF	Nov.	1897	2	Inmate
Morris, Francis	WM	Sept.	1897	2	Inmate
Morris, Harold	WM	Mar.	1896	4	Inmate
Morris, Richard	WM	Nov.	1897	2	Inmate
Morris, Roberta	WF	June	1899	1	Inmate
Morris, Vincent	WM	July	1899	0	Inmate

Morten, John	WM	Apr.	1900	0	Inmate
Morton, Alma	WM*	Apr.	1899	1	Inmate
Moss, Ellen	WF	Mar.	1860	40	Inmate
Mossey, Francis	WM	Dec.	1899	0	Inmate
Mow, Edward	WM	Feb.	1897	3	Inmate
Mulcahy, Helen	WF	Feb.	1825	75	Sister
Mulchinock, Anna	WF	Apr.	1900	0	Inmate
Mullaly, Annie	WF	Aug.	1899	0	Inmate
Mullane, Wm.	WM	Oct.	1895	4	Inmate
Mullen, Florence	WF	July	1897	2	Inmate
Muller, Nettie	WF	May	1880	20	Inmate
Mulligan, Alphonsus	WM	Mar.	1900	0	Inmate
Mulligan, Kate	WF	Dec.	1878	21	Inmate
Mullin, Annie	WF	Feb.	1899	1	Inmate
Mulry, Irene	WF	Apr.	1900	0	Inmate
Mulvaney, Caroline	WF	May	1870	30	Sister
Muphy, Ethel	WF	Dec.	1899	0	Inmate
Murgalus, Martha	WF	July	1897	2	Inmate
Murphy, Aloysius	WM	Sept.	1899	0	Inmate
Murphy, Annie	WF	Jan.	1876	24	St. Ann's
Murphy, Elaine	WF	Nov.	1899	0	Inmate
Murphy, Florence	WF	Jan.	1900	0	Inmate
Murphy, Francis	WM	Feb.	1899	1	Inmate
Murphy, James	WM	Sept.	1899	0	Inmate
Murphy, Margaret	WF	June	1882	18	Inmate
Murphy, Mary	WF	Aug.	1899	1	Inmate
Murphy, Mary	WF	Sept.	1897	2	Inmate
Murray, James	WM	July	1897	2	Inmate
Murray, Joseph	WM	Apr.	1898	2	Inmate
Murray, Josephine	WF	June	1882	18	Inmate
Murray, Loretto	WF	Mar.	1897	3	Inmate
Murray, Louise	WF	May	1898	2	Inmate
Murray, Margaret	WF	July	1897	2	Inmate
Murray, Mary	WF	Dec.	1899	0	Inmate
Murray, Mary	WF	Nov.	1897	2	Inmate
Murray, Thomas	WM	Mar.	1899	1	Inmate
Murray, Thomas	WM	Nov.	1899	0	Inmate
Murray, William	WM	Aug.	1899	1	Inmate
Murtha, James	WM	May	1899	1	Inmate
Naale, Anne	WF	Jan.	1899	1	Inmate
Nanninger, Michael	WM	Feb.	1900	0	Inmate
Nara, Margaret	WF	Aug.	1860	39	Sister

Neal, Joseph	WM	July	1897	2	Inmate
Neary, Joseph	WM	May	1899	1	Inmate
Nelson, Agnes	WF	Aug.	1875	24	Inmate
Nelson, Edgar	WM	June	1899	1	Inmate
Nelson, Joseph	WM	Feb.	1900	0	Inmate
Nelson, Percy	WM	Aug.	1898	1	Inmate
Newman, Florence	WF	Oct.	1899	0	Inmate
Newman, Rose	WF	Mar.	1900	0	Inmate
Nicholas, George	WM	Sept.	1898	1	Inmate
Nicholas, Paul	WM	Sept.	1899	0	Inmate
Noel, Mary	WF	Dec.	1898	1	Inmate
Nolan, Bernard	WM	May	1898	2	Inmate
Nolan, Maggie	WF	July	1898	1	Inmate
Nolan, Mary	WF	Mar.	1900	0	Inmate
Nolasco, Agnes	WF	Jan.	1899	1	Inmate
Noonan, Margaret	WF	Sept.	1897	2	Inmate
Norbert, Mary	WF	June	1898	2	Inmate
Norman, Louis	WM	Feb.	1899	1	Inmate
Norman, Oliver	WM	Nov.	1899	0	Inmate
Norton, Vitiline	WF	Nov.	1899	0	Inmate
Noval, Mary	WF	June	1898	2	Inmate
Nunez, Andrew	WM	Nov.	1898	1	Inmate
O'Brein, Andrew	WM	Jan.	1900	0	Inmate
O'Brein, John	WM	Nov.	1899	0	Inmate
O'Brien, James	WM	July	1899	0	Inmate
O'Brien, Joseph	WM	June	1897	2	Inmate
O'Brien, Mary	WF	Mar.	1900	0	Inmate
O'Brien, Willie	WM	Apr.	1897	3	Inmate
Obriesti, Amelia	WF	Oct.	1897	2	Inmate
O'Connor, Dennis	WM	Feb.	1899	1	Inmate
O'Connor, Donald	WM	Feb.	1898	2	Inmate
O'Connor, Eliza	WF	Oct.	1899	0	Inmate
O'Connor, Joseph	WM	Aug.	1898	1	Inmate
O'Connor, Mary	WF	Mar.	1900	0	Inmate
O'Connor, Mary	WF	Oct.	1897	2	Inmate
O'Connor, Maurice	WM	Feb.	1897	3	Inmate
O'Dowd, Edward	WM	Feb.	1898	2	Inmate
O'Hara, Florence	WF	Mar.	1897	3	Inmate
Ohlrich, Benny	WM	June	1897	2	Inmate
O'Keefe, Annie	WF	Dec.	1899	0	Inmate
O'Keefe, Delia	WF	Oct.	1875	24	Inmate
O'Keefe, Margaret	WF	Sept.	1896	3	Inmate

O'Keefe, Stephen	WM	Dec.	1898	1	Inmate
Olcott, Mary	WF	Apr.	1898	2	Inmate
Oliver, William	WM	Apr.	1898	2	Inmate
Olsen, Marie	WF	Oct.	1899	0	Inmate
Ondis, Joseph	WM	Jan.	1900	0	Inmate
O'Neil, Catherine	WF	June	1899	0	Inmate
O'Neil, Clare	WF	Jan.	1900	0	Inmate
O'Neil, Mildred	WF	Jan.	1900	0	Inmate
O'Niel, Margaret	WF	Mar.	1898	2	Inmate
O'Niel, Thomas	WM	Aug.	1896	3	Inmate
O'Niel, Winifred	WF	Mar.	1899	1	Inmate
Oppenheimer, Mariel	WF	July	1897	2	Inmate
O'Reilly, Lizzie	WF	Dec.	1871	28	Inmate
Ormond, Adeline	WF	Dec.	1899	0	Inmate
O'Rouke, Marie	WF	May	1899	1	Inmate
O'Rourke, Alice	WF	Feb.	1899	1	Inmate
Orr, Delephinie	WF	Sept.	1899	0	Inmate
Orr, Mary	WF	Oct.	1899	0	Inmate
Osborne, George	WM	July	1893	3	Inmate
Osborne, Leonora	WF	Dec.	1899	0	Inmate
Oswald, Aurelia	WF	Mar.	1898	2	Inmate
Owens, Josephine	WF	July	1899	0	Inmate
Packer, Clarence	WF	Aug.	1897	2	Inmate
Page, Reginald	WM	Feb.	1897	3	Inmate
Paladino, Joseph	WM	Apr.	1900	0	Inmate
Palm, Dolores	WF	Apr.	1900	0	Inmate
Palmer, Joseph	WM	Mar.	1898	2	Inmate
Parks, Mary	WF	May	1870	30	Inmate
Parmento, Joseph	WM	July	1897	2	Inmate
Parslow, Amy	WF	Aug.	1899	0	Inmate
Parslow, Amy	WF	Feb.	1878	22	Inmate
Parsons, Marg't.	WF	July	1899	0	Inmate
Pauling, Genevieve	WF	May	1899	1	Inmate
Paulis, Mary	WF	Nov.	1897	2	Inmate
Payne, Edward	WM	May	1897	3	Inmate
Payne, Mary	WF	Oct.	1888	11	Inmate
Peace, Albert	WM	Oct.	1897	2	Inmate
Pearlsteim, Flora	WF	Dec.	1897	2	Inmate
Peckingham, Edward	WM	Mar.	1898	2	Inmate
Peiffer, John	WM	Apr.	1898	2	Inmate
Penedispki, Clara	WF	Nov.	1897	2	Inmate
Pepple, Julia	WF	July	1898	1	Inmate

Perry, Charles	WM	June	1898	1	Inmate
Petray, Walter	WM	July	1898	1	Inmate
Petroski, Leander	WM	Feb.	1898	2	Inmate
Pfortner, Bertha	WF	June	1898	1	Inmate
Phalen, Joseph	WM	Jan.	1900	0	Inmate
Phalon, Charlotte	WF	Feb.	1880	20	Inmate
Phelan, Richard	WM	Sept.	1898	1	Inmate
Phillips, Julia	WF	Nov.	1899	0	Inmate
Phillips, Monica	WM*	May	1899	1	Inmate
Phillips, Namoi	WF	May	1899	1	Inmate
Piderit, William	WM	Dec.	1894	5	Inmate
Pierce, Katie	WF	Mar.	1880	20	Inmate
Pierce, William	WM	Oct.	1899	0	Inmate
Pierson, Leon	WM	May	1897	3	Inmate
Pieter, George	WM	Apr.	1897	3	Inmate
Piggott, Aubrey	WF	Apr.	1900	0	Inmate
Pitt, Marie	WF	July	1899	0	Inmate
Plimkett, Ellen	WF	Apr.	1879	21	St. Ann's
Plumite, Mary	WF	Mar.	1899	1	Inmate
Plunket, Maud	WF	Jan.	1870	30	Sister
Polatshek, Rosa	WF	Sept.	1897	2	Inmate
Polinski, Frank	WM	Nov.	1897	2	Inmate
Polita, Jennie	WF	Apr.	1900	0	Inmate
Pollard, Mary	WF	July	1895	4	Inmate
Pollester, Madeline	WF	Apr.	1898	2	Inmate
Porter, Albert	WM	Jan.	1900	0	Inmate
Porter, Lucille	WF	Oct.	1897	2	Inmate
Posener, James	WM	Jan.	1900	0	Inmate
Powell, Paul	WF	June	1899	1	Inmate
Powers, Gerald	WM	Aug.	1896	3	Inmate
Powers, William	WM	Apr.	1896	4	Inmate
Prescott, Marie	WF	Sept.	1899	0	Inmate
Preston, Leo.	WM	Mar.	1900	0	Inmate
Price, Lizzie	WF	Dec.	1869	30	Inmate
Proctor, Winifred	WM	July	1897	2	Inmate
Provinco, Gregory	WM	Dec.	1899	0	Inmate
Pryor, Catherine	WF	Apr.	1876	24	Inmate
Pulman, Lillian	WF	Feb.	1871	29	Inmate
Pulman, Philomena	WF	Feb.	1900	0	Inmate
Puloso, Cecilia	WF	July	1899	0	Inmate
Purcell, Anna	WF	July	1849	50	Sister
Purcell, John	WM	Apr.	1896	4	Inmate

Quigley, Catherine	WF	Jan.	1900	0	Inmate
Quigley, Michael	WM	Mar.	1899	1	Inmate
Quilan, Angela	WF	May	1897	3	Inmate
Quinlan, George	WM	Dec.	1897	2	Inmate
Quinn, Agnes	WF	Mar.	1876	24	Inmate
Quinn, Frank	WM	Oct.	1897	2	Inmate
Quinn, John	WM	May	1898	2	Inmate
Quinn, Mary	WF	Aug.	1899	1	Inmate
Quintard, Genevieve	WF	Jan.	1900	0	Inmate
Quintard, Mary	WF	Oct.	1870	29	Inmate
Quinton, Henry	WM	Oct.	1898	1	Inmate
Quirk, Catherine	WF	Apr.	1899	1	Inmate
Rader, William	WM	Apr.	1900	0	Inmate
Rafferty, Frank	WM	May	1897	3	Inmate
Rafferty, Joseph	WM	Sept.	1899	0	Inmate
Rapalo, Paul	WM	Apr.	1897	3	Inmate
Raphy, Maria	WF	Oct.	1898	1	Inmate
Raplayea, Julia	WF	Jan.	1897	3	Inmate
Rath, Pauline	WF	July	1899	0	Inmate
Raw, William	WM	May	1896	4	Inmate
Raymond, Edward	WM	Dec.	1899	0	Inmate
Raymond, Joseph	WM	Dec.	1899	0	Inmate
Raymond, Joseph	WM	Dec.	1898	1	Inmate
Raymond, Mary	WF	Jan.	1900	0	Inmate
Ready, Anna	WF	May	1859	41	Sister
Reardon, Loretto	WF	Jan.	1895	5	Inmate
Reddin, Marion	WF	Jan.	1900	0	Inmate
Redmond, Rose	WF	Feb.	1899	1	Inmate
Reed, Lulu	WF	May	1900	0	Inmate
Reeves, Joseph	WM	Dec.	1898	1	Inmate
Regalia, Annie	WF	Oct.	1871	28	St. Ann's
Regan, William	WM	Sept.	1899	0	Inmate
Regen, Celestine	WF	Dec.	1898	1	Inmate
Reid, Jennie	WF	Oct.	1899	0	Inmate
Reilly, Alice	WF	Jan.	1900	0	Inmate
Reilly, Catherine	WF	Feb.	1898	2	Inmate
Reilly, Joseph	WM	July	1899	0	Inmate
Reilly, Joseph	WM	May	1898	2	Inmate
Reilly, Kate	WF	Dec.	1863	36	Inmate
Reilly, Margaret	WF	Mar.	1884	16	Inmate
Reilly, Mary	WF	Feb.	1899	1	Inmate
Reilly, Rose	WF	Jan.	1900	0	Inmate

Reilly, Thomas	WM	Apr.	1900	0	Inmate
Reilly, Thomas	WM	Apr.	1896	4	Inmate
Reilly, Walter	WM	Apr.	1900	0	Inmate
Reinmuth, Alfred	WM	Nov.	1899	0	Inmate
Reman, Bertha	WF	Mar.	1899	1	Inmate
Rempsen, Laura	WF	Sept.	1898	1	Inmate
Reneski, Anna	WF	Feb.	1897	3	Inmate
Revens, John	WM	Aug.	1891	8	Inmate
Reymond, Stanislaus	WM	May	1898	2	Inmate
Reynolds, James	WM	Jan.	1900	0	Inmate
Reynolds, Lottie	WF	Jan.	1898	2	Inmate
Rezvelert, Susan	WF	Mar.	1900	0	Inmate
Rhen, George	WM	July	1899	0	Inmate
Rhodes, Magaret	WF	May	1900	0	Inmate
Rice, Margaret	WF	Jan.	1897	3	Inmate
Richaddese, John	WM	Jan.	1897	3	Inmate
Ricton, Sadie	WF	July	1896	3	Inmate
Ridley, Mary	WF	Mar.	1873	27	St. Ann's
Riendew, Victoria	WF	Dec.	1899	0	Inmate
Riley, Harry	WM	July	1898	1	Inmate
Riley, John	WM	Mar.	1899	1	Inmate
Ripp, Annie	WF	DEc.	1899	0	Inmate
Riston, Mary	WF	Nov.	1872	27	Inmate
Riston, Robert	WM	Mar.	1900	0	Inmate
Roach, John	WM	Aug.	1897	2	Inmate
Roberts, Charles	WM	Apr.	1900	0	Inmate
Roberts, Florence	WF	Jan.	1900	0	Inmate
Robertson, Robert	WM	Apr.	1896	4	Inmate
Robins, Albert	WM	Dec.	1899	0	Inmate
Robinson, Antoin	WM	May	1899	1	Inmate
Robinson, Harold	WM	Dec.	1896	3	Inmate
Robinson, Marg't.	WF	Apr.	1884	16	St. Ann's
Robinson, Robert	WM	July	1899	0	Inmate
Roche, Clarence	WF*	Feb.	1898	2	Inmate
Rochel, Carrie	WF	Nov.	1897	2	Inmate
Rochford, Anna	WF	Aug.	1873	26	Sister
Rock, Annie	WF	Mar.	1900	0	Inmate
Rock, Michael	WM	Aug.	1899	0	Inmate
Roderick, Richard	WM	June	1898	1	Inmate
Rodgers, Wm.	WM	Oct.	1898	1	Inmate
Rogen, Kate	WF	Feb.	1878	22	Inmate
Rogere, Mary	WF	May	1894	6	Inmate

Rogers, Augustine	WF	Nov.	1899	0	Inmate
Rogers, Mark	WM	Apr.	1899	1	Inmate
Rolick, Matilda	WF	Dec.	1895	4	Inmate
Romana, Emma	WF	July	1898	1	Inmate
Romani, Mary	WF	Sept.	1893	6	Inmate
Romanski, Reinhold	WF*	Nov.	1897	2	Inmate
Ronan, Elizabeth	WF	Nov.	1897	2	Inmate
Roosevelt, Oscar	WM	Oct.	1899	0	Inmate
Rose, Angeline	WF	July	1899	0	Inmate
Rose, James	WM	Oct.	1895	4	Inmate
Rosen, Arthur	WM	June	1898	1	Inmate
Rosen, Esther	WF	Apr.	1899	1	Inmate
Rosen, James	WM	Aug.	1899	0	Inmate
Rosen, Sara	WF	Nov.	1898	1	Inmate
Rosenberg, Annie	WF	Oct.	1899	0	Inmate
Rosenberg, Fannie	WF	Dec.	1882	17	Inmate
Rosenberg, Lena	WF	Nov.	1899	0	Inmate
Rosenberg, Maurice	WM	July	1898	1	Inmate
Rosenblum, Cecilia	WF	Oct.	1899	0	Inmate
Rosendorf, Joseph	WM	Aug.	1897	2	Inmate
Rosevelt, Stell	WF	Dec.	1895	4	Inmate
Ross, Albert	WM	Aug.	1899	0	Inmate
Ross, Edwin	WM	July	1898	1	Inmate
Ross, Lucinda	WF	Feb.	1899	1	Inmate
Rossi, Andrew	WM	Oct.	1898	1	Inmate
Roubler, Josephine	WF	June	1899	1	Inmate
Rowland, Joseph	WM	Oct.	1897	2	Inmate
Rowland, Theodore	WM	Oct.	1897	2	Inmate
Rubin, Dora	WF	Dec.	1899	0	Inmate
Rucomski, Frank	WM	Mar.	1897	2	Inmate
Ruggeri, Antonio	WM	Nov.	1899	0	Inmate
Rush, John	WM	Aug.	1897	2	Inmate
Rush, Sarah	WF	Jan.	1870	30	Sister
Russell, Genevieve	WF	Aug.	1899	0	Inmate
Russell, Gertrude	WF	June	1898	1	Inmate
Russell, Mary	WF	June	1870	29	Inmate
Ruthmuick, Emma	WF	Mar.	1872	28	Inmate
Ruthwick, Albert	WM	Nov.	1895	4	Inmate
Ryan, Alice	WF	June	1896	3	Inmate
Ryan, Annie	WF	Nov.	1899	0	Inmate
Ryan, George	WM	Jan.	1899	1	Inmate
Ryan, James	WM	May	1900	0	Inmate

Ryan, John	WM	Jan.	1899	1	Inmate
Ryan, Lawrence	WM	May	1898	2	Inmate
Ryan, Margaret	WF	June	1867	32	Sister
Ryan, Mary	WF	Mar.	1900	0	Inmate
Ryan, Mary	WF	June	1898	2	Inmate
Ryan, Mary	WF	Jan.	1875	25	Inmate
Ryan, Paul	WM	Apr.	1900	0	Inmate
Ryan, Rose	WF	Nov.	1878	21	Inmate
Ryan, Thomas	WM	Nov.	1893	6	Inmate
Ryan, William	WM	Jan.	1899	1	Inmate
Ryani, Charles	WM	Sept.	1899	0	Inmate
Ryder, Martha	WF	Feb.	1900	0	Inmate
Sabbal, Joseph	WM	Feb.	1898	2	Inmate
Sabbas, Joseph	WM	Dec.	1898	1	Inmate
St. John, Genevieve	WF	Feb.	1898	2	Inmate
St. John, George	WM	Apr.	1898	2	Inmate
St. John, Joseph	WM	May	1898	2	Inmate
Salono, Joseph	WM	July	1899	0	Inmate
Salzer, Merice	WF	June	1899	1	Inmate
Sanders, Eleanor	WF	Apr.	1898	2	Inmate
Sanders, Robert	WM	Dec.	1898	1	Inmate
Sands, Daniel	WM	Aug.	1898	1	Inmate
Sands, Samuel	WM	Apr.	1897	3	Inmate
Saubert, Agnes	WF	May	1900	0	Inmate
Sawyer, Henry	WM	Jan.	1896	4	Inmate
Scally, Magaret	WF	Feb.	1875	25	Inmate
Scanlon, Mary	WF	Mar.	1850	50	Sister
Scanton, Lillian	WF	May	1900	0	Inmate
Scarpi, Anthony	WM	Sept.	1897	2	Inmate
Schaeffer, Anthony	WM	May	1897	3	Inmate
Schaughnessy, Geo.	WM	Jan.	1899	1	Inmate
Schilling, James	WM	Feb.	1900	0	Inmate
Schmidt, Anna	WF	Mar.	1899	1	Inmate
Schmidt, Anna	WF	Mar.	1896	4	Inmate
Schmidt, John	WM	Jan.	1900	0	Inmate
Schmidt, Julia	WF	Dec.	1898	1	Inmate
Schmidt, Lena	WF	Mar.	1878	22	Inmate
Schmidt, Peter	WM	Nov.	1895	4	Inmate
Schneider, Caroline	WF	Jan.	1899	1	Inmate
Schneider, Joseph	WM	May	1898	2	Inmate
Schneider, Mamie	WF	May	1898	2	Inmate
Scholz, George	WM	Sept.	1899	0	Inmate

Schoomer, Thomas	WF*	Dec.	1896	3	Inmate
Schoron, Mary	WF	June	1894	5	Inmate
Schriber, Alice	WF	Jan.	1898	2	Inmate
Schroeder, Rudolph	WM	Feb.	1900	0	Inmate
Schultz, Annie	WF	May	1881	19	St. Ann's
Schultz, Teresa	WF	May	1898	2	Inmate
Schwartz, Gussie	WF	Apr.	1898	2	Inmate
Schwartz, Mary	WF	Sept.	1897	2	Inmate
Schwitzer, Marg't.	WF	Jan.	1900	0	Inmate
Sciacca, Josephine	WF	Mar.	1900	0	Inmate
Scodoors, John	WM	Dec.	1896	3	Inmate
Scott, Alice	WF	Feb.	1898	2	Inmate
Scott, James	WM	Jan.	1897	3	Inmate
Scott, Joseph	WM	Oct.	1896	3	Inmate
Scott, Laura	WF	Jan.	1897	3	Inmate
Scott, Marie	WF	Dec.	1893	6	Inmate
Scott, Rosabel	WF	Oct.	1899	0	Inmate
Seamon, Esther	WF	Sept.	1898	1	Inmate
Sedestrum, Albert	WF*	Apr.	1897	3	Inmate
Seegar, Arthur	WM	Jan.	1900	0	Inmate
Seeger, Elizabeth	WF	May	1880	20	Inmate
Selig, Thomas	WM	Sept.	1899	0	Inmate
Sever, William	WM	Mar.	1898	2	Inmate
Shane, Mary	WF	Apr.	1897	3	Inmate
Shanley, John	WM	June	1898	2	Inmate
Shannahan, Ellen	WF	June	1898	1	Inmate
Shannon, Thomas	WM	June	1898	1	Inmate
Shapiro, Maurice	WM	Feb.	1900	0	Inmate
Sharks, Frances	WF	May	1896	4	Inmate
Shaunnon, Thomas	WM	Aug.	1899	0	Inmate
Shay, Annie	WF	Mar.	1898	2	Inmate
Shay, Annie	WF	Jan.	1872	28	Inmate
Shay, Elizabeth	WF	Dec.	1899	0	Inmate
Shay, Michael	WM	Sept.	1896	3	Inmate
Sheardon, William	WM	Feb.	1898	2	Inmate
Sheehy, Wm.	WM	Apr.	1895	5	Inmate
Sheldon, Alice	WF	June	1899	0	Inmate
Shellard, Jas.	WM	Sept.	1899	0	Inmate
Shenk, Elsie	WF	May	1898	2	Inmate
Sheoffin, Thomasina	WF	June	1898	2	Inmate
Shepherd, Louis	WM	May	1898	2	Inmate
Shepperd, Violet	WF	Aug.	1897	2	Inmate

Shiegler, Edward	WM	Jan.	1900	0	Inmate
Shinoli, Frank	WM	Oct.	1899	0	Inmate
Shralley, Nicholas	WM	Apr.	1894	6	Inmate
Shunk, Englebert	WM	Jan.	1895	5	Inmate
Sibas, Joseph	WM	July	1898	1	Inmate
Simms, Wm.	WM	June	1892	8	Inmate
Simon, Agnes	WF	Dec.	1898	1	Inmate
Simon, Thomas	WM	Nov.	1894	5	Inmate
Simpson, Annie	WF	July	1898	1	Inmate
Simpson, Anto	WM	Apr.	1897	3	Inmate
Simpson, Mary	WF	Jan.	1893	7	Inmate
Simpson, Walter	WM	Dec.	1898	1	Inmate
Sirame, Rose	WF	Feb.	1900	0	Inmate
Skahen, Peter	WM	Sept.	1896	3	Inmate
Skidmore, Dorothy	WF	Aug.	1896	3	Inmate
Slarch, William	WM	July	1899	0	Inmate
Slier, Joseph	WM	Feb.	1898	2	Inmate
Slyvia, Mary	WF	Feb.	1898	2	Inmate
Smeltz, Willie	WM	Apr.	1897	3	Inmate
Smith, Annie	WF	June	1898	1	Inmate
Smith, Anthony	WM	Oct.	1898	1	Inmate
Smith, Bertha	WF	June	1898	2	Inmate
Smith, Bertrand	WF	Sept.	1897	2	Inmate
Smith, Charlotte	WF	Oct.	1899	0	Inmate
Smith, Charlotte	WF	July	1896	3	Inmate
Smith, Constance	WF	Apr.	1893	7	Inmate
Smith, Ellen	WF	June	1898	1	Inmate
Smith, Emma	WF	Dec.	1897	2	Inmate
Smith, Emma	WF	May	1882	18	Inmate
Smith, George	WM	Aug.	1898	1	Inmate
Smith, George	WM	Mar.	1899	1	Inmate
Smith, George	WM	Nov.	1894	5	Inmate
Smith, Harold	WM	Feb.	1900	0	Inmate
Smith, Harold	WM	May	1897	3	Inmate
Smith, Harry	WM	Nov.	1899	0	Inmate
Smith, Harry	WM	Nov.	1894	5	Inmate
Smith, Henry	WM	May	1898	2	Inmate
Smith, Irwin	WM	Jan.	1897	3	Inmate
Smith, John	WM	June	1899	0	Inmate
Smith, Joseph	WM	Mar.	1900	0	Inmate
Smith, Joseph	WM	Dec.	1898	1	Inmate
Smith, Joseph	WM	Jan.	1898	2	Inmate

Smith, Joseph	WM	June	1896	4	Inmate
Smith, Julia	WF	Mar.	1900	0	Inmate
Smith, Lillian	WF	May	1898	2	Inmate
Smith, Lizzie	WF	Dec.	1895	4	Inmate
Smith, Maggie	WF	Feb.	1898	2	Inmate
Smith, Marg't.	WF	Feb.	1898	2	Inmate
Smith, Marie	WF	Sept.	1899	0	Inmate
Smith, Mary	WF	May	1898	2	Inmate
Smith, Mary	WF	June	1898	2	Inmate
Smith, Mary	WF	July	1895	4	Inmate
Smith, Mary	WF	May	1876	24	Inmate
Smith, Mildred	WF	Sept.	1899	0	Inmate
Smith, Mildred	WF	Sept.	1898	1	Inmate
Smith, Minnie	WF	July	1897	2	Inmate
Smith, Penelope	WF	Oct.	1898	1	Inmate
Smith, Peter	WM	Sept.	1896	3	Inmate
Smith, Sarah	WF	Jan.	1898	2	Inmate
Smith, Senora	WM*	Nov.	1895	4	Inmate
Smith, Veronica	WF	Aug.	1898	1	Inmate
Smith, William	WM	Nov.	1897	2	Inmate
Smith, Williamana	WF	Sept.	1899	0	Inmate
Smith, Winifred	WF	Mar.	1869	31	Inmate
Snee, Raymond	WM	Sept.	1894	5	Inmate
Somers, Isabella	WF	Dec.	1899	0	Inmate
Somson, Beatrice	WF	Dec.	1898	1	Inmate
Sott, Frank	WM	Oct.	1899	0	Inmate
Souiler, Lester	WM	Apr.	1898	2	Inmate
Spang, Marion	WF	June	1898	1	Inmate
Spence, Francis	WM	Dec.	1899	0	Inmate
Spencer, George	WM	May	1898	2	Inmate
Spencer, Ida	WF	Mar.	1900	0	Inmate
Stallman, Louis	WM	July	1899	0	Inmate
Stanley, Harry	WM	Jan.	1900	0	Inmate
Stanley, Innocent	WF	Dec.	1899	0	Inmate
Stanton, Marie	WF	Nov.	1899	0	Inmate
Stapleton, Edward	WM	Dec.	1899	0	Inmate
Statska, Annie	WF	Feb.	1900	0	Inmate
Stearn, Helen	WF	Dec.	1898	1	Inmate
Stein, Henry	WM	Dec.	1899	0	Inmate
Sterch, Mary	WF	Oct.	1899	0	Inmate
Stevens, Annie	WF	Feb.	1897	3	Inmate
Stevens, Arthur	WM	Mar.	1900	0	Inmate

Stevens, Christina	WF	Dec.	1898	1	Inmate
Stevens, Herbert	WM	May	1898	2	Inmate
Stevens, Mary	WF	May	1898	2	Inmate
Stevens, Rita	WF	Jun.	1898	2	Inmate
Stevenson, Joseph	WM	Jan.	1897	3	Inmate
Stewart, Geneve	WF	Feb.	1898	2	Inmate
Stewart, Kate	WF	Aug.	1898	1	Inmate
Stiner, Catherine	WF	Apr.	1900	0	Inmate
Stone, Agnes	WF	Sept.	1899	0	Inmate
Stone, George	WM	Apr.	1898	2	Inmate
Stone, Ignatius	WM	Oct.	1897	2	Inmate
Strobel, George	WM	Sept.	1897	2	Inmate
Strum, George	WM	Mar.	1900	0	Inmate
Student, John	WM	Dec.	1897	2	Inmate
Sullivan, Daniel	WM	Jan.	1897	3	Inmate
Sullivan, Ellen	WF	Jan.	1900	0	Inmate
Sullivan, Ellen	WF	Feb.	1872	28	Inmate
Sullivan, John	WM	Jan.	1900	0	Inmate
Sullivan, John	WM	Nov.	1894	5	Inmate
Sullivan, Julia	WF	Sept.	1880	19	Inmate
Sullivan, Julia	WF	June	1880	19	Inmate
Sullivan, Martin	WM	Dec.	1899	0	Inmate
Sullivan, Mary	WF	Jan.	1900	0	Inmate
Sullivan, Mary	WF	Jan.	1899	1	Inmate
Sullivan, Mary	WF	July	1898	1	Inmate
Sullivan, Mary	WF	Jan.	1897	3	Inmate
Sullivan, Mary	WF	Dec.	1870	29	Sister
Sullivan, Mary	WF	Feb.	1870	30	Inmate
Sullivan, Michael	WM	Jan.	1898	2	Inmate
Sullivan, Rachel	WF	Apr.	1900	0	Inmate
Sullivan, Thomas	WM	Sept.	1899	0	Inmate
Suminig, Sara	WF	July	1898	1	Inmate
Summer, Catherine	WF	Nov.	1897	2	Inmate
Sundatali, Jos.	WM	May	1898	2	Inmate
Sunstran, Cath.	WF	Aug.	1899	0	Inmate
Sussman, Henry	WM	Sept.	1899	0	Inmate
Sutton, Eliza	WF	Jan.	1875	25	St. Ann's
Swamt, Joseph	WM	Dec.	1899	0	Inmate
Sweeney, Aloysius	WM	June	1898	1	Inmate
Sweeny, James	WM	Oct.	1899	0	Inmate
Swerster, Thomas	WM	Jan.	1898	2	Inmate
Swetzer, Lucy	WF	Jan.	1898	2	Inmate

Swift, Albert	WM	Aug.	1895	4	Inmate
Symth, Mary	WF	Jan.	1899	1	Inmate
Symthe, Hyman	WM	July	1897	2	Inmate
Szocobo, Anna	WF	Oct.	1895	5	Inmate
Tangley, Maria	WF	Dec.	1898	1	Inmate
Tanni, Angela	WF	Mar.	1899	1	Inmate
Taunebaum, Rose	WF	Mar.	1897	3	Inmate
Taylor, Alfred	WM	Mar.	1900	0	Inmate
Taylor, Rebecca	WF	May	1874	26	Inmate
TenBrock, Christine	WF	May	1900	0	Inmate
Tenny, Goldie	WF	May	1882	18	St. Ann's
Terry, Genevieve	WF	Apr.	1900	0	Inmate
Theal, George	WM	Aug.	1895	4	Inmate
Thirston, Edward	WM	Sept.	1895	4	Inmate
Thomas, Frank	WM	Nov.	1895	4	Inmate
Thomas, Maggie	WF	Feb.	1882	28	Inmate
Thomas, Margaret	WF	May	1898	2	Inmate
Thomas, Octavia	WM*	Jan.	1900	0	Inmate
Thomas, Thedore	WM	Mar.	1900	0	Inmate
Thompkins, Alice	WF	Mar.	1898	2	Inmate
Thompson, Cecillia	WF	Mar.	1899	1	Inmate
Thompson, Joseph	WM	Dec.	1895	4	Inmate
Thompson, Lizzie	WF	May	1870	30	Inmate
Thompson, Paul	WM	Mar.	1898	2	Inmate
Thompson, Thomas	WM	Apr.	1900	0	Inmate
Thompson, Willie	WM	Oct.	1890	9	Inmate
Thurst, George	WM	Sept.	1897	2	Inmate
Tierney, Robert	WM	July	1895	4	Inmate
Tighe, Helena	WF	Nov.	1898	1	Inmate
Titus, Cecillia	WF	Jan.	1897	3	Inmate
Tobin, Joseph	WM	Sept.	1897	2	Inmate
Tomney, Elizabeth	WF	Aug.	1854	45	Sister
Tracey, Loretto	WF	Oct.	1871	28	Inmate
Tracy, Marietta	WF	May	1900	0	Inmate
Traut, Augusta	WF	Jan.	1897	3	Inmate
Travers, Teresa	WF	Oct.	1899	0	Inmate
Travers, Veronica	WF	Oct.	1881	18	Inmate
Treen, Jennie	WF	June	1899	0	Inmate
Trent, Sylvester	WM	Mar.	1900	0	Inmate
Trinizi, Irmine	WM*	Dec.	1895	4	Inmate
Tully, Anna	WF	May	1854	46	Sister
Tully, Benjamin	WM	June	1895	4	Inmate

Tunny, Joseph	WM	Apr.	1897	3	Inmate
Turm, Charles	WM	May	1897	3	Inmate
Twomey, Irene	WF	Nov.	1899	0	Inmate
Uhl, George	WM	Oct.	1898	1	Inmate
Uhly, Charles	WM	Jan.	1899	1	Inmate
Ulner, Lucy	WF	July	1899	0	Inmate
Ulrich, Lucy	WF	July	1897	2	Inmate
Uniack, Mary	WF	Feb.	1900	0	Inmate
Uradi, Marcella	WF	Jan.	1900	0	Inmate
Urban, Andrew	WM	Nov.	1899	0	Inmate
Vacaro, Angelo	WM	Sept.	1899	0	Inmate
Valdman, Joseph	WM	Feb.	1899	1	Inmate
Vale, Gertrude	WF	Dec.	1899	0	Inmate
Valeton, Ralph	WM	Oct.	1898	1	Inmate
VanBuren, James	WM	Nov.	1897	2	Inmate
Vance, Gertrude	WF	Jan.	1900	0	Inmate
Vand, George	WM	Feb.	1899	1	Inmate
VanDorn, Kenneth	WM	July	1899	0	Inmate
VanKuren, Ada	WF	Jan.	1878	22	St. Ann's
Vaulkner, John	WM	Feb.	1900	0	Inmate
Veitch, Maria	WF	Jan.	1880	20	Inmate
Veleto, Marie	WF	Aug.	1893	6	Inmate
Veloy, Blanche	WF	Feb.	1900	0	Inmate
Vemitz, Herbert	WM	Oct.	1893	6	Inmate
Veret, Helen	WF	Dec.	1899	0	Inmate
Vernon, Anna	WM	Mar.	1900	0	Inmate
Vesey, Robert	WM	Jan.	1900	0	Inmate
Vesey, Sylvester	WM	Jan.	1897	3	Inmate
Vetter, Rose	WF	May	1899	1	Inmate
Vianney, Annie	WF	Feb.	1900	0	Inmate
Vincent, Joseph	WM	Nov.	1897	2	Inmate
Vincent, Mary	WF	Mar.	1900	0	Inmate
Vincent, Michael	WM	May	1900	0	Inmate
Vincent, Stella	WF	Mar.	1900	0	Inmate
Vincenzo, Beatrice	WF	May	1899	1	Inmate
Vincenzo, Pauline	WF	May	1899	1	Inmate
Vinton, Louis	WM	Jan.	1899	1	Inmate
Vinton, Thomas	WM	Nov.	1899	0	Inmate
Vioski, John	WM	Sept.	1899	0	Inmate
Vogel, Charles	WM	Dec.	1899	0	Inmate
Vogel, Louis	WM	June	1894	5	Inmate
Vogel, William	WM	May	1899	1	Inmate

Volitti, Anthony	WM	Jan.	1900	0	Inmate
Volz, Louis	WM	Jan.	1900	0	Inmate
Voneski, Rose	WF	Feb.	1900	3m	Inmate
Vopianski, Rebec	WF	June	1898	1	Inmate
Vought, James	WM	Sept.	1899	0	Inmate
Vrea, Kate	WF	Apr.	1873	27	Inmate
Vreas, Joseph	WM	Jan.	1900	0	Inmate
Vreeland, Leo	WM	Mar.	1900	0	Inmate
Wagner, Mary	WF	Mar.	1897	3	Inmate
Walker, Grace	WF	May	1877	23	St. Ann's
Wall, Catherine	WF	Jan.	1900	0	Inmate
Wallace, Arthur	WM	Mar.	1900	0	Inmate
Wallace, Leo	WM	Mar.	1900	0	Inmate
Wallace, Thomas	WM	Dec.	1896	3	Inmate
Walsh, Joseph	WM	Dec.	1898	1	Inmate
Walsh, Joseph	WM	Mar.	1899	1	Inmate
Walsh, Mary	WF	Dec.	1899	0	Inmate
Walsh, Mary	WF	Apr.	1900	0	Inmate
Walsh, Mary	WF	Mar.	1870	30	Inmate
Walter, Louise	WF	Apr.	1899	1	Inmate
Ward, Isabella	WF	May	1895	5	Inmate
Ward, Joseph	WM	May	1899	1	Inmate
Ward, Mary	WF	Mar.	1895	5	Inmate
Ward, Sarah	WF	Oct.	1893	6	Inmate
Ward, William	WM	Sept.	1898	1	Inmate
Wardell, Joseph	WM	Apr.	1899	1	Inmate
Warner, Annie	WF	May	1877	23	St. Ann's
Warner, Ethel	WF	Apr.	1900	0	Inmate
Warren, Gertrude	WF	May	1877	23	Inmate
Warren, Thomas	WM	Oct.	1898	1	Inmate
Warwick, Joseph	WM	May	1898	2	Inmate
Wasbauer, Bertha	WF	Feb.	1898	2	Inmate
Washington, Frank	WM	June	1898	1	Inmate
Washington, Vincent	WM	Feb.	1900	0	Inmate
Wasil, Annie	WF	Nov.	1899	0	Inmate
Watson, James	WM	Jan.	1899	1	Inmate
Wayant, Gertrude	WF	Nov.	1898	1	Inmate
Weber, George	WM	Feb.	1900	0	Inmate
Weber, George	WM	Nov.	1898	1	Inmate
Weeks, Annie	WF	Sept.	1887	12	Inmate
Weinstein, Henry	WM	May	1895	5	Inmate
Weller, Edward	WM	Jan.	1900	0	Inmate

Welsh, Delia	WF	Mar.	1873	27	Inmate
Welsh, John	WM	Nov.	1899	0	Inmate
Welsh, Josephine	WF	Mar.	1897	3	Inmate
Welsh, Louis	WM	May	1893	7	Inmate
Wench, Rose	WF	Nov.	1897	2	Inmate
Wentling, Marie	WF	Jan.	1898	2	Inmate
Wesser, Jeanette	WF	Aug.	1896	3	Inmate
West, Emile	WF*	June	1898	2	Inmate
Whalaren, Joseph	WM	June	1898	1	Inmate
Wheller, Edward	WM	Dec.	1897	2	Inmate
White, Alfred	WM	Apr.	1897	3	Inmate
White, Arbrahm	WM	Dec.	1897	2	Inmate
White, Carrol	WM	Nov.	1898	1	Inmate
White, Charles	WM	June	1898	2	Inmate
White, Joseph	WM	Mar.	1898	2	Inmate
White, Lucy	WF	Dec.	1899	0	Inmate
White, Marie	WF	Aug.	1898	1	Inmate
Whiting, Agnes	WF	Apr.	1897	3	Inmate
Whiting, Mary	WF	Apr.	1900	0	Inmate
Whitlow, Albert	WM	Feb.	1897	3	Inmate
Whitton, James	WM	Sept.	1898	1	Inmate
Wilde, Helen	WF	Jan.	1899	1	Inmate
Wilkins, William	WM	Sept.	1898	1	Inmate
Willard, Frank	WM	Nov.	1898	1	Inmate
Willett, Lillian	WF	Apr.	1898	2	Inmate
Williams, Arthur	WM	Mar.	1898	2	Inmate
Williams, Catherine	WF	Mar.	1900	0	Inmate
Williams, Charles	WM	June	1898	2	Inmate
Williams, Dominick	WM	Aug.	1896	3	Inmate
Williams, Ethel	WF	May	1897	3	Inmate
Williams, Eugene	WM	Feb.	1897	3	Inmate
Williams, Fred	WM	June	1898	2	Inmate
Williams, James	WM	Sept.	1899	0	Inmate
Williams, Jeanette	WF	June	1896	3	Inmate
Williams, Joseph	WM	May	1898	2	Inmate
Williams, Teresa	WF	Jan.	1900	0	Inmate
Wilmouth, Robert	WM	Dec.	1897	2	Inmate
Wilson, Charles	WM	Apr.	1900	0	Inmate
Wilson, David	WM	June	1898	2	Inmate
Wilson, Edward	WM	Apr.	1899	1	Inmate
Wilson, Edward	WM	Jan.	1898	2	Inmate
Wilson, George	WM	Nov.	1897	2	Inmate

Wilson, Marg't.	WF	May	1900	0	Inmate
Wilson, Marg't.	WF	Aug.	1898	1	Inmate
Wilson, Sadie	WF	Sept.	1880	19	Inmate
Wiltzer, Catherine	WF	Oct.	1897	2	Inmate
Windsor, Herbert	WM	July	1899	0	Inmate
Winthorpe, Ida	WF	Apr.	1879	21	St. Ann's
Witcoski, Joseph	WM	Apr.	1895	5	Inmate
Wolf, Isabella	WF	Feb.	1900	0	Inmate
Wolz, Jennie	WF	Apr.	1895	5	Inmate
Wood, Ruth	WF	Feb.	1900	0	Inmate
Woods, Christina	WF	Dec.	1899	0	Inmate
Woods, John	WM	Nov.	1895	4	Inmate
Woods, Mary	WF	Dec.	1869	30	Inmate
Woods, Robert	WM	July	1899	0	Inmate
Wortheimer, Harold	WM	Sept.	1899	0	Inmate
Wortheimer, Sadie	WF	Dec.	1878	21	Inmate
Wrede, Julius	WM	Oct.	1893	6	Inmate
Wright, Eleanor	WF	Aug.	1898	1	Inmate
Wyckoff, Carl	WF*	Mar.	1898	2	Inmate
Wynn, Josephine	WF	Mar.	1900	0	Inmate
Yadatali, Cecillia	WF	June	1898	2	Inmate
Yeugles, Marie	WF	Apr.	1870	30	Inmate
Yoanna, Stella	WF	June	1897	2	Inmate
Yon, Marie	WF	Dec.	1897	2	Inmate
Yonifini, Josephine	WF	July	1898	1	Inmate
Young, Aloysius	WM	July	1899	0	Inmate
Young, John	WM	May	1900	0	Inmate
Young, Rose	WF	Oct.	1898	1	Inmate
Young, Walter	WM	Mar.	1900	0	Inmate
Young, William	WM	Oct.	1898	1	Inmate
Yule, Stephen	WM	Dec.	1899	0	Inmate
Zellman, Martin	WM	Dec.	1896	3	Inmate
Zellner, Josephine	WF	Sept.	1898	1	Inmate
Zera, Arcadius	WF	Jan.	1900	0	Inmate
Zettler, Louis	WM	Apr.	1899	1	Inmate
Zimmer, Harry	WM	Sept.	1896	3	Inmate
Zinek, Mary	WF	Feb.	1872	28	Inmate
Zuccaro, Martha	WF	Dec.	1899	1	Inmate
Zuccaro, Martha	WF	Nov.	1880	19	Inmate
Zugner, William	WM	Jan.	1899	1	Inmate

Index to the
New York State Enumeration of the Inhabitants of

The New York Foundling Hospital

175 East 68th Street
New York, New York

June 1, 1905

Assembly District No. 26
Election District No. 4
Pages 1 - 45

Charles F. Smith, Enumerator

Guide to Column Headings

in the

1905 New York State Enumeration Index

Name　　　　Name of each person whose usual place of abode was in the institution on June 1, 1905. The census includes the name of every person living on June 1, 1905. Children born since June 1, 1905 were omitted. The surname is listed first, then the given name and middle initial.

R-G　　　　Race and gender. White is designated by the letter "W", black by the letter "B" and Mulatto by the letters "Mu". Males are designated by the letter "M" and females are designated by the letter "F".

*　　　　Notes that the enumerator may have reported the name or gender incorrectly.

A　　　　Age at last birthday. Designated in years, unless otherwise noted with an "m" for "months". Generally, children who were less than one year old were described in terms of months.

Relation　　　　Relationship of each person to the institution.

Note　　　　The Nativity of each child was listed as "United States". Refer to the orginal census for the Nativity, Citizenship, and Occupation of adult occupants. Some of the older children attended school. Refer to the original census for this information.

Name	R-G	A	Relation
Abbott, Mary	WF	1	Inmate
Abernnwitz, Linus	WM	4	Inmate
Adamos, Joseph	WM	1	Inmate
Adams, Jennie	WF	7m	Inmate
Adams, Marion	WF	1	Inmate
Adams, Vincent	WM	2	Inmate
Addison, Joseph	WM	1	Inmate
Addison, May	WF	30	Nurse
Adomick, Helen	WF	7m	Inmate
Agazzi, Paul	WM	4m	Inmate
Ahearn, Elizabeth	WF	1	Inmate
Aiello, Eulemia	WF	1m	Inmate
Ainsley, Vincent	WM	8m	Inmate
Ajax, Marie	WF	1m	Inmate
Aldrich, Edward	WM	2	Inmate
Allegro, Margaret	WF	1	Inmate
Allen, Francis	WM	1, 6m	Inmate
Allen, Harold	WM	2	Inmate
Allen, Leopold	WM	2	Inmate
Allen, Milton	WF*	1	Inmate
Allston, Vincent	WM	8m	Inmate
Alma, Edward	WM	5	Inmate
Alorrango, Krauline	WF	2	Inmate
Altzuller, Josephine	WF	5m	Inmate
Ambler, James	BM	7	Inmate
Amerigo, Rosa	WF	2	Inmate
Amherst, Joseph	WM	2	Inmate
Anbrusko, Matilda	WF	8m	Inmate
Anderson, Alma	WF	20	Nurse
Anderson, Charles	WM	7	Inmate
Anderson, John P.	WM	6m	Inmate
Anderson, Leo V.	WM	6m	Inmate
Anderson, Vincent	WM	1	Inmate
Andrew, Mary	WF	4	Inmate
Anewert, Agnes	WF	1	Inmate
Appleton, Adam	WM	15	Inmate
Appleton, Mary A.	WF	3	Inmate
Apply, Frederick	WM	2	Inmate
Archangelo, Frederick	WM	1	Inmate
Archer, Nellie	WF	40	Nurse

Archman, John	WM	1	Inmate
Arles, Concepta	WF	2	Inmate
Armstrong, Margaret	WF	2	Inmate
Arnold, Thomas	WM	1	Inmate
Arvine, Martin	WM	7m	Inmate
Ashley, Percy	WM	3	Inmate
Atkins, Arthur	WM	1	Inmate
Atkinson, Mabel	WF	3	Inmate
Atte, Anna	WF	21	Seamstress
Atwood, Miriam	WF	6m	Inmate
Austin, Constance	WF	2	Inmate
Bagclensitis, Isidore	WM	2	Inmate
Bailey, Frank	WM	1	Inmate
Bailey, Ruth	WF	2	Inmate
Bairnzz, Antonio	WM	1	Inmate
Baker, James	WM	4	Inmate
Balfred, John	WM	3	Inmate
Ball, James	WM	3m	Inmate
Ball, Matthew	WM	1	Inmate
Balletto, Berriette	WF	1	Inmate
Banbrick, Edgar	WM	3	Inmate
Banks, Arthur	WM	1	Inmate
Banks, Constance	WF	1	Inmate
Banks, Evelyn	BF	4	Inmate
Barbieri, Raphael	WM	3	Inmate
Barica, Marco	WM	1m	Inmate
Barker, Gertrude	WF	8m	Inmate
Barker, Paul	WM	1m	Inmate
Barnes, Louisa	WF	15	Seamstress
Barnett, Rose	WF	20	Nurse
Barns, Julia	WF	33	Nurse
Baroca, Mary	WF	27	Nurse
Baron, Sophie	WF	1m	Inmate
Barrett, Emily	WF	3	Inmate
Barrett, Sidney	WM	3m	Inmate
Barron, Cecilia	WF	26	Housework
Barry, Rita	WF	1	Inmate
Bartolini, Margaret	WF	1	Inmate
Baruts, Veronica	WF	1	Inmate
Battell, Richard	WM	7m	Inmate
Bauer, Herbert	WM	4	Inmate
Baugor, Evelyn	WF	1	Inmate

Baxter, Helena	WF	1m	Inmate
Baxter, Mary	WF	22	Nurse
Bayarsky, Mary	WF	1	Inmate
Beacken, Reginald	WM	2m	Inmate
Beckendorf, Charles	WM	7	Inmate
Becker, Gordon	WM	2	Inmate
Beelis, Mary	WF	37	Nurse
Beggaus, Mary	WF	2	Inmate
Behrens, Rebecca	WF	2	Inmate
Bell, Elizabeth	WF	17	Nurse
Bell, Rose	WF	0m	Inmate
Bellin, Maria	WF	8	Inmate
Bellotti, Mary	WF	5m	Inmate
Belschev, Rita	WF	1	Inmate
Belt, Mary	WF	4	Inmate
Bendstrup, Delia	WF	32	Nurse
Bendstrup, Gertrude	WF	7m	Inmate
Bendstrup, Laura	WF	1	Inmate
Benneker, Edwin	WM	6m	Inmate
Bennett, David	WM	1	Inmate
Bennett, Margaret	WF	1m	Inmate
Bennett, Marion	WF	17	Housework
Bennett, Martha	WF	2	Inmate
Berchman, John	WM	2m	Inmate
Bergen, Clara	WF	5	Inmate
Bergen, Grace	WF	4m	Inmate
Bergen, Sadie	WF	1	Inmate
Bergrn, Frank	WM	1	Inmate
Berkeley, Francis	WM	1	Inmate
Berntha, Victor	WM	2m	Inmate
Bernthal, Esther	WF	17	Nurse
Berrier, Jean	WM	2	Inmate
Bertram, John	WM	1	Inmate
Bigley, William	WM	2	Inmate
Bird, Josephine	WF	20	Nurse
Birmingham, Margaret	WF	20	Nurse
Birmingham, Wilson	WM	1m	Inmate
Bischoff, Richard	WM	1	Inmate
Bittner, Emma	WF	2	Inmate
Bittschen, Freda	WF	4m	Inmate
Blackson, Arthur	BM	1	Inmate
Blain, Catherine	WF	2	Inmate

Blanchard, Jennie	WF	24	Nurse
Blaney, William	WM	6m	Inmate
Blatek, Gertrude	WF	2	Inmate
Bleakford, Martha	WF	1	Inmate
Block, Lizzie	WF	5m	Inmate
Bloomfield, Lula	WF	4	Inmate
Blum, Jules	WM	4	Inmate
Bogart, Catharine	WF	4	Inmate
Bolles, Josephine	WF	3m	Inmate
Bonde, Irene	WF	2	Inmate
Bonecaze, Jennie	WF	19	Seamstress
Bordan, Otto	WM	1	Inmate
Boromes, Carlotte	WF	2	Inmate
Bostler, Thomas	WM	5	Inmate
Bouger, Joseph	WM	4	Inmate
Bowen, John	WM	6	Inmate
Bower, Harry	WM	1	Inmate
Boylan, George	WM	2	Inmate
Boylan, Joseph	WM	6	Inmate
Boyle, Agnes	WF	1	Inmate
Bradley, James	BM	6	Inmate
Bradley, John	WM	1	Inmate
Bradley, Margaret	WF	2	Inmate
Bradshaw, Arthur	WM	2	Inmate
Brady, Adeline	WF	7	Inmate
Brady, Delia	WF	21	Nurse
Brady, Florence	WF	1m	Inmate
Brady, Irene	WF	4m	Inmate
Brady, Margaret	WF	1m	Inmate
Brady, Mary	WF	30	Nurse
Brady, Susie	WF	18	Nurse
Brady, William	WM	2	Inmate
Bragg, Dorothy	BF	2	Inmate
Brantigan, Florence	WF	4m	Inmate
Braut, Margaret	WF	6	Inmate
Brazil, Richard	WM	8m	Inmate
Breenach, Walter	WM	1	Inmate
Breenwald, Edith	WF	3	Inmate
Breitung, Lena	WF	41	Laundress
Brennan, John	WM	3	Inmate
Breslin, Catherine	WF	24	Housework
Bretani, Guiseppuice	WF	50	Seamstress

Brian, Mary	WF	1	Inmate
Bridge, Constance	WF	8m	Inmate
Brien, William	WM	4	Inmate
Bright, Elizabeth	WF	1m	Inmate
Bright, Lawrence	WM	5	Inmate
Brock, Rose	WF	7	Inmate
Brogan, Joseph	WM	5	Inmate
Brogan, Mary E.	WF	4m	Inmate
Brondi, Teresa	WF	1m	Inmate
Broskey, John	WM	7m	Inmate
Brown, Catherine	WF	1	Inmate
Brown, Charles	BM	6	Inmate
Brown, Clare	WF	5m	Inmate
Brown, Clementine	WF	8m	Inmate
Brown, Edna	BF	4m	Inmate
Brown, Ella	WF	1	Inmate
Brown, Florence	BF	5m	Inmate
Brown, George	WM	1m	Inmate
Brown, Helen	WF	2	Inmate
Brown, James	WM	3m	Inmate
Brown, John	WM	7	Inmate
Brown, Joseph	WM	4	Inmate
Brown, Leo	WM	1	Inmate
Brown, Louis	WM	10m	Inmate
Brown, Mabel	WF	1	Inmate
Brown, Madeline	WF	1	Inmate
Brown, Margaret	WF	22	Nurse
Brown, Margaret	WF	24	Nurse
Brown, Pricilla	WF	36	Nurse
Brown, Sarah	WF	18	Seamstress
Brown, Thomas	WM	3	Inmate
Brownstone, Mark	WM	0m	Inmate
Buchanan, Robert	WM	1	Inmate
Buckingham, Mary	WF	2	Inmate
Buckley, Mary	WF	2	Inmate
Bull, Pauline	Wf	6m	Inmate
Bullog, Anna	WF	1	Inmate
Bulonaski, James	WM	1	Inmate
Bunn, Michael	WM	2	Inmate
Burek, Helen	WF	23	Kitchen Maid
Burek, Louise	WF	1	Inmate
Burgess, Blanch	WF	24	Nurse

Burgess, Florence	WF	4	Inmate
Burke, Catherine	WF	11m	Inmate
Burke, John M.	WM	11m	Inmate
Burke, Josephine	WF	6m	Inmate
Burke, Katie	WF	10	Inmate
Burke, Sadie	WF	21	Nurse
Burke, Vincent	WM	4	Inmate
Burnes, William	WM	1	Inmate
Burns, Annie	WF	26	Seamstress
Burns, Cecilia	WF	22	Nurse
Burns, Dominic	WM	4	Inmate
Burns, Edward	WM	3	Inmate
Burns, Joseph	WF*	1m	Inmate
Burns, Margaret	WF	2	Inmate
Burns, Maria	WF	1	Inmate
Burns, Sr. Mary Raphael	WF	67	Head of Day Nursery
Burns, Muriel	WF	0m	Inmate
Burns, Thomas	WM	11m	Inmate
Burr, Chester	WM	3	Inmate
Burres, Catharine	WF	21	Nurse
Burton, Mildred	WF	4	Inmate
Bush, William	WM	3	Inmate
Butler, Claud	WM	3	Inmate
Butler, Ida	BF	1	Inmate
Butler, James	WM	7m	Inmate
Butley, Joseph	WM	1	Inmate
Buttner, George	WM	1	Inmate
Byrnes, Hubert	WM	7m	Inmate
Cahill, Rose	WF	1	Inmate
Calacciati, Fabio	WM	0m	Inmate
Callahan, Frank	WM	2	Inmate
Callahan, Harold	WM	1	Inmate
Callahan, Helen	WM*	3	Inmate
Callahan, James	WM	1	Inmate
Callahan, Mary	WF	27	Nurse
Calligan, Annie	WF	2	Inmate
Calpin, Nora	WF	26	Nurse
Calvin, Loretto	WF	2	Inmate
Camari, Ferdinand	WM	2	Inmate
Camh, David	WM	1	Inmate
Camistruice, Mary	WF	38	Nurse
Camnezzo, Giovanna	WF	1	Inmate

Camorata, Marie	WF	8m	Inmate
Campbell, Clarence	WM	1	Inmate
Campbell, Mary	WF	1	Inmate
Canistiaci, Giovanina	WF	0m	Inmate
Canistraccio, John	WM	1m	Inmate
Canivet, Annie	WF	21	Nurse
Canivet, Harold	WM	0m	Inmate
Canning, Beatrice	WF	38	Nurse
Cannon, Teresa	WF	2	Inmate
Capone, Alphonse	WM	5m	Inmate
Cappas, Luigi	WM	1	Inmate
Cappuccio, Leon	WM	2	Inmate
Cappuzzo, Antony	WM	2	Inmate
Captin, Joseph	WM	2	Inmate
Carden, John	WM	9m	Inmate
Carey, Alice	WF	40	Nurse
Carey, Charles	WM	6m	Inmate
Carey, Irene	WF	5	Inmate
Carey, Katherine	WF	17	Teacher's Asst.
Carig, Kathleen	WF	1	Inmate
Carlin, Laurence	WM	1	Inmate
Carlos, Jerome	WM	8m	Inmate
Carlton, John	WM	4m	Inmate
Carmody, Anna	WF	2	Inmate
Carney, William	WM	6m	Inmate
Carroccio, Vincenzo	WM	3m	Inmate
Carroll, Agnes	WF	8m	Inmate
Carroll, Anna	WF	1	Inmate
Carroll, Anthony	WM	1	Inmate
Carroll, Arthur	WM	2	Inmate
Carroll, Francis	WM	3	Inmate
Carroll, George	WM	2	Inmate
Carroll, Harry S.	WM	1m	Inmate
Carroll, Louise	WF	7m	Inmate
Carssen, Victoria	BF	4m	Inmate
Cartelyon, Beatrice	BF	6	Inmate
Carter, Inez	WF	82	Nurse
Cashim, Helen	WF	4	Inmate
Cassezza, Aloysius	WM	1	Inmate
Cassidy, Joseph	WM	0m	Inmate
Cassidy, Lillian	WF	16	Nurse
Cassidy, Lillian	WF	16	Seamstress

Castle, Mary	WF	4	Inmate
Caulfield, Margaret	WF	23	Nurse
Cavanagh, Catharine	WF	22	Nurse
Cerencava, Christopher	WM	2	Inmate
Chaquette, Adrian	WM	3m	Inmate
Charbat, Joseph	WM	4m	Inmate
Charles, Francesca	WF	1	Inmate
Charlot, Josephine	WF	28	Nurse
Chatoney, Joseph	WM	2	Inmate
Cheney, Arthur	WM	4m	Inmate
Chibas, Susan	WF	11m	Inmate
Chlebasa, Anthony	WM	2	Inmate
Christianson, Francis	BM	6	Inmate
Christie, Agatha	WF	2m	Inmate
Ciascone, Marie	WF	2	Inmate
Clancey, Mary	WF	1	Inmate
Clancey, Mary	WF	38	Nurse
Clark, Anna	WF	1	Inmate
Clark, Florence	WF	2	Inmate
Clark, Genevieve	WF	2	Inmate
Clark, Harold	WM	1	Inmate
Clark, Jeanne	WF	3m	Inmate
Clark, Margaret	WF	5m	Inmate
Clark, Marie	WF	1	Inmate
Clark, William	WM	1	Inmate
Clask, Sr. Mary Paulete	WF	48	Nursery
Cleary, Margaret	WF	1	Inmate
Clenlaud, Alice	WF	9m	Inmate
Clews, Catharine	WF	10m	Inmate
Clifford, Margaret	BF	4	Inmate
Cline, George	WM	2	Inmate
Cody, Edard	WM	2	Inmate
Coffee, Jerry	WM	6	Inmate
Cohen, Bernard	WM	1m	Inmate
Cohen, John	WM	6m	Inmate
Cohen, Rosie	WF	1	Inmate
Cohen, Sophie	WF	2m	Inmate
Cole, William	WM	1	Inmate
Coleman, James	WM	11m	Inmate
Collins, Daniel	WM	1	Inmate
Collins, John H.	WM	1	Inmate
Collins, Josephine	WF	2m	Inmate

Collins, May	WF	19	Nurse
Collins, William	WM	4	Inmate
Commerce, Edna	WF	9	Inmate
Comparata, Marie	WF	10m	Inmate
Compton, Evelyn	WF	6m	Inmate
Concannon, Patrick	WM	1	Inmate
Condy, Annie	WF	72	Cutter
Cone, Veronica	WF	1	Inmate
Conecky, William	WM	2	Inmate
Conkley, Katie	WF	31	Chambermaid
Conklin, Stella	WF	1	Inmate
Connell, Paul	WM	5m	Inmate
Connelly, Anna	WF	22	Nurse
Connelly, John	WM	4	Inmate
Connelly, Mary	WF	7	Inmate
Connelly, Sr. Mary Helen	WF	28	Asst. Informarian
Connelly, Sr. M. Syrilla	WF	34	Asst. Secretary
Connelly, Sebastan	WM	3	Inmate
Conners, James	WM	3	Inmate
Connolly, Charles	WM	6m	Inmate
Connolly, Helen	WF	1	Inmate
Conquest, Frank	WM	4	Inmate
Conrey, Katie	WF	1	Inmate
Convery, Joseph	WM	1	Inmate
Conway, Bridget	WF	31	Nurse
Conway, Francis	WM	1	Inmate
Conway, John	WM	11m	Inmate
Conway, William	WM	0m	Inmate
Cooher, Homer	WM	1	Inmate
Cook, Frances	WF	17	Nurse
Cooney, Catharine	WF	1	Inmate
Coook, Mary E.	WF	2m	Inmate
Corbett, Sarah	WF	25	Cook
Corcary, John	WM	1	Inmate
Corcoran, Mary E.	WF	4m	Inmate
Corcoran, Mary	WF	0m	Inmate
Cosenza, Virtu	WM	1	Inmate
Costello, Kate	WF	60	Nurse
Cotter, Richard	WM	2	Inmate
Cotticchio, Jennie	WF	7m	Inmate
Coutts, Catherine	WF	4	Inmate
Cox, Alfred	WM	2	Inmate

Cox, Esther	WF	2	Inmate
Cox, Mary	WF	7	Inmate
Coyle, Helen	WF	5m	Inmate
Coyle, John	WM	2	Inmate
Coyne, Andrew	WM	3	Inmate
Cramen, Imelda	WF	2	Inmate
Crane, Gertrude	WF	1	Inmate
Crane, Matthew	WM	8m	Inmate
Crawford, Robert	WM	11m	Inmate
Cregan, Nellie	WF	2m	Inmate
Crevier, Gerard	WM	2	Inmate
Crieghton, Sr. Sarah Angela	WF	54	Informarian
Cromer, Joseph	WM	1	Inmate
Cromie, Harry	WM	3	Inmate
Cronan, Annie	WF	18	Nurse
Cronin, Mary	WF	6	Inmate
Cronnie, Mary	WF	24	Laundress
Cross, Sr. Corsini Andrew	WF	56	Head of Wardrobe
Crowley, Helen	WF	1	Inmate
Crowley, Maggie	WF	30	Laundress
Cryvalika, Mary	WF	24	Nurse
Cuasolla, Agnes	WF	4m	Inmate
Culbertson, Arthur	WM	2	Inmate
Cullen, Alice	WF	3	Inmate
Cummings, Hannah	WF	33	Nurse
Cummings, Thomas	WM	1m	Inmate
Cummisky, Edward	WM	5	Inmate
Cummisky, Irene	WF	2	Inmate
Cunningham, Anna	WF	4	Inmate
Cunningham, Grace	WF	3	Inmate
Cunningham, John	WM	2m	Inmate
Cunningham, Margaret	WF	39	Nurse
Cunningham, Mary	WF	5	Inmate
Curran, Mary	WF	4	Inmate
Curry, Paul	WM	11m	Inmate
Curry, Roland	WM	2	Inmate
Curtin, Margaret	WF	5	Inmate
Dade, Julia	WF	21	Nurse
Dady, George	WM	9m	Inmate
Daganan, Eva	WF	3m	Inmate
Daley, Anna J.	WF	1m	Inmate
Daley, Annie	WF	3	Inmate

Daley, Catherine	WF	2	Inmate
Daley, Cecelia	WF	2	Inmate
Daley, Viola	WF	2m	Inmate
Daly, John	WM	3	Inmate
Daly, John	WM	4	Inmate
Daly, John R.	WM	4m	Inmate
Daly, Mary	WF	22	Nurse
Daly, Patrick	WM	1	Inmate
Damasse, Bertha	WF	20	Nurse
Dan, Ruth	WF	7m	Inmate
Danna, Elle	WF	2	Inmate
Darlington, Justine	WF	2	Inmate
Dasje, Hans	WM	1	Inmate
Davidson, Mary	WF	3m	Inmate
Davidson, William	WM	3	Inmate
Davis, Arthur	WM	1	Inmate
Davis, Harold J.	WM	4m	Inmate
Davis, Margaret	WF	2	Inmate
Davis, Maria	WF	25	Nurse
Day, Cathareine	WF	7m	Inmate
Day, Mary	WF	11m	Inmate
Dean, Julia	WF	25	Nurse
Deanan, Grace	WF	2	Inmate
DeBaum, Edger	WM	3	Inmate
DeChalzne, Joseph	WM	3	Inmate
Dechop, Frank	WM	1	Inmate
DeFord, Effie	BF	2	Inmate
Dejmsiara, Annina	WF	7m	Inmate
Delahanty, Eva	WF	16	Nurse
Delahoid, Daniel	WM	3	Inmate
Delaney, Alice	WF	29	Nurse
Delaney, Francis	WM	0m	Inmate
Delaney, Walter	WM	1	Inmate
Demka, Mary	WF	1	Inmate
Demko, Margurite	WF	8m	Inmate
Denchaus, William	WM	4m	Inmate
Deolin, Mary	WF	5	Inmate
Deorio, Concilia	WF	3m	Inmate
Deppo, Henry	WM	4m	Inmate
DeRalm, Marie	WF	1	Inmate
DeRosa, Katie	WF	11m	Inmate
Derrickson, Robert	WM	11m	Inmate

Devine, John	WM	5	Inmate
Devlin, Mary	WF	41	Laundress
Dickson, Frances	WF	4	Inmate
Diemer, Angeline	WF	2	Inmate
Dillman, Emily	WF	23	Nurse
Dilman, Josephine	WF	1	Inmate
DiMarco, Giuseppe	WM	0m	Inmate
Dimlock, Louis	WM	2	Inmate
Dingley, Dorothy	WF	1	Inmate
Dioch, Charles	WM	5m	Inmate
Disbrow, Victor	WM	2	Inmate
Dixon, Emma	WF	31	Nurse
Dodd, Laurence	WM	9m	Inmate
Doherty, Anna	WF	4	Inmate
Dolle, August	WM	4	Inmate
Domassa, Theodore	WM	0m	Inmate
Donacchi, Sante	WF	1	Inmate
Donohue, John	WM	5	Inmate
Donohue, Rose	WF	6m	Inmate
Donovan, Mary	WF	36	Nurse
Doody, Bernardine	WF	3m	Inmate
Doogan, Francis	WM	4	Inmate
Dooley, James	WM	5	Inmate
Doran, Anthony	WM	6	Inmate
Dorge, Hannah	WF	25	Nurse
Dotson, William	BM	1m	Inmate
Dougherty, Anna	WF	4	Inmate
Douglas, Agnes	WF	1	Inmate
Dowd, Frances	WF	6	Inmate
Dowling, Paul	WM	2	Inmate
Downing, Marie	WF	23	Nurse
Doyle, Alphonse	WM	4	Inmate
Doyle, Cecilia	WF	1	Inmate
Doyle, Helen	WF	7m	Inmate
Doyle, Katie	WF	22	Nurse
Doyle, Thomas	WM	7	Inmate
Doyle, Thomas V.	WM	1	Inmate
Dressell, Mary	WF	4	Inmate
Dricoll, Sr. Agnes Joseph	WF	51	Nursery
Drummond, Helen	WF	6	Inmate
DuBois, Marie	WF	2	Inmate
Dudley, James	WM	5	Inmate

Duffy, Annie	WF	17	Nurse
Duffy, Charles	WM	5	Inmate
Duffy, Joseph	WM	5	Inmate
Duffy, Julia	WF	1	Inmate
Duffy, Margaret	WF	1	Inmate
Duffy, Regina	WF	1m	Inmate
Duffy, Sabina	WF	29	Waitress
Dugan, William	WM	3	Inmate
Dumac, Mary V.	WF	33	Nurse
Duman, Gustave	WM	1m	Inmate
Dumont, Mary	WF	17	Nurse
Duner, Thomas	WM	3	Inmate
Dunn, Annie	WF	42	Laundress
Dunn, Esther	WF	11m	Inmate
Dunn, Irene	WF	1	Inmate
Dunn, John J.	WM	1	Inmate
Dunn, Lillian	BF	2	Inmate
Dunn, Martin	WM	1	Inmate
Dunn, Sr. Mary Firando	WF	46	Nursery
Dunn, William T.	WM	1	Inmate
Dwinecz, Sylvester	WM	4m	Inmate
Dyer, Vincent	WM	2	Inmate
Eckert, Charles	WM	2	Inmate
Eddy, Vincent	WM	3	Inmate
Ederline, Mary	WF	8m	Inmate
Ederstine, Charles	WM	6m	Inmate
Edgerton, Leo	WM	3	Inmate
Edlstine, Selia	WF	19	Nurse
Edward, Beatrice	WF	3	Inmate
Edwards, Irene	WF	11m	Inmate
Edwards, Stephen	WM	3	Inmate
Edwarks, Francis	WM	7	Inmate
Egan, Thomas	WM	2	Inmate
Eigner, Francis	WM	1	Inmate
Eldrech, May	WF	2	Inmate
Eldredge, Frank	WM	2m	Inmate
Eliott, Grace	WF	9m	Inmate
Elliott, Michael	WM	4	Inmate
Ellis, Bridget	WF	9	Inmate
Ellis, Tillie	WF	2	Inmate
Elsmere, Joseph	WM	2m	Inmate
Emerald, Cecilia	WF	9m	Inmate

Engel, Irene	WF	1	Inmate
English, Lillie	WF	11m	Inmate
Ennes, Ruth	WF	1	Inmate
Eppstein, Jeromita	WF	3	Inmate
Erder, Margaret	WF	2m	Inmate
Erdman, Pauline	WF	1	Inmate
Ereghind, Lena	WF	6m	Inmate
Erickson, Anna	WF	11m	Inmate
Erlonson, Dorothy	WF	3m	Inmate
Erne, Joseph	WM	1	Inmate
Eskes, Mary	WF	9m	Inmate
Evans, Alphonse	WM	2	Inmate
Evans, Elizabeth	WF	2	Inmate
Evers, Sr. Frances Marie	WF	27	Nursery
Evers, Jennie	WF	24	Nurse
Evers, Joseph	WM	2m	Inmate
Evers, Mary	WF	2m	Inmate
Ewing, John	WM	3m	Inmate
Eymer, Samuel	WM	1	Inmate
Faber, Philip	WM	2	Inmate
Fabrik, Stephen	WM	1	Inmate
Fagan, Grace	WF	1	Inmate
Fagan, Margaret	WF	38	Nurse
Fair, Augusta	WF	1	Inmate
Faller, Christina	WF	2	Inmate
Fallon, Rose	WF	2	Inmate
Fanell, Margaret	WF	2	Inmate
Fanning, Herbert	WM	7m	Inmate
Farrell, Mary	WF	4	Inmate
Farrell, Michael	WM	1	Inmate
Farrell, William	WM	6m	Inmate
Farron, Sr. Mary Merceline	WF	34	Nursery
Farvalls, Francis	WM	10m	Inmate
Fasans, Joseph	WM	7	Inmate
Fay, Annie	WF	3	Inmate
Fay, Catharine	WF	1	Inmate
Fee, Helen	WF	1m	Inmate
Feehan, Madeline	WF	16	Nurse
Feeny, Helen	WF	1	Inmate
Feery, Charles	WM	3	Inmate
Feinburg, Mary T.	WF	4m	Inmate
Feker, Marguerite	WF	2	Inmate

Fennessy, John	WM	1m	inmate
Ferguson, Alice	WF	1	Inmate
Fernand, Louise	WF	1	Inmate
Feuser, Joseph	WM	1	Inmate
Fiereck, Joseph	WM	1	Inmate
Finney, Joseph	WM	4	Inmate
Fisher, Anna	WF	7m	Inmate
Fisher, Grace	WF	12	Inmate
Fisher, Marie	WF	1	Inmate
Fitzgerald, Agnes	WF	9m	Inmate
Fitzgerald, Annie	WF	14	Inmate
Fitzgerald, Charles	WM	0m	Inmate
Fitzgerald, Elizabeth	WF	18	Nurse
Fitzgerald, Florence	WF	20	Nurse
Fitzgerald, Julia	WF	6	Inmate
Fitzgerald, Ruth	WF	2	Inmate
Fitzhenry, Angela	WF	5	Inmate
Fitzhenry, Marie	WF	20	Nurse
Fitzpatrick, Catherine	WF	3	Inmate
Fitzpatrick, Marion	WF	4	Inmate
Fitzpatrick, Mary	WF	30	Nurse
Fitzpatrick, Rose	WF	9m	Inmate
Flannery, Catharine	WF	1	Inmate
Fleming, Margaret	WF	6	Inmate
Fleming, William	WM	4	Inmate
Fletcher, Rachael	WF	3	Inmate
Flick, Lena	WF	0m	Inmate
Flond, Ethel	WF	3	Inmate
Flood, Leonelda	WF	3	Inmate
Flynn, Harry	WM	2	Inmate
Flynn, Mary	WF	35	Nurse
Fogel, Simon	WM	1	Inmate
Foley, Henry	WM	2	Inmate
Foley, Irene	WF	11m	Inmate
Foley, Lizzie	WF	24	Nurse
Folina, Marie	WF	3	Inmate
Foran, May	WF	26	Seamstress
Foraus, Mary	WF	9m	Inmate
Fordan, Antonia	WF	36	Nurse
Forden, Helen	WF	3m	Inmate
Foreman, Agnes	WF	22	Nurse
Foreman, William	WM	1	Inmate

Forn, Mary	WF	0m	Inmate
Forrinni, Florence	WF	1	Inmate
Forster, Alma	WF	3	Inmate
Fortunato, Antonio	WM	2m	Inmate
Foster, Elizabeth	WF	1	Inmate
Foster, Ralph	WM	1	Inmate
Fox, Arthur	WM	1	Inmate
Fox, Elizabeth	WF	38	Nurse
Fox, Genevieve	WF	2m	Inmate
Fradcucci, Amerigo	WM	2	Inmate
Francis, Anson	WM	4	Inmate
Frank, Margaret	WF	2m	Inmate
Franks, Bella	WF	2	Inmate
Frans, Helen	WF	1m	Inmate
Fraus, Catharine	WF	23	Nurse
Frawley, George	WM	2	Inmate
Frayer, Louis	WM	6m	Inmate
Frazer, Isabella	WF	1	Inmate
Freeman, Loretto	WF	26	Nurse
Freeman, Mary	WF	1	Inmate
Freeman, Mary	WF	19	Nurse
Freeman, Walter	WM	1	Inmate
Friedman, Gregory	WM	2m	Inmate
Friedman, Henry	WM	4m	Inmate
Friedman, Thomas	WM	2	Inmate
Fries, Myron	WM	2	Inmate
Frisbee, Edward	WM	4	Inmate
Friza, Alma	WF	2	Inmate
Fromm, Elsie	WF	1	Inmate
Fubur, Joseph	WM	8m	Inmate
Fuhrman, Joseph	WM	3	Inmate
Fulton, Maude	WF	2	Inmate
Furlong, Minnie	WF	29	Nurse
Furst, Anna	WF	2	Inmate
Gabrino, Francesca	WF	1	Inmate
Gaffney, William	WM	3	Inmate
Gainey, Juan	WM	3	Inmate
Galeus, Antonio	WM	0m	Inmate
Gallagher, Bernard	WM	9m	Inmate
Gallagher, Mary	WF	29	Nurse
Galletzon, Luke	WM	1m	Inmate
Gambinello, Collette	WF	25	Nurse

Gambinello, Marie	WF	1	Inmate
Ganaway, Marion	BF	5m	Inmate
Gannon, Alice	WF	2	Inmate
Gannon, Francis	WM	2m	Inmate
Gannyra, Louisa	WF	22	Seamstress
Gardiner, Charles	WM	3	Inmate
Garland, Lillie	WF	3m	Inmate
Garland, Rose	WF	31	Nurse
Gasperdomi, Francesca	WF	1m	Inmate
Gates, Cecilia	WF	8m	Inmate
Gates, Marid	WF	19	Nurse
Geitz, Christina	WF	5m	Inmate
Gelleortz, Bella	WF	0m	Inmate
Gelman, Ida	WF	2	Inmate
Gentosa, Gartano	WM	1	Inmate
Geoghan, Gertrude	WF	3	Inmate
George, Mary	WF	7m	Inmate
Gerker, Frederick	WM	3	Inmate
Gerone, Maria	WF	2	Inmate
Gervuvix, Anne	WF	20	Nurse
Gibbons, Herbert	WM	4m	Inmate
Gibbons, John	WM	1	Inmate
Gibbons, Regina	WF	4	Inmate
Gibson, Edward	WM	4	Inmate
Gibson, Edward	WM	4	Inmate
Gilbert, Leroy	WM	1m	Inmate
Gilbert, Step.	WM	2	Inmate
Gilchrist, Minnie	WF	2	Inmate
Gile, Thomas	WM	1	Inmate
Gilhooley, Richard	WM	2m	Inmate
Gilks, George	WM	3m	Inmate
Gillen, Joseph	WM	2	Inmate
Gilligan, Nellie	WF	25	Nurse
Gillis, Valentine	WM	3m	Inmate
Gilmartin, William	WM	1	Inmate
Gilosky, Sarah	WF	1	Inmate
Giraud, Adrian	WM	3	Inmate
Giroux, Sr. Mary M.	WF	44	Asst. Secretary
Gleason, Edward	WM	2	Inmate
Gleason, Teresa	WF	5	Inmate
Glenn, Gerald	WM	6	Inmate
Glick, Herman	WM	6m	Inmate

Glick, Sadie	WF	1	Inmate
Glick, Sadie	WF	2	Inmate
Gloss, John	WM	4m	Inmate
Glynn, Margaret	WF	1	Inmate
Godson, Julia	WF	3	Inmate
Goggin, Sr. Rose Angela	WF	44	Nursery
Goldback, Julia	WF	10	Inmate
Goldberg, Andrian	WM	5	Inmate
Goldberg, Ella	WF	2	Inmate
Golden, Dora	WF	23	Nurse
Golden, John	WM	1	Inmate
Golden, Max	WM	10m	Inmate
Golding, Joseph	WM	4	Inmate
Goldstein, Charles	WM	3	Inmate
Goldstein, Harry	WM	2	Inmate
Goldstein, Jesse	WF	1	Inmate
Goldstein, Walter	WM	2	Inmate
Golemme, Fannie	WF	3m	Inmate
Goodman, Edwin	WM	3	Inmate
Goodman, Lucy	WF	6m	Inmate
Goodman, Matthew	WM	4m	Inmate
Goodman, William	WM	2	Inmate
Goodrich, Charles	WM	1	Inmate
Graham, Frank	WM	1	Inmate
Graham, Mary	WF	1	Inmate
Graham, Minora	WF	1	Inmate
Graimble, Mary	WF	7m	Inmate
Gramella, Rosa	WF	2	Inmate
Grander, Frank	WM	6	Inmate
Grant, Sr. Mary Immaculate	WF	50	Kindergarten
Grasser, Margaret	WF	17	Seamstress
Graus, Catharine	WF	3m	Inmate
Gray, John	WM	2	Inmate
Greber, Arthur	WM	11m	Inmate
Green, Arthur	WM	1	Inmate
Green, Bertha	WF	1	Inmate
Green, Charles	WM	8m	Inmate
Green, Ladie	WF	3	Inmate
Green, Mary	BF	5	Inmate
Green, Rosie	WF	1	Inmate
Green, Sadie	WF	3	Inmate
Green, Samuel	WM	2m	Inmate

Greenburg, Charles	WM	7m	Inmate
Greensberg, Francis	WM	3	Inmate
Gregor, Mary	WF	3	Inmate
Gregory, Catharine	WF	39	Housekeeper
Griefer, August	WM	2	Inmate
Griffin, Adeline	BF	6	Inmate
Griffin, Marie	WF	1	Inmate
Grinvalk, Joseph	WM	2	Inmate
Grossman, Dora	WF	1	Inmate
Guinan, Anthony	WM	2	Inmate
Guiney, Michael	WM	1	Inmate
Gunn, Alice	WF	1	Inmate
Gunn, Margaret	WF	1	Inmate
Gutzig, Rose	WF	9m	Inmate
Hack, Henry	WM	2	Inmate
Hagan, Maggie	WF	27	Cutter
Haggerty, Agnes	WF	3	Inmate
Halaizzat, Peter	WM	1	Inmate
Halloran, Josephine	WF	2	Inmate
Halomene, Antonia	WF	1	Inmate
Hamburger, Mary	WF	1	Inmate
Hamill, Robert	WM	6m	Inmate
Hamilton, Amy	WF	37	Housework
Hamilton, Bessie	WF	21	Waitress
Hamilton, Maurice	WM	4	Inmate
Hamilton, Richard	WM	3	Inmate
Hamm, Mary	WF	3	Inmate
Hanahan, Sr. Mary Emervitu	WF	70	Refectorian
Hand, Joseph	WM	5	Inmate
Handen, Mary	WF	5	Inmate
Hanes, Nellie	WF	22	Nurse
Hanley, Ambrose	WM	4m	Inmate
Hanlon, Catherine	WF	32	Housekeeper
Hannigan, Annie	WF	30	Domestic
Hannigan, John	WM	6	Inmate
Hanteville, Angela	WF	11m	Inmate
Hardy, Joseph	WM	2	Inmate
Hared, Catherine	WF	5m	Inmate
Harmon, Annie	WF	7	Inmate
Harold, Frederic	WM	0m	Inmate
Harrigan, Catharine	WF	2	Inmate
Harrington, John	WM	2	Inmate

Harris, Agatha	WF	5	Inmate
Harris, Agnes	WF	70	Nurse
Harris, May	WF	22	Domestic
Harrison, Joseph	WM	6m	Inmate
Hart, Delia	WF	29	Nurse
Hart, Florence	WF	2	Inmate
Harvey, Catherine A.	WF	83	Nurse
Harvey, Clarence	WM	3	Inmate
Harvey, Florence	WF	3m	Inmate
Hasinone, Thomas	WM	4	Inmate
Haskins, Esther	WF	1	Inmate
Hasnett, Mary	WF	1	Inmate
Hasselring, Raphael	WM	6m	Inmate
Hauteville, Mary	WF	4	Inmate
Hautville, Mary	WF	29	Nurse
Hayden, Gertrude	WF	42	Laundress
Hayes, George	WM	8m	Inmate
Hayes, John	WM	11m	Inmate
Hayes, Mary	WF	1	Inmate
Hazard, Robert	WM	1	Inmate
Healey, Bridget	WF	3	Inmate
Healy, Margaret	WF	4m	Inmate
Healy, Mary	WF	3	Inmate
Heeren, Mary	WF	11m	Inmate
Heery, Margaret	WF	3m	Inmate
Hefele, Philip	WM	7m	Inmate
Hefferin, William	WM	5m	Inmate
Heffernan, Henry	WM	5m	Inmate
Heffernan, Irene	WF	2	Inmate
Heffon, Anna	WF	85	Seamstress
Heidtman, Lillian	WF	24	Nurse
Helzel, Maurice	WM	2	Inmate
Henderson, Vivian	BF	8m	Inmate
Hennessy, Anna	WF	5m	Inmate
Hennessy, Julia	WF	1	Inmate
Hennessy, Mary	WF	0m	Inmate
Hennessy, Mary	WF	17	Nurse
Henry, Catharine	WF	2	Inmate
Herke, Annie	WF	7	Inmate
Herman, Frank	WM	4m	Inmate
Herman, Joseph	WM	0m	Inmate
Hicka, Paula	WM*	1	Inmate

Hickey, William	WM	4	Inmate
Higgins, Charles	WM	5	Inmate
Higgson, Sarah	WF	63	Nurse
Higley, Mary	WF	1	Inmate
Hill, Gabriel	WM	1	Inmate
Hill, John	WM	8m	Inmate
Hill, Joseph	WM	6	Inmate
Hill, Walter	BM	4	Inmate
Hilll, Katie	WF	1	Inmate
Hines, Emma	WF	1	Inmate
Hines, Margaret	WF	4	Inmate
Hirsch, Harold	WM	4m	Inmate
Hitzig, Moses	WM	8m	Inmate
Hoagland, Clarence	WM	0m	Inmate
Hoagland, Jennie	WF	19	Nurse
Hoch, Edward	WM	3m	Inmate
Hodan, Charles	WM	3m	Inmate
Hodestetter, Vincent	WM	4	Inmate
Hodgins, Richard	WM	9m	Inmate
Hoffman, Arthur	BM	3	Inmate
Hoffman, Charles	WM	1	Inmate
Hoffman, Louise	WF	4	Inmate
Hoffman, Walter	BM	4	Inmate
Hogan, Anna	WM*	4	Inmate
Hogan, James	WM	2	Inmate
Hogan, John	WM	2	Inmate
Holdman, William	WM	3	Inmate
Holeitza, Frank	WM	8m	Inmate
Holmes, George	WM	1	Inmate
Holmes, William	WM	1	Inmate
Holstein, Margaret	WF	4	Inmate
Holtman, Robert	WM	1m	Inmate
Holzka, Blanche	WF	5	Inmate
Honan, Joseph	WM	2	Inmate
Honhilan, Lizzie	WF	17	Nurse
Honick, Frederick	WM	2	Inmate
Hooker, Drusilla	BF	6	Inmate
Hope, Ernest	WM	3m	Inmate
Hopkins, John	WM	2	Inmate
Horan, Thomas	WM	4	Inmate
Horton, Edwin	WM	1	Inmate
Horwitz, Henry	WM	4	Inmate

Howard, John V.	WM	4m	Inmate
Howell, Frederick	BM	8	Inmate
Howorth, James	WM	0m	Inmate
Hoy, Mary	WF	1	Inmate
Huber, Anna	WF	0m	Inmate
Hudson, Richard	WM	2	Inmate
Hughes, Alma	WF	3	Inmate
Hughes, Joseph	WM	6	Inmate
Hughes, Mary	WF	10m	Inmate
Hughes, Mary	WF	31	Nurse
Humme, Minnie	WF	1	Inmate
Humphrey, Edward	WM	3	Inmate
Hunt, Cecilia	WF	6m	Inmate
Hunt, Francws	WF	2m	Inmate
Hunter, Margaret	WF	1	Inmate
Hurley, Mary	WF	29	Laundress
Hurley, Sr. Rose Perpetual	WF	41	Kindergarten
Hurnity, Sarah	WF	32	Nurse
Hurt, Bertha	WF	1	Inmate
Hurwitz, Lena	WF	7m	Inmate
Hustory, Albert	WM	1	Inmate
Hutchings, Mary	WF	59	Nurse
Hyde, Fannie	WF	26	Nurse
Iba, Isidore	WM	2	Inmate
Iisley, Stephen	WM	1	Inmate
Ilion, Beatrice	WF	1	Inmate
Ilona, Juliana	WF	5m	Inmate
Ilsley, Eudora	WF	3	Inmate
Imhern, Aloysius	WF*	11m	Inmate
Indarf, Franics	WM	4	Inmate
Ingalls, John	WM	1m	Inmate
Ingerman, Francis	WM	9m	Inmate
Ingleton, Katie	WF	1	Inmate
Inkelas, Andrew	WM	9m	Inmate
Innick, John	WM	1	Inmate
Insley, Mary	WF	3m	Inmate
Inwood, Benedict	WM	2m	Inmate
Isling, Miriam	WF	6m	Inmate
Isola, Patricio	WM	2m	Inmate
Iverson, Leo	WM	2	Inmate
Izett, Alfred	WM	9m	Inmate
Jackson, Emily	BF	1	Inmate

Jackson, Florence	WF	2	Inmate
Jackson, Frances	WF	5	Inmate
Jackson, William	BM	9	Inmate
Jacobi, Angelo	WM	1	Inmate
Jalker, Mark	WM	2	Inmate
James, Daniel	WM	2	Inmate
James, Dorothy	WF	25	Housework
James, William	BM	3	Inmate
James, Winifred	BF	4m	Inmate
Jameson, Peter	WM	8m	Inmate
Janco, John	WM	2	Inmate
Janik, Christina	WF	30	Nurse
Jasper, Anna	WF	1m	Inmate
Jdsco, Benjamin	WM	6m	Inmate
Jdsco, Julia	WF	18	Nurse
Jeffrey, James	WM	5	Inmate
Jelalniska, Ludwig	WM	1	Inmate
Jennison, Nicholas	WM	5m	Inmate
Jerze, Joseph	WM	11m	Inmate
Jeter, Ruth	BF	1	Inmate
Jewett, Cyril	WM	2	Inmate
Johanson, Hedwig	WF	2	Inmate
Johnson, Alham J.	WM	1	Inmate
Johnson, Allston	WM	1	Inmate
Johnson, Anna	BF	8m	Inmate
Johnson, Austin	WM	10m	Inmate
Johnson, Christopher	WM	3m	Inmate
Johnson, Clare	BF	1	Inmate
Johnson, Dorothy	BF	1	Inmate
Johnson, Mary I.	WF	8m	Inmate
Johnson, Percy	BM	1m	Inmate
Johnson, Rita	WF	8m	Inmate
Johnson, Rose	WF	4	Inmate
Johnson, Victor	WM	1	Inmate
Johnstone, Edith	WF	21	Nurse
Johson, Marie	WF	7m	Inmate
Johson, Mary	WF	9	Housekeeper
Jones, Bessie	WF	15	Inmate
Jones, Florence	WF	6m	Inmate
Jones, Marion	WF	1m	Inmate
Jones, Nicholas	WM	2	Inmate
Jones, Raymond	WM	10m	Inmate

Jones, William	BM	7m	Inmate
Joseph, Stella	WF	6m	Inmate
Joyce, John	WM	5	Inmate
Joyce, Martha	WF	5m	Inmate
Joyce, Mary	WF	21	Nurse
Joyce, Mary	WF	22	Nurse
Joyce, Stella	WF	1	Inmate
Joyner, Andrew	BM	4	Inmate
Jube, Nicholas	WM	1	Inmate
Judge, Francis	WM	2	Inmate
Judson, Monica	WF	10m	Inmate
Judson, Paul	WM	2	Inmate
Juhasz, Mary	WF	5m	Inmate
Julian, Margaret	WF	1	Inmate
Kaan, Loretto	WF	3m	Inmate
Kahn, Edna	WF	3	Inmate
Kane, Elizabeth	WF	2	Inmate
Kane, Gerald	WM	2	Inmate
Kane, Hannah	WF	4	Inmate
Kane, John	WM	6	Inmate
Kane, Loretto	WF	4	Inmate
Kane, Margaret	WF	1	Inmate
Kane, Margaret	WF	32	Housekeeper
Kane, Maud	WF	21	Nurse
Kane, Stephen	WM	1	Inmate
Kaplan, Ernest	WM	1	Inmate
Kaplan, Eugene	WM	1	Inmate
Kaplan, Nellie	WF	4m	Inmate
Kaplan, Samuel	WM	4m	Inmate
Kapler, Susie	WF	5m	Inmate
Kapper, Emily	WF	3m	Inmate
Kasolsky, Helen	WF	1	Inmate
Kasper, Mary	WF	30	Nurse
Kassack, Emma	WF	6m	Inmate
Katchonorick, Mary	WF	25	Nurse
Kaufman, Helen	WF	8m	Inmate
Kaufman, Victor	WM	10m	Inmate
Kaufmann, Walter	WM	1	Inmate
Kavanagh, Elizabeth	WF	31	Nurse
Kearney, Edward	WM	3	Inmate
Kearney, Margaret	WF	21	Nurse
Keefe, James	WM	3	Inmate

Keegan, Helena	WF	2	Inmate
Keenan, Lawrence	WM	2	Inmate
Keenan, William	WM	2	Inmate
Kellan, Sr. Frances Ligorni	WF	65	Sacristan
Keller, Christina	WF	4	Inmate
Keller, James	WM	2	Inmate
Keller, Rita	WF	1	Inmate
Kelly, Alice	WF	2	Inmate
Kelly, Camelius	WM	9m	Inmate
Kelly, Catharine	WF	2	Inmate
Kelly, Cecelia	WF	20	Nurse
Kelly, Elizabeth	WF	3	Inmate
Kelly, Felix	WM	2	Inmate
Kelly, Frank	WM	5	Inmate
Kelly, John	WM	1	Inmate
Kelly, John F.	WM	2	Inmate
Kelly, John T.	WM	8m	Inmate
Kelly, Joseph	WM	2	Inmate
Kelly, Josephine	WF	1	Inmate
Kelly, Margaret	WF	24	Seamstress
Kelly, Mary V.	WF	3m	Inmate
Kelly, Sylvester	WM	5m	Inmate
Kelly, Vincent	WM	3	Inmate
Kendrick, Pearl	WF	3	Inmate
Kengley, Emily	WF	2	Inmate
Kennedy, Clare	WF	4m	Inmate
Kennedy, Henry	WM	7m	Inmate
Kennedy, Raymond	WM	5	Inmate
Kennnedy, Paul	WM	1	Inmate
Kenny, Janier	WM	4	Inmate
Kenny, Louise	WF	1	Inmate
Kenny, Mary	WF	2	Inmate
Kent, James	WM	3	Inmate
Kent, Robert	WM	2	Inmate
Kentan, Ronald	WM	7m	Inmate
Kenyon, Helen	BF	4m	Inmate
Kepplera, Frank	WM	2	Inmate
Kerbs, Charles	WM	4	Inmate
Kern, John	WM	1	Inmate
Kerns, Helen	WF	1	Inmate
Kerrigan, Antoinette	WF	11m	Inmate
Kerswell, Ethel	WF	6m	Inmate

Keyes, James	WM	2	Inmate
Kidsberk, Jennie	WF	1	Inmate
Kiernan, Mary	WF	1	Inmate
Kiley, Thomas	WM	1	Inmate
Kilroy, Margaret	WF	7m	Inmate
Kimball, Andrew	WM	1	Inmate
Kinasley, Anita	WF	1	Inmate
King, Casper	WM	5m	Inmate
King, Harry	WM	5	Inmate
King, John J.	WM	8m	Inmate
King, Michael	WM	8m	Inmate
King, Oswald	WM	3	Inmate
King, Stella	WF	1	Inmate
Kingsley, Angela	WF	2	Inmate
Kisheto, Rosa	WF	20	Nurse
Kishetz, Martin	WM	7m	Inmate
Klein, Aloysius	WM	2m	Inmate
Klein, Florence	WF	2	Inmate
Klein, Helen	WF	5m	Inmate
Kline, Godfrey	WM	0m	Inmate
Klinsack, Mary	WF	2	Inmate
Klopsky, Annie	WF	1m	Inmate
Klotzke, Lillian	WF	5m	Inmate
Klselesky, Joseph	WF	2	Inmate
Kluttz, Marion	WF	4m	Inmate
Knapp, Harold	WM	2	Inmate
Knight, Valentine	WM	2	Inmate
Koch, Emma	WF	1	Inmate
Koebler, Rudolph	BM	8	Inmate
Koehn, Margery	WF	8m	Inmate
Koerrner, Harold	WM	9m	Inmate
Kolder, Richard	WM	2	Inmate
Koll, Harry	WM	4	Inmate
Konick, Chas.	WM	9m	Inmate
Konn, Sarah	WF	3	Inmate
Kontan, Mary	WF	23	Nurse
Kopac, Joseph	WM	2	Inmate
Kosuck, Helen	WF	7m	Inmate
Kotchmorich, Josephine	WF	5m	Inmate
Kovitch, Charles	WM	5m	Inmate
Kozelka, John	WM	4	Inmate
Krever, William	WM	2	Inmate

Krieger, Augusta	WF	1	Inmate
Krieger, William	WM	5m	Inmate
Kuhn, Helen	WF	1	Inmate
Kulaki, Francesca	WF	20	Nurse
Kulitz, Anna	WF	3	Inmate
Kutorska, Joseph	WM	2m	Inmate
Kutorska, Stella	WF	30	Nurse
Lahty, Gretta	WF	1	Inmate
Lally, John	WM	3m	Inmate
Lama, Vincenzo	WF	3m	Inmate
Lamb, Ambrose	WM	4	Inmate
Lambert, Ross	BM	4m	Inmate
Lamke, George	WM	8m	Inmate
Lampton, Raymond	WM	0m	Inmate
Lancaster, Raphael	WM	3	Inmate
Laneschruk, John	WM	4m	Inmate
Lang, Charles	WM	4	Inmate
Lang, Lillian	WF	5m	Inmate
Lansman, Frances	WF	17	Nurse
LaPorta, Maria	WF	3	Inmate
Lard, James	WM	1	Inmate
Lardner, Margaret	WF	40	Cook
Lardres, Maria	WF	1	Inmate
Larkin, Maggie	WF	29	Domestic
Larkin, Thomas	WM	7m	Inmate
LaRosa, Guipe	WF	9m	Inmate
Larwick, Violet	WF	3	Inmate
Laucks, Harold	WM	1	Inmate
Lausman, Dolores	WF	1m	Inmate
Lavelle, John	WM	5	Inmate
Lavocca, Emma	WF	11m	Inmate
Lawlor, Beatrice	WF	6m	Inmate
Lawlor, Thomas	WM	4	Inmate
Lawrence, Edward	WM	3	Inmate
Layten, Eva	WF	17	Seamstress
Layton, Vincent	WM	2m	Inmate
Lazer, Isidore	WM	1	Inmate
Leader, Gertrude	WF	2m	Inmate
Leahy, Kathleen	WF	1m	Inmate
Lear, William	WM	3	Inmate
Leary, George	WM	4	Inmate
Leary, William	WM	5	Inmate

Leathon, Margaret	WF	2m	Inmate
Leathone, Margaret	WF	20	Nurse
Lee, Ernest	WM	1	Inmate
Leigh, Bridget	WF	28	Nurse
Leigh, Helen	WF	10m	Inmate
Leigh, James	WM	2	Inmate
Leitner, Veronica	WF	0m	Inmate
Lemerle, Charles	WM	2	Inmate
Lenahan, Sr. Mary Rosalie	WF	58	Nursery
Lenihan, Owen	WM	1	Inmate
Lenihon, Elizabeth	WF	11m	Inmate
Lennies, Helen	WF	1	Inmate
Lent, Helen	WF	1	Inmate
Lentz, Teresa	wF	1	Inmate
Leonard, George	WM	6	Inmate
Leopold, Aloysius	WM	9m	Inmate
Leroy, Harry	WM	1	Inmate
Levegne, May	WF	4	Inmate
Levet, Helen	WF	6	Inmate
Levie, Theodore	WM	1	Inmate
Levitz, Helen	WF	1	Inmate
Lewis, Charles	WM	3m	Inmate
Lewis, Francis	WM	2	Inmate
Lewis, Marguerite	WF	10m	Inmate
Lichtman, Norbert	WM	2	Inmate
Lieb, George	WM	3	Inmate
Liebener, George	WM	4	Inmate
Lieberman, Sarah	WF	8m	Inmate
Ligiati, Edwin	WM	2	Inmate
Lilly, Ambrose	WM	4	Inmate
Lindwehi, Stella	WF	0m	Inmate
Lingquist, Stephen	WM	6m	Inmate
Lingwher, Annie	WF	17	Nurse
Lischnek, Antoinette	WF	11m	Inmate
Lischnek, Rosa	WF	29	Nurse
Lockwood, Nellie	WF	32	Portress
Lohmann, William	WM	5m	Inmate
Lomberd, Julia	WF	28	Nurse
Lorenzo, Dorothy	WF	4m	Inmate
Lorizan, Susie	WF	19	Nurse
Lougen, Theodore	WM	1	Inmate
Lova, Isabella	WF	9	Inmate

Lowell, Joseph	WM	10m	Inmate
Lucania, Angela	WF	2m	Inmate
Lucky, Katie	WF	24	Nurse
Luco, Marie	WF	6	Inmate
Luddy, Bridget	WF	31	Nurse
Ludlow, Mary	WF	1	Inmate
Luppe, George	WM	4	Inmate
Lutz, Josephine	WF	1	Inmate
Lutzke, Annie	WF	2	Inmate
Lutzke, Charles	WM	1	Inmate
Lutzke, Maria	WF	24	Kitchen Maid
Lyman, Anna	WF	27	Houswork
Lynan, Kathryn	WF	19	Nurse
Lynch, Agnes	WF	11m	Inmate
Lynch, Bridget	WF	28	Housework
Lynch, Elizabeth	WF	2m	Inmate
Lynch, John	WM	2	Inmate
Lynch, Margaret	WF	23	Nurse
Lynch, Mary F.	WF	4m	Inmate
Lynch, Thomas A.	WM	1	Inmate
Lyon, Addie	WF	27	Nurse
Lyonas, Carroll	WM	3	Inmate
Lyons, John	WM	3	Inmate
Lyons, Sr. Mary Regis	WF	47	Housekeeper
Lyons, Miriam	WF	1	Inmate
Lyons, Philip	WM	2	Inmate
Mack, Gladys	WF	32	Nurse
Mack, Joseph	WM	4	Inmate
Mackesey, Mary	WF	1	Inmate
Mackey, Grace	WF	26	Stenographer
Mackwood, John	WM	10m	Inmate
Macky, Clara	WF	7m	Inmate
Magluson, George	WM	2m	Inmate
Maguire, Lizzie	WF	22	Housework
Maher, Daniel	WM	1	Inmate
Maital, John	WM	2	Inmate
Malinka, Catherine	WF	8m	Inmate
Malo, Angela	WF	6m	Inmate
Malone, John	WM	2	Inmate
Maloney, Hannah	WF	32	Nurse
Maloney, Joseph	WM	2m	Inmate
Maltas, Edward	WM	3m	Inmate

Mandell, Cecelia	WF	2	Inmate
Manders, Sylvester	WM	2	Inmate
Manley, Cecilia	WF	7	Inmate
Mannaing, Esther	WF	4m	Inmate
Manning, Bridget	WF	19	Housework
Manning, Sr. Stella Marie	WF	36	Housekeeper
Mannix, Eugene	WM	10m	Inmate
Mara, Philomena	WF	1	Inmate
Maranz, Florence	WF	1m	Inmate
Maravigliano, Catharine	WF	1	Inmate
Marcus, Anna	WF	30	Nurse
Marcus, Annie	WF	25	Nurse
Marcus, John	WM	10m	Inmate
Maresca, Antonio	WM	11m	Inmate
Marie, Agnes	WF	1m	Inmate
Marion, Marion	WF	9m	Inmate
Marisa, Antonia	WF	22	Nurse
Mark, Marie	WF	6	Inmate
Markell, Frank	WM	1	Inmate
Marks, Louis	WM	4	Inmate
Marrochi, Elvira	WF	2	Inmate
Marshall, Alfred	BM	7	Inmate
Marshall, Genevieve	WF	2	Inmate
Marshall, James	WM	3	Inmate
Martens, Dorothy	WF	2	Inmate
Martin, Bertha	WF	4	Inmate
Martin, Harold	WM	1	Inmate
Martin, Katie	WF	22	Nurse
Martin, Lauren	WM	3	Inmate
Martin, Louise	WF	9m	Inmate
Martin, Mark	WM	5	Inmate
Martin, Mary	WF	1	Inmate
Martin, Mary T.	WF	1	Inmate
Martin, Nellie	WF	25	Waitress
Martinez, Edna	WF	4	Inmate
Martinka, Agnes	WF	1	Inmate
Martrika, Martha	WF	18	Nurse
Martzles, John	WM	2	Inmate
Marvin, Eugene	WM	2	Inmate
Marx, Diana	BF	5	Inmate
Maseski, Vincent	WM	5	Inmate
Mashire, Agnes	WF	18	Seamstress

Masilina, Anna	WF	2	Inmate
Mason, Alice	WF	1	Inmate
Masten, Francis	WM	6m	Inmate
Master, Lucella	WF	28	Nurse
Masterson, Annie	WF	38	Nurse
Mastro, Antonus	WM	4	Inmate
Matew, John	WM	1	Inmate
Mather, Sadie	WF	2m	Inmate
Matthews, Lillian	WF	1	Inmate
Mauchen, Catherine	WF	3m	Inmate
May, Bernardo	WF*	5	Inmate
Mayer, Gerard	WM	3	Inmate
Mayers, Christine	WF	6m	Inmate
McAdams, Francis	WM	4m	Inmate
McAleer, Alice	WF	20	Nurse
McAleer, Sr. Cecilia Ann	WF	29	Asst. Secretary
McAleer, Mary	WF	1m	Inmate
McAllister, Walter	BM	4	Inmate
McBride, Augustine	WM	0m	Inmate
McBride, Rita	WF	3	Inmate
McCabe, Ellen	WF	19	Nurse
McCabe, Genevieve	WF	2	Inmate
McCann, Elizabeth	WF	5	Inmate
McCann, Elizabeth	WF	38	Nurse
McCartem, Aloysius	WM	4	Inmate
McCarthy, Katie	WF	7m	Inmate
McCarthy, Katie	WF	18	Nurse
McCarthy, Margaret	WM*	1	Inmate
McCarthy, Monica	WF	10	Inmate
McCarthy, Sebastian	WM	2	Inmate
McCauley, Teresa	WF	1	Inmate
McClennen, Thomas	WM	4	Inmate
McConville, Aloysius	WM	1	Inmate
McCooy, Marie	WF	4	Inmate
McCormack, Gerald	WM	2	Inmate
McCormick, Sr. Mary C.	WF	35	Head of Laundry
McCrystal, Michael	WM	64	Superintendant
McCrystio, Sr. Teresa V.	WF	60	Head; Treasurer
McCullough, Mary	WF	4	Inmate
McDay, Elizabeth	WF	2	Inmate
McDermott, Alice	WF	3	Inmate
McDermott, Mary	BF	4	Inmate

McDevitt, Bella	WF	23	Nurse
McDonald, Henry	WM	9m	Inmate
McDonald, James	WM	1	Inmate
McDonald, Mary	WF	1	Inmate
McDonall, Blanch	WF	1	Inmate
McDoneugh, Hannah	WF	27	Nurse
McDonough, John	WM	1	Inmate
McDonough, Mary	WF	8m	Inmate
McDowell, Francis	WM	0m	Inmate
McFarlane, Charles	WM	10m	Inmate
McFarlane, Joseph	WM	4	Inmate
McGee, Rose	WF	36	Laundress
McGenty, Mrs. Nellie	WF	39	Nurse
McGhee, Charles	WM	2	Inmate
McGovern, Helen	WF	4m	Inmate
McGovern, James	WM	7	Inmate
McGovern, Maggie	WF	32	Laundress
McGowan, Rose	WF	7m	Inmate
McGrath, James	WM	2	Inmate
McGrath, Jeannetta	WF	5	Inmate
McGrath, Madeline	WF	1	Inmate
McGratton, Anna	BF	6	Inmate
McGuinness, Edward	WM	4	Inmate
McGuire, Cephas	WM	2	Inmate
McGuire, Josephine	WF	3	Inmate
McGuire, Julia	WF	20	Nurse
McGuire, Margaret	WF	5m	Inmate
McGuire, Mary	WF	1	Inmate
McGuire, Walter	WM	3	Inmate
McIntosh, Robert	WM	4	Inmate
McKenna, Gertrude	WF	1	Inmate
McKenna, Sr. Marie Anne	WF	45	Dressmaker
McKenne, John	WM	4	Inmate
McKeon, John	WM	9m	Inmate
McKillan, Joseph	WM	2	Inmate
McKnight, George	WM	1	Inmate
McLain, Gertrude	WF	1	Inmate
McLaughlin, Fanny	WF	33	Domestic
McLaughlin, Nora	WF	21	Nurse
McMahon, Helena	WF	6m	Inmate
McMahon, Margaret	WF	3	Inmate
McMann, Mary	WF	25	Nurse

McNally, Grace	WF	9m	Inmate
McNeal, George	WM	1	Inmate
McNulty, Catharine	WF	2	Inmate
McNulty, Sr. Mary Joseph	WF	48	Nursery
McQuade, Sarah	WF	1	Inmate
McRoberts, Jeanette	WF	1	Inmate
McSherry, Cormick	WM	2	Inmate
McTighe, Catherine	WF	32	Nurse
McVeigh, Florence	WF	5m	Inmate
McVey, William	WM	1	Inmate
Means, Madeline	WF	2	Inmate
Mecepolis, Bella	WF	2m	Inmate
Meehan, James	WM	1	Inmate
Meehan, Maggie	WF	1	Inmate
Menoerg, Sophie	WF	1	Inmate
Merkle, Arthur	WM	4m	Inmate
Messina, Mary	WF	1	Inmate
Messmer, Eugene	WM	1	Inmate
Metaller, Michael	WM	11m	Inmate
Meyer, Felix	WM	1	Inmate
Meyers, Edward	BM	8	Inmate
Meyers, Rose	WF	1	Inmate
Michalka, Susie	WF	23	Nurse
Michalla, Jennie	WF	1	Inmate
Michallka, Jennie	WF	7m	Inmate
Michels, Edward	WM	2	Inmate
Michels, Helen	WF	2	Inmate
Mignone, Pasqualina	WF	3	Inmate
Miles, Ralph	WM	5m	Inmate
Miller, Amelia	WF	4	Inmate
Miller, Charles	WM	2	Inmate
Miller, Dora	WF	2	Inmate
Miller, Ethel	WF	0m	Inmate
Miller, Flora	WF	5m	Inmate
Miller, Frank	WM	2	Inmate
Miller, George C.	WM	0m	Inmate
Miller, Kate	WF	35	Nurse
Miller, Margaaret	WF	2	Inmate
Miller, Mary C.	WF	5m	Inmate
Miller, Mary J.	WF	1	Inmate
Miller, Rita	WF	8m	Inmate
Miller, Victor	WM	4m	Inmate

Millerick, Dorothy	WF	8m	Inmate
Millet, Herbert	WM	1	Inmate
Millo, Helen	WF	3	Inmate
Mills, Libbie	WF	20	Portress
Milue, Dorothy	WF	1	Inmate
Milward, Maggie	WF	19	Seamstress
Miskell, Mary	WF	1	Inmate
Misogna, Mary	WF	6m	Inmate
Mitchell, John H.	WM	1	Inmate
Mitchell, Mary C.	WF	8m	Inmate
Moncella, Marie	WF	1	Inmate
Monhahan, Rita	WF	1	Inmate
Montgomery, Agnes	WF	4m	Inmate
Montifrisco, Vincent	WM	3	Inmate
Mooney, Bridget	WF	3	Inmate
Mooney, Sr. Teresa Gertrude	WF	61	Dormitorian
Moore, Frances	WF	7m	Inmate
Moore, Francis	WM	1	Inmate
Moran, Annie Y.	WF	29	Nurse
Moran, Catherine	WF	1	Inmate
Moran, Delia	WF	25	Kitchen Maid
Moran, Edmund	WM	3	Inmate
Moran, Elizabeth	WF	1	Inmate
Moran, James	WM	2	Inmate
Moran, Sr. Joseph Angela	WF	40	Head of Hospital
Moran, Leo	WM	2	Inmate
Moran, Mary	WF	1	Inmate
Moran, Thomas	WM	2	Inmate
Moreland, Mary	WF	1	Inmate
Morgan, Angela	WF	1	Inmate
Morgan, Joseph	WM	3	Inmate
Morgan, Mary E.	WF	1	Inmate
Moriara, Filna	WF	6m	Inmate
Moriarty, Irene	WF	1	Inmate
Moriarty, Katie	WF	18	Seamstress
Morris, Dorothy	WF	3	Inmate
Morrison, Mabel	WF	23	Housework
Moss, Ellen	WF	58	Nurse
Moss, Leopold	WM	8m	Inmate
Moxon, George	WM	2	Inmate
Mozarti, John	WM	5	Inmate
Mugelska, Joseph	WM	6m	Inmate

Mulcahey, John	WM	9m	Inmate
Mulcahy, Mamie	WF	18	Nurse
Mulhern, Edward	WM	3	Inmate
Muligan, John	WM	3	Inmate
Mullane, Mary	WF	72	Nurse
Mullen, Agnes	WF	3	Inmate
Mullen, Annie	WF	38	Laundress
Mullen, Catharine	WF	1	Inmate
Mullen, Margaret	WF	1	Inmate
Mullens, Gertrude	WF	3	Inmate
Mullerky, Annie	WF	2m	Inmate
Mulligan, Amanda	WF	1	Inmate
Mulligan, Vincent	WM	3	Inmate
Mulligen, Alphonse	WF*	5	Inmate
Mulroy, Teresa	WF	35	Laundress
Murphy, Agnes	WF	1	Inmate
Murphy, Anthony	WM	3	Inmate
Murphy, Catharine	WF	2	Inmate
Murphy, George	WM	2	Inmate
Murphy, Henry	WM	4	Inmate
Murphy, Joseph	WM	5	Inmate
Murphy, Mary E.	WF	2	Inmate
Murphy, Mary F.	WF	2	Inmate
Murphy, Rose	WF	1	Inmate
Murphy, Ruth	WF	1	Inmate
Murphy, Sarah	WF	2	Inmate
Murphy, Thomas	WM	1	Inmate
Murphy, Vincent	WM	3	Inmate
Murphy, Viola	WF	10m	Inmate
Murray, Agnes	WF	4m	Inmate
Murray, Edwin	WM	11m	Inmate
Murray, Loretto	WF	2	Inmate
Murray, Madeline	WF	9m	Inmate
Murray, Marie	WF	2	Inmate
Murray, Mary M.	WF	8m	Inmate
Murray, Matilda	WF	1	Inmate
Murray, William	WM	5	Inmate
Murtha, Joseph	WM	3	Inmate
Murtha, Mary	WF	1	Inmate
Muskow, Rose	WF	2	Inmate
Myrick, Sidney	WM	2	Inmate
Nadel, Rosa	WF	6m	Inmate

Nadesku, Maria	WF	23	Housework
Nagle, Florence	WF	2	Inmate
Narkabone, Lewis	WM	1	Inmate
Narkabone, Michael	WM	1	Inmate
Nash, Genevieve	WF	4	Inmate
Naudika, Monica	WF	3m	Inmate
Naw, Charles	WM	9m	Inmate
Neany, Edward	WM	2	Inmate
Neary, Joseph	WM	6	Inmate
Neely, William	WM	5m	Inmate
Neilson, Edwina	WF	0m	Inmate
Neimuth, Anne	WF	2	Inmate
Nella, Andrea	WM	0m	Inmate
Nelsen, Catharine	WF	20	Nurse
Neltzen, Assunta	WF	10m	Inmate
Neri, Ignazio	WM	10m	Inmate
Nesbit, Seth	WM	6m	Inmate
Nestle, Mark	WM	9m	Inmate
Neuhaus, Marie	WF	2	Inmate
Neuman, Eva	WF	3m	Inmate
Nevins, William	WM	11m	Inmate
Newberg, Charles	WM	7m	Inmate
Nicholas, Catharine	WF	1	Inmate
Nicholl, Joseph	WM	8m	Inmate
Nierensohn, Emily	WF	2	Inmate
Nixon, Thomas	WM	5m	Inmate
Noble, Raymond	WM	4	Inmate
Noel, Ruth	WF	6m	Inmate
Nolan, Edward	WM	1	Inmate
Nolan, Gertrude	WF	4m	Inmate
Nolasco, Mark	WM	4m	Inmate
Nolda, Robert	WM	3m	Inmate
Noleda, Lucy	WF	2	Inmate
Noonan, Annie	WF	27	Housework
Noonan, Mary H.	WF	0m	Inmate
Norman, Joseph	WM	4	Inmate
Noroella, Francis	WM	2	Inmate
Norris, Ella	WF	3	Inmate
North, Eleanor	WF	8m	Inmate
Northrop, Minnie	WF	21	Nurse
Norton, Lawrence	WM	8m	Inmate
Norton, Maria	WF	29	Nurse

Norton, William	WM	3	Inmate
Nosuk, Helen	WF	20	Nurse
Noyes, Sr. Marie Elsie	WF	48	Asst. Secretary
Nutt, Anna	WF	4	Inmate
Nutt, Joseph	WM	4	Inmate
Nutt, Mary	WF	32	Laundress
Nylands, Francis	WM	10m	Inmate
Oakes, Mary	WF	60	Seamstress
O'Brien, Annie	WF	34	Housekeeper
O'Brien, Edward	WM	3	Inmate
O'Brien, John	WM	3m	Inmate
O'Brien, Leo	WM	2	Inmate
O'Brien, Martha	WF	1	Inmate
O'Brien, Sr. Mary M.	WF	36	Nursery
O'Brien, Mary	WF	19	Nurse
O'Brien, Theodore	WM	3	Inmate
O'Connell, John	WM	2	Inmate
O'Connor, Dennis	WM	6	Inmate
O'Day, Margaret	WF	8m	Inmate
O'Dey, Joseph	WM	1	Inmate
O'Donnell, Joseph	WM	1	Inmate
O'Donohue, Annie	WF	50	Teacher
O'Donohue, Mary	WF	1	Inmate
O'Dowd, Edward	WM	7	Inmate
O'Hara, Delia	WF	34	Housework
O'Hara, Marie	WF	2	Inmate
Ohlsen, George	WM	1	Inmate
Ohlsen, Gustave	WF*	3m	Inmate
Oiner, Mary	WF	1	Inmate
O'Keefe, Annie	WF	5	Inmate
O'Keefe, Delia	WF	37	Laundress
Oler, Sophie	WF	2	Inmate
Oliven, Mary	WF	1	Inmate
Oliver, Homer	WM	4	Inmate
O'Malley, Teresa	WF	3	Inmate
O'Neill, Bessie	WF	1	Inmate
O'Neill, Eleanor	WF	8m	Inmate
O'Neill, John	WM	3m	Inmate
O'Neill, Marguerite	WF	5m	Inmate
O'Neill, Mary	WF	26	Seamstress
Ooington, Mary	WF	8m	Inmate
Orbiston, Felix	WM	2	Inmate

Orkey, Laurentine	WF	10m	Inmate
Ormsby, Harold	WM	2	Inmate
Orne, Marie	WF	1	Inmate
O'Rorke, Helen	WF	1	Inmate
O'Rourka, Alice	WF	7	Inmate
O'Rourke, Mary	WF	26	Nurse
Orr, Andrew	WM	2	Inmate
Orr, Augustine	WM	2	Inmate
Orr, Josephine	WF	21	Domestic
Orrenstein, Lena	WF	1	Inmate
Osborne, Leanor	WF	5	Inmate
Oser, Vincent	WM	1	Inmate
Osgood, Cecilia	WF	6m	Inmate
O'Toole, Agnes	WF	2	Inmate
Owens, Eugene	BM	3	Inmate
Owens, John	WM	3	Inmate
Page, Raymond	WM	2	Inmate
Pahanga, Lizzie	WF	19	Laundress
Palmer, Lillian	WF	1	Inmate
Pan, Joseph	WM	3	Inmate
Parks, Alice	WF	23	Nurse
Parks, Edward	WM	4m	Inmate
Parks, Mary	WF	5	Inmate
Pasteu, Clarence	WM	3	Inmate
Patrick, Carl	WM	3	Inmate
Patterson, Arthur	WM	3m	Inmate
Patterson, Mary	WF	1	Inmate
Pauco, George	WM	3m	Inmate
Paul, Esther	WF	1m	Inmate
Payne, Edward	BM	8	Inmate
Payne, Gabriella	WF	2	Inmate
Payne, Justin	BM	3	Inmate
Peiffer, John	WM	7	Inmate
Penosa, Lena	WF	1	Inmate
Perez, Allen	WM	1	Inmate
Perl, Rose	WF	5m	Inmate
Perora, Giuspa	WF	1	Inmate
Perry, Agnes	WF	1	Inmate
Peters, Adele	WF	3	Inmate
Petrona, Antonio	WM	1	Inmate
Phelan, Catharine	WF	2	Inmate
Phelan, Gerald	WM	1	Inmate

Phelan, Stephen	WM	1	Inmate
Phelps, Joseph	WM	2	Inmate
Pick, Frederick	WM	1	Inmate
Pilger, John	WM	4	Inmate
Piliosky, Michael	WM	2	Inmate
Pirkes, Helen	WF	1	Inmate
Pitt, Mary	WF	1	Inmate
Pius, Joseph	WM	1	Inmate
Plunkett, Sr. Cecilia M.	WF	35	Pharmacist
Plunkett, Jerome	WM	1	Inmate
Politzka, Margaret	WF	1	Inmate
Poolgrac, Anthony	WM	1	Inmate
Powers, Sr. Josephine M.	WF	20	Nursery
Powers, Kate	WF	29	Housekeeper
Powers, Margaret	WF	65	Nurse
Powers, Veronica	WF	2	Inmate
Preston, Agatha	WF	2	Inmate
Price, Thomasina	WF	2m	Inmate
Principe, Antony	WM	2	Inmate
Proctu, Winifield	BF	7	Inmate
Prospero, Alberta	WF	3	Inmate
Pryar, Gladys	BF	5	Inmate
Pryar, Mary	WF	5	Inmate
Pryor, Catharine	WF	29	Nurse
Pulsen, Christian	WM	4m	Inmate
Pulsen, Christina	WF	19	Nurse
Purcell, Sr. Mary Bernadette	WF	60	Dressmaker
Pushkovitz, Annie	WF	4m	Inmate
Pyne, Josephine	WF	1	Inmate
Quigley, Mary R.	WF	1m	Inmate
Quinlan, Agnes	WF	66	Nurse
Quinn, Arthur	WM	1	Inmate
Quinn, Lilly	WF	21	Nurse
Quinn, May	WF	28	Nurse
Quinn, Paul	WM	1	Inmate
Quinones, Walter	WM	6m	Inmate
Quintard, Genevieve	WF	5	Inmate
Quirk, Arthur	WM	3m	Inmate
Quirk, Catherine	WF	6	Inmate
Radner, Walter	WM	3	Inmate
Raffela, Joseph	WM	4m	Inmate
Raguzina, Carmela	WF	2	Inmate

Ramsay, Gilbert	WM	3	Inmate
Rasen, James	WM	5	Inmate
Rawley, Magdalen	WF	1	Inmate
Raymond, Angela	WF	7m	Inmate
Raymond, Louisa	WF	22	Nurse
Raymond, Mary	WF	5m	Inmate
Raymore, Grace	WF	3m	Inmate
Raynoi, Dorothy	WF	2	Inmate
Reak, Valerie	WF	3m	Inmate
Reardon, Louis	WM	4	Inmate
Redden, Lizzie	WF	30	Kitchen Maid
Reddy, Sr. Cecilia Anthony	WF	45	Nursery
Redington, John	WM	1	Inmate
Redmond, Frauds	WM	3	Inmate
Regen, James	WM	1m	Inmate
Reid, Herman	WM	3	Inmate
Reid, Lillian	WF	2	Inmate
Reidy, Agnes	WF	24	Laundress
Reilly, Alice	WF	2	Inmate
Reilly, Bernard	WM	1	Inmate
Reilly, John	WM	6	Inmate
Reilly, Marie A.	WF	0m	Inmate
Reilly, Mary	WF	4	Inmate
Reilly, Sr. Mary Ernestine	WF	61	Asst. Secretary
Reilly, Stephen	WM	1	Inmate
Reilly, William	WM	1	Inmate
Reilly, William	WM	2	Inmate
Remson, Mary	WF	2	Inmate
Rensk, Annie	WF	4m	Inmate
Renyolds, Mary	WF	39	Nurse
Restano, James	WM	4m	Inmate
Reynolds, Howard	WM	2m	Inmate
Rhen, George	WM	5	Inmate
Riccio, Mary	WF	4	Inmate
Rich, Joseph	WM	1	Inmate
Richards, Gerald	WM	2	Inmate
Richards, Mary	WF	3	Inmate
Richards, Oscar	WM	2	Inmate
Richardson, Agnes	WF	2	Inmate
Richardson, Bessie	BF	1	Inmate
Richardson, Gertrude	WF	2	Inmate
Richmond, Catharine	WF	1	Inmate

Richter, William	WM	6m	Inmate
Rick, Joseph	WM	1	Inmate
Rieger, Frank	WM	1	Inmate
Riker, Mary	WF	2	Inmate
Riley, Joseph	WM	5	Inmate
Riley, Matilda	WF	5m	Inmate
Rioers, Edward	WM	1	Inmate
Risari, Charles	WM	2	Inmate
Riss, Martha	WF	2m	Inmate
Rivers, Reginald	WM	3	Inmate
Rizzo, John	WM	3	Inmate
Roben, Robert	WM	2m	Inmate
Roberts, Annie	WF	17	Seamstress
Robins, Amelia	BF	3	Inmate
Robinson, Adelade	WF	23	Nurse
Robinson, Cornelia	WF	3	Inmate
Robinson, George	WM	1	Inmate
Robinson, Helen	WF	1m	Inmate
Robinson, Louise	WF	1	Inmate
Robinson, Mamie	Wf	22	Seamstress
Robinson, Wilfred	WM	1	Inmate
Roblech, John	WM	3m	Inmate
Rochesi, Anna	WF	8m	Inmate
Rochford, Sr. Dominique M.	WF	33	Nursery
Rochford, Mary	WF	1	Inmate
Rockwell, Alma	WF	3	Inmate
Roesener, Clara	WF	1	Inmate
Rogen, Augustine	WM	5	Inmate
Rogers, Bertha	WF	4m	Inmate
Rogers, Bertha	WF	5m	Inmate
Rogers, Francis	WM	2m	Inmate
Romano, Antoinette	WF	11m	Inmate
Romano, Mary	WF	10m	Inmate
Ronycos, Isabel	WF	4m	Inmate
Rorke, Joseph	WM	3	Inmate
Rose, Harry	WM	1	Inmate
Rose, Joseph V.	WM	1	Inmate
Rosemani, Louis	WM	1	Inmate
Rosen, Morrise	WF	6m	Inmate
Rosen, Teresa	WF	1	Inmate
Rosenfeld, Lottie	WF	0m	Inmate
Ross, Harold	WM	2	Inmate

Ross, Joseph	WM	4	Inmate
Rossell, Joseph	WM	1	Inmate
Rossi, Marco	WM	1	Inmate
Roth, Philip	WM	3	Inmate
Rotsford, Mary	WF	31	Waitress
Rousle, Elizabeth	WF	50	Nurse
Rovitch, Alexander	WM	4m	Inmate
Rowan, Kenneth	BM	2m	Inmate
Rowen, Sr. Anna M.	WF	42	Asst. Secretary
Rowland, Joseph	WM	8	Inmate
Rubens, Alphonsus	WM	2	Inmate
Rubens, Mary	WF	1	Inmate
Rubes, Rosa	WF	4	Inmate
Ruser, Leo	WM	3	Inmate
Rusesell, Edmund	WM	2m	Inmate
Rush, Matthew Miriam	WF	34	Sister, Nursery
Russell, Antoinette	WF	4	Inmate
Russell, Mary	WF	37	Nurse
Russell, Mary	WF	44	Seamstress
Rutledge, Paul	WM	1	Inmate
Ryan, Annie	WF	5	Inmate
Ryan, Annie	WF	29	Portress
Ryan, David	WM	4	Inmate
Ryan, Elizabeth	WF	11m	Inmate
Ryan, Harry	WM	4m	Inmate
Ryan, Helen	WF	6m	Inmate
Ryan, Jerome	WM	2	Inmate
Ryan, Joseph	WM	4	Inmate
Ryan, Joseph C.	WM	1	Inmate
Ryan, Katie	WF	24	Nurse
Ryan, Mary F.	WF	3	Inmate
Ryan, Norah	WF	23	Cook
Ryan, Timothy	WM	8m	Inmate
Ryan, William E.	WM	0m	Inmate
Sadler, William	WM	1	Inmate
Sadowski, Clara	WF	1	Inmate
Salier, Raymond	WM	1	Inmate
Saloi, Rosa	WF	0m	Inmate
Salva, Frank	WM	1	Inmate
Salvatorei, Helen	WF	2	Inmate
Salzer, Merice	WM	5	Inmate
Salzo, George	WM	4	Inmate

Sanford, Clarid	WM	3	Inmate
Sarkison, Takoolue	WF	25	Seamstress
Sarlay, Joseph	WM	4	Inmate
Satanella, Margaret	WF	2	Inmate
Satterlee, Frederick	WM	4m	Inmate
Savoy, Sophie	WF	40	Cook
Scalley, Dorothy	WF	1	Inmate
Scanlon, Sr. Mary Dolorosa	WF	55	Informarian
Scanlon, Mary	WF	1	Inmate
Scanloy, Lillie	WF	5	Inmate
Schaefer, Caroline	WF	5m	Inmate
Schaefer, Edward	WM	0m	Inmate
Schaefer, Loretto	WF	2	Inmate
Schaefer, Marion	WF	3m	Inmate
Schaeffer, Anna	WF	2	Inmate
Schaeffer, Henry	WM	2	Inmate
Schilling, Charles	WM	1	Inmate
Schlegel, William	WM	5m	Inmate
Schmidt, Henry	WM	4	Inmate
Schmist, John	WM	3	Inmate
Schraudner, Francis	WM	2	Inmate
Schraudner, James	WM	6m	Inmate
Schuelar, Anna	WF	1	Inmate
Schultz, Teresa	WF	3	Inmate
Schuty, Tillie	WF	28	Nurse
Schutz, Jacob	WM	1	Inmate
Schutz, Marion	WF	7m	Inmate
Schwab, Alfred	WM	2	Inmate
Schwartz, Clara	WF	4	Inmate
Schwartz, Teresa	WF	2m	Inmate
Schwiler, Richard	WM	4	Inmate
Scott, Lulu	WF	2	Inmate
Scott, Veronica	WF	3	Inmate
Scozza, Antoinette	WF	2	Inmate
Scully, Maggie	WF	35	Nurse
Seaman, Elsie	WF	7m	Inmate
Seegar, Henry	WM	1	Inmate
Seguine, George	WM	3	Inmate
Seibert, Viola	WF	0m	Inmate
Seigle, Dora	WF	20	Nurse
Seiteu, Joseph	WM	0m	Inmate
Seroiss, James	WM	0m	Inmate

Severina, Elista	WF	3m	Inmate
Seymoure, Teresa	WF	3	Inmate
Shackelford, John	WM	1	Inmate
Shackelford, Stella	WF	32	Nurse
Shaler, Albert	WM	1	Inmate
Shandnew, Nellie	WF	24	Nurse
Shanlen, Jerome	WM	4	Inmate
Shannon, Joseph	WM	2	Inmate
Shannon, Thomas	WM	5	Inmate
Sharkey, Reginald	WM	1	Inmate
Shaughnessy, William	WM	1	Inmate
Shea, Josephine	WF	5m	Inmate
Shea, Sr. Mary Leondella	WF	28	Nursery
Sheahan, James	WM	5	Inmate
Sheehan, Bridget	WF	22	Nurse
Sheigler, Edward	WM	5	Inmate
Shellman, Tillie	WF	29	Nurse
Shepard, Winifred	WF	2	Inmate
Sheperd, Earl	WM	1m	Inmate
Sheridan, Aloysius	WM	2	Inmate
Sheucer, Raymond	WM	4	Inmate
Shewn, Frederick	WM	3	Inmate
Shortall, Marie	WF	50	Nurse
Siegel, Anthony	WM	3m	Inmate
Silva, Dora	WF	5m	Inmate
Simmons, Helena	BF	3m	Inmate
Sisco, Maude	WF	1	Inmate
Sizwa, Anna	WF	3	Inmate
Slattery, Veronica	WF	2	Inmate
Smirda, Mary	WF	1	Inmate
Smith, Alice	WF	2	Inmate
Smith, Clarence	WM	1	Inmate
Smith, Claudia	WF	3m	Inmate
Smith, Elmira	BF	6m	Inmate
Smith, Emma	WF	32	Laundress
Smith, Franklin	WM	1	Inmate
Smith, Genieve	WF	11m	Inmate
Smith, Harold	WM	5	Inmate
Smith, John	WM	4	Inmate
Smith, John E.	WM	3	Inmate
Smith, Mabel	WF	3	Inmate
Smith, Maggie	WF	6	Inmate

Smith, Maggie	WF	34	Laundress
Smith, Margery	WF	3	Inmate
Smith, Marion	WF	2	Inmate
Smith, Mary	WF	9	Inmate
Smith, Mary P.	WF	1	Inmate
Smith, Michael	WM	3	Inmate
Smith, Otto	WM	11	Inmate
Smith, Paul	WM	1m	Inmate
Smith, Peter	WM	1m	Inmate
Smith, Susie	WF	36	Laundress
Smith, Viola	WF	5m	Inmate
Smith, Walter	WM	2	Inmate
Snow, Raphael	WM	5m	Inmate
Snyder, Bessie	WF	17	Nurse
Sobeliski, Frank	WM	1	Inmate
Solomon, Myrtle	WF	4	Inmate
Sorice, Salvator	WM	1	Inmate
Souri, Maria	WF	4m	Inmate
Southard, Edwin	WM	3	Inmate
Spellman, Joseph	WM	2m	Inmate
Srustkewiezz, Harold	WM	2	Inmate
Stafford, John	WM	1	Inmate
Stanley, Agnes	WF	4	Inmate
Stanley, Richard	BM	1	Inmate
Stanofsky, Mary	WF	20	Nurse
Stanofsky, Stephen	WM	7m	Inmate
Stanton, John H.	WM	3	Inmate
Stark, Mary	WF	1	Inmate
Steele, Gertrude	WF	1	Inmate
Stelig, Mary	WF	20	Nurse
Stelmk, John	WM	1m	Inmate
Stengallouna, Frederick	WM	3	Inmate
Stengel, Joseph	WM	1	Inmate
Stephans, Herbert	WM	10m	Inmate
Stewart, Alonzo	WM	1	Inmate
Stewart, Marguerite	WF	0m	Inmate
Stone, Irene	WF	4m	Inmate
Stone, Louis	WM	2	Inmate
Stone, Peter	WM	1m	Inmate
Strachma, Johanna	WF	2	Inmate
Strauss, Adelaide	WF	9m	Inmate
Stroh, Frederick	WM	2	Inmate

Stures, Edward	WM	3m	Inmate
Sturke, Mary	WF	60	Housekeeper
Sucky, Louise	WF	1	Inmate
Sullivan, Alice	WF	1	Inmate
Sullivan, Constance	WF	11m	Inmate
Sullivan, Elizabeth	WF	11m	Inmate
Sullivan, Ellen	WF	32	Nurse
Sullivan, Ernestine	WF	3	Inmate
Sullivan, Francis	WM	1	Inmate
Sullivan, John	WM	2	Inmate
Sullivan, John	WM	4	Inmate
Sullivan, John	WM	5	Inmate
Sullivan, John C.	WM	3	Inmate
Sullivan, Joseph	WM	2	Inmate
Sullivan, Sr. Joseph Carmela	WF	34	Housekeeper
Sullivan, Kate	WF	4m	Inmate
Sullivan, Kate	WF	33	Nurse
Sullivan, May	WF	2m	Inmate
Sullivan, May	WF	18	Nurse
Sullivan, Thomas	WM	5	Inmate
Sullivan, Tomothy	WM	1	Inmate
Surin, Elizabeth	WF	32	Nurse
Sutton, Ann	WF	4m	Inmate
Sweeney, Alousia	WF	5	Inmate
Sweeney, James	WM	5	Inmate
Sweeney, Mary	WF	3	Inmate
Sweeney, Mary	WF	36	Nurse
Sweeney, Patrick	WM	3	Inmate
Sweeny, Michael	WM	1	Inmate
Swift, James	WM	3m	Inmate
Swyda, Annie	WF	22	Nurse
Talbot, Adeline	WF	2	Inmate
Taniscio, Guiseppe	WM	9m	Inmate
Tarmenski, Maria	WF	29	Nurse
Taxter, Annie	WF	18	Nurse
Taxter, Harold	WM	1m	Inmate
Taylor, Agnes	BF	1	Inmate
Taylor, Anna	WF	3	Inmate
Taylor, Arthur	WM	3	Inmate
Taylor, Donald	BM	2m	Inmate
Taylor, Marion	WF	28	Nurse
Taylor, Mary H.	WF	7m	Inmate

Taylor, Rebecca	WF	17	Seamstress
Teatu, Aloysius	WM	3m	Inmate
Tecan, Agnes	WF	27	Nurse
Tecan, Edith	WF	3m	Inmate
Teen, Loretto	WF	27	Housework
TenEyck, Frederick	WM	10m	Inmate
Terhune, Virginia	WF	8m	Inmate
Terrill, Vivian	WF	2	Inmate
Testarda, Mark	WM	0m	Inmate
Testol, Frederic	WM	1m	Inmate
Thayer, Vincent	WM	2	Inmate
Thomas, Clarence	WM	2	Inmate
Thomas, Margaret	WF	19	Portress
Thomas, Mary	WF	27	Nurse
Thomas, Robert	WM	5m	Inmate
Thomas, Rose	WF	1	Inmate
Thompson, Charlotte	WF	1	Inmate
Thompson, Irma	WF	2	Inmate
Thompson, John	BM	4	Inmate
Thomson, Agnes	WF	3	Inmate
Thomson, George	WM	1	Inmate
Thornton, Elizabeth	WF	40	Seamstress
Thornton, Francis	WM	2	Inmate
Thull, Louis	WM	2	Inmate
Tierney, Sr. Ann Aloysia	WF	58	Asst. Secretary
Tiffany, Vincent	WM	2	Inmate
Timmins, George	WM	11m	Inmate
Timothy, Sarah	WF	1	Inmate
Tinall, Mary	WF	1m	Inmate
Tindall, Anna	WF	3	Inmate
Tiot, Joseph	WM	1	Inmate
Toal, Loretto	WF	3	Inmate
Tobani, Margaret	WF	9m	Inmate
Tobin, John	WM	4	Inmate
Tobin, Mary	WF	23	Nurse
Tobin, Mary F.	WF	3m	Inmate
Tohn, Bertha	WF	3m	Inmate
Tomasi, Nicholas	WM	3	Inmate
Tomney, Sr. Mary Fidele	WF	46	Asst. Secretary
Tornienski, Michael	WM	2m	Inmate
Toth, Wilhelmina	WF	1	Inmate
Toukey, Veronica	WF	3	Inmate

Townsend, Augusta	WF	1m	Inmate
Townsend, Berence	WF	1	Inmate
Townsend, John	WM	1	Inmate
Townsend, John	WM	5m	Inmate
Tracey, Cornelia	WF	2	Inmate
Tracey, Francis	WM	1	Inmate
Traut, Augusta	WF	8	Inmate
Travers, Viola	WF	2	Inmate
Traynor, Ellen	WF	23	Nurse
Traynor, Joseph	WM	1m	Inmate
Treanac, John	WM	8m	Inmate
Treut, Adolph	WM	3	Inmate
Triebe, Richard	WM	1	Inmate
Truddle, Mary	WF	26	Domestic
Tulle, Joseph D.	WM	2	Inmate
Tulley, Joseph	WM	2	Inmate
Tulley, Sr. Marie Joseph	WF	51	Nursery
Turenne, Catharine	WF	2	Inmate
Turenne, John	WM	2	Inmate
Turentz, William	WM	9	Inmate
Turintz, Josephine	WF	22	Nurse
Turner, Florence	WF	6m	Inmate
Tyler, Leo.	WM	1	Inmate
Tynnan, Daniel	WM	4m	Inmate
Tyrrell, May	WF	1	Inmate
Ubazo, Joseph	WM	11m	Inmate
Ubberoth, Robert	WM	11m	Inmate
Udell, Arthur	WM	11m	Inmate
Ughetta, Mary	WF	7m	Inmate
Uhling, Mary	WF	10m	Inmate
Uhloufirky, Annie	WF	30	Nurse
Uker, Joseph	WM	10m	Inmate
Ulick, Peter	WM	1	Inmate
Ulier, Marie	WF	2m	Inmate
Uliton, Miriam	WF	6m	Inmate
Ulman, Jennie	WF	2m	Inmate
Ulworth, Augusta	WF	1	Inmate
Underwood, Alice	WF	2m	Inmate
Urlton, Theodore	WM	11m	Inmate
Utzinger, Virginia	WF	1	Inmate
Vacca, Sr. Mary Vincenzo	WF	34	Asst. Refectorian
Vailey, John	WM	4	Inmate

Valentine, Helen	WF	3	Inmate
Valk, Thomas	WM	4m	Inmate
Valley, George	WM	3	Inmate
VanRiper, Dorothy	WF	1	Inmate
VanRiper, Richard	WM	4	Inmate
VanTassell, Herbert	WM	3	Inmate
VanZile, Jerome	WM	10m	Inmate
Vargar, Mary	WF	5m	Inmate
Vassi, Bianca	WF	2m	Inmate
Vaughn, Evelyn	WF	1	Inmate
Vaugle, James	WM	9m	Inmate
Vazile, Vincenzo	WM	4m	Inmate
Veital, Ella	WF	2m	Inmate
Veitch, Maude	WF	22	Chambermaid
Vellazza, Carlotta	WF	4m	Inmate
Ventino, Rosie	WF	20	Nurse
Ventner, Mary	WF	4m	Inmate
Vernon, Mary	WF	6m	Inmate
Vervain, Etta	WF	1	Inmate
Vesely, Francis	WM	3m	Inmate
Viancort, Clotilde	WF	1	Inmate
Victory, John	WM	10m	Inmate
Viertel, Paul	WM	2	Inmate
Virrito, Maria	WF	1m	Inmate
Voccaro, Angelo	WM	5	Inmate
Volk, Catherine	WF	25	Nurse
Volts, Marie	WF	2	Inmate
Volz, Bessie	WF	1	Inmate
Voorhess, Josephine	WF	1	Inmate
Wade, Agnes	WF	10m	Inmate
Wadworth, George	WM	3	Inmate
Wagner, Francis	WM	2	Inmate
Wakefield, Agnes	WF	21	Seamstress
Wakely, Edward	WM	1	Inmate
Walker, Mary	WF	2	Inmate
Wallace, Vincent	WM	7m	Inmate
Walser, Carrie	WF	1	Inmate
Walsh, Annie	WF	1	Inmate
Walsh, Annie	WF	21	Nurse
Walsh, Gabrielle	WF	3	Inmate
Walsh, Harry	WM	2	Inmate
Walsh, John J.	WM	0m	Inmate

Walsh, Josephine	WF	25	Nurse
Walsh, Margaret	WF	2	Inmate
Walsh, Margaret	WF	25	Nurse
Walsh, Thomas	WM	1m	Inmate
Walsh, Walter	WM	1m	Inmate
Wants, Michael	WM	1	Inmate
Ward, Agnes	WF	9m	Inmate
Ward, Agnes	WF	1	Inmate
Ward, James	WM	1	Inmate
Ward, Lizzie	WF	40	Nurse
Ward, Sarah	WF	10	Inmate
Ward, Vera	WF	2	Inmate
Warner, Ethel	BF	5	Inmate
Warner, Irene	BF	4	Inmate
Warren, Clotilde	WF	0m	Inmate
Warren, Leonard	WM	2	Inmate
Warst, Angeline	WF	3	Inmate
Washington, Francis	BM	6	Inmate
Wasser, Jeanette	WF	8	Inmate
Waterman, Irving	WM	5	Inmate
Waters, John	WM	5m	Inmate
Waters, Mary	WF	2m	Inmate
Watson, George	WM	2	Inmate
Weber, George	WM	5	Inmate
Weeks, Annie	WF	16	Seamstress
Wegan, Mary	WF	45	Nurse
Weinberg, Arthur	WM	8m	Inmate
Weingart, Henry	WM	10m	Inmate
Weir, Andrew	WM	3m	Inmate
Weiss, Anna	WF	1	Inmate
Weiss, Louis	WM	1	Inmate
Weiss, Margaret	WF	1	Inmate
Weller, Charles	WM	2	Inmate
Welsh, Jerome	WM	2	Inmate
Welsh, John V.	WM	10m	Inmate
Welsh, Joseph	WM	2	Inmate
Wendel, Flora	WF	3	Inmate
Wentworth, Edna	WF	2	Inmate
Wentworth, Joseph	WM	3	Inmate
West, Isidore	WM	1	Inmate
Weymann, Lillian	WF	1	Inmate
Whalen, Charles	WM	5m	Inmate

Whales, Annie	WF	23	Nurse
Wheeler, Beatrice	WF	4	Inmate
Wheeler, Dorothy	WF	4	Inmate
Wheeler, Edward	WM	2	Inmate
Whelen, Grace	WF	3	Inmate
Whipple, Francis	WM	0m	Inmate
White, Alice	WF	25	Nurse
White, George	WM	1	Inmate
White, Louise	WF	1	Inmate
White, Lucy	WF	5	Inmate
White, Mary	WF	2	Inmate
White, Max	WM	1	Inmate
White, Philip	WM	0m	Inmate
Whitefield, William	WM	3	Inmate
Whitely, Catharine	WF	7m	Inmate
Whiting, Agnes	WF	8	Inmate
Whiting, Mary	WF	5	Inmate
Whittendale, Frederick	WM	1	Inmate
Wienig, John	WM	2	Inmate
Wilde, Antoinette	WF	2	Inmate
Williams, Arthur	WM	7	Inmate
Williams, Ethel	WF	2	Inmate
Williams, Eugene	WM	8	Inmate
Williams, Patrick	WM	5	Inmate
Willis, Emily	WF	24	Nurse
Willis, Henry	WM	1	Inmate
Willoughby, Arnold	WM	2	Inmate
Wilson, Charles	WM	5	Inmate
Wilson, Edward	WM	6	Inmate
Wilson, Francis	WM	2	Inmate
Wilson, Frank	WM	2	Inmate
Wilson, Helena	WF	2m	Inmate
Wilson, John	WM	3	Inmate
Wilson, Marguerite	WF	5	Inmate
Wilson, Mary C.	WF	1m	Inmate
Wilson, William	WM	2	Inmate
Winburne, Jerome	WM	2	Inmate
Winslow, Josephine	WF	4	Inmate
Winters, Jean	WM	1	Inmate
Wizeleska, Annie	WF	34	Nurse
Wolf, Catharine	WF	7m	Inmate
Wolfe, Margaret	WF	1	Inmate

Wolfe, Marguerite	WF	3m	Inmate
Wolfe, Percy	WM	9m	Inmate
Wolffe, Joseph	WM	3	Inmate
Wood, Hillard	WM	7m	Inmate
Woods, Mary	WF	39	Nurse
Worthington, Charles	WM	2	Inmate
Wright, Wilhied	WM	8m	Inmate
Wukrentowiecz, Sophie	WF	5m	Inmate
Wyatt, Ella	WF	2	Inmate
Wybientowiecy, Appoline	WF	21	Nurse
Yanik, Romanus	WM	0m	Inmate
Yanika, Rosie	WF	32	Nurse
Yank, Stephen	WM	9m	Inmate
Yanso, Leo	WM	2	Inmate
Yarrington, Leopold	WM	9m	Inmate
Yates, Margaret	WF	21	Nurse
Ybaum, Stephen	WM	1	Inmate
Yeacey, Loretto	WF	37	Nurse
Yeatman, Thomas	WM	2m	Inmate
Yeldo, Maria	WF	0m	Inmate
Yenley, Dominic	WM	10m	Inmate
Yesler, Raymond	WM	2	Inmate
Yeugles, Marie	WF	30	Cook
Ygaravidez, John	WM	3	Inmate
Yoerg, Irene	WF	3m	Inmate
Yoest, Adrian	WM	11m	Inmate
Yorke, Raymond	WM	3	Inmate
Young, Catherine	WF	14	Nurse
Young, Charles	WM	1	Inmate
Young, Regina	WF	2	Inmate
Young, Rose	WF	5m	Inmate
Young, Tillie	WF	2	Inmate
Yovin, Paul	WM	7m	Inmate
Yvo, John	WM	1	Inmate
Zandell, Augustine	WM	1m	Inmate
Zang, Lena	WF	2	Inmate
Zappar, Lizzie	WF	2	Inmate
Zardetti, Natal	WF	3	Inmate
Zauger, Raphael	WM	1	Inmate
Zboys, Anna	WF	10m	Inmate
Zell, Gilbert	WM	3	Inmate
Zem, Lillian	WF	2m	Inmate

Zemh, Anthony	WM	1	Inmate
Zenta, Marie	WF	6m	Inmate
Zentgraf, Ernestine	WF	1	Inmate
Zerega, Jerome	WM	5m	Inmate
Zertz, Miriam	WF	1	Inmate
Zies, Louis	WM	9m	Inmate
Zigalotti, Bianca	WF	9m	Inmate
Zilla, Veronica	WF	2	Inmate
Zimmer, Stella	WF	2	Inmate
Zinn, Jerome	WM	5m	Inmate
Zinnek, Adele	WF	5	Inmate
Zireck, James	WM	1m	Inmate
Zobbiat, John	WM	1	Inmate
Zolz, Eugene	WM	1	Inmate
Zucker, Lucy	WF	1	Inmate
Zulma, Annie	WF	10m	Inmate
Zundel, Teresa	WF	5m	Inmate
Zutilli, Jennie	WF	3m	Inmate
Zutman, Thomas	WM	2	Inmate

Index to the
Federal Enumeration of the Inhabitants of

The New York Foundling Hospital

175 East 68th Street
New York, New York

April 15, 1910

Ward No. 19
Supervisor's District No. 1
Election District No. 1068
Pages 1A - 28A

Beatrice Wolffsohn, Enumerator

Guide to Column Headings

in the

1910 Federal Enumeration Index

Name   Name of each person whose usual place of abode
                   was in the institution on April 15, 1910. The
                   census includes the name of every person living
                   on April 15, 1910. Children born since April
                   15, 1910 were omitted. The surname is listed
                   first, then the given name and middle initial.

R-G   Race and gender. White is designated by the let-
                   ter "W", black by the letter "B", Mulatto by the
                   letters "Mu" and Japanese by the letter "J".
                   Males are designated by the letter "M" and fe-
                   males are designated by the letter "F".

*   Notes that the enumerator may have reported
                   the name or gender incorrectly.

A   Age at last birthday. Designated in years, un-
                   less otherwise noted with an "m" for "months".
                   Generally, children who were less than three
                   years old were described in terms of months or
                   in terms of years and months.

Relation   Relationship of each person to the institution.

Continued...

Note All persons were listed as "Single". The birthplace of each child was listed as "New York",
and the Nativity of his mother and father was
sometimes given. Refer to the original census
for this information. Also, refer to the orginal
census for the Nativity of each adult occupant
and her parents, the Language she spoke, and
her Occupation.

The enumerator occasionally ran a line through
through an Inmate's name and left the rest of
the entry blank. In such cases, the name has
been underlined in this index.

Name	R-G	A	Relation
Abbate, Mariano	WF	4	Inmate
Abbott, Mark	WM	1, 4m	Inmate
Abbott, Mary	WF	2, 2m	Inmate
Accetto, Matteo	WM	2, 9m	Inmate
Acker, Francis	WM	1, 2m	Inmate
Adams, Edith	WF	3	Inmate
Adinolf, Teresa	WF	4	Inmate
Adler, Anna	WF	2, 9m	Inmate
Adler, Annie	WF	23	Servant
Adler, John	WM	1, 11m	Inmate
Adler, Michael	WM	1, 2m	Inmate
Agnello, Guiseppina	WF	1, 10m	Inmate
Agnew, Anthony	WM	1, 10m	Inmate
Ahearn, Mary	WF	26	Nurse
Ahrens, Sarah	WF	3	Inmate
Aillinane, Edward	WM	1, 5m	Inmate
Albanese, Antonio	WM	2, 3m	Inmate
Alberti, Ella	WF	2, 10m	Inmate
Albina, Philomina	WF	1, 2m	Inmate
Alcott, Edna	WF	1, 9m	Inmate
Alexander, Veronica	WF	1, 3m	Inmate
Alirno, Edward	WM	4	Inmate
Allen, Joseph	WM	2m	Inmate
Allen, Lillian	WF	6m	Inmate
Allgaier, Clara	WF	2, 1m	Inmate
Alter, Marion	WF	1, 1m	Inmate
Alvino, Alvira	WF	2, 4m	Inmate
Alvord, Edwin	WM	2, 7m	Inmate
Alymer, Mary	WF	24	Servant
Alymn, Cahtherine	WF	38	Sister
Amaro, Giuseppe	WM	1, 8m	Inmate
Anderson, Arthur	WM	2, 4m	-
Anderson, Beatrice	WF	30	Servant
Anderson, Charles	WM	3m	Inmate
Anderson, David	WM	1, 10m	Inmate
Anderson, Helen	WF	5m	Inmate
Anderson, John	WM	5	Inmate
Andrews, Anna	WF	4m	Inmate
Andrews, Cecilia	WF	5m	Inmate
Andrews, Genevieve	WF	3m	Inmate

Andrews, Herbert	WM	2, 3m	Inmate
Andrews, Julius	WM	8m	Inmate
Anne, Madeline	WF	1, 11m	Inmate
Anniello, Assunta	WF	1m	Inmate
Anson, Margaret	WF	3	Inmate
Antilla, Mary	WF	1, 5m	Inmate
Antizi, Grethe	WF	2m	Inmate
Appel, Raphael	WM	1, 5m	Inmate
Appell, Helen	WF	21	Servant
Appleton, Aloysius	WM	20	Stenographer
Arance, Mary	WF	83	Servant
Archer, Elbie	WM	11m	Inmate
Archer, Ellen	WF	45	Nurse
Areson, Berthold	WM	2, 4m	Inmate
Ariglan, Michael	WM	8m	Inmate
Arisi, Joseph	WM	1m	Inmate
Armstrong, Franceis	WM	4m	Inmate
Armstrong, Matthis	WM	1m	Inmate
Arnot, Elizabeth	WF	30	Servant
Arnot, Margaret	WF	1, 6m	Inmate
Arnot, Miriam	WF	3	Inmate
Aroks, Mary	WF	55	Servant
Arthur, Alice	WF	5m	Inmate
Arthur, Charles	WM	4	Inmate
Artilli, Michael	WM	2, 6m	Inmate
Arvini, Tony	WM	4	Inmate
Aseardi, Carmela	WM	1, 11m	Inmate
Ashe, Kenneth	WM	8m	Inmate
Ashmand, Edward	WM	1, 10m	Inmate
Ashton, Eliza	BF	1, 1m	Inmate
Assella, Mary	WF	4	Inmate
Aster, John	WM	1, 9m	Inmate
Atkinson, James	BM	1	Inmate
Attas, Rudolph	WM	2, 3m	Inmate
Aukin, Philip	WM	1	Inmate
Auseloma, Henry	WM	2, 1m	Inmate
Austin, Joseph	WM	5m	Inmate
Autocha, Edward	WM	2, 9m	Inmate
Avendis, Joseph	WM	2, 11m	Inmate
Ayers, Benjamin	WM	1, 10m	Inmate
Aylmer, Mary	WF	9m	Inmate
Ayne, Lily	WF	2, 10m	Inmate

Ayne, Martin	WM	8m	Inmate
Babbett, Anna	WF	1m	Inmate
Babione, Aloysius	-	-	-
Babott, Julia	WF	19	Servant
Back, Harold	WM	6m	Inmate
Badrick, Leo	WM	2	Inmate
Baer, George	WM	1, 2m	Inmate
Baerlein, Augustus	WM	2, 10m	Inmate
Bagonetta, Albert	WM	2m	Inmate
Baiata, Maria	WF	1, 1m	Inmate
Bailey, Agnes	WF	26	Servant
Baker, Caroline	BF	2m	Inmate
Bala, Susie	WF	1	Inmate
Balfe, Marion	WF	9m	Inmate
Bali, Mary	WF	22	Kitchen Helper
Balleth, John	WM	3	Inmate
Ban, George	WM	1, 5m	Inmate
Baraglimca, Antonio	WM	1, 9m	Inmate
Barbara, Alice	WF	24	Servant
Barker, Miria	WF	1, 11m	Inmate
Barnes, Albert	WM	1, 2m	Inmate
Barrett, Francis	WM	10m	Inmate
Barrett, John	WM	2	Inmate
Barrett, Lilliian	WF	19	Servant
Barrett, Mary	WF	7m	Inmate
Barry, Agnes	WF	1, 2m	Inmate
Barry, David	WM	1, 2m	Inmate
Barry, James	WM	2, 10m	Inmate
Barry, Joseph	WM	2, 10m	Inmate
Bartee, Frederic	WM	1, 10m	Inmate
Barter, Mariana	BF	2, 1m	Inmate
Bartoloni, Carmelina	WF	4m	Inmate
Bastardy, Joseph	WM	2m	Inmate
Bastnofsky, Ida	WF	1m	Inmate
Batmann, Margaret	WF	3	Inmate
Bauer, Eugene	WM	3	Inmate
Bauman, William	WM	2m	Inmate
Baumann, Eugene	WM	2, 6m	Inmate
Beatty, Raymond	WM	7m	Inmate
Beck, Joseph	WM	5m	Inmate
Becker, Emma	WF	1, 6m	Inmate
Becker, Katherine	WF	1m	Inmate

Beckies, Antonetta	WF	2, 1m	Inmate
Beekman, Russell	WM	11m	Inmate
Bekely, Mary	WF	1, 5m	Inmate
Belfield, John	WM	8	Inmate
Bell, Mary	WF	5m	Inmate
Bell, Mary	WF	2, 1m	Inmate
Bellantini, Joseph	WM	1, 9m	Inmate
Bendel, Stephen	WM	2, 11m	Inmate
Benett, Helena	WF	2, 6m	Inmate
Bennett, Eleanor	WF	1m	Inmate
Bennett, Mary L.	WF	10m	Inmate
Bennett, Teresa	WF	1m	Inmate
Bennett, Violet	WF	1, 6m	Inmate
Bennett, William J.	WM	4	Inmate
Bentzel, Doleres	WM*	1, 11m	Inmate
Berg, Harry	WM	2, 3m	Inmate
Bergin, Catherine	WF	1, 7m	Inmate
Berneska, Michael	WM	10m	Inmate
Berry, James	WM	1, 11m	Inmate
Bertisky, Joseph	WM	3	Inmate
Besner, Joseph	WM	6m	Inmate
Bettigeno, Frances	WF	2, 9m	Inmate
Beuler, Angela	WF	1, 8m	Inmate
Beuson, Mary	WF	1, 4m	Inmate
Beuzel, Dolorsa	WF	19	Servant
Bhyman, Frances	WF	1, 6m	Inmate
Bianco, Alfredo	WM	1, 8m	Inmate
Biddle, Margaret	WF	21	Servant
Biddle, Rita	WF	2m	Inmate
Biegal, Catherine	WF	22	Servant
Biegel, Edward	WM	1, 4m	Inmate
Bilschen, Freda	WF	5	Inmate
Binos, John	WM	2, 8m	Inmate
Bivacqua, Josie	WF	2, 2m	Inmate
Black, Harry	WM	9m	Inmate
Black, Lillian	WF	3m	Inmate
Blackburn, George	WM	3	Inmate
Blackson, Arthur	WM	6	Inmate
Blair, Frederic	WM	1, 9m	Inmate
Blair, Henry	WM	3m	Inmate
Blake, Joseph	WM	1, 7m	Inmate
Blanchard, Julia	WF	25	Servant

Blanchard, Thelma	WF	1	Inmate
Blauss, Mary	WF	10m	Inmate
Bleakford, Mashta	WF	6	Inmate
Bleni, Rose	WF	2, 1m	Inmate
Bley, Edith	WF	2m	Inmate
Blow, James	WM	1, 10m	Inmate
Blumenthal, Charles	-M	-	-
Blumitti, Joseph	WM	6m	Inmate
Boak, Alfred	WM	8m	Inmate
Boboth, Julius	WM	2, 7m	Inmate
Bohdrum, Joseph	WM	1	Inmate
Bohdwin, Yetta	WF	16	Servant
Bole, Joseph	WM	3	Inmate
Bolger, Helen	WF	6m	Inmate
Bolla, Annie	WF	1, 3m	Inmate
Bons, Thomas	WM	1, 4m	Inmate
Bonugle, David	WM	1, 7m	Inmate
Bonwell, Frank	WM	5	Inmate
Borak, George	WM	1, 8m	Inmate
Borand, Margaret	WF	1, 9m	Inmate
Borons, Charles	WM	1, 3m	Inmate
Botz, Charles	WM	10m	Inmate
Bouen, Carrie	WF	3	Inmate
Bower, Catherine Irene	WF	46	Sister
Bowey, Anna E.	WF	67	Boarder
Bowman, Ruth	WF	1m	Inmate
Boyce, Raymond	WM	3	Inmate
Boyle, Grace	WF	4m	Inmate
Brace, Evelyn	WF	6m	Inmate
Bracken, Harold	WM	1	Inmate
Bradford, Ansyin	WM	1m	Inmate
Bradish, Philip	WM	2	Inmate
Bradley, Andrew	WM	2, 2m	Inmate
Bradley, Harry	WM	?m	Inmate
Bradly, William	WM	7	Inmate
Bradshaw, Nora	WF	2, 1m	Inmate
Brady, Agnes	WF	1, 6m	Inmate
Brady, Alice	WF	3m	Inmate
Brady, Clara	WF	35	Servant
Brady, Mary	WF	1, 5m	Inmate
Brady, Mary J.	WF	7	Inmate
Brainard, Lillian	WF	36	Servant

Brajes, Ceale	WF	1m	Inmate
Bramerd, Joseph	WM	2, 4m	Inmate
Braun, Leo	WM	1m	Inmate
Breen, Teresa	WF	19	Nurse
Breene, Anna	WF	9m	Inmate
Brehart, Elizabeth	WF	11m	Inmate
Breiting, Agnes	WF	13	Inmate
Breitrig, Lena	WF	46	Servant
Brendic, Katie	WF	25	Servant
Brennan, Agnes	WF	24	Servant
Brennan, John	WM	1, 1m	Inmate
Brennan, John F.	WM	1, 9m	Inmate
Brennan, William	WM	10m	Inmate
Brennan, William	WM	1, 2m	Inmate
Brennan, William	WM	2	Inmate
Brennan, William	WM	2, 9m	Inmate
Brent, Charles	WM	11m	Inmate
Bresler, Mary	WF	5m	Inmate
Breslin, Anna	WF	1, 11m	Inmate
<u>Brick, Joseph</u>	-	-	-
Brickman, Catherine	WF	18	Servant
Brien, Francis	WM	1, 9m	Inmate
Bright, Clarence	BM	1m	Inmate
Brill, Lillian	WF	1, 1m	Inmate
Brinkman, Eleanor	WF	4	Inmate
Briscoe, John	WM	0m	Inmate
Briskin, Aaron	WM	8m	Inmate
Brook, Staplo	WM	2, 4m	Inmate
Brooks, Robert	WM	3m	Inmate
Brown, Alice	WF	7m	Inmate
Brown, Andrew	WM	8m	Inmate
Brown, Annie	WF	20	Servant
Brown, Carrie	WF	1, 8m	Inmate
Brown, Clara	WF	2, 3m	Inmate
Brown, Edward	WM	1, 1m	Inmate
Brown, Elsie	WF	1, 1m	Inmate
Brown, Emily	WF	1, 1m	Inmate
Brown, Ernest	WM	3	Inmate
Brown, George	WM	2, 4m	Inmate
Brown, Grace	WF	1, 4m	Inmate
Brown, Helen	WF	8m	Inmate
Brown, Helen	WF	1, 7m	Inmate

Brown, Hope	WF	1, 7m	Inmate
Brown, John	WM	9m	Inmate
Brown, John	WM	1, 10m	Inmate
Brown, John	WM	2, 1m	Inmate
Brown, Joseph	WM	2, 4m	Inmate
Brown, Lillian	WF	21	Servant
Brown, Mary	WF	1, 10m	Inmate
Brown, Mary	WF	24	Servant
Brown, Paula	WF	2m	Inmate
Brown, Richard	WM	4m	Inmate
Brown, Rita	WF	6m	Inmate
Brown, Sarah	WF	4	Inmate
Brown, Thomas	WM	4m	Inmate
Browne, Harold	WM	8m	Inmate
Bruch, Percy	WM	4	Inmate
Bruidise, Victoria	WF	2m	Inmate
Bruster, Charles	WM	10m	Inmate
Bryant, Marie	WF	5m	Inmate
Buckley, John	-	-	-
Buckley, John	WM	1, 6m	Inmate
Buckridge, Laura	WF	23	Servant
Buckridge, William	WM	10m	Inmate
Bucsik, John	WM	11m	Inmate
Budkovitz, Elizabeth	WF	2, 2m	Inmate
Bulok, Martha	WF	2, 2m	Inmate
Bunchman, Eva	WF	1, 7m	Inmate
Burek, Louise	WF	7	Inmate
Burgers, William	WM	6m	Inmate
Burgy, Irene	WF	1, 2m	Inmate
Burke, Edmond	WM	2, 1m	Inmate
Burke, Luke	WM	1m	Inmate
Burke, Madeline	WF	1, 2m	Inmate
Burke, Margaret	WF	1, 6m	Inmate
Burke, Mary	WF	20	Servant
Burke, Thomas	WM	2m	Inmate
Burke, William V.	WM	2, 9m	Inmate
Burken, James	WM	2, 2m	Inmate
Burkhart, John	WM	1, 1m	Inmate
Burman, Fanny	WF	9m	Inmate
Burnes, Edward	WM	1, 2m	Inmate
Burns, Bridget	WF	1, 8m	Inmate
Burns, David	WM	3m	Inmate

Burns, Hilda	WF	2	Inmate
Burns, John	WM	1, 1m	Inmate
Burns, Lucy	WF	1, 3m	Inmate
Burns, Marguerite	WF	2, 3m	Inmate
Burns, Mrs. John	WF	78	Servant
Burns, Regina	WF	9m	Inmate
Burns, Thomas	WM	6	Inmate
Burtin, Clarence	WM	2, 5m	Inmate
Bussanik, William	WM	1	Inmate
Bussloft, Bella	WF	6m	Inmate
Buszak, Frances	WF	4m	Inmate
Butler, Helen	WF	1	Inmate
Butler, John M.	WM	1, 11m	Inmate
Butler, Joseph	WM	7m	Inmate
Buvyak, John	WM	2, 7m	Inmate
Buzzeo, Amelia	-	-	-
Byers, Bertha	WF	2	Inmate
Bylansky, Mary	WF	1, 3m	Inmate
Byrnees, Carl	WM	2, 3m	Inmate
Caballo, Joseph	WF	8m	Inmate
Cabuccio, Walter	WM	4	Inmate
Cacher, Thomas	WM	1, 5m	Inmate
Cadonia, Josie	WF	2, 11m	Inmate
Cahill, Eileen	WF	1, 5m	Inmate
Cahill, Ellen	WF	1, 7m	Inmate
Caimona, Mary	WF	-	Inmate
Calisi, Serafina	WF	1, 8m	Inmate
Callahan, Margaret	WF	1	Inmate
Calleria, Vincenza	WF	9m	Inmate
Callicci, Ester	WF	1m	Inmate
Camera, Michael	WM	2, 2m	Inmate
Camp, Charles	WM	7m	Inmate
Campanello, Frances	WF	1	Inmate
Campbell, George	WM	10m	Inmate
Campbell, Mary	WF	9m	Inmate
Campbell, Pearl	BF	5m	Inmate
Campbell, William	WM	8m	Inmate
Campomensi, Louise	WF	2, 9m	-
Canie, Basil	WM	10m	Inmate
Cannon, Delia	WF	24	Servant
Capitola, Frank	WM	1, 10m	Inmate
Capola, Alphonsus	WM	7m	Inmate

Capputo, Dominick	WM	1	Inmate
Capputo, Michael	WM	1, 9m	Inmate
Caprighone, Raffaela	WF	4m	Inmate
Capuzzo, Antony	WM	6	Inmate
Carboryl, Mary	WF	21	Servant
Cardella, Annie	WF	2m	Inmate
Cardinuto, Salvador	WM	2	Inmate
Carey, Edward	WM	4	Inmate
Carey, Eugene	WM	3	Inmate
Carey, Kohn	WM	3	Inmate
Carissa, Nicolo	WM	1, 11m	Inmate
Carlin, Gerald	WM	2, 6m	Inmate
Carlino, Carl	WM	3	Inmate
Carlson, George	WM	1, 3m	Inmate
Carlson, Lucy	WF	6m	Inmate
Carlston, Helen	WF	1, 5m	Inmate
Carmela, Maria	WF	9m	Inmate
Carmody, Ellen	WF	1, 1m	Inmate
Carney, James	WM	1, 1m	Inmate
Carnopla, Frank	WM	1	Inmate
Carolin, Patrick H.	WM	2, 2m	Inmate
Carr, Mary	WF	1, 11m	Inmate
Carroll, Catherine	WF	25	Servant
Carroll, Edward	WM	3	Inmate
Carroll, Elizabeth	WF	28	Servant
Carroll, Emanuel	WM	5m	Inmate
Carroll, John B.	WM	1, 1m	Inmate
Cartegena, Josephine	WF	4m	Inmate
Carter, Gertrude	WF	10m	Inmate
Carter, Hattie	BF	1, 5m	Inmate
Carter, Marim	WF	11	Inmate
Cartzers, Mary	WF	5m	Inmate
Casa, John	WM	1, 4m	Inmate
Casa, Joseph	WM	3m	Inmate
Casaguenda, Joseph	WM	1m	Inmate
Casale, Amaedoe	WM	1, 9m	Inmate
Casalo, Nicholas	WM	1, 1m	Inmate
Cassalo, Louis	WM	1, 9m	Inmate
Cassarena, Anna	WF	10m	Inmate
Castella, John	WM	9m	Inmate
Castle, Ida	WF	2, 11m	Inmate
Castoldi, Lizzie	WF	2, 7m	Inmate

Catani, John	WM	1, 3m	Inmate
Catauzaro, Joseph	WM	1, 10m	Inmate
Caularva, Mary	WF	2m	Inmate
Cemino, Irene	WF	1	Inmate
Chaft, Veronica	WF	1m	Inmate
Chalmers, James	WM	2, 4m	Inmate
Chamara, John	WM	2, 7m	Inmate
Chanley, Gilbert	WM	1, 5m	Inmate
Chapis, Harry	WM	3	Inmate
Chapman, Thomas	WM	1, ?m	Inmate
Chena, Margaret	WF	3m	Inmate
Chilak, Anna	WF	1m	Inmate
Chinni, John	WM	4m	Inmate
Christian, John	WM	1, 4m	Inmate
Christman, Herbert	WM	4m	Inmate
Chumley, Helen	WF	14	Servant
Cibrauck, Josephine	WF	4	Inmate
Cirdelo, Annie	WF	1, 2m	Inmate
Cisona, George	WM	1m	Inmate
Clamoskie, Anna	WF	29	Servant
Clancey, Catherine	WF	7m	Inmate
Clark, Ada Bertha	WF	44	Sister
Clark, Bridget	WF	52	Sister
Clark, Helen	WF	19	Servant
Clark, John A.	WM	2, 4m	Inmate
Clark, John F.	WM	1, 4m	Inmate
Clark, Margaret	WF	23	Servant
Clark, Mary	WF	1, 11m	Inmate
Clark, Regina	WF	2m	Inmate
Clarrser, Charles	WM	1, 9m	Inmate
Cleary, Gertrude	WF	1m	Inmate
Clertak, Anna	WF	20	Servant
Clesoka, Lillian	WF	2, 1m	Inmate
Clifford, James	WM	1, 7m	Inmate
Clinton, Patrick	WM	2, 6m	Inmate
Clinton, Ruth	WF	1	Inmate
Clover, Anthony	-	-	-
Cluccia, Jennia	WF	6m	Inmate
Cohen, Annie	WF	1, 4m	Inmate
Cohen, Julius	WM	1m	Inmate
Cohen, William	WM	1, 8m	Inmate
Cohn, Rose	WF	1	Inmate

Cohson, Lily	WF	5m	Inmate
Colas, Henry	WM	6m	Inmate
Cole, Julia	WF	21	Servant
Collins, Agnes	WF	1, 2m	Inmate
Collins, Bernard	WM	9m	Inmate
Collins, Bertha	WF	1, 9m	Inmate
Collins, David	WM	1, 4m	Inmate
<u>Collins, Gerald</u>	-	-	-
Collins, Gerald	WM	1m	Inmate
Collins, Josephine	WF	26	Nurse
Collins, Mary	WF	1m	Inmate
Collins, Thomas	WM	4	Inmate
Cologiro, Josephine	WF	1, 1m	Inmate
Colombo, Mary	WF	1, 5m	Inmate
Colville, Loretto	WF	4m	Inmate
Conchman, Wilfred	WM	1, 5m	Inmate
Concillio, Mara	WF	2, 1m	Inmate
Coneez, Elizabeth	WF	24	Servant
Conforto, Rose	WF	1, 2m	Inmate
Coniglan, Elen T.	WF	50	Sister
Conk, George	WM	1, 2m	Inmate
Conklin, Helen	WF	2, 1m	Inmate
Connell, Alice	WF	1m	Inmate
Connelly, Eleanor	WF	39	Sister
Conners, Bertrand	WM	4m	Inmate
Connolly, George	WM	11m	Inmate
Connolly, Joseph	WM	11m	Inmate
Connolly, William	WM	6m	Inmate
Connoly, Margaret	WF	1, 1m	Inmate
Connor, Margaret	WF	2, 3m	Inmate
Conquest, Jennie	BF	5m	Inmate
Conroy, Gertrude	WF	4m	Inmate
Conroy, Leonard	WM	1	Inmate
Considini, James	WM	2, 1m	Inmate
Conway, Thomas F.	WM	2, 5m	Inmate
Conzo, Michael	WM	2, 5m	Inmate
Cook, Alexander	WM	1, 5m	Inmate
Cook, Elizabeth	WF	2m	Inmate
Cook, Margaret	WF	2, 1m	Inmate
Cooper, Mary	WF	6m	Inmate
CopensaChuch, Charles	WM	4	Inmate
Coppolino, Sadie	WF	1, 10m	Inmate

Corcoran, Joseph	WM	3	Inmate
Corey, Charles	WM	10m	Inmate
Coriaci, Michale	WM	2, 10m	Inmate
Corrella, Frank	WM	1, 1m	Inmate
Corson, Achian	WM	2m	Inmate
Cortes, Philomena	WF	1, 6m	Inmate
Cosbada, Joseph	WM	0m	Inmate
Costella, Kate	WF	60	Servant
Courtney, Hannah	WF	18	Nurse
Cousin, Charles	BM	?m	Inmate
Coven, Emanuel	WM	2, 9m	Inmate
Coyle, Bernard	WM	11m	Inmate
Coyle, Edward	WM	6m	Inmate
Coyle, Frances	WF	11m	Inmate
Coyser, Sophie	WF	2, 2m	Inmate
Craad, Elizabeth	WF	30	Servant
Crane, Paul	WM	2m	Inmate
Creemant, Helen	WF	1, 9m	Inmate
Creighton, Marguerite M.	WF	60	Sister
Creighton, Mary	WF	49	Sister
Cristal, Joseph	WM	1, 7m	Inmate
Croad, Rose M.	WF	2, 1m	Inmate
Crome, Harry	WM	11m	Inmate
Crome, Mary	WF	24	Servant
Cromie, Harry	WM	8	Inmate
Cronin, Rosana	WF	10m	Inmate
Cronin, Thomas	WM	1, 2m	Inmate
Crook, James	WM	3m	Inmate
Croparie, Carmela	WF	4	Inmate
Cropsey, Alfred	WM	2m	Inmate
Crosse, John	WM	1, 5m	Inmate
Crowley, Mary	WF	11m	Inmate
Cuccinota, Mary	WF	25	Servant
Cucinotta, Alponso	WM	4	Inmate
Cullen, Christine	WF	2, 4m	Inmate
Cullen, Rose	WF	1, 2m	Inmate
Culliton, Terrance	WM	2	Inmate
Cummings, Francis	WM	2, 6m	Inmate
Cunningham, Elsie	WF	1, 7m	Inmate
Cunningham, John	WM	3	Inmate
Cunningham, Margaret	WF	44	Nurse
Cunningham, Walter	WM	1m	Inmate

Cuomo, Salvatore	WM	1, 9m	Inmate
Cupputo, Michael	WM	4	Inmate
Curcio, Antonio	WM	3	Inmate
Curran, Margaret	WF	0m	Inmate
Curran, Mary	WF	0m	Inmate
Curry, Irene	WF	23	Servant
Curtin, Mary	WF	11m	Inmate
Curtis, Lillian	WF	1, 4m	Inmate
Cyriacks, Frederic	WM	3m	Inmate
Czmor, Michael	WM	1, 9m	Inmate
Dadis, Henry	-	-	-
Dale, Regina	WF	8m	Inmate
Daley, Charles	-	-	-
Daley, Mary	WF	3m	Inmate
Daley, Paul	WM	5m	Inmate
Dalglish, Jane	WF	1, 3m	Inmate
D'Allessandro, Albina	WF	1, 5m	Inmate
Daltery, Arthur	WM	1, 6m	Inmate
Dalton, Alury V.	WM	5m	Inmate
Dalton, Eugena	WF	2, 4m	Inmate
Dalton, Harled	WM	1m	Inmate
Dalton, Robert	WM	11m	Inmate
Daly, John	WM	1m	Inmate
Daly, Joseph	WM	2, 6m	Inmate
Dampsay, Edward	WM	4	Inmate
Dan, Margaret	WF	8m	Inmate
DanBuskey, Mamie	WF	1, 3m	Inmate
Dane, Margaret	WF	1, 9m	Inmate
Danelly, Frederic	WM	1, 6m	Inmate
Daniels, Christopher	WM	1, 1m	Inmate
Dannhovitz, Joseph	WM	4m	Inmate
Dante, Beatrice	WF	10m	Inmate
Darcey, Walter	WM	10m	Inmate
Dargo, Edward	WM	1, 5m	Inmate
Darling, Vincent	WM	6m	Inmate
Darling, Walter	WM	1, 4m	Inmate
Daskell, Theodore	WM	5m	Inmate
Dausch, Gertrude	WF	8m	Inmate
Dauson, Harry	WM	2, 6m	Inmate
Dauz, Caroline	WF	2m	Inmate
Davis, Gladys	BF	1, 5m	Inmate
Davis, Grace	WF	1, 8m	Inmate

Davis, James	WM	3m	Inmate
Davis, Mary	WF	1, 9m	Inmate
Davis, Mary E.	WF	9m	Inmate
Davis, Molly	WF	2, 1m	Inmate
Davis, Nodey	WF	2, 11m	Inmate
Davis, Theodore	BM	1	Inmate
Day, Ethel	WF	8m	Inmate
Day, Joseph	WM	4	Inmate
Day, Raymond	WM	1m	Inmate
Day, Vincent	WM	5	Inmate
Deah, Ruth	WF	5	Inmate
Deas, Frederic	WM	1m	Inmate
Deas, Grace	WF	20	Servant
Deater, Paul	WM	5m	Inmate
DeDio, Maria	WF	5	Inmate
Deegan, William	WM	4	Inmate
Defio, Donato	WM	3m	Inmate
DeFord, Effie	BF	7	Inmate
DeFrance, Frances	WF	7	Inmate
DeFranco, Jennie	WF	1, 1m	Inmate
DeFranczo, Carlo	WM	2m	Inmate
Deime, Helen	WF	11m	Inmate
Delancy, Edith M.	WF	1, 10m	Inmate
Delaney, Charles	WM	4	Inmate
Delaney, Elizabeth	WF	1, 11m	Inmate
Delaney, Harvey	WM	2, 1m	Inmate
Delaney, Martin	WM	6m	Inmate
Delaney, Mary E.	WF	11m	Inmate
DeMass, Josephine	WF	6m	Inmate
Dempsey, Frances	WF	1m	Inmate
Dempsey, Mary	WF	6m	Inmate
Denka, John	WM	3	-
Denny, Marion	WF	6m	Inmate
Densco, Joseph	WM	1m	Inmate
DeRosa, Antonio	WF*	2m	Inmate
DeSimone, Eugene	WM	4	Inmate
Desola, Carolina	WF	2m	Inmate
DeStefano, Annie	WF	2, 2m	Inmate
Devan, John	WM	10m	Inmate
Devans, John	WM	2, 4m	Inmate
Devine, Alice	WF	4	Inmate
Devine, Nicholas	WM	4	Inmate

DeVito, Marie	WF	4	Inmate
Devoti, Rosa	-	-	-
Devoto, Rose	WF	1, 6m	Inmate
Dewey, Charles	WM	3	Inmate
Dewey, Oswald	WM	2, 8m	Inmate
Dey, Anna	WF	19	Servant
Dibella, Lily	WF	1, 7m	Inmate
Dicartre, Maria	WF	2, 1m	Inmate
Diehl, William	WM	1, 11m	Inmate
Digohanis, Maria	WF	11m	Inmate
Dillon, Thomas	WM	10m	Inmate
DiMaggio, Marie	WF	9m	Inmate
Dime, Rose	WF	22	Servant
Dimicelli, Thomas	WM	1, 5m	Inmate
Dinaw, Tony	WM	7m	Inmate
Dineen, Francis	WM	2m	Inmate
Diocon, Frances	WF	9	Inmate
Discopka, Nicholas	WM	2, 4m	Inmate
Dittrich, Joseph	WM	1, 6m	Inmate
Dobsai, Ella	WF	23	Servant
Dobscu, Helen	WF	2, 1m	Inmate
Docker, Cora	WF	1, 1m	Inmate
Dodd, Marie	WF	7m	Inmate
Dodge, Charles	WM	2, 11m	Inmate
Doherty, Anna	WF	1, 1m	Inmate
Doherty, Catherine	WF	2, 1m	Inmate
Doherty, Daniel	WM	0m	Inmate
Doherty, Rose	WF	19	Servant
Dolan, Edward	WM	1, 8m	Inmate
Dolson, Anne	WF	9, 5m	Inmate
Dom, Michael	WM	1, 5m	Inmate
Donacchi, Santa	WF	6	Inmate
Donahue, Francis	WM	2, 2m	Inmate
Dondeas, Joseph	WM	10m	Inmate
Donelson, Anna	-	-	-
Donnelly, Bernard	WM	6m	Inmate
Donnelly, Dorothy	WF	3	Inmate
Donnelly, Florence	WF	20	Servant
Donnelly, Joseph	WM	1, 7m	Inmate
Donnelly, Mary	WF	5m	Inmate
Donnelly, Stanislaus	WM	3	Inmate
Donohue, Charlotte	WF	1, 3m	Inmate

Donohue, George	WM	5m	Inmate
Donohue, Harold	WM	2, 6m	Inmate
Donohue, Martin	WM	1, 10m	Inmate
Donohue, Mary	WF	2, 10m	Inmate
Donovan, Julia	WF	1, 3m	Inmate
Donovan, Mary	WF	18	Nurse
Donovari, Thomas	WM	1, 9m	Inmate
Doorlon, Gerald	WM	10m	Inmate
Doran, William	WM	2, 7m	Inmate
Dorge, Hannah	WF	30	Kitchen Helper
Dorne, Tessie	WF	4m	Inmate
Dosje, Haus	WM	6	Inmate
Dotte, Pietro	WM	2, 11m	Inmate
Dottorel, Gregory	WM	1, 9m	Inmate
Douglass, Edward	WM	4	Inmate
Doville, Vincenzo	WM	11m	Inmate
Dowd, Anna	WF	1, 2m	Inmate
Dowd, Katherine	WF	15	Stenographer
Doyle, Mary	WF	2m	Inmate
Doyle, Mary	WF	10m	Inmate
Driscoll, Marguerite	WF	3	Inmate
Driscoll, Rita	WF	1, 1m	Inmate
Dryseuse, Josephine	WF	1m	Inmate
Duff, John F.	WM	1, 3m	Inmate
Duffeo, Charles	WM	5m	Inmate
Duffy, Elinor	WF	2m	Inmate
Duffy, John J.	WM	1, 9m	Inmate
Duffy, Letitia	WF	24	Servant
Duffy, Salma	WF	20	Teacher
Dugan, Mary	WF	20	Servant
Duggan, Clare	WF	1m	Inmate
Duhain, Frencis	BM	5	Inmate
Duhrkoppe, Chriistina	WF	21	Servant
Dull, Alfred	WM	2, 1m	Inmate
Dulton, Samuel	WM	3m	Inmate
Dumas, Elizabeth	WF	20	Servant
Dumest, Margaret	WF	1, 2m	Inmate
Dunn, Anna	WF	4m	Inmate
Dunn, Annie	WF	54	Servant
Dunn, Bessie	WF	4	Inmate
Dunn, Elen	WF	49	Sister
Dunn, Mary	WF	10m	Inmate

Dunning, Norman E.	WM	2, 3m	Inmate
Dunphy, Eleanor	WF	2, 8m	Inmate
Dunphy, James	WM	4m	Inmate
Duprez, Joseph	WM	1m	Inmate
Durant, Dorothy	WF	10m	Inmate
Durkin, Rosaline	WF	2m	Inmate
Durr, Martha	WF	2m	Inmate
Dusen, Joseph	WM	2, 2m	Inmate
Duston, Florence	WF	2m	Inmate
Dwyer, Catherine	WF	3	Inmate
Dwyer, Gertrude	WF	1, 6m	Inmate
Eagan, Mary	WF	1m	Inmate
Eagan, Thomas	WM	1, 4m	Inmate
Earle, Charles	WM	1m	Inmate
Easton, Marjorie	WF	0m	Inmate
Eber, Mary	WF	2, 7m	Inmate
Echternacht, Philip	WM	1, 6m	Inmate
Eckeal, Charles	WM	3	Inmate
Eckert, Edward	WM	2, 7m	Inmate
Eckstein, Louis	WM	7m	Inmate
Edler, Raymond E.	WM	2	Inmate
Eisner, Mary	WF	2, 1m	Inmate
Eldridge, Maria	WF	2m	Inmate
Eliner, Laurence	WM	1, 11m	Inmate
Elling, Hubert	WM	2, 11m	Inmate
Elliott, James	WM	1, 7m	Inmate
Ellis, Dorothy	WF	1, 1m	Inmate
Elsmith, Dorothy	WF	1m	Inmate
Engel, Elsie	WF	4m	Inmate
Eno, Jennie	WF	1, 1m	Inmate
Enrico, Albino	WM	6m	Inmate
Enright, Mary	WF	3	Inmate
Enwright, Annie	WF	9m	Inmate
Epps, Agnes	BF	-	-
Erikson, Arne	WM	2, 11m	Inmate
Erikson, George	WM	2, 11m	Inmate
Esposito, Nicholas	WM	6m	Inmate
Etzel, Joseph	WM	2, 5m	Inmate
Evanels, Peter	WM	1, 10m	Inmate
Evans, Elaine	-	-	-
Evia, Lorenzo	WM	10m	Inmate
Fagan, Joseph	WM	2, 1m	Inmate

Name			
<u>Fagan, Thomas</u>	-	-	-
Falaney, Magdalen	WF	1, 8m	Inmate
Faliska, Amy	WF	1, 8m	Inmate
Fallon, Arthur	WM	2m	Inmate
Fallon, Charles	WM	3	Inmate
Fanell, Francis	WM	8m	Inmate
Fanicelli, Louis	WM	2, 7m	Inmate
Fanning, Stephen	WM	3	Inmate
Farley, Harry	WM	4	Inmate
Farley, Helen	WF	3m	Inmate
Farley, John F.	WM	2, 9m	Inmate
Farley, John	WM	4	Inmate
Farnum, Francis	WM	1, 5m	Inmate
Farrell, Helen	WF	3	Inmate
Farrell, Mary	WF	5m	Inmate
Farrell, Veronic	WF	3	Inmate
Farrens, Michael	WM	6m	Inmate
Faruna, Jennie	WF	4m	Inmate
Fasolio, Giovanni	WM	3	Inmate
Fedeska, Mark	WM	4m	Inmate
Feeney, William	WM	2, 1m	Inmate
Feinan, Francis	WM	2, 3m	Inmate
Feit, Teresa	WF	3	Inmate
Felk, Ellen	WF	1, 3m	Inmate
Fennell, Charles	WM	1, 2m	Inmate
Ferguson, Bernard	WM	1, 8m	Inmate
Ferguson, James	WM	9m	Inmate
Ferguson, Mary	WF	22	Servant
Fermondy, Louise	WF	6	Inmate
Feron, Sarah	WF	35	Sister
Ferris, Irene	WF	1, 3m	Inmate
Ferro, Jennie	WF	1, 1m	Inmate
Ferro, Joseph	WM	1, 4m	Inmate
Ferrucha, Angelina	WF	10m	Inmate
Fiala, Rose	WF	1, 9m	Inmate
Fiancor, Jay	WM	1, 4m	Inmate
Fields, Catherine	WF	1, 10m	Inmate
Fields, James	WM	1, 9m	Inmate
Fields, Jeanette	WF	1, 4m	Inmate
Fierman, Wasgel	WM	1, 2m	Inmate
Figan, Stephen	WM	1, 1m	Inmate
Filiardi, Louis	WM	2, 8m	Inmate

Finebery, Maurice	WM	11m	Inmate
Finegan, Charles	WM	1, 3m	Inmate
Finellis, Frank	WM	1, 9m	Inmate
Finely, James	WM	23	Fireman
Finley, Ralph	WM	1, 5m	Inmate
Finnegan, Matthew	WM	2, 7m	Inmate
Firdelo, Frances	WF	2, 2m	Inmate
Fische, William	WM	1m	Inmate
Fischer, William	WM	0m	Inmate
Fishbein, Beatrice	WF	3m	Inmate
Fisher, Arthur	BM	4m	Inmate
Fisher, Edward	WM	2, 6m	Inmate
Fisher, Mary	WF	1, 10m	Inmate
Fitspatrick, Myra	WF	1, 2m	Inmate
Fitus, Mary A.	WF	1, 8m	Inmate
Fitz, Justis	-	-	-
Fitzgerald, Agnes	WF	5	Inmate
Fitzgerald, Helen	WF	11m	Inmate
Fitzgerald, Helen	WF	2	Inmate
Fitzgerald, John	WM	10m	Inmate
Fitzgerald, John	WM	1, 5m	Inmate
Fitzgerald, Winnie	WF	21	Servant
Fitzharris, Edward	WM	1	Inmate
Fitzhenry, Angela	WF	10	Inmate
Fitzhenry, Maria	WF	25	Servant
Fitzpatrick, Lewis	WM	1, 3m	Inmate
Fitzpatrick, Philip	WM	1	Inmate
Fitzsimmins, Mabel	WF	3m	Inmate
Fitzsimmons, John	WM	1, 3m	Inmate
Flaherty, Eugene	WM	1m	Inmate
Flanagan, John	WM	1, 5m	Inmate
Fleck, Rudolph	WM	2m	Inmate
Fletcher, Margaret	WF	3m	Inmate
Fletcher, Rachel	WF	8	Inmate
Floward, Loretto	WF	30	Servant
Flynn, Arnelius	WM	1, 6m	Inmate
Flynn, Mary E.	WF	3	Inmate
Fogert, Olaga	WF	1, 11m	Inmate
Foote, Frances	WF	2, 6m	Inmate
Ford, Mabel	BF	1m	Inmate
Ford, William	WM	1, 4m	Inmate
Forrest, John	WM	2, 4m	Inmate

Fortunata, Jennie	WF	1, 9m	Inmate
Foss, Tony	WM	2, 3m	Inmate
Foster, Marion	WF	11m	Inmate
Fouth, Stephen	WM	1m	Inmate
Fox, Adelbert	WF	1, 5m	Inmate
Fox, Arthur	WM	4m	Inmate
Fox, Catherine	WF	3	Inmate
Fox, Mary	-	-	Inmate
Fox, Mary	WF	1, 3m	Inmate
Frama, Mary	WF	7m	Inmate
Francis, Ellen	WF	10m	Inmate
Franklin, Felix	WM	11m	Inmate
Franklin, Mary	WF	2m	Inmate
Franks, Frank	WM	1	Inmate
Fraser, Anthony	WM	1	Inmate
Fredericks, Rudolph	WM	1, 1m	Inmate
Frederico, Nunziato	WM	2, 11m	Inmate
Frederico, Samuel	WM	7m	Inmate
Freedman, Henry	WM	5	Inmate
Freeman, Alveria	WF	2, 2m	Inmate
Freneyour, Henrietta	WF	10m	Inmate
Frich, Annie	WF	1, 5m	Inmate
Friedman, Freda	WF	10m	Inmate
Friedman, Lily	WF	2m	Inmate
Friedman, Rebecca	WF	19	Servant
Friel, Mary E.	WF	1	Inmate
Friel, Mary	WF	27	Servant
Friesbee, Harold	WM	3m	Inmate
Frisella, Ermete	WM	1, 5m	Inmate
Frisk, James	WM	4	Inmate
Fritch, John	WM	1, 6m	Inmate
Frosperino, Josephine	WF	1, 2m	Inmate
Frutter, Maurice	WM	2, 7m	Inmate
Fugginallo, Francisco	WM	5m	Inmate
Fuller, James	WM	1m	Inmate
Funn, William	BM	1, 8m	Inmate
Furst, Mary	WF	1, 8m	Inmate
Futchie, Catherine	WF	1	Inmate
Gabe, Josephine	WF	2	Inmate
Gaeghanan, Rose	WF	1, 2m	Inmate
Gaiel, Peter	WM	1, 3m	Inmate
Gale, William	WM	2, 9m	Inmate

Gali, Clement	WM	4m	Inmate
Gallager, Mary	WF	6m	Inmate
Gallagher, Edward	WM	4	Inmate
Gallagher, Margaret	WF	1, 8m	Inmate
Galli, Antonio	WM	2, 2m	Inmate
Gallizzi, Alfonso	WM	2, 11m	Inmate
Gallner, Agnes	WF	1m	Inmate
Galvin, Florence	WF	2, 10m	Inmate
Gambino, Angeline	WF	8m	Inmate
Gammel, Margaret	WF	1, 11m	Inmate
Ganey, William	WM	6m	Inmate
Gannon, Teresa	WF	1, 2m	Inmate
Gannon, Thomas	WM	2, 4m	Inmate
Ganzuroli, Francis	WM	2, 2m	Inmate
Ganzuroli, Joseph	WM	2, 2m	Inmate
Gappizzo, Guiseppe	WM	2	Inmate
Gardiner, Clara	WF	7m	Inmate
Gardiner, Edna	WF	11m	Inmate
Gardiner, Helen	WF	11m	Inmate
Gargario, Gaetanio	WM	1, 1m	Inmate
Garrett, Elizabeth	-	-	-
Garrity, Dorothy	WF	10m	Inmate
Garuppa, Mary	WF	2, 6m	Inmate
Gateson, Joseph	WM	3	Inmate
Gault, Gussie	W-	-	-
Gauser, Yetta	WF	1m	Inmate
Gay, Winifred	WF	1, 5m	Inmate
Geames, Michael	WM	1, 7m	Inmate
Geary, Louis	WM	1, 11m	Inmate
Gebhart, Constance	WF	4m	Inmate
Geighio, Genevieve	WF	2, 4m	Inmate
Geillitzen, Luke	WM	4	Inmate
Generard, James	WM	3	Inmate
George, Wilfred	WM	7m	Inmate
Gerlach, William	WM	7m	Inmate
Geruna, Giovanni	WM	3m	Inmate
Geyner, Annie	WF	1, 5m	Inmate
Ghetto, May	WF	3	Inmate
Giacome, Jennie	WF	2	Inmate
Giamina, Lucy	WF	2, 2m	Inmate
Gianio, Ersilia	WF	1	Inmate
Gibberio, Jules	WM	10m	Inmate

Gibson, Mary	WF	34	Servant
Gierney, Michael	WM	6	Inmate
Gilbert, Bernard	WM	1m	Inmate
Gilbert, Daniel	WM	2, 5m	Inmate
Gilbert, Mary	WF	1m	Inmate
Gilchrist, Thomas	WM	2	Inmate
Gilento, Joseph	WM	1m	Inmate
Gill, John	WM	8m	Inmate
Gillen, Agnes	WF	2, 6m	Inmate
Gillespie, Charles	WM	2m	Inmate
Gilsen, Joseph	WM	1, 5m	Inmate
Gilson, Margaret	WF	3m	Inmate
Ginder, Nicholas	WM	2, 3m	Inmate
Ginsberg, Ella	WF	1, 3m	Inmate
Ginter, Miriam	WF	1, 1m	Inmate
Giroux, Anna	WF	56	Sister
Gladstone, Guthbert	WM	4m	Inmate
Gladys, May	WF	3	Inmate
Gleason, Annie	WF	4	Inmate
Glennon, Howard	WM	5m	Inmate
Glennon, James	WM	2m	Inmate
Glica, Rosa	WF	9m	Inmate
Gloeggler, Elizabeth	WF	1, 4m	Inmate
Glover, Annie	BF	1, 3m	Inmate
Glynn, Margaret	WF	6	Inmate
Gochman, Fannie	WF	4m	Inmate
Goddard, William	WM	3m	Inmate
Godgos, Annie	WF	1, 1m	Inmate
Goedtel, Frank	WM	7m	Inmate
Goetz, Anna	WF	?m	Inmate
Goetz, Edward	WM	10m	Inmate
Gold, Helen	WF	1, 9m	Inmate
Goldberg, Abraham	WM	1, 9m	Inmate
Goldberg, Gerard	WM	1	Inmate
Goldblack, Julia	WF	21	Inmate
Goldblatt, Grace	WF	1	Inmate
Goldchinsky, Charles	WM	10m	Inmate
Golden, Helen	WF	1, 5m	Inmate
Goldenberg, Charles	WM	3	Inmate
Goldstein, Frances	WF	1, 9m	Inmate
Goldstein, Herman	WM	0m	Inmate
Goldstein, Miriam	WF	1m	Inmate

Goleste, Rose	WF	2m	Inmate
Gomez, Vincent	WM	9m	Inmate
Goodman, Frances	WF	10m	Inmate
Goodman, Mary	WF	11m	Inmate
Goodnough, Margaret	WF	1	Inmate
Goodrich, Elizabeth	WF	4	Inmate
Goodyear, Vera	WF	1, 2m	Inmate
Gordon, Edwin	BM	5m	Inmate
Gordon, Elizabeth	WF	1m	Inmate
Gordon, Margaret	WF	1, 1m	Inmate
Gordon, Rose	WF	0m	Inmate
Gorman, John	WM	9m	Inmate
Gotlieb, Gussie	WF	2, 9m	Inmate
Gould, Magdalen	WF	4m	Inmate
Grace, Anna	WF	1	Inmate
Grace, Maria	WF	1m	Inmate
Grace, Sarah	WF	23	Servant
Graft, William	WM	1m	Inmate
Graham, Joseph	WM	1, 3m	Inmate
Graham, William	WM	2, 6m	Inmate
Graiska, John	WM	1, 1m	Inmate
Grant, Catharine	WF	57	Sister
Grant, John	WM	2, 6m	Inmate
Grarritano, Melo	WM	1, 2m	Inmate
Grasuer, Charles	WM	2, 10m	-
Graturs, Dolores	WM*	1, 5m	Inmate
Gray, Philip	WM	1, 8m	Inmate
Gray, Robert	WM	3m	Inmate
Greco, Louis	WM	11m	Inmate
Green, Florence	WF	2, 6m	Inmate
Green, Ida	WF	1, 6m	Inmate
Green, Jennie	WF	1, 6m	Inmate
Green, Stanislaus	WM	5m	Inmate
Greenberg, Mary	WF	9m	Inmate
Greenberg, Mary	WF	1, 7m	Inmate
Grey, Joseph	WM	4m	Inmate
Grey, Molly	WF	28	Servant
Grey, Sergius	WM	5m	Inmate
Grie, Rose	WF	5	Inmate
Griesman, Antonio	WM	4m	Inmate
Griffin, Joseph	WM	1, 11m	Inmate
Griffin, Leon	WM	2, 2m	Inmate

Griffin, Teresa	WF	1, 8m	Inmate
Griffin, Terresa	BF	1, 1m	Inmate
Griffith, May	WF	24	Servant
Griffiths, Agnes	WF	2, 10m	Inmate
Griffiths, Amelia	WF	5	Inmate
Griffiths, Walter	WM	1, 9m	Inmate
Grifpu, Charles	WM	2, 1m	Inmate
Grilotti, Carmella	WF	1, 1m	Inmate
Grilotti, Stephanie	WF	4m	Inmate
Grimardi, Elizabeth	WF	1, 3m	Inmate
Grimchan, Joseph	WM	1, 11m	Inmate
Gristo, Magdalen	WF	2, 1m	Inmate
Grobotz, Katie	WF	3	Inmate
Grole, Anna	WF	6m	Inmate
Gross, Henrietta	WF	8m	Inmate
Gross, James	WM	1, 5m	Inmate
Grote, Charlotte	WF	1m	Inmate
Gruber, Isidore	WM	2, 2m	Inmate
Gruber, Ludwig	WM	1, 11m	Inmate
Gruon, Annie	WF	10m	Inmate
Gugari, Felicia	WF	6m	Inmate
Gugriotta, Salvadore	WM	6m	Inmate
Guidler, Mary	WF	2, 3m	Inmate
Guilombosky, Rosa	WF	1, 2m	Inmate
Gunn, Lena	WF	22	Servant
Gunning, Joseph	WM	10m	Inmate
Guss, Andrew	WM	2, 5m	Inmate
Gussi, Tony	WM	1, 4m	Inmate
Guwn, Annie	WF	23	Servant
Guzarde, Philip	WM	1m	Inmate
Haberbosch, Anna	WF	1, 3m	Inmate
Hackett, Margaret	WF	3	Inmate
Hadden, Gertrude	WF	43	Servant
Hagen, Harold	WM	6m	Inmate
Hagerdon, Marguerite	WF	5m	Inmate
Haggerty, John	WM	2, 9m	Inmate
Halbeg, Frederic	WM	1, 8m	Inmate
Hall, Constance	WF	2m	Inmate
Hall, Harold	WM	1, 5m	Inmate
Hall, Joseph	WM	2	Inmate
Halleck, John	WM	1m	Inmate
Halligan, Margaret	WF	2, 2m	Inmate

Halomene, Antonia	WF	6	Inmate
Halpin, Margaret	WF	10m	Inmate
Hamilton, Francis	WM	6m	Inmate
Hampton, Violet	WF	1, 9m	Inmate
Hanan, Gladys	WF	10m	Inmate
Hand, Bernardine	WF	4	Inmate
Haning, Annie	WF	35	Servant
Haningam, Patrick	WM	3	Inmate
Hank, Ann	WF	3	Inmate
Hannah, Mary	WF	2, 1m	Inmate
Hannigan, James	WM	4	Inmate
Hannon, James	WM	1, 7m	Inmate
Hanrihan, Jennie	WF	23	Servant
Hansknecht, Joseph	WM	8m	Inmate
Hansy, Catherine	WF	4	Inmate
Harder, Edna	WF	2m	Inmate
Harding, James	WM	2, 7m	Inmate
Harmon, William	WM	3	Inmate
Harnike, George	WM	3m	Inmate
Harrington, John	WM	1, 5m	Inmate
Harrington, Mary P.	WF	1, 9m	Inmate
Harrington, Vincent	WM	3	Inmate
Harris, Hazel	WF	9m	Inmate
Harris, Helen	WF	1, 1m	Inmate
Hart, Delia	WF	40	Servant
Hart, Florence	WF	7	Inmate
Hart, John	WM	6m	Inmate
Hartlieb, Lena	WF	9m	Inmate
Hartman, Edith	WF	1m	Inmate
Harvey, Clarence	BM	8	Inmate
Harvey, Raymond	WM	1m	Inmate
Haspel, Anna	WF	4m	Inmate
Haupaka, Annie	WF	20	Servant
Hausen, Dorothy	WF	9m	Inmate
Hayes, Helen	WF	2	Inmate
Hayes, Josephine	WF	9m	Inmate
Hazlewood, Agnes	WM	1, 9m	Inmate
Healey, Gertrude	WF	19	Servant
Healey, Marion	WF	10m	Inmate
Healey, William	WM	4m	Inmate
Hearing, Elsie	WF	7m	Inmate
Hearns, Nellie	WF	1, 3m	Inmate

Heffering, William	WM	3	Inmate
Heffernan, Geraldine	WF	8m	Inmate
Hegerts, Mary	WF	9m	Inmate
Heinz, Elizabeth	WF	5m	Inmate
Heistus, Muriel	WF	1m	Inmate
Heitzman, James	WM	2, 2m	Inmate
Helfer, Felise	WM*	1, 11m	Inmate
Heltzinger, Harry	WM	2, 11m	Inmate
Henderson, Albert	WM	6m	Inmate
Hendrickson, Alfred	WM	5m	Inmate
Henry, James	WM	3	Inmate
Henry, Margaret	WF	18	Servant
Henschka, Willie	WM	2, 1m	Inmate
Heppner, Robert	WM	3	Inmate
Hermann, Miriam	WF	2, 11m	Inmate
Herrick, Mabel	WF	2, 8m	Inmate
Herring, Veronica	WF	1, 3m	Inmate
Hess, Edward	WM	1, 6m	Inmate
Hess, Joseph	WM	2m	Inmate
Hess, Mary	WF	18	Servant
Hessian, Mary E.	WF	3	Inmate
Heusunot, Nellie	WF	18	Servant
Heusworth, Francis	WM	7m	Inmate
Heyman, Bernard	WM	6m	Inmate
Hickey, Jennie	WF	19	Servant
Hickey, Margaret	WF	20	Servant
Hickey, Rita	WF	1m	Inmate
Hickey, Rose	WF	21	Servant
Hickney, Gertrude	WF	2m	Inmate
Hidsey, Margaret	WF	2m	Inmate
Higgins, Gertrude	WF	9m	Inmate
Higgins, James	WM	1, 1m	Inmate
Hill, James	WM	3	Inmate
Hill, William	WM	6	Inmate
Hinman, John	WM	8m	Inmate
Hirsch, Louise	WF	9m	Inmate
Hoar, Manuel	WM	2, 1m	Inmate
Hockstille, Vincent	BM	9	Inmate
Hocman, John	WM	3	Inmate
Hodgim, Richard	WM	5	Inmate
Hoffman, Alexander	WM	3	Inmate
Hoffman, Anna	WF	22	Servant

Hoffman, Annie	WF	8m	Inmate
Hoffman, Arthur	WM	4	Inmate
Hoffman, Bessie	WF	2, 3m	Inmate
Hoffman, Joseph	WM	1, 2m	Inmate
Hoffman, Mary	WF	1, 1m	Inmate
Hoffman, Rose	WF	1, 8m	Inmate
Hogan, Elizabeth	WF	11m	Inmate
Hogan, Leonorees	WF	4	Inmate
<u>Hogan, Robert</u>	WM	-	-
Hogan, Stephen	WM	3	Inmate
Holden, William	WM	3	Inmate
Holland, John	WM	2, 3m	Inmate
Holland, Joseph	WM	1, 11m	Inmate
Holland, Rosamond	WM*	1, 4m	Inmate
Holtage, Celia	WF	1m	Inmate
Holtman, Robert	WM	4	Inmate
Holtz, Lillian	WF	2, 3m	Inmate
Homolka, Mildred	WF	5m	Inmate
Homug, Mabel	WF	10m	Inmate
Hopkins, Ethel	WF	3	Inmate
Hoppuer, Edward	WM	1, 1m	Inmate
Horan, William	WM	1	Inmate
Horn, Frederic	WM	3	Inmate
Horn, John	WM	8m	Inmate
Horn, Mabel	WF	2, 3m	Inmate
Horring, Louis	WM	1, 3m	Inmate
Hourihan, Maria	WF	8m	Inmate
Howard, Emma	WF	1, 11m	Inmate
Howard, Mary	WF	1, 4m	Inmate
Howell, Agnes	WF	3	Inmate
Hoyt, Clarence	WM	8m	Inmate
Hubom, Arthur	WM	2, 3m	Inmate
Hudden, Stephen	WM	2, 3m	Inmate
Hughes, Michael	WM	6m	Inmate
Humbert, Dagni	WF	8m	Inmate
Hungerberger, Lina	WF	20	Servant
Hungervergerr, Agnes	WF	2, 2m	Inmate
Hunt, Hugh	WM	1, 7m	Inmate
Hunt, Joseph	WM	2, 9m	Inmate
Hurley, Anna F.	WF	47	Sister
Hurley, Mary	WF	78	Housekeeper
Husehones, Dora	WF	11m	Inmate

Hussey, Maurice	WM	2, 3m	Inmate
Hyatt, Madeline	WF	7m	Inmate
Hyde, Fanny	WF	56	Servant
Hyland, Adele	WF	8m	Inmate
Hyland, Irene	WF	4	Inmate
Hyland, Joseph	WM	2	Inmate
Hzydu, Stephen	WM	2, 2m	Inmate
Idelstret, Benjamin	WM	1, 4m	Inmate
Igmanz, Anny	WF	1, 11m	Inmate
Ignolo, John	WM	1, 10m	Inmate
Ingram, Sadie	WF	2, 2m	Inmate
Ireland, Patrick	WM	4	Inmate
Irving, Raymond	WM	9m	Inmate
Iselt, Aloysius	WM	2, 3m	Inmate
Isen, Anna	WF	8m	Inmate
Italia, Jerome	WM	1, 7m	Inmate
Ivanovich, Anna	WF	1	Inmate
Iverson, Cyril	WM	?m	Inmate
Ives, Jerome	WM	1, 10m	Inmate
Jabiska, Jennie	WF	1, 11m	Inmate
Jackel, Rosina	WF	3m	Inmate
Jackson, Harold	BM	9m	Inmate
Jacobs, Rose	WF	2	Inmate
Jacovski, Michael	WM	11m	Inmate
Jadon, Francis	WM	1, 1m	Inmate
Jambarato, Jospehine	WF	6m	Inmate
Jambarato, Maria	WF	1, 4m	Inmate
James, Francis	WM	1, 2m	Inmate
James, Francis	WM	3	Inmate
Janeway, Mary	WF	11m	Inmate
Jansen, Madeline	WF	1m	Inmate
Jarvis, Paul	WM	2, 2m	Inmate
Jausen, Mary	WF	1, 10m	Inmate
Jaushopky, Frank	WM	3	Inmate
Jawas, Vincent	WM	1m	Inmate
Jefferson, Ida	WF	2	Inmate
Jenda, Henry	WM	3	Inmate
Jenkels, Mary	WF	40	Kitchen Helper
Jenkins, Alonia	WF	3	Inmate
Jenkins, Thomas	WM	1, 7m	Inmate
John, Arthur	WM	1, 10m	Inmate
Johnson, Annie	WF	24	Servant

Johnson, Charles	BM	5m	Inmate
Johnson, Edward	WM	2, 1m	Inmate
Johnson, Jane	WF	66	Maid
Johnson, Joseph	WM	1, 10m	Inmate
Johnson, Lizzie	WF	25	Servant
Johnson, Martin	WM	6m	Inmate
Johnson, Mary	WF	1, 3m	Inmate
Johnson, Mary	WF	17	Servant
Johnson, Miriam	WF	1, 4m	Inmate
Johnson, Oscar	WM	1	Inmate
Johnson, Raymond	WM	2m	Inmate
Johnson, Richard	WM	5m	Inmate
Johnson, Sarah	WF	11m	Inmate
Jollo, Patricia	WF	2	Inmate
Jones, Carl	WM	5m	Inmate
Jones, Caroline	WF	2, 7m	Inmate
Jones, Denis	WM	37	Clerk
Jones, Harold	WM	1, 5m	Inmate
Jones, Henrietta	WF	1m	Inmate
Jones, Joseph	WM	10m	Inmate
Jones, Lizzie	WF	1, 9m	Inmate
Jones, Surion	WM	30	Porter
Jordan, Philomena	WF	6m	Inmate
Jordon, Edward	WM	1, 7m	Inmate
Josef, Mary	WF	2	Inmate
Joyce, Lillian	WF	1, 6m	Inmate
Jubert, Veronica	WF	6m	Inmate
Jucbin, Monica	WF	5	Inmate
Justman, Paul	WM	1m	Inmate
Kaden, William	WM	5m	Inmate
Kahlenberg, Ruth	WF	1, 7m	Inmate
Kaiser, Annie	WF	22	Servant
Kaiser, Samuel	WM	7m	Inmate
Kakin, Christina	WF	4m	Inmate
Kalbiskie, Mary	WF	3	Inmate
Kamin, Margaret	WF	2	Inmate
Kane, Catherine	WF	3	Inmate
Kane, Francis	WM	2, 1m	Inmate
Kane, George	WM	1, 1m	Inmate
Kane, Harry	WM	1m	Inmate
Kane, Mary	WF	1	Inmate
Kantar, Charles	WM	1, 3m	Inmate

Kaplan, Eugene	WM	6	Inmate
Kaplan, Sarah	WF	3m	Inmate
Kapper, Emily	WF	5	Inmate
Karen, Minnie	WF	5	Inmate
Karkurtch, Louis	WM	1, 4m	Inmate
Karrabeen, Annie	WF	1	Inmate
Kaskoun, Frank	WM	11m	Inmate
Kathnowsky, Helen	WF	2, 7m	Inmate
Katz, Edward	WM	1, 5m	Inmate
Katz, Mary	WF	19	Servant
Kaufman, Joseph	WM	2	Inmate
Kaufman, Margaret	WF	1, 9m	Inmate
Kaufman, Victor	BM	5	Inmate
Kavney, John	WM	8m	Inmate
Kawkin, Marion	WF	7m	Inmate
Kayser, Harold	WM	1, 4m	Inmate
Kealis, Mary	WF	19	Servant
Keane, Agnes	WF	2	Inmate
Kearney, John	WM	10m	Inmate
Kearns, Harold	WM	8m	Inmate
Kearns, Mary	WF	40	Servant
Keating, Bernard	WM	1, 1m	Inmate
Keefe, James	WM	8	Inmate
Keeler, Maria	WF	2, 2m	Inmate
Keeley, Charles	WM	10m	Inmate
Keeley, Richard	WM	1, 7m	Inmate
Keir, Evelyn	WF	5m	Inmate
Keleke, Margaret	WF	1, 5m	Inmate
Kellar, Francis	WM	1m	Inmate
Kelleher, Annie	WF	24	Servant
Kelleher, John	WM	8m	Inmate
Keller, Helen	WF	63	Sister
Keller, Louis	WM	3	Inmate
Kelley, Bernard	WM	2, 7m	Inmate
Kellog, Florence	WF	2	Inmate
Kelly, Catherine	WF	24	Servant
Kelly, Edward	WM	1m	Inmate
Kelly, George	WM	1, 1m	Inmate
Kelly, Harriet	WF	3m	Inmate
Kelly, Kate	WF	1, 5m	Inmate
Kelly, Kathleen	WF	6	Inmate
Kelly, Loretto	WF	4m	Inmate

Kelly, Margaret	WF	3	Inmate
Kelly, Margaret	WF	24	Nurse
Kelly, Mary	WF	6m	Inmate
Kelly, Mary	WF	10m	Inmate
Kelly, Mary	WF	18	Servant
Kelly, Mary R.	WF	1	Inmate
Kelly, Patrick	WM	2m	Inmate
Kelly, Susan	-	-	-
Kelly, Thomas	WM	1, 8m	Inmate
Kelly, Walter	WM	4	Inmate
Kelly, William	WM	3	Inmate
Kempen, Viola	WF	7m	Inmate
Ken, Ruth	WF	1, 7m	Inmate
Kennedy, Elizabeth	WF	1, 8m	Inmate
Kennedy, Francis	WM	9	Inmate
Kennedy, Irene	WF	2, 10m	Inmate
Kennedy, John F.	WM	10m	Inmate
Kennedy, Thomas	WM	1m	Inmate
Kennedy, Thomas	WM	30	Coachman
Kenny, Frank	WM	35	Servant
Kenny, John	WM	1, 9m	Inmate
Kenoni, Elizabeth	WF	3m	Inmate
Kentan, Maria	WF	25	Maid
Kentan, Ronald	WM	5	Inmate
Kenton, Isabel	WF	5m	Inmate
Keohn, Margery	WF	5	Inmate
Kerlea, Laura	WF	8m	Inmate
Kern, Mary	WF	15	Inmate
Kerr, Arthur	WM	2, 3m	Inmate
Kerrigan, Mary	WF	2, 7m	Inmate
Kerse, Clements	WM	11m	Inmate
Kescinio, Rose	WF	1m	Inmate
Kevan, Willie	WM	2, 2m	Inmate
Kewwin, Margaret	WF	18	Servant
Kidder, Grace	WF	9m	Inmate
Kiely, Annie	WF	29	Servant
Kift, Mary	WF	2m	Inmate
Kignan, Elizabeth	-	2, 2m	-
Kilday, Mary	WF	2	Inmate
King, Dorothy	BF	9m	Inmate
King, Grace	WF	1, 4m	Inmate
King, John	WM	8m	Inmate

King, Leo	WM	1, 6m	Inmate
King, Vincent	WM	1, 2m	Inmate
Kinnane, Thomas	WM	3	Inmate
Kirby, Elizabeth	WF	2m	Inmate
Kirsch, Gregory	WM	4m	Inmate
Kirtesales, Eva	WF	10m	Inmate
Kisma, Anne	WF	1, 11m	Inmate
Kissuer, Carrie	WF	2, 11m	Inmate
Klamiskie, Ella	WF	2m	Inmate
Klepper, Lewis	WM	0m	Inmate
Klepper, Lewis	WM	1m	Inmate
Knapp, Miriam	WF	2m	Inmate
Knight, Margaret	WF	6m	Inmate
Knight, Victor	WM	1	Inmate
Kohlunski, Pauline	WF	3m	Inmate
Kohn, Abraham	WM	1, 6m	Inmate
Kohn, Anna	WF	9m	Inmate
Kolack, Joseph	WM	1, 11m	Inmate
Koldrizz, Catherine	WF	22	Servant
Kolochriez, Edward	WM	0m	Inmate
Kondelka, Antonio	WM	2, 2m	Inmate
Konnor, Dorothy	WF	1, 10m	Inmate
Korchinsky, Annie	WF	9m	Inmate
Korchinsky, John	WM	1	-
Korise, Marguerita	-	1, 11m	Inmate
Kormack, Annie	WF	1, 7m	Inmate
Kortsella, Mary	WF	4	Inmate
Kosinski, Mary	WF	2, 2m	Inmate
Kosok, Joseph	WM	9m	Inmate
Kosyak, Emma	WF	1, 1m	Inmate
Kotchmorich, Joseph	-	-	-
Kovatz, Joseph	WM	1, 3m	Inmate
Kracheska, Annie	WF	1, 5m	Inmate
Krane, Robert	-	-	-
Kraus, David	WM	1, 10m	Inmate
Krause, Elsie	WF	3	Inmate
Kreamer, Minnie	WF	21	Servant
Kreames, Teresa	WF	9m	Inmate
Krebel, Charles	WM	1, 7m	Inmate
Kress, Anna	WF	2, 4m	Inmate
Krewson, Joseph	WM	1, 9m	Inmate
Kripefiz, Julia	WF	2, 1m	Inmate

Kronenberg, Ethel	WF	11m	Inmate
Kruse, Gertrude	WF	1, 3m	Inmate
Kruwl, John	WM	1, 10m	Inmate
Kulez, Annie	WF	7	Inmate
Kummick, Cecilia	WF	1, 6m	Inmate
Kupke, Margaret	WF	3m	Inmate
Kurnicia, John	WM	2m	Inmate
Kutzer, William	WM	11m	Inmate
Labo, Luigi	WM	4	Inmate
Ladislow, Wenceslaus	WM	4m	Inmate
Laffoso, Josephine	WF	1, 5m	Inmate
Lago, Carrie	WF	2, 3m	Inmate
Lagrille, Robert	WM	1, 4m	Inmate
Lahey, Elizabeth	WF	1, 4m	Inmate
Lahey, Paul	WM	1, 5m	Inmate
Laitzer, Natalie	WF	1	Inmate
Lambardi, Marie	WF	3	Inmate
Lambert, Angela	WF	8m	Inmate
Lambert, Bertie	WM	5m	Inmate
Lambert, Rose	WF	5	Inmate
Lampinene, Annie	WF	28	Servant
Lampmen, John	WM	5m	Inmate
Land, Alice	WF	3m	Inmate
Lannon, Catherine	WF	1m	Inmate
Lansbury, Albert	WM	3	Inmate
Lansing, James	WM	3	Inmate
Laparta, Jennie	WF	1, 2m	Inmate
Lardner, Margaret	WF	50	Cook
Larkin, William	WM	4	Inmate
Laugfelt, Margaret	WF	11m	Inmate
Laulle, Margaret T.	WF	1, 9m	Inmate
Lauria, Salvador	WM	11m	Inmate
Lauson, Lillian	WF	11m	Inmate
Lavelle, Frances	WF	1, 11m	Inmate
Laveri, Garmelia	WF	11m	Inmate
Lawler, Gertrude	WF	1, 4m	Inmate
Lawlor, David	WM	2, 3m	Inmate
Lawlor, Fred	WM	2m	Inmate
Lawlor, Kenneth	WM	2, 6m	Inmate
Lawlor, Margaret	WF	11m	Inmate
Lawlor, Thomas	WM	4	Inmate
Lawrence, Gertrude	WF	1, 3m	Inmate

Lawson, Kathleen	WF	23	Servant
Lederer, Bertha	WF	1	Inmate
Lee, Alma	WF	3	Inmate
Lee, Arthur	WM	3	Inmate
Lee, Elizabeth	WF	1, 9m	Inmate
Lee, Joseph	WM	2	Inmate
Lee, Thomas	WM	2, 5m	Inmate
Leeder, Howard	WM	1, 9m	Inmate
Leggan, Mary	WF	1, 6m	Inmate
Lehman, Mary	WF	2m	Inmate
Lehman, William	WM	5	Inmate
Lehr, Yetta	WF	1m	Inmate
Leiflure, Sarah	WF	9m	Inmate
Leirrie, Adelaide	WF	2m	Inmate
Lenahan, Mary	WF	63	Sister
Lenihan, Julia	WF	1, 2m	Inmate
Lenihan, Jullian	WM	9m	Inmate
Lennon, Bertha	WF	10m	Inmate
Lennon, Nettie D.	WF	2, 5m	Inmate
Leonard, Mary	WF	1, 3m	Inmate
Leone, James	WM	1, 4m	Inmate
Lepper, Mary	WF	16	Servant
Lester, James	WM	1, 5m	Inmate
Letterio, Mary	WF	1, 2m	Inmate
Letto, Nancy	WF	1, 6m	Inmate
Levan, Ida	WF	1, 8m	Inmate
Levine, Eugene	WM	1, 11m	Inmate
Levine, Sarah	WF	1, 3m	Inmate
Levy, Joseph	WM	9m	Inmate
Levy, Pearl	WF	1, 3m	Inmate
Lewis, Alexander	WM	2	Inmate
Lewis, Andrew	WM	2m	Inmate
Lewis, Philip	WM	3	Inmate
Liberto, Leo	WM	1m	Inmate
Lica, Leo	WM	1, 3m	Inmate
Licata, Elena	WF	1, 2m	Inmate
Lidwood, Jessie	WF	9m	Inmate
Liener, Dora	WF	23	Servant
Lienn, Frank	WM	1m	Inmate
Lilleto, Leo	WM	1, 1m	Inmate
Lindsley, Eleanor	WF	1, 10m	Inmate
Linekren, Josephine	WF	1, 7m	Inmate

Lingotte, Agatha	WF	2m	Inmate
Linkovitch, Thomas	WM	1, 8m	Inmate
Lipaght, George	WM	6m	Inmate
Lipaight, Delia	WF	18	Servant
Lipps, Emma	WF	1, 8m	Inmate
Litanthie, Marguerite	WF	2, 1m	Inmate
Liverro, Lucy	WF	4m	Inmate
Livingston, Mary	WF	4	Inmate
Livingstone, Eveline	WF	2, 6m	Inmate
Livingtone, John	WM	1, 4m	Inmate
Locani, Vincent	WM	8m	Inmate
Locka, Annie	WF	4	Inmate
Loftas, Margaret	WF	20	Servant
Loftus, Margaret	WF	1m	Inmate
Loiselle, Joseph	WM	2, 10m	Inmate
Lokowitz, Antonio	WM	4m	Inmate
Long, Ester	WF	25	Servant
Longinotti, Rugela	WF	25	Servant
Longinotti, Virginia	WF	2	Inmate
Loomis, Edith	WF	2, 3m	Inmate
Lopez, Howard	WM	2, 9m	Inmate
Lopez, Joseph	WM	2, 10m	Inmate
LoPio, Antoinette	WF	1, 5m	Inmate
Lorden, Annie	WF	1, 9m	Inmate
Lory, Joseph	WM	1, 11m	Inmate
Losquadi, Concella	WF	8m	Inmate
Loughram, Nellie	WF	37	Servant
Louis, Florence	WF	8m	Inmate
Louis, James	WM	1m	Inmate
Louise, Michael	WM	2, 2m	Inmate
Lowe, Florence	WF	9m	Inmate
Luckhursh, Mary	WF	1, 2m	Inmate
Ludlum, Ella	WF	40	Nurse
Luigi, Charlotte	WF	3, 5m	Inmate
Luipoche, Mary	WF	20	Servant
Lulus, Amy	WF	1, 9m	Inmate
Lupino, Catherine	WF	10m	Inmate
Lupino, Mary	WF	28	Servant
Lurch, William	WM	2, 1m	Inmate
Lutski, Anne	WF	7	Inmate
Lutski, Charles	WM	6	Inmate
Lutzke, Mary	WF	30	Kitchen Helper

Lynch, Annie	WF	11m	Inmate
Lynch, Florence	WF	10m	Inmate
Lynch, Joseph	WM	8m	Inmate
Lynch, Loretto	WF	1, 8m	Inmate
Lynch, Margaret	WF	2m	Inmate
Lynis, Charles	WM	1m	Inmate
Lyons, Catharine	WF	54	Sister
Lyons, John	WM	6	Inmate
Lyons, Teresa	WF	1, 5m	Inmate
Lyston, Mary	WF	3m	Inmate
Macey, Abraham	WM	1, 5m	Inmate
Mack, Theodore	WM	1, 1m	Inmate
Mack, Tilly	WF	3	Inmate
Mackey, Anastasia	WF	7m	Inmate
Macom, Nellie	WF	2, 7m	Inmate
Madden, Martha	WF	1m	Inmate
Madden, Rita	WF	1, 7m	Inmate
Maggio, Joseph	WM	7m	Inmate
Maglin, Hattie	WF	1	Inmate
Mahon, John	WM	1, 5m	Inmate
Mahon, William	WM	1, 4m	Inmate
Mahoney, Peter	WM	3	Inmate
Mahoney, Thomas	WM	1, 4m	Inmate
Mainrano, Marie	WF	3	Inmate
Makak, Mary	WF	2, 3m	Inmate
Maliluson, George	WM	5	Inmate
Malmey, Alice	WF	4	Inmate
Malone, Dolores	WM*	4	Inmate
Maloney, Edward	WM	7m	Inmate
Maloney, Mary	WF	1, 5m	Inmate
Malun, Margaret	WF	3	Inmate
Maluney, John	WM	4	Inmate
Manahan, Jovh	WM	3	Inmate
Manakhan, Alice	WF	1, 8m	Inmate
Mandell, Rose	WF	11m	Inmate
Mangera, Giuseppina	WF	1, 8m	Inmate
Manning, Elizabeth	WF	41	Sister
Manning, Mary F.	WF	63	Sister
Manuelaerts, Stanislaus	WM	11m	Inmate
Marachio, Joseph	WM	2, 10m	Inmate
Maravik, John	WM	2, 1m	Inmate
Marble, Vincent	WM	4	Inmate

Marconi, Adele	WF	4m	Inmate
Marena, Angela	WF	3	Inmate
Marhart, Catherine	WF	19	Servant
Maria, John	WM	2, 7m	Inmate
Marino, Antonette	WF	8m	Inmate
Marion, Clemintina	WF	5	Inmate
Marion, Ignatius	WM	4	Inmate
Mark, Benny	WM	2	Inmate
Maroni, John	WM	1, 7m	Inmate
Marose, Gertrude	WF	1	Inmate
Marrow, Catherine	WF	4	Inmate
Martin, Charles	WM	11m	Inmate
Martin, Grace	WF	7m	Inmate
Martin, Harold J.	WM	2, 1m	Inmate
Martin, John	WM	3	Inmate
Martin, John V.	WM	3	Inmate
Martin, Joseph	WM	3	Inmate
Martin, Josephine	WF	1	Inmate
Martin, Lillian	WF	1m	Inmate
Martin, Mary	WF	11m	Inmate
Martin, Mary	WF	4	Inmate
Martin, Mary	WF	19	Servant
Martin, Mary C.	WF	2	Inmate
Martin, Walter	WM	4	Inmate
Martinus, Vincent	WM	1, 9m	Inmate
Marx, Gerald	WM	1	Inmate
Mascevell, Loretto	WF	1, 10m	Inmate
Mashart, Charles	WM	3m	Inmate
Masure, Mary	WF	9m	Inmate
Matacchiere, Mamie	WF	2, 4m	Inmate
Matacchiere, Michael	WM	1m	Inmate
Matera, Serafina	WF	2, 3m	Inmate
Mathens, Anna	WF	1, 10m	Inmate
Matje, Catherine	WF	1, 1m	Inmate
Mato, Maria	WF	1, 1m	Inmate
Matolo, Mary	WF	9m	Inmate
Matthew, Mary	WF	1, 10m	Inmate
Matthews, Paul	WM	11m	Inmate
Mauger, Mary D.	WF	3	Inmate
Mauley, Violet A.	WF	2, 1m	Inmate
Maurey, Catherine	WF	3	Inmate
Mauritz, William	WM	7m	Inmate

Mauro, Joseph	WM	4m	Inmate
Mause, Mary	WF	23	Servant
Mauspeld, Paul	WM	4m	Inmate
May, Julia	WF	2, 3m	Inmate
McAlen, Jane I.	WF	42	Sister
McAllister, Albert	WM	1, 6m	Inmate
McCabe, Gerye	WM	3	Inmate
McCabe, James	WM	3m	Inmate
McCabe, Margaret	WF	27	Servant
McCann, James	WM	3	Inmate
McCann, Lizzie	WF	36	Servant
McCanse, Violet	WF	1, 8m	Inmate
McCarthy, Annie	WF	1, 7m	Inmate
McCarthy, Augustine	WF	4	Inmate
McCarthy, Charles	WM	1, 7m	Inmate
McCarthy, Charles A.	WM	26	Doctor
McCarthy, Joseph	WM	4	Inmate
McCarthy, Julia	WF	4	Inmate
McCarthy, Mary	WM*	3m	Inmate
McCarthy, Mary	WF	7m	Inmate
McCarthy, Mary	WF	1, 1m	Inmate
McCauley, Ethel	WF	1, 7m	Inmate
McCausland, George	WM	2, 4m	Inmate
McClelland, Annie	WF	14	Inmate
McClickey, Edward	WM	2m	Inmate
McCluskey, Esther	WF	1, 3m	Inmate
McCluskey, Jennie	WF	16	Servant
McComsky, Charles	WM	2, 11m	Inmate
McConnell, Francis	WM	7m	Inmate
McCormack, Catherine	WF	40	Sister
McCormack, James	WM	7m	Inmate
McCormic, Agnes	WF	2, 2m	Inmate
McCrystal, Jane C.	WF	67	Sister
McCrystal, Michael	WM	75	Superintendant
McDermott, Edward	WM	5m	Inmate
McDermott, Helen	WF	3	Inmate
McDermott, Mary	WF	20	Servant
McDermott, Mildred	WF	19	Servant
McDermott, Virginia	WF	8m	Inmate
McDonald, Daniel	WM	5	Inmate
McDonald, Gene	WM	3	Inmate
McEvoy, Agnes	WF	3	Inmate

McFadden, Charles	WM	2, 2m	Inmate
McFoul, Elizabeth	WF	4m	Inmate
McGarry, Charles	WM	2, 10m	Inmate
McGee, Mary	WF	1, 1m	Inmate
McGee, Rose	WF	35	Servant
McGinnis, Marie	WF	3	Inmate
McGonitas, Nellie	WF	1, 8m	Inmate
McGovern, Helen	WF	6	Inmate
McGowan, Catherine	WF	19	Servant
McGowan, Frances	WF	2m	Inmate
McGowan, John	WM	7m	Inmate
McGowan, Mary	WF	1, 7m	Inmate
McGowan, Mary	WF	28	Sister
McGrath, Carrie	WF	1	Inmate
McGrath, Rickard	WM	2, 9m	Inmate
McGrory, John	WM	1	Inmate
McGrory, Margaret	WF	25	Servant
McGuin, Frank	WM	2, 4m	Inmate
McGuire, Charles	WM	1, 6m	Inmate
McGuire, Helen	WF	3m	Inmate
McGuire, Julia	WF	21	Servant
McKay, Alice	WF	1	Inmate
McKeever, Catherine	WF	4m	Inmate
McKeever, Marie	WF	24	Servant
McKeever, Robert	WM	2m	Inmate
McKeever, Rose	WF	21	Servant
McKeever, Russell	WM	2m	Inmate
McKenna, Agnes	WF	1, 4m	Inmate
McKenna, Clara	WF	50	Sister
McKenna, Irene	WF	4m	Inmate
McKenny, Frances	WF	1, 6m	Inmate
McKeogh, James	WM	8m	Inmate
McKeon, Olive	WF	14	Servant
McKieman, Agnes	WF	9m	Inmate
McKnight, Mary	WF	8m	Inmate
McKupky, Katie	WF	1, 2m	Inmate
McLaine, Thomas	WM	3	Inmate
McLane, Eleanor	BF	1, 8m	Inmate
McLarney, Mary	WF	1, 4m	Inmate
McLaughlin, Julia	WF	46	Kitchen Helper
McLaughlin, Margaret	WF	2m	Inmate
McLaughlin, Ruth	WF	2, 7m	Inmate

McLean, Thomas	WM	5m	Inmate
McLoughlin, Bridget	WF	44	Servant
McLoughlin, Francis	WM	1, 1m	Inmate
McLoughlin, Joseph	WM	7m	Inmate
McMahon, Daniel	WM	2, 5m	Inmate
McMahon, Thomas	WM	1, 11m	Inmate
McMalion, Mary	WF	1, 1m	Inmate
McMartin, Bertha	WF	1, 5m	Inmate
McMenomey, Catherine	WF	2	Inmate
McMurrough, Marie	WF	8m	Inmate
McNamara, Delia	WF	28	Servant
McNamara, Margaret	WF	4	Inmate
McNamara, Thomas	WM	1, 5m	Inmate
McNamee, Mary	WF	2m	Inmate
McNeil, Thomas	WM	1	Inmate
McNulty, Margery	WF	50	Sister
McOrmond, Wilson	WM	5	Inmate
McPhee, Catherine	WF	3	Inmate
McPherson, Carrie	WF	2, 1m	Inmate
McQuade, Francis	WM	0m	Inmate
McQuaird, Annie	WF	33	Servant
McRae, Helen	WF	28	Servant
McSherry, Harriet	WF	1, 5m	Inmate
McVey, William	WM	5	Inmate
Meade, James	WM	10m	Inmate
Mealet, Bernard	WM	2, 2m	Inmate
Mebloume, Isabel	BF	10m	Inmate
Medniger, Vincent	WM	1m	Inmate
Medralor, Helen	WF	2, 10m	Inmate
Melody, John	WM	1	Inmate
Mercadante, Lily	WF	1, 1m	Inmate
Meroney, Margaret	WF	63	Sister
Merriam, Francis	WM	4m	Inmate
Merserovich, Mary	WF	7m	Inmate
Merta, Clare	WF	2m	Inmate
Mesiniro, Josephine	WF	2, 4m	Inmate
Messina, Rosina	WF	11m	Inmate
Messman, Joseph	WM	6m	Inmate
Meurer, William	WM	3	Inmate
Meurer, William	WM	4	Inmate
Meyer, Helen	WF	3	Inmate
Meyers, Kathleen	WF	2, 11m	Inmate

Meyers, Vincent	WM	11m	Inmate
Michabe, John	WM	2m	Inmate
Michak, Anna	WF	33	Servant
Michalka, Jannie	WF	5	Inmate
Michels, Catherine	WF	11m	Inmate
Michelson, Annie	WF	2	Inmate
Middaustraw, Emil	-	-	-
Middleton, Thomas	WM	2m	Inmate
Migliaco, Loretto	WF	18	Servant
Mignalli, Mary	WF	5m	Inmate
Mignone, Pasquelina	WF	7	Inmate
Miklus, Andrew	WM	1, 11m	Inmate
Milazo, Charles	WM	2, 3m	Inmate
Mildusak, Petra	WM	1, 3m	Inmate
Miles, Ernest	WM	1m	Inmate
Miller, Antoni	WM	6m	Inmate
Miller, Catherine	WF	4	Inmate
Miller, Harold	BM	10m	Inmate
Miller, Hattie	WF	1, 6m	Inmate
Miller, Howard	WM	6m	Inmate
Miller, Joseph	WM	1m	Inmate
Miller, Joseph	WM	2m	Inmate
Miller, Lostrair	WF	1, 4m	Inmate
Miller, Margaret	WF	1, 5m	Inmate
Miller, Mary	WF	0m	Inmate
Miller, Mary	WF	1, 3m	Inmate
Miller, Mary	WF	21	Servant
Miller, Nicholas	-	-	-
Miller, Oswald	WM	2m	Inmate
Miller, Tedda	WF	11m	Inmate
Miller, William	WM	1, 11m	Inmate
Milton, George	WM	2, 11m	Inmate
Milton, Mary	W-	-	Inmate
Milza, Katie	WF	1, 4m	Inmate
Mitchell, James	WM	5m	Inmate
Mittcell, Mary	WF	1, 2m	Inmate
Mitzeger, George	WM	4m	Inmate
Moccia, Emma	WF	2, 1m	Inmate
Molotesta, Rose	WF	9m	Inmate
Mondiso, Carmela	WF	4m	Inmate
Moneald, Paoli	WF	9m	Inmate
Monroe, Florence	WF	5m	Inmate

Montagrino, Frances	WF	1, 9m	Inmate
Montrose, Sidney	WM	1, 3m	Inmate
Mooder, Anna	WF	2, 6m	Inmate
Mooney, Rachel	WF	63	Sister
Moophie, Carmella	WF	1m	Inmate
Moore, Augustin	WF	2, 11m	Inmate
Moore, George	WM	3m	Inmate
Moore, James	WM	1, 2m	Inmate
Moore, John P.	WM	2, 10m	Inmate
Moore, Kate	WF	77	Servant
Moore, Mary	WF	11m	Inmate
Moran, Annie	WF	45	Sister
Moran, Beatrice	WF	2, 10m	Inmate
Moran, Ida	WF	23	Servant
Moran, Justin	WM	3	Inmate
Moran, Mary	WF	1m	Inmate
Morano, Salvatore	WM	2m	Inmate
Morarty, John	WM	1, 3m	Inmate
Moraxo, Francis	WM	7m	Inmate
Morgan, Kathleen	WF	1, 1m	Inmate
Morgan, Margaret	WF	1, 5m	Inmate
Morre, Rose	WF	2	Inmate
Morris, Lillian	WF	1	Inmate
Morrison, Louis	WM	3	Inmate
Morse, Helen	WF	1, 6m	Inmate
Morse, Helen	WF	2, 9m	Inmate
Morton, Sarah	BF	2m	Inmate
Moscowitz, Mary	WF	1	Inmate
Mosea, Mary	WF	1, 4m	Inmate
Mosiella, Louis	WM	1, 3m	Inmate
Movanti, Mary	WF	1m	Inmate
Mucciom Margaret	WF	1, 9m	Inmate
Muir, Catherine	WF	0m	Inmate
Mulholland, Susanna	WF	45	Sister
Mullane, Mary	WF	78	Servant
Mullen, Hugh	WM	3	Inmate
Mullen, William	WM	5m	Inmate
Muller, Angel	WF	10m	Inmate
Mulligan, Joseph	WM	2, 7m	Inmate
Mulligan, Nellie	WF	31	Servant
Mullins, Jeremiah	WM	1, 2m	Inmate
Mullins, Mamie	WF	2, 9m	Inmate

Mullohan, William	WM	4	Inmate
Mulroy, Teresa	WF	38	Servant
Mulry, Parthenia	WF	28	Sister
Mulvihill, John	WM	9m	Inmate
Murphy, Annie	WF	35	Kitchen Helper
Murphy, Catherine	WF	1, 7m	Inmate
Murphy, Catherine	WF	27	Servant
Murphy, Daniel	WM	1, 4m	Inmate
Murphy, Edwin	WM	4	Inmate
Murphy, Elizabeth	WF	4m	Inmate
Murphy, Frances	WF	1, 11m	Inmate
Murphy, George	WM	2, 5m	Inmate
Murphy, Josephine	WF	3	Inmate
Murphy, Margaret	-	-	-
Murphy, Margaret	WF	1, 6m	Inmate
Murphy, Margaret	WF	2, 6m	Inmate
Murphy, Margaret	WF	17	Servant
Murphy, Mary	WF	9m	Inmate
Murphy, Mary	WF	2, 1m	Inmate
Murphy, Mary C.	WF	9m	Inmate
Murphy, Nellie	WF	1, 11m	Inmate
Murphy, Nora	WF	4m	Inmate
Murphy, Stephen	WM	2, 2m	Inmate
Murphy, Thomas	WM	3m	Inmate
Murray, Anna	WF	1, 4m	Inmate
Murray, Francis	WM	1, 2m	Inmate
Murray, James	WM	2, 2m	Inmate
Murray, Mary	WF	3m	Inmate
Museirek, Louise	WF	5m	Inmate
Muzelska, Joseph	WM	5	Inmate
Naavski, Catherine	WF	1m	Inmate
Nadler, Francis	WM	2, 5m	Inmate
Napolita, Tony	WM	8m	Inmate
Neal, Ernest	WM	7m	Inmate
Nealis, Marie	WF	8m	Inmate
Neary, Patrick	WM	2	Inmate
Neilson, Edward	WM	10m	Inmate
Neilson, Esther	WF	21	Servant
Nelson, Agnes	WF	1	Inmate
Nelson, Cyril	WM	4	Inmate
Nelson, Esther	WF	2m	Inmate
Nelson, Mary	WF	8m	Inmate

Nemitz, Julia	WF	11m	Inmate
Newman, Anna	WF	1, 8m	Inmate
Nigro, Selina	WF	5m	Inmate
Nocito, Julia	WF	1, 6m	Inmate
Noe, Mary Irene	WF	21	Nurse
Nolan, Annie	WF	1, 5m	Inmate
Nolan, Josephine	WF	7m	Inmate
Nolan, Nellie	WF	16	Servant
Nolan, Veronica	WF	2, 1m	Inmate
Nolan, Walter	WM	2	Inmate
Nolasco, Mark	WM	5	Inmate
Noonan, Annie	WF	23	Servant
Nooney, John	WM	1, 8m	Inmate
Norgush, John	WM	1, 9m	Inmate
Norman, Ellen	WF	1	Inmate
Norman, Helen	WF	1, 1m	Inmate
Norton, Irene	WF	1, 5m	Inmate
Norton, Lew	WM	17	Carpenter
Norton, Margaret	WF	35	Servant
Norton, Maria	WF	31	Servant
Notan, Mary	WF	24	Teacher
Noyes, Mary E.	WF	54	Sister
Nuellay, Catherine	WF	1, 11m	Inmate
Nuzzo, Charles	WM	6m	Inmate
Oazarillo, Maria	WF	1, 2m	Inmate
O'Brien, Bertrand	WM	2m	Inmate
O'Brien, Bridget	WF	27	Servant
O'Brien, Briget	WF	1m	Inmate
O'Brien, George F.	WM	2, 1m	Inmate
O'Brien, Gerald	WM	1, 11m	Inmate
O'Brien, Helen	WF	2, 5m	Inmate
O'Brien, James	WM	3	Inmate
O'Brien, John	WM	2	Inmate
O'Brien, Joseph	WM	1, 8m	Inmate
O'Brien, Leonora	WF	5m	Inmate
O'Brien, Margaret	WF	2, 10m	Inmate
O'Brien, Mary	WF	1, 5m	Inmate
O'Brien, Mary A.	WF	38	Sister
O'Brien, Ralph	WM	2m	Inmate
O'Brien, Timothy	WM	1, 5m	Inmate
O'Brien, William	WM	1, 10m	Inmate
O'Connell, Daniel	WM	4	Inmate

O'Connell, Mary V.	WF	2, 1m	Inmate
O'Conner, Catherine	WF	7m	Inmate
O'Connor, Anna	WF	1, 6m	Inmate
O'Connor, Annie	-	-	-
O'Connor, Bernard	WM	3	Inmate
O'Connor, Caroline	WF	22	Nurse
O'Connor, Catherine	WF	3	Inmate
O'Connor, Katie	WF	2, 2m	Inmate
O'Connor, Marguerite	WF	1, 3m	Inmate
Odell, Cecilia	WF	2, 3m	Inmate
Odell, Ralph	WM	1, 6m	Inmate
O'Donnell, Frances	WF	1, 2m	Inmate
O'Donnell, John	WM	2m	Inmate
O'Donnell, Mary	WF	1	Inmate
O'Donnell, May	WF	22	Servant
Oetner, Frederic	WM	10m	Inmate
Ogden, Mathew	WM	1, 11m	Inmate
O'Hara, Alice	WF	53	Sister
O'Hara, Annie	WF	10m	Inmate
O'Hare, Mary	WF	1m	Inmate
Oiven, Catherine	WF	21	Servant
O'Keefe, Ethel	WF	3m	Inmate
O'Keefe, Helen	WF	18	Servant
Olack, Annie	WF	1, 7m	Inmate
Ole, Norman	WM	2, 10m	Inmate
Olieska, Anna	WF	1, 5m	Inmate
Oliso, Salvatore	WM	2, 11m	Inmate
Oliver, Dominica	WM*	1m	Inmate
Oliverti, Frank	WM	1, 10m	Inmate
Oliveto, Joseph	WM	6m	Inmate
Oltner, Louise	WF	10m	Inmate
Olwell, Matthew	WM	2, 5m	Inmate
O'Malley, Josephine	WF	3	Inmate
O'Mara, Mary	WF	65	Servant
O'Neill, Gerard	WM	1, 1m	Inmate
O'Neill, Ida	WF	4	Inmate
O'Neill, Nellie	WF	7m	Inmate
O'Niel, Henry	WM	1, 1m	Inmate
O'Niel, Nora	WF	20	Servant
O'Niell, John	WM	1	Inmate
O'Niell, John	WM	6m	Inmate
Oor, Andrew	WM	7	Inmate

Name	Race/Sex	Age	Status
<u>Oprolio, Joseph</u>	-	-	-
Opsalil, Harold	WM	11m	Inmate
O'Reilly, Francis	WM	2	Inmate
O'Reilly, Mildred	WF	8m	Inmate
Orogrioan, Elizabeth	WF	1m	Inmate
O'Rourke, John	WM	3m	Inmate
O'Rourke, Peter	WM	6m	Inmate
Orr, Josephine	WF	24	Servant
Osborne, Julia	WF	2, 9m	Inmate
Osen, Oscar	WM	3m	Inmate
Oskerte, Catherine	WF	2, 1m	Inmate
Oswald, Leonard	WM	1, 11m	Inmate
Otrein, William	WM	1, 10m	Inmate
Owan, Annie	WF	2	Inmate
Owens, Annette	WF	1, 4m	Inmate
Pace, Clayton	WM	4	Inmate
Padilla, Angelina	WM*	2, 6m	Inmate
Padillo, Louise	BF	1, 5m	Inmate
Pafalik, Margaret	WF	7m	Inmate
Paigna, Vincenza	WF	2, 7m	Inmate
Pan, Joseph	WM	8	Inmate
Panrano, Ida	WF	1, 11m	Inmate
Panzella, Josephine	WF	3	Inmate
Paolo, Ecanilla	WM	2m	Inmate
Papiolenkm, John	WM	2	Inmate
Parelli, Raymond	WM	2, 7m	Inmate
Parisino, Julius	WM	1, 1m	Inmate
Parke, Norman	WM	7m	Inmate
Parker, Florence	WF	5m	Inmate
Parlak, Rose	WF	1, 8m	Inmate
Parley, Carrie	WF	23	Servant
Paroni, Joseph	WM	2, 9m	Inmate
Partysilli, Maria	WF	11m	Inmate
Pascal, Jennie	WF	2m	Inmate
Pashrirtz, Paul	WM	1, 3m	Inmate
Paskelto, Garibaldi	WM	1, 9m	Inmate
Passaro, Antonio	WM	1, 3m	Inmate
Passaro, Sylvester	WM	1, 3m	Inmate
Paster, Isidore	WM	1, 5m	Inmate
Patterson, Charles	WM	3	Inmate
Patterson, Madeline	WF	3	Inmate
Patumbo, Regina	WF	1, 2m	Inmate

Paulo, Helena	WF	5m	Inmate
Payer, Albert	WM	3	Inmate
Payne, Frances	WF	3m	Inmate
Payne, Gabriella	WF	7	Inmate
Payne, William	WM	1, 1m	Inmate
Peal, David	WM	4	Inmate
Pechman, Benjamin	WM	1, 2m	Inmate
Pechonia, Mary	WF	5m	Inmate
Pegburn, Justia	WF	2m	Inmate
Pegirella, Gasper	WM	1, 11m	Inmate
Pelatzki, Rose	WF	2	Inmate
Perlstein, Hubert	WM	5m	Inmate
Perrilion, Leon	WM	2m	Inmate
Perrino, William	WM	1, 5m	Inmate
Person, Emily	WF	2	Inmate
Peterson, Louise	WF	6m	Inmate
Peterson, Rose	WF	1, 9m	Inmate
Petrelli, Casmir	WM	2, 11m	Inmate
Petrus, Helen	WF	2, 4m	Inmate
Pettenieto, Assunta	WF	2m	Inmate
Phelan, Margaret	WF	1, 5m	Inmate
Phelps, Caroline	WF	1, 5m	Inmate
Phillips, Genevieve	WF	1, 11m	Inmate
Pica, Gaetana	WF	4m	Inmate
Picarelli, Leopold	WM	2, 1m	Inmate
Pierson, Harold	WM	2, 6m	Inmate
Pilchinni, Lily	WF	1, 2m	Inmate
Pillings, Walter	WM	1, 7m	Inmate
Pilluys, Walter	WM	3	Inmate
Pinacew, Sadie	WF	10m	Inmate
Pinto, Angelo	WM	3m	Inmate
Piremalli, Allesandro	WM	3	Inmate
Pisa, Harold	WM	7m	Inmate
Pittarelli, Millie	WF	1, 5m	Inmate
Pleezner, Joseph	WM	1, 10m	Inmate
Pleshinger, Emil	WM	4	Inmate
Pliffear, Annie	WF	1, 3m	Inmate
Pliffear, Kate	WF	3m	Inmate
Plumar, Regina	WF	4m	Inmate
Plummer, Thomas	WM	1, 2m	Inmate
Plunkitt, Maud	WF	40	Sister
Polack, Charles	WM	1, 9m	Inmate

Polcowitz, Edward	WM	7	Inmate
Ponty, Leo F.	WM	1, 6m	Inmate
Poole, Nora	WF	3	Inmate
Porter, Donald	WM	2	Inmate
Potovania, Maria	WF	1m	Inmate
Potter, Bertha	WF	6m	Inmate
Powers, Helen	WF	27	Nurse
Powers, Joseph	WM	8m	Inmate
Prefort, Charles	WM	1	Inmate
Preiser, Anna	WF	2	Inmate
Press, Harry	WM	2, 4m	Inmate
Presta, Arthur	WM	3m	Inmate
Presto, Lillian	WF	24	Servant
Preston, John	WM	1, 4m	Inmate
Price, Thomasina	WF	5	Inmate
Probe, Clara	WF	5m	Inmate
Probert, Ernest	WM	1, 1m	Inmate
Procida, Angelita	WF	1, 6m	Inmate
Prollnar, Elizabeth	WF	3m	Inmate
Prossea, Elizabeth	WF	2, 1m	Inmate
Prosser, Catherine	WF	1, 1m	Inmate
Prowley, Joseph	WM	2, 6m	Inmate
Prunty, Rose	WF	1, 11m	Inmate
Purell, Anna	WF	64	Sister
Purr, Pauline	WF	2, 3m	Inmate
Purskey, Jennie	WF	2, 1m	Inmate
Quartaro, Lucy	WF	3	Inmate
Quenser, Anna	WF	8m	Inmate
Quigley, Frances	WF	5m	Inmate
Quincey, Adrian	WM	2, 1m	Inmate
Quinn, Annie	WF	10m	Inmate
Quinn, Eugene	WM	2, 11m	Inmate
Quinn, James H.	WM	27	Doctor
Quinn, Joseph	WM	2, 4m	Inmate
Quintavalo, Giuseppina	WF	4	Inmate
Quirk, Mary	WF	5m	Inmate
Rabienin, Isabel	WF	4m	Inmate
Rabinovich, Rose	WF	19	Servant
Rabowintz, Helen	WF	7m	Inmate
Rafanelli, Ida	WF	2, 8m	Inmate
Raims, George	WM	5	Inmate
Raiser, Leo	WM	8	Inmate

Randolph, Dolores	WF	1m	Inmate
Rappuzzi, Margaret	WF	1m	Inmate
Rauber, Sarah	WF	2, 1m	Inmate
Raulton, Edward	WM	2m	Inmate
Raven, John	WM	1, 1m	Inmate
Ray, John	WM	2m	Inmate
Readdy, Anna	WF	49	Sister
Ready, Lizzie	WF	35	Servant
Reahl, Edward	WM	1, 5m	Inmate
Redican, Rose	WF	1, 6m	Inmate
Reed, Ambrose	WM	2, 9m	Inmate
Regans, Joseph	WM	11m	Inmate
Reilley, Mary E.	WF	2, 10m	Inmate
Reilly, Bridgett	WF	65	Sister
Reilly, Catherine	WF	9m	Inmate
Reilly, Catherine	WF	1, 4m	Inmate
Reilly, Flora	WF	1, 7m	Inmate
Reilly, George	WM	4	Inmate
Reilly, George F.	WM	7m	Inmate
Reilly, John	WM	4	Inmate
Reilly, Joseph	WM	1, 4m	Inmate
Reilly, Joseph	WM	2, 10m	Inmate
Rello, Romando	WM	4	Inmate
Remman, John	WM	8m	Inmate
Rentz, Hilary	WF	5m	Inmate
Repipe, Mary	WF	24	Servant
Reppyse, John	WM	9m	Inmate
Retz, William	WM	1, 10m	Inmate
Revere, Winifred	WF	2, 6m	Inmate
Reynolds, Herbert	WM	10m	Inmate
Reynolds, Mary	WF	50	Servant
Rheinhart, James	WM	3	Inmate
Rhodes, Clarence A.	WM	33	Doctor
Richards, Laurine	WM*	1, 7m	Inmate
Richards, Marie	WF	11m	Inmate
Rickey, William	WM	6m	Inmate
Rico, Loretto	WF	2, 7m	Inmate
Riddick, Clara	BF	1, 7m	Inmate
Riden, Joseph	WM	1, 8m	Inmate
Rider, Emma	WF	1, 6m	Inmate
Ridiardo, Frances	WF	0m	Inmate
Riem, George	WM	1, 4m	Inmate

Rikard, Veronica	WF	2m	Inmate
Riley, Catherine	WF	35	Servant
Riley, Dorothy	BF	5	Inmate
Rilly, Mary	WF	1, 4m	Inmate
Rindle, Paul	WM	2, 3m	Inmate
Ripkin, Rosie	WF	1, 7m	Inmate
Ritzo, Joseph	WM	2, 2m	Inmate
Ritzo, Vita	WF	2, 2m	Inmate
Robbina, Vitallo	WM	10m	Inmate
Roberto, Stephen	WM	2, 4m	Inmate
Roberts, Arthur	WM	9m	Inmate
Roberts, Bertha	WF	1, 4m	Inmate
Roberts, Frances	WF	1, 6m	Inmate
Robertson, Joseph	-	-	-
Robinskey, Mary	WF	9m	Inmate
Robinson, Agnes	WF	1, 3m	Inmate
Robinson, Alexander	WM	2, 6m	Inmate
Robinson, Augusta	WF	2m	Inmate
Robinson, Jeanette	WF	1, 4m	Inmate
Robinson, Thomas	WM	9m	Inmate
Robinson, Thomas D.	WM	7m	Inmate
Robinstein, Louis	WM	3m	Inmate
Roche, Annie	WF	1, 2m	Inmate
Roche, Maria J.	WF	47	Sister
Roche, Mary E.	WF	1, 8m	Inmate
Rochford, Annabel	WF	36	Sister
Rock, Angela	WF	1, 5m	Inmate
Rock, Janet	WF	1, 4m	Inmate
Rock, Josephine	WF	10m	Inmate
Rock, Mary	WF	20	Servant
Rodeck, William	WM	4	Inmate
Roesener, Clara	WF	6	Inmate
Rogers, Anna	WF	1m	Inmate
Rolfe, Lucia	WF	6m	Inmate
Rolos, Joseph	WM	2, 10m	Inmate
Roman, Joseph	WM	1, 11m	Inmate
Romana, Albina	WF	5m	Inmate
Romana, Frances	WF	14	Servant
Romeo, Amaizrata	WF	2, 11m	Inmate
Rooney, Catherine	WF	1	Inmate
Roony, Georgiana	WF	1, 1m	Inmate
Roopert, Genevieve	WF	1, 4m	Inmate

Rosckley, Peter	WM	2, 2m	Inmate
Rosczak, Amelia	-	-	-
Rose, Frank	WM	4	Inmate
Rose, Harry	WM	5	Inmate
Rose, Mary	WF	1, 11m	Inmate
Rosen, Henry	WM	10m	Inmate
Rosen, Ida	WF	10m	Inmate
Rosenbaum, Sadie	WF	2, 10m	Inmate
Rosenbaum, Samuel	WM	1, 4m	Inmate
Rosenberg, Joseph	WM	9m	Inmate
Rosenberg, Thomas	WM	1, 4m	Inmate
Rosencranz, Elizabeth	WF	2, 1m	Inmate
Rosenfeld, Rose	WF	11m	Inmate
Rosenstein, Florence	-	-	-
Rosenthal, Rose	WF	2, 3m	Inmate
Rosenthal, Rosie	WF	2, 10m	Inmate
Ross, Amelia	WF	2, 9m	Inmate
Ross, John	WM	1, 8m	Inmate
Rosseido, Alexander	WM	2, 6m	Inmate
Rotella, Antoniette	-	-	-
Rothleive, Mollie	WF	6m	Inmate
Rotzig, Charlotte	WM*	4	Inmate
Rovitch, Valentine	WM	2m	Inmate
Rowalska, Maria	WF	9m	Inmate
Rowan, Kenneth F.	WM	5	Inmate
Roweska, Thecla	WF	24	Servant
Rowieca, Feliz	WM	3	Inmate
Royal, Grace	BF	3	Inmate
Royster, Robert	WM	2, 9m	Inmate
Roze, Annie	WF	1, 4m	Inmate
Ruber, Charles	WM	1	Inmate
Rubiano, Josephine	WF	1m	Inmate
Rubin, Mabel	WF	1, 1m	Inmate
Rubmovich, Rose	WF	1m	Inmate
Ruddy, John	WM	2m	Inmate
Ruderson, Grace	WF	1m	Inmate
Rukin, Vincent	WM	6m	Inmate
Runge, John	WM	1, 10m	Inmate
Runger, Francis	WM	6m	Inmate
Ruse, Caroline	WF	10m	Inmate
Ruser, Rose	WF	27	Servant
Rusla, Sarah	WF	39	Sister

Russell, Mary	WF	48	Servant
Russo, Micholena	WF	1, 1m	Inmate
Rutaga, Joseph	WM	2, 1m	Inmate
Rutledge, Helen	WF	1, 6m	Inmate
Ruton, Maurice	-	-	Inmate
Rutzer, Mary	WF	19	Servant
Ryan, Annie	WF	2, 1m	Inmate
Ryan, Edward	WM	1, 8m	Inmate
Ryan, Edward	WM	4	Inmate
Ryan, Florence	WF	2, 1m	Inmate
Ryan, Georgianna	WF	19	Servant
Ryan, John	WM	1	Inmate
Ryan, John	WM	1, 6m	Inmate
Ryan, Julia	WF	1, 8m	Inmate
Ryan, Mary	WF	1, 3m	Inmate
Ryan, Mary	WF	1, 5m	Inmate
Ryan, William	WM	5m	Inmate
Sadilak, John	WM	2, 1m	Inmate
Sagmeister, Alice	WF	3m	Inmate
St. Lester, Charles	BM	3m	Inmate
Sajker, Edmond	WM	2m	Inmate
Salska, John	WM	2m	Inmate
Salucora, Lucy	WF	1, 11m	Inmate
Salupsky, Fannie	WF	1m	Inmate
Salva, Frank	WM	5	Inmate
Samiskey, Frank	WM	10m	Inmate
Samiskey, Kate	WF	33	Servant
Sancci, Mary	WF	2, 8m	Inmate
Sanders, James	WM	2, 6m	Inmate
Sanders, Rose	WF	1, 2m	Inmate
Sandutte, Viola	WF	5m	Inmate
Sannaconne, Carmine	WF	1, 1m	Inmate
Sareccia, Rosie	WF	1, 4m	Inmate
Sarkism, Helen	WF	14	Inmate
Sarkison, Teknoe	WF	38	Seamstress
Sarvanak, Pauline	WF	3m	Inmate
Satrcuno, Alphonse	WM	1, 4m	Inmate
Saunders, Edward	WM	7m	Inmate
Sauser, Mary	WF	2	Inmate
Savarese, Madeline	WF	1, 1m	Inmate
Scanlon, John	WM	4	Inmate
Scardilli, Salvador	WM	1, 10m	Inmate

Scere, Maria	WF	1, 5m	Inmate
Schall, Frederic	WM	9m	Inmate
Scherkert, Elizabeth	WF	4m	Inmate
Schillinger, Pauline	WF	20	Nurse
Schindler, Samuel	WM	1, 5m	Inmate
Schmidt, Eugene	WM	1	Inmate
Schmidt, Helen	WF	1, 8m	Inmate
Schmidt, Levcadia	WF	5m	Inmate
Schmidt, Maria	WF	22	Kitchen Helper
Schneider, Arnold	WM	1	Inmate
Schneider, Sabina	WF	1, 7m	Inmate
Schneider, Teresa	WF	2, 7m	Inmate
Schnich, Rose	WF	2, 9m	Inmate
Schryska, Ludwig	WM	4	Inmate
Schulback, Clades	WM	2, 2m	Inmate
Schultz, William	WM	1, 5m	Inmate
Schur, Alfred	WM	4	Inmate
Schwartz, Clara	WF	9	Inmate
Schwartz, Mary	WF	11m	Inmate
Schwartz, Urban	WM	3m	Inmate
Schwarz, Sadie	WF	2, 3m	Inmate
Schwintzer, Nathan	WM	1	Inmate
Sciccs, Maggie	WF	2, 8m	Inmate
Scilionraskie, Edward	WM	1, 4m	Inmate
Scitchman, Jennie	WF	4m	Inmate
Scobi, Mary	WF	1, 5m	Inmate
Scola, Emilio	WM	2m	Inmate
Scott, Denivig	WF	0m	Inmate
Scott, Robert	WM	2, 1m	Inmate
Sean, Theodore	WM	3m	Inmate
Searpati, Mary	WF	1, 2m	Inmate
Seding, Charles	WM	4m	Inmate
Seedbald, Theodore	WM	2, 2m	Inmate
Seguine, Elizabeth	WF	1m	Inmate
Seibert, James	WM	2, 6m	Inmate
Seidow, Martha	WF	2, 5m	Inmate
Seigel, Rose	WF	11m	Inmate
Seitti, Henry	WM	1, 9m	Inmate
Seliski, Frank	WM	11m	Inmate
Sell, William	WM	2, 3m	Inmate
Senemer, Annie	WF	1, 7m	Inmate
Seradt, Rose	WF	4	Inmate

Serbi, Andrew	WM	2, 6m	Inmate
Serden, Sadie	WF	6m	Inmate
Serinu, Florence	WF	1, 2m	Inmate
Sese, Dorothy	WF	11m	Inmate
Sessa, Antoinette	WF	7m	Inmate
Setley, Alice	WF	1, 2m	Inmate
Seton, Eunice	WF	1, 1m	Inmate
Setti, Americoz	WM	1, 11m	Inmate
Seukow, Helen	WF	3	Inmate
Sever, Anna	WF	6m	Inmate
Seymour, Louis	WM	1m	Inmate
Shady, Hannah	WF	1, 4m	Inmate
Shalett, Leon	WM	2m	Inmate
Shanahan, Alexander	WM	2m	Inmate
Shankey, Mary	WF	46	Sister
Shannon, Harry	WM	1m	Inmate
Shapiro, Bertha	WF	4m	Inmate
Sharp, Annie	WF	2m	Inmate
Sharp, Matthew	WM	2m	Inmate
Shaw, Sidney	WM	2, 3m	Inmate
Shea, Briget	WF	26	Servant
Shea, Clara	WF	1, 6m	Inmate
Shea, John	WM	9m	Inmate
Sheahan, Mary	WF	1, 4m	Inmate
Shelow, Alice	WF	1, 10m	Inmate
Shelton, Albert	BM	3m	Inmate
Shentsky, Elizabeth	WF	20	Servant
Sherer, John	WM	3m	Inmate
Sheridan, Lillian	WF	1	Inmate
Sheridan, Marion	WF	19	Servant
Sheridan, Martha	WF	11m	Inmate
Sherlock, Thomas	WM	2, 6m	Inmate
Sherman, Edward	WM	1m	Inmate
Sherman, Herbert	WM	1, 3m	Inmate
Sherror, James	WM	2, 9m	Inmate
Sheurer, John G.	WM	2, 1m	Inmate
Shevolin, Thomas	WM	8m	Inmate
Shields, Gertrude	WF	1, 1m	Inmate
Shields, Kathleen	WF	1m	Inmate
Shilith, Helen	WF	28	Servant
Shimco, John	WM	4	Inmate
Shirr, William	WM	1, 10m	Inmate

Shohn, Alped	WM	2, 9m	Inmate
Shore, John	WM	2, 1m	Inmate
Shrivak, Anna M.	WF	2	Inmate
Shugg, Joseph	WM	11m	Inmate
Shultz, James	WM	4m	Inmate
Shusdack, Beatrice	WF	4m	Inmate
Shuster, Rose	WF	2, 5m	Inmate
Sidesky, Abraham	WM	3	Inmate
Siegel, Annie	WF	2, 3m	Inmate
Siegel, Gregory	WM	2m	Inmate
Sign, Nicholas	WM	4m	Inmate
Siler, Edith	WF	1, 4m	Inmate
Silva, Mary	WF	1	Inmate
Silvergold, Leopold	WM	3	Inmate
Silverman, Daniel	WM	1m	Inmate
Silverman, Joseph	WM	6m	Inmate
Silvernman, Anna	WF	2, 2m	Inmate
Simmons, Harry	WM	2	Inmate
Simmons, Harry	WM	11m	Inmate
Simon, Emma	WF	2, 6m	Inmate
Simon, Jennie	WF	10m	Inmate
Sims, Clifford	WM	1, 2m	Inmate
Sinclair, Hubert	WM	4	Inmate
Singleton, Catherine	WF	1, 6m	Inmate
Sinsky, Stephen	WM	1, 4m	Inmate
Sinylebon, Margaret	WF	10m	Inmate
Sisco, Donald R.	WM	3	Inmate
Skennett, Leona	WF	5m	Inmate
Skewka, Mary	WF	22	Servant
Skidell, Sadie	WF	16	Servant
Skidgill, Margaret	WF	0m	Inmate
Skora, Henry	WF	8m	Inmate
Skully, Mamie	WF	1, 5m	Inmate
Skully, Margaret	WF	40	Servant
Slack, Frances	WF	29	Nurse
Slader, Mary	WF	1, 8m	Inmate
Slevin, Daniel	WM	1, 9m	Inmate
Smit, Rose	WF	1, 5m	Inmate
Smith, Ann M.	WF	1, 10m	Inmate
Smith, Anna	WF	1m	Inmate
Smith, Anna	WF	22	Servant
Smith, Antony	WM	4	Inmate

Smith, Bertha	WF	1	Inmate
Smith, Catherine	WF	1, 9m	Inmate
Smith, Elizabeth	WF	2m	Inmate
Smith, Florence	WM	3m	Inmate
Smith, Frank	WM	2, 6m	Inmate
Smith, Grace	WF	3	Inmate
Smith, Harry	WM	1, 5m	Inmate
Smith, Helen	WF	5m	Inmate
Smith, Helen	WF	1, 4m	Inmate
Smith, Ida	WF	1, 8m	Inmate
Smith, James	WM	?m	Inmate
Smith, James	WM	1, 4m	Inmate
Smith, James	WM	2, 4m	Inmate
Smith, James	WM	6	Inmate
Smith, John	WF	9m	Inmate
Smith, John	WM	1, 8m	Inmate
Smith, John	WM	2, 8m	Inmate
Smith, Kenneth	WM	11m	Inmate
Smith, Lillie	WF	6m	Inmate
Smith, Louisa	WF	4m	Inmate
Smith, Margaret	WF	2m	Inmate
Smith, Margaret	WF	1, 1m	Inmate
Smith, Marion	WF	1m	Inmate
Smith, Mary	WF	29	Servant
Smith, Mary P.	WF	6	Inmate
Smith, Michael, J.	WM	4	Inmate
Smith, Susie	WF	41	Servant
Smith, Tille	WF	20	Servant
Smith, William	WM	0m	Inmate
Smith, William	BM	1, 2m	Inmate
Snabel, Victor	WM	4	Inmate
Snazzo, Teresa	WF	22	Servant
Snow, Patrick	WM	2, ?m	Inmate
Sobeliski, Frank	WM	6	Inmate
Soden, May	WF	2, 8m	Inmate
Sohaick, Carl	WF	4m	Inmate
Somola, Anna	WF	5m	Inmate
Sono, Thomas	WM	2	Inmate
Sorenson, Oswald	WM	2, 4m	Inmate
Sortino, Jennie	WF	4m	Inmate
Sothern, Edgar	WM	3	Inmate
Souzzo, Josephine	WF	1	Inmate

Souzzo, Mary	WF	2, 2m	Inmate
Spadafnir, Anna	WF	1, 4m	Inmate
Sparks, Albert	WM	7m	Inmate
Spartzmina, Toby	WM	2m	Inmate
Spazetto, Demetrio	WM	3m	Inmate
Speadutis, Anglelina	WF	2, 1m	Inmate
Speigel, Katie	WF	1m	Inmate
Spellman, Jerome	WM	1, 2m	Inmate
Spiegel, Josephine	WF	1, 3m	Inmate
Spisack, Mary	WF	1, 9m	Inmate
Spitalski, Joseph	WM	1, 11m	Inmate
Spitalski, Josephine	WF	24	Servant
Spragafiga, Annie	WF	1, 3m	Inmate
Stacey, Abraham	WM	1, 3m	Inmate
Stafferi, John	WM	10m	Inmate
Stafuskey, John	WM	8m	Inmate
Stanely, Raymond	WM	2, 9m	Inmate
Stanisloskay, John	WM	1, 4m	Inmate
Stanton, Anastasia	WF	18	Servant
Stanton, Joseph	WM	2m	Inmate
Stantpu, John F.	WM	1, 8m	Inmate
Stauber, Frederic	WM	1	Inmate
Stazio, Frances	WF	5m	Inmate
Steele, Adrian	WM	1, 4m	Inmate
Stein, Edward	WM	1, 4m	Inmate
Stein, Mary	WF	4m	Inmate
Steinbicker, Albert	WM	3m	Inmate
Steiner, Harold	WM	2, 6m	Inmate
Steinman, Luke	WM	1, 6m	Inmate
Stenson, Reuberta	WF	1, 3m	Inmate
Stepheus, Edna	WF	1, 3m	Inmate
Stern, Edward	WM	3m	Inmate
Sternweiss, Andrew	WM	5m	Inmate
Stevens, Anna	WF	2, 3m	Inmate
Stevens, Frances	WF	23	Servant
Stevens, John	WM	8m	Inmate
Stevens, Joseph	WM	8m	Inmate
Stewart, Alonzo	WM	6	Inmate
Stewart, Thomas	WM	2, 1m	Inmate
Steyer, Rose	WF	11m	Inmate
Stillwell, Miriam	WF	1, 8m	Inmate
Stone, Gallista	WF	5m	Inmate

Stradetski, William	WM	2, 3m	Inmate
Stratton, Grace	WF	6m	Inmate
Strazinsky, Stephen	WM	0m	Inmate
Strentzky, John	WM	3m	Inmate
Strep, Willie	WM	1, 9m	Inmate
Strocono, Margaret	WF	1, 1m	Inmate
Stuart, Barbara	WF	2m	Inmate
Stuart, Elizabeth	WF	9m	Inmate
Stuart, Viola	WF	6m	Inmate
Stumph, Clarence	WM	7m	Inmate
Stutts, James	WM	2, 7m	Inmate
Suchicki, Vincent	WM	2m	Inmate
Suchy, Louisa	WF	6	Inmate
Sullivan, Anna	WF	3m	Inmate
Sullivan, Edward	WM	1	Inmate
Sullivan, Ernest	WM	2m	Inmate
Sullivan, George	WM	3	Inmate
Sullivan, Helen	WF	1, 1m	Inmate
Sullivan, John	WM	2m	Inmate
Sullivan, John	WM	10m	Inmate
Sullivan, John	WM	7	Inmate
Sullivan, Mary	WF	1, 3m	Inmate
Sullivan, Mary	WF	19	Servant
Sullivan, Mary	WF	24	Servant
Sullivan, Mary	WF	39	Sister
Sullivan, May	WF	22	Servant
Sullivan, Thomas	WM	3	-
Sully, Annie	WF	55	Sister
Suno, Elizabeth	WF	6m	Inmate
Suror, Edward	wM	6m	Inmate
Susanska, Victoria	WF	10m	Inmate
Sussi, Sylvan	WM	1, 3m	Inmate
Suzarde, John	WM	3	Inmate
Sweeney, Walter	WM	2, 5m	Inmate
Sweeny, Thomas	WM	2, 6m	Inmate
Taillon, George	WM	1m	Inmate
Taillon, Leontine	WF	23	Servant
Tann, Joseph	WM	1, 5m	Inmate
Tarallo, Peter	WM	1, 1m	Inmate
Tart, Frederick	WM	4	Inmate
Taubner, Harry	WM	8m	Inmate
Tavana, Salire	WM	3	Inmate

Taylor, Adrian	WM	2, 10m	Inmate
Taylor, Agnes	WF	6	Inmate
Taylor, Arthur	WM	2, 7m	Inmate
Taylor, Marion	WF	35	Nurse
Taylor, Robert	WM	3m	Inmate
Tayn, Herman	WM	1, 1m	Inmate
Teachman, Josephine	WF	1, 10m	Inmate
Teberskie, Annie	WF	4m	Inmate
Teiaroni, Paul	WM	4	Inmate
Teresam, Rose	WF	11m	Inmate
Terifori, Elizabeth	WF	27	Servant
Terrell, Margaret	WF	3	Inmate
Terriford, Marguerite	WF	3	Inmate
Tesetora, Ricarrdo	WM	3	Inmate
Tessitore, Andrew	WM	2, 9m	Inmate
Tharen, Thomas	WM	10m	Inmate
Therry, Edith	WF	11m	Inmate
Thick, Loretto	WF	2, 11m	Inmate
Thomas, Charles	BM	2m	Inmate
Thomas, Elizabeth	WF	3	Inmate
Thomas, George	WM	2, 6m	Inmate
Thomas, Mabel	WF	3	Inmate
Thomas, Ruth	BF	2m	Inmate
Thomas, Thomas D.	WM	1, 11m	Inmate
Thompson, Walter	WM	3m	Inmate
Thorndyke, George	WM	4m	Inmate
Tierney, Annette	WF	1, 5m	Inmate
Tierney, Arthur	WM	2, 2m	Inmate
Tighe, Eleanor	WF	11m	Inmate
Tighe, Mary	WF	0m	Inmate
Tillock, Carlton J.	WM	1, 11m	Inmate
Tilman, George	WM	3	Inmate
Timoney, Edward	WM	2, 10m	Inmate
Timoney, Lily	WF	3	Inmate
Tobensky, Mary	WF	20	Servant
Tobin, Mary	WF	1, 2m	Inmate
Tonelli, Joseph	WM	4m	Inmate
Tonellie, Carrie	WF	30	Servant
Tonisson, Evelyn	WF	24	Servant
Tooker, Joseph	WM	3	Inmate
Toomey, Mary	WF	19	Nurse
Topez, Manuela	WF	21	Servant

Torickey, Helen	WF	3	Inmate
Torisco, Frances	WF	4m	Inmate
Torok, Mary	WF	6m	Inmate
Torre, Peter	WM	3m	Inmate
Torre, Rosina	WF	2	Inmate
Torrenti, Adele	WF	1, 9m	Inmate
Toska, Florence	WF	6m	Inmate
Tovientino, Antoinette	WF	2m	Inmate
Tower, Nathan	WM	3m	Inmate
Tracey, Glenna	WF	18	Servant
Trapper, Frances	WF	1, 5m	Inmate
Triebe, Richard	WM	4	Inmate
Trimbly, Mildred	WF	1, 11m	Inmate
Trimby, Helen	WF	30	Kitchen Helper
Trott, Dolores	WF	11m	Inmate
Trovata, Salvadore	WM	4m	Inmate
Trovetello, Mary	WF	4m	Inmate
Trudiair, Ignatius	WM	0m	Inmate
Truman, Andrew	WM	4m	Inmate
Tuck, Raphael	WM	1, 4m	Inmate
Tuffie, John	WM	2, 3m	Inmate
Tully, Mary	WF	25	Servant
Turco, John	WM	1, 1m	Inmate
Tutorella, Joseph	WM	2	Inmate
Tuttle, Pear	WF	1, 8m	Inmate
Udile, Albert	WM	1, 5m	Inmate
Uhler, Agnes	WF	2	Inmate
Ulman, Ethel	WF	1, 6m	Inmate
Ulrich, Francis	WM	2m	Inmate
Ultra, Philomena	WF	1, 5m	Inmate
Underwood, Agetha	WF	1, 6m	Inmate
Underwood, Margaret	WF	7m	Inmate
Unterberger, Thomas	WM	2m	Inmate
Untermeyer, Camille	WF	1, 4m	Inmate
Uriharra, Joseph	WM	7m	Inmate
Urso, Isidore	WM	2	Inmate
Utley, Ruth	WF	2, 2m	Inmate
Uttner, Louis	WM	1, 11m	Inmate
Vaccia, Maria	WF	35	Sister
Valentz, Ignaria	WF	3	Inmate
Valenza, Joseph	WM	1, 10m	Inmate
Vallamount, James	WM	2, 2m	Inmate

Valmouth, Charles	WM	1, 8m	Inmate
VanEschun, Thomas	WM	3m	Inmate
VanHerten, Henrietta	WF	8m	Inmate
Vanna, Edwarda	WF	1, 3m	Inmate
VanNess, William	WM	1, 8m	Inmate
VanNostrand, Clifford	WM	2, 8m	Inmate
VanVechter, Richard	WM	2, 1m	Inmate
Varga, Anna	WF	4m	Inmate
Varga, Bertha	WF	27	Servant
Varzruski, Lilly	WF	1	Inmate
Vaule, Edmund	WM	5m	Inmate
Veera, Angelo	WM	1, 1m	Inmate
Veershan, Arthur	WM	9m	Inmate
Venere, Mary	WF	2, 10m	Inmate
Venies, William	WM	9m	Inmate
Veola, Velina	WF	2, 4m	Inmate
Veranda, Maria V.	WF	1, 11m	Inmate
Veres, Annie	WF	2, 3m	Inmate
Vernas, Teresa	WF	2, ?m	Inmate
Vernet, Walter	WM	2, 4m	Inmate
Veronovitz, Mary	WF	8m	Inmate
Verotz, Joseph	WM	8m	Inmate
Verson, Vincent	WM	1, 11m	Inmate
Vichontovitch, Pauline	WF	27	Servant
Victor, Francis	WM	3	Inmate
Victor, Otho	BM	1, 10m	Inmate
Vida, Victor	WM	2, 5m	Inmate
Vierenza, Angela	WF	6m	Inmate
Vincenjes, Julia	WF	20	Servant
Vinchizso, Peter	WM	6m	Inmate
Vineste, Rosie	WF	8m	Inmate
Viole, Ada	WF	1, 7m	Inmate
Virgensky, Stephen	WM	9m	Inmate
Vise, Samuel	WM	1	Inmate
Visoopky, Elizabeth	WF	21	Servant
Visoskay, Barnard	WM	9m	Inmate
Vito, Philipp	WM	2, 2m	Inmate
Volk, Catherine	WF	29	Servant
Volk, Thomas	WM	5	Inmate
Volker, Aloysius	WM	9m	Inmate
VonRapacki, Raymond	WM	2m	Inmate
Voydi, Joseph	WM	2m	Inmate

Voydi, Teressa	WF	20	Servant
Vulkowski, Joseph	WM	1, 4m	Inmate
Vurano, Annie	WF	2, 3m	Inmate
Wagner, Bertha	WF	5m	Inmate
Wagoner, George W.	WM	2, 10m	Inmate
Wakley, Mabel	WF	2, 7m	Inmate
Walker, Alice	WF	3	Inmate
Wallace, Elsie	WF	1, 10m	Inmate
Wallace, Joseph	WM	9m	Inmate
Walsh, Anna	WF	17	Servant
Walsh, Briget	WF	51	Sister
Walsh, Catherine	WF	3	Inmate
Walsh, Claire	WF	1, 5m	Inmate
Walsh, Helen	WF	1, 11m	Inmate
Walsh, James	WM	8m	Inmate
Walsh, Margaret	WF	5m	Inmate
Walsh, Margaret	WF	8m	Inmate
Walsh, Margaret	WF	9m	Inmate
Walsh, Margaret	WF	1, 5m	Inmate
Walters, Ignatius	WM	2, 10m	Inmate
Walters, Thomas	WM	3	Inmate
Wans, Elizabeth	WF	8m	Inmate
Ward, Harry	WM	2, 7m	Inmate
Ward, Loretto	WF	3m	Inmate
Warner, Edna	WF	1, 1m	Inmate
Warren, Gertrude	WF	1, 6m	Inmate
Warren, Ralph	WM	1, 8m	Inmate
Warren, Rita	WF	1, 11m	Inmate
Wasserstein, Mary	WF	1m	Inmate
Waters, Joseph	WM	3	Inmate
Watkins, Elinor	BF	11m	Inmate
Watson, William	WM	3m	Inmate
Weeks, Mary	WF	4	Inmate
Weeks, Paul	WM	1, 10m	Inmate
Wein, Sarah	WF	1, 9m	Inmate
Weinberg, Adolph	WM	10m	Inmate
Weinman, Herbert	WM	1, 6m	Inmate
Weintraub, Alexander	WM	1	Inmate
Weintrone, Yedda	WF	1, 1m	Inmate
Weise, Mary	WF	1, 5m	Inmate
Weiss, Albert	WM	1, 1m	Inmate
Weiss, Rose	WF	2	Inmate

Weith, Katherine	WF	3m	Inmate
Wellington, Frederic	WM	2m	Inmate
Wells, Louis	WM	4	Inmate
Welsh, Aloysius	WM	4	Inmate
Welta, Rosa	WF	1, 5m	Inmate
Wendel, Florence	WF	8	Inmate
Wenzel, Dora	WF	4	Inmate
West, John	WM	9m	Inmate
Whalen, Francis	WM	1, 7m	Inmate
Wheeler, John	WM	2m	Inmate
Whelan, Cecilia	WF	2	Inmate
Whelan, George	WM	9m	Inmate
Whiner, Helen	WF	21	Servant
White, Agnes	WF	23	Servant
White, Dorothy	WF	4m	Inmate
White, Edmund	WM	1, 4m	Inmate
White, Ethel	WF	3m	Inmate
White, John	WM	1, 2m	Inmate
White, Leslie	WF	2m	Inmate
Whitman, Jacob	WM	2, 4m	Inmate
Whitney, Donald	WM	1, 3m	Inmate
Whitney, Francis	WM	1m	Inmate
Whittaker, Dorothy	BF	1, 7m	Inmate
Whonan, Ruby	WF	2m	Inmate
Wick, Jack	WM	2, 5m	Inmate
Widdicomb, William	WM	2	Inmate
Widlake, Harold	WM	2	Inmate
Wilkins, Mary	WF	1, 1m	Inmate
William, Mary	WF	2, 3m	Inmate
Williams, Adele	BF	2m	Inmate
Williams, Catherine	BF	4m	Inmate
Williams, Ethel	WF	7	Inmate
Williams, Helen	WF	8m	Inmate
Williams, John A.	WM	2, 2m	Inmate
Williams, William	WM	2, 2m	Inmate
Williskey, Eva	WF	1, 5m	Inmate
Wilson, Anna	WF	5m	Inmate
Wilson, Charles	WM	1, 8m	Inmate
Wilson, Dorothy	WF	2, 5m	Inmate
Wilson, Edward	WM	3m	Inmate
Wilson, Frances	WF	28	Servant
Wilson, Francis	WM	4m	Inmate

Wilson, John	WM	3m	Inmate
Wilson, James F.	WM	2	Inmate
Wilson, Mabel	WF	2, 2m	Inmate
Wilson, William	WM	1, 2m	Inmate
Wingut, Mary C.	WF	1, 10m	Inmate
Winnie, Esther	WF	?m	Inmate
Winters, Dorothy	BF	1, 3m	Inmate
Winters, Margaret	WF	5m	Inmate
Winters, William	WM	1	Inmate
Wise, Helen	WF	1, 9m	Inmate
Wiseman, David	WM	1, 1m	Inmate
Withers, Adrian H.	WM	2, 11m	Inmate
Wiver, Cecilia	WF	4	Inmate
Wohle, Maurice	WM	1m	Inmate
Wolze, Margeret	WF	5	Inmate
Woods, Amelia	WF	1, 2m	Inmate
Woods, Clara	WF	9m	Inmate
Woods, Clarissa	BF	1, 4m	Inmate
Woods, Florence	WF	1m	Inmate
Woods, Gertrude	WF	11m	Inmate
Woods, Josepha	WF	5m	Inmate
Woods, Marion	WF	10m	Inmate
Woods, Mary	WF	55	Servant
Wornisley, Josephine	BF	8m	Inmate
Wright, Agnes	WF	23	Servant
Wuyciak, Joseph	WM	4	Inmate
Wykrentowiecz, Sophie	WF	5	Inmate
Wymbs, Mary	WF	1, 1m	Inmate
Wynn, Margaret	WF	3	Inmate
Wynn, Nellie	WF	4	Inmate
Yale, Augustin	WF	1, 11m	Inmate
Yasko, William	WM	2	Inmate
Yeaslanck, Marie	WF	9m	Inmate
Yeck, Joseph	WM	1, 8m	Inmate
Yeschiner, Annie	WF	4	Inmate
Yespa, John	WM	7m	Inmate
Yoemaus, Winifred	WF	7m	Inmate
Young, Rose S.	WF	1, 11m	Inmate
Yunkel, Eva	WF	1, 2m	Inmate
Yvkata, Taka	JM	1	Inmate
Zabo, Thomas	WM	1, 4m	Inmate
Zaddell, Josephine	WF	1	Inmate

Zahn, Elsie	WF	11m	Inmate
Zakel, Mary	WF	1, 11m	Inmate
Zamper, Anthony	WM	3	Inmate
Zdenick, Anna	WF	10m	Inmate
Zender, Ignatius	WF	1, 6m	Inmate
Zepit, Carmelina	WF	1, 2m	Inmate
Zeunieta, Maria	WF	1, 11m	Inmate
Zibbilie, Raffael	WM	1m	Inmate
Zizza, Mary	WF	11m	Inmate
Zmakel, Anna	WF	2, 2m	Inmate
Zuba, Maey	WF	3	Inmate
Zulch, Margaret	WF	1, 6m	Inmate

Index to the
New York State Enumeration of the Inhabitants of

The New York Foundling Hospital

175 East 68th Street
New York, New York

June 1, 1915

Assembly District No. 29
Election District No. 13
Pages 29, 31 - 48

Edwin A. Smith, Enumerator

Guide to Column Headings

in the

1915 New York State Enumeration

Name   Name of each person whose usual place of abode
                    was in the institution on June 1, 1915. The cen-
                    sus includes the name of every person living on
                    June 1, 1915. Children born since June 1, 1915
                    were omitted. The surname is listed first, then
                    the given name and middle initial.

R-G   Race and gender. White is designated by the let-
                    ter "W", black by the letter "B" and Mulatto by
                    the letters "Mu". Males are designated by the
                    letter "M" and females are designated by the
                    letter "F".

*   Notes that the enumerator may have reported
                    the name or gender incorrectly.

A   Age at last birthday. Designated in years, un-
                    less otherwise noted with an "m" for "months"
                    or "d" for "days". Generally, children who were
                    less than one year old described in terms
                    of days, although some were described in terms
                    of years and months.

Relation   Relationship of each person to the institution.

Note   The Nativity of each child was listed as "United
                    States". Refer to the orginal census for the Na-
                    tivity, Citizenship, and Occupation of adult oc-
                    cupants.

Name	R-G	A	Relation
Adamo, Rosairo	WF	80d	Patient
Adonska, Anna	WF	21	Patient
Adonska, Antonio	WM	204d	Patient
Aimee, Ruth	WF	26	Patient
Allen, May	WF	28	Patient
Allen, Ruth	WF	72d	Patient
Alocike, Joseph	WM	2	Patient
Anderson, Elizabeth	WF	4	Patient
Antello, John	WM	3	Patient
Appleton, Aloysius V.	WM	25	Stenographer
Archambault, Charlotte	WF	16	Patient
Archambault, Gabriel	WM	234d	Patient
Arnold, John	WM	178d	Patient
Ashley, Antonio	WM	3	Patient
Ashlingdon, Anna	WF	4	Patient
Atkins, Charles	WM	28d	Patient
Azabodors, Annie	WF	21	Patient
Babik, Edward	WM	1	Patient
Babik, Mary	WF	27	Patient
Bablolowski, Josephine	WF	22	Patient
Baker, Ignatius	WM	111d	Patient
Baldino, Louis	WM	55d	Patient
Barnett, Isabella	WF	3	Patient
Barthom, Mary	WF	16	Patient
Baskwillie, William	WM	3	Patient
Bastardy, Joseph	WM	5	Patient
Baxter, Edward	WM	4	Patient
Baxter, Elsie	WF	24	Patient
Baylan, John	WM	3	Patient
Beally, Walter	WM	2	Patient
Beck, Lucy	WF	59d	Patient
Becker, Herbert	WM	5	Patient
Bellino, Angelo	WF	4	Patient
Benkoski, Daris	WF	216d	Patient
Benso, Anthony	WM	4	Patient
Bernie, Francis	WM	2	Patient
Bernstein, Ralph	WM	4	Patient
Bertsole, Michael	WM	4	Patient
Beruch, Frances	WF	5	Patient
Betamie, Josephine	WF	69	Clothes Room Maid

Biazoska, John	WM	297d	Patient
Birkenbush, John	WM	27d	Patient
Bisazlio, Joseph	WM	3	Patient
Blanchfield, Catherine	WF	20	Patient
Blanchfield, Filbert	WM	246d	Patient
Blum, Midred	WF	88d	Patient
Blum, Mildred	WF	20	Patient
Bobeck, Francis J.	WM	41d	Patient
Bobeck, Gertrude	WF	22	Patient
Bohlman, Edwin	WM	4	Patient
Bonner, John	WM	70d	Patient
Bonner, Sophia	WF	20	Patient
Borkoles, Anna	WF	77d	Patient
Bosze, Kalman	WM	314d	Patient
Botsford, Anna	WF	5	Patient
Bowen, Catherine I.	WF	52	Sister of Charity
Bower, Isabella	WF	2	Patient
Bowst, Julius	WM	5	Patient
Boyle, James	WM	4	Patient
Bradley, Marie	WF	20	Patient
Brady, Thomas	WM	330d	Patient
Brantigan, Agnes	WF	301d	Patient
Braum, William	WM	4	Patient
Bray, Helen	WF	18	Nurse
Bray, Myrtle	WF	21	Nurse
Breen, Esther	WF	35	Patient
Bremen, Irene	WF	18	Nurse
Brennan, Francis	WM	3	Patient
Brennan, Gertrude	WF	17	Clothes Room Maid
Brennan, Margaret	WF	65	Sister of Charity
Brennan, Ruth	WF	4	Patient
Brent, Matilda	WF	241d	Patient
Brierso, Nettie	WF	27	Patient
Brocato, Tony	WM	4	Patient
Brocken, Stephen	WM	5	Patient
Brody, Anna	WF	5	Patient
Bronslova, Joseph	WM	246d	Patient
Brosseau, Mary	WF	26	Patient
Brown, Charles	WM	16	Carpenter App.
Brown, John	-M	275d	Patient
Brown, Mildred	WF	3	Patient
Brown, Neil	WM	4	Patient

Browne, William	WM	4	Patient
Brozoska, Catherine	WF	20	Patient
Brummer, Edward	WM	2	Patient
Brummer, Howard	WM	183d	Patient
Budley, Veronica	WF	195d	Patient
Buise, Charles	WM	3	Patient
Burbage, Mary	WF	29	Nurse
Burger, Henry	WM	117d	Patient
Burke, Mary	WF	22	Patient
Burke, Minnie	WF	19	Patient
Burke, Thomas	WM	4	Patient
Burke, Walter	WM	46d	Patient
Burnet, Sarah	WF	25	Patient
Burns, Catherine	WF	19	Patient
Burns, David	WM	6	Patient
Burns, George	WM	7d	Patient
Burns, Gertrude	WF	18	Seamstress
Burns, Josephine	WF	21	Patient
Burns, Margaret	WF	143d	Patient
Burns, Mary	WF	15d	Patient
Burns, Sadie	WF	20	Patient
Burpinbush, Mary	WF	18	Patient
Butler, Julian	WM	5	Patient
Cafara, Gertrude R.	WF	16	Seamstress
Caffora, Rita	WF	158d	Patient
Caleagono, Alfredo	WM	103d	Patient
Callahan, Anna	WF	3	Patient
Callahan, Eugene	WM	2	Patient
Callahan, Helen	WF	38	Patient
Calli, Antonina	WF	5	Patient
Callo, Elizabeth	WF	100d	Patient
Camera, Michael	WM	7	Patient
Cameron, Daniel	WM	4	Patient
Campbell, Alice	WF	6	Patient
Campbell, Peter	WM	5	Patient
Campbell, Sarah	WF	21	Patient
Campbell, William	WM	3	Patient
Cardello, Marie	WF	3	Patient
Carey, Alice	WF	50	Clothes Room Maid
Caroicle, Angelo	WM	293d	Patient
Carpentaro, Rose	WF	20	Patient
Carpenter, Camella	WF	1	Patient

Carper, Sophie	WF	8	Patient
Carrol, Elizabeth	WF	35	Clothes Room Maid
Carson, Aliver	WM	1	Patient
Cartier, Marie I.	WF	88d	Patient
Carvey, Anna	WF	19	Nurse
Casey, Jane	WF	25	Patient
Casey, Joseph M.	WM	271d	Patient
Casey, Mary	WF	24	Patient
Cashing, Fredrick	WM	3	Patient
Cassfer, Alfred	WM	83d	Patient
Catalino, Andrew	WM	5	Patient
Cerra, Anna	WF	18d	Patient
Chacles, Anna	WF	20	Patient
Charles, Sarah	WF	44	Sister of Charity
Charleston, Catherine	BF	21	Stenographer
Chase, Miriam	WF	2	Patient
Chervine, Anton	WM	4	Patient
Chinonick, Alexander	WM	3	Patient
Christopher, Anthony	WM	196d	Patient
Clair, Veronica	WF	54d	Patient
Clarendon, Hattie	WF	29	Patient
Clark, Bridget	WF	57	Sister of Charity
Cody, Agnes	WF	169d	Patient
Codz, Elizabeth	WF	22	Patient
Cogle, Elizabeth	WF	3	Patient
Cogswell, Bessie	WF	20	Seamstress
Cogswell, Rose	WF	271d	Patient
Cohen, Bella	WF	25	Patient
Cohen, Fanny	WF	20	Patient
Cohen, Lann	WM	72d	Patient
Cohen, Lillian	WF	310d	Patient
Collins, Alexander	WM	5	Patient
Collins, Bernard	WM	5	Patient
Collins, Nora	WF	181d	Patient
Comforti, Raphael	WF*	3	Patient
Connelly, Eleanor F.	WF	46	Sister of Charity
Connelly, Mary	WF	38	Waitress
Connolly, Francis	WM	5	Patient
Connolly, Harold	WM	5	Patient
Connolly, James	WM	6	Patient
Connolly, Sarah	WF	35	Sister of Charity
Cooney, Anna	WF	24	Patient

Corbin, Francis	WM	3	Patient
Corbin, Gerald	WM	6	Patient
Corcoran, Helen	WF	116d	Patient
Corcoran, Mary	WF	19	Patient
Cornell, Edward	WM	47d	Patient
Costa, Joseph	WM	4	Patient
Costello, Katherine	WF	70	Nursery Maid
Cranslon, Anna M.	WF	52d	Patient
Crearon, Mary	WF	4	Patient
Creighton, Margaret M.	WF	65	Sister of Charity
Cremer, Edith	WF	181d	Patient
Crogenti, William	WM	290d	Patient
Crood, Elizabeth	WF	37	Matron of Nursery
Crosse, John	WM	7	Patient
Crowley, Minnie	WF	21	Nurse
Crupko, Paula	WF	9d	Patient
Cucinnetta, Maria	WF	24	Patient
Cullen, Anthony T.	WM	95d	Patient
Cullen, Helen	WF	21	Patient
Cullen, Lillian	WF	5	Patient
Cullen, Regina	WF	1	Patient
Cummings, Elsie	WF	27	Patient
Cunningham, Margaret	WF	50	Nurse
Cuomo, Raffaela	WF	4	Patient
Curon, Mary	WF	32	Patient
Currie, Edna	WF	62d	Patient
Czbanja, Marie	WF	3	Patient
Czupko, Teresa	WF	29	Patient
Dailey, Jane	WF	24	Patient
Daniels, Joseph	WM	47d	Patient
Dapolitana, Rosie	WF	31	Patient
Dareb, Mary	WF	21d	Patient
Darey, Katherine	WF	23	Patient
Darkerson, Helen	WF	20	Clothes Room Maid
Darkerson, Lakarita	WF	39	Clothes Room Maid
Davis, Henry	WM	104d	Patient
Deegan, Ceceilia	WF	1	Patient
Delaney, Nora	WF	29	Nurse
DeLia, Frank	WM	7	Patient
DelPescio, Angeline	WF	1	Patient
Demike, Anna	WF	5	Patient
Dening, Mollie	WF	23	Patient

Deodata, Alfredo	WM	1	Patient
Desmith, Paula	WF	340d	Patient
Devery, Mary	WF	3	Patient
Devlin, Charles	WM	52d	Patient
Deyneka, Michalina	WF	210d	Patient
DiCicco, Eva	WF	70d	Patient
DiCicco, Minnie	WF	20	Patient
Diffenback, Gertrude	WF	243d	Patient
Digbey, Mary	WF	17	Nurse
Dill, Mary	WF	6	Patient
Dinsdor, Frank	WM	3	Patient
Ditomo, Nicholas	WM	4	Patient
Dolan, Nellie	WF	4	Patient
Donahue, Agnes	WF	20	Patient
Drewbeka, Appolia	WF	89d	Patient
Due, Dorothy	WF	16	Patient
Duffenback, Louise	WF	18	Seamstress
Dugan, Maria	WF	18	Seamstress
Duggan, Margaret	WF	22d	Patient
Duggan, Margaret	WF	32	Patient
Duggan, Teresa	WF	17d	Patient
Dumphy, Agnes	WF	35d	Patient
Dumphy, Bridget	WF	30	Patient
Dumphy, Edward	WF*	98d	Patient
Dunn, Anna	WF	37	Patient
Dunn, Charles	WM	5	Patient
Dunn, Delia	WF	28	Patient
Dunn, Ella	WF	55	Sister of Charity
Dunn, Margaret	WF	26	Patient
Dwyer, Joseph	WM	2	Patient
Dwyer, William	WM	4	Patient
Eacuvetto, Anthony	WM	1	Patient
Edgerton, Elizabeth	WF	1	Patient
Edgnon, James	WM	166d	Patient
Edvanak, William	WM	132d	Patient
Edwards, Joseph	WM	3	Patient
Egan, Catherine O.	WF	31	Sister of Charity
Egan, Johanna	WF	2	Patient
Egan, Margaret	WF	17	Patient
Egan, Mary	WF	5	Patient
Egan, Nellie	WF	37	Patient
Elder, Helen	WF	19	Patient

Elder, Joseph	WM	14d	Patient
Elsner, Virginia	WF	143d	Patient
English, Adelaide	WF	4	Patient
Esposito, Nicholas	WM	6	Patient
Evens, Alexander	WM	40d	Patient
Falino, Margaret	WF	260d	Patient
Farrell, Anna	WF	2	Patient
Farrell, Margaret	WF	23	Patient
Fatara, Mary	WF	4	Patient
Fedozyk, Maria	WF	2	Patient
Ferguson, Harold	WM	109d	Patient
Ferguson, Leonia	WF	4	Patient
Fern, Sarah	WF	50	Sister of Charity
Finley, Elizabeth	WF	36	Patient
Finley, Nettie	WF	22	Patient
Finley, Robert	WM	49d	Patient
Finn, Margaret	WF	3	Patient
Finnegan, Catherine	WF	289d	Patient
Finnegan, Catherine	WF	40	Patient
Finnegan, Thomas	WM	289d	Patient
Finnelly, John	WM	4	Patient
Fitch, Helen	WF	33d	Patient
Fitzgerald, Matthew	WM	3	Patient
Flaherty, Francis	WM	3	Patient
Flaherty, Mary	WF	50d	Patient
Flaherty, Minnie	WF	25	Patient
Flannigan, Mercella	WF	4	Patient
Fleer, Leanor	WF	102d	Patient
Fletcher, Anna	WF	16	Nurse
Ford, Myrtle F.	WF	3	Patient
Forquignon, Howard	WM	6	Patient
Fox, Catherine	WF	18	Patient
Fox, James	WM	279d	Patient
Fox, Joseph	WM	61d	Patient
Fredricks, Margaret	WF	248d	Patient
Fredwitz, Helen	WF	170d	Patient
Fredwitz, Helen	WF	30	Patient
Fretzni, Samuel	WM	2	Patient
Gabittello, Anna	WF	5	Patient
Gaffney, Alice	WF	24	Patient
Gaffney, Clare	WF	14d	Patient
Gaffney, Illeen	WF	23	Patient

Gaffney, Julia	WF	219d	Patient
Gaffney, Mary	WF	35	Patient
Gagens, Richard	WM	3	Patient
Galagher, Helen	WF	23	Ass't. Cook
Gali, Clement	WM	6	Patient
Gallagan, Madeline	WF	26	Patient
Gallagher, Anna	WF	20	Patient
Gallagher, Mary	WF	290d	Patient
Gallamore, Mary	WF	24	Patient
Ganluccics, Giuseppena	WF	129d	Patient
Garney, James	WM	77d	Patient
Garvey, Mary	WF	22	Patient
Gassey, Cecilia	WF	142d	Patient
Gaynoski, Clara	WF	177d	Patient
Gebbous, Joseph	WM	133d	Patient
Gennan, Victoria	WF	3	Patient
Geraghty, Margaret	WF	3	Patient
Gessler, Milton	WM	2	Patient
Giardini, Raoul	WM	4	Patient
Gilchrist, Agnes	WF	35	Patient
Gilchrist, Thomas	WM	7	Patient
Gillen, Winifred	WF	20	Nurse
Gilligan, James	WM	1	Patient
Gilligan, John	WM	1	Patient
Gillon, Gertrude	WF	320d	Patient
Gioia, Edward	WM	3	Patient
Giroux, Anna	WF	55	Sister of Charity
Gleason, Elizabeth	WF	20	Patient
Gleason, Joseph	WM	46d	Patient
Goerb, Katherine	WF	271d	Patient
Goetz, Frances	WF	19	Patient
Goff, Thomas	WM	4	Patient
Goldner, Catherine	WF	5	Patient
Golula, Amelia	WF	256d	Patient
Goodman, Stella	WF	264d	Patient
Goodnough, Margaret	WF	7	Patient
Goodwin, Louise	WF	5	Patient
Goody, Margaret	WF	21	Patient
Goody, Margaret R.	WF	171d	Patient
Gordon, Vincent	WM	153d	Patient
Graham, Fredrick	WM	34d	Patient
Graham, Mary	WF	32	Patient

Gramar, Rose	WF	267d	Patient
Gramar, Rose	WF	19	Patient
Granan, James	WM	3	Patient
Grant, Katherine	WF	57	Sister of Charity
Grasso, Mary	WF	21	Patient
Gray, Anna	WF	313d	Patient
Gray, Robert	WM	5	Patient
Grayenisk, Anna	WF	21	Patient
Green, Ruben	WM	1	Patient
Greesh, Mary	WF	32	Patient
Griffin, Delia	WF	24	Patient
Griffin, Veronica	WF	85d	Patient
Griffiths, Mary	WF	28	Patient
Grimm, Thomas	WM	4	Patient
Gross, Joseph	WM	3	Patient
Gunn, Lena	WF	23	Seamstress
Guppo, Louise	WF	18	Seamstress
Gusick, John	WM	5	Patient
Guson, Anna	WF	22	Patient
Guyders, John	WM	4	Patient
Guzari, Felicia	WM*	5	Patient
Habecht, Stella	WF	22	Patient
Habicha, Frank	WM	183d	Patient
Hakes, Mary	WF	30	Patient
Halie, Edwin	WM	3	Patient
Hannigan, Anna	WF	40	Waitress
Hanson, Anthony	WM	121d	Patient
Hanson, Ellen	WF	42	Patient
Harquial, Anna	WF	36	Sister of Charity
Harrington, Alice	WF	199d	Patient
Harris, Betty	WF	20	Patient
Harris, Helen	WF	232d	Patient
Harris, Mary	WF	35	Patient
Harris, Thomas	WM	258d	Patient
Hart, Delia	WF	35	Patient
Harting, Paul	WM	144d	Patient
Harting, Tillie	WF	19	Patient
Hartman, Charles	WM	6	Patient
Hawkins, William	BM	6	Patient
Hayes, Marion	WF	21	Patient
Hearne, Margaret	WF	4	Patient
Hefferman, Josephine	WF	1	Patient

Helderbrand, Robert	WM	4	Patient
Henderson, Stephen	WM	4	Patient
Hessler, Harold	WM	126d	Patient
Hessler, Jennie	WF	20	Seamstress
Hill, Reimgius	WM	4	Patient
Himalka, Mildred	WF	6	Patient
Hoffman, Isabella	WF	134d	Patient
Hogan, Mary	WF	3	Patient
Holland, Gabriella	WF	172d	Patient
Hoorihan, Jennie	WF	24	Waitress
Hornkamp, Esther	WF	3	Patient
Horowitz, Catherine	WM	4	Patient
Hughes, Isabella	WF	108d	Patient
Hurley, Anna F.	WF	53	Sister of Charity
Hurley, Margaret	WF	23	Patient
Huss, William	WM	1	Patient
Hyde, Fannie	WF	54	Nursery Maid
Ippolito, Catherine	WF	18	Patient
Ippolito, Catherine	WF	70d	Patient
Irving, Andrew	WM	3	Patient
Irving, Francis	WF	60d	Patient
Irwin, Thomas	WM	2	Patient
Isold, Rose	WF	24	Patient
James, Horace	WM	3	Patient
Janack, Anna	WF	23	Patient
Janack, Dorothy	WF	184d	Patient
Johngkoff, Mary	WF	26	Patient
Johningkoff, Helen	WF	334d	Patient
Johnson, Esther	WF	29	Patient
Johnson, Russell	WM	52d	Patient
Johnson, William O.	WM	6	Patient
Jones, Carl	WM	6	Patient
Jones, Eugene	WM	5	Patient
Jones, Stephen	WM	109d	Patient
Jordon, Julius	WM	4	Patient
Joyce, James	WM	4	Patient
Judge, Blanche	WF	17	Patient
Kagel, Catherine	WF	26	Patient
Kain, Joseph	WM	3	Patient
Kalendowitz, Joseph	WM	4	Patient
Kann, Thomas	WM	4	Patient
Kariam, Anna	WF	24	Patient

Kariam, Mary	WF	1	Patient
Karney, John	WM	5	Patient
Kasel, John	WM	50d	Patient
Kaufman, John	WM	30d	Patient
Kaymuska, Jennie	WF	228d	Patient
Kealos, Augusta	WF	37	Patient
Kealos, Felix	WM	348d	Patient
Kearel, Richard	WM	173d	Patient
Kearn, Joseph	WM	156d	Patient
Kearn, Mary	WF	30	Patient
Kearns, Margaret	WF	62d	Patient
Kearns, Theadore	WF	4	Patient
Keasel, Agens	WF	22	Patient
Kellar, Louise	WF	22	Patient
Kellard, William	WM	4	Patient
Kelleher, Thomas	WM	5	Patient
Keller, Alfred	WM	331d	Patient
Keller, Mary H.	WF	68	Sister of Charity
Kelly, Mary	WF	4	Patient
Kenny, Annabelle	WF	23	Waitress
Kenny, Francis	WM	5	Patient
Keppe, Josephine	WF	19	Patient
Kerrigan, Margaret	WF	29	Nurse
Ketna, Edward	WM	107d	Patient
Keyes, Augusta	WF	19	Stenographer
Kiely, Mary	WF	90d	Patient
Kiley, Mary	WF	23	Patient
Kilna, Bertha	WF	20	Patient
Kimcles, Catherine	WF	82d	Patient
Kindler, Pauline	WF	3	Patient
Kingman, Mary	WF	4	Patient
Kippe, Elizabeth	WF	176d	Patient
Klatt, Louis	WM	318d	Patient
Klatts, Pauline	WF	38	Patient
Knox, Mary	WF	20	Patient
Kochler, William	WM	4	Patient
Kogel, Catherine	WF	150d	Patient
Kouval, Anna	WF	235d	Patient
Kowal, Mary	WF	26	Patient
Kowalika, Marie	WF	5	Patient
Kramer, Gertrude	WF	21	Patient
Krouch, Anna	WF	24	Patient

Kubele, Mary	WF	3	Patient
Kugles, Josephine	WF	32	Sister of Charity
Kumanowin, Ama	WF	75d	Patient
Kunder, Starsia	WF	28	Patient
Kundis, Catherine	WF	21	Patient
Kustofk, Lena	WF	22	Patient
Kuzzini, Sophia	WF	32	Patient
Kuzzini, Josephine	WF	126d	Patient
Laffet, Mary	WF	24	Ass't. Cook
LaRosco, Joseph	WM	3	Patient
Lastfoget, Margaret M.	WF	17	Patient
Lavin, Mary	WF	33	Patient
Lawrence, Helen	WF	28	Head Cook
Leary, Mary	WF	29	Patient
Leary, Michael	WM	5	Patient
Leary, William	WM	303d	Patient
LeBarre, Dolores	WF	5	Patient
LeBlanc, Grace	WF	68d	Patient
Leigh, Blanch	WF	116d	Patient
Lenahan, George	WM	3	Patient
Lenahan, Mary	WF	78	Sister of Charity
Lesita, Catherine	WF	20	Patient
Lesley, Adele	WF	3d	Patient
Leslie, May	WF	18	Patient
Levanduski, Elizabeth	WF	238d	Patient
Levin, Anne M.	WF	321d	Patient
Levy, Nathan	WM	2	Patient
Linenberg, Marion	WF	7d	Patient
Linenberg, Olga	WF	21	Patient
Lockhart, Mary	WF	21	Nurse
Lockman, John	WM	3	Patient
Lodge, Eliza	WF	27	Seamstress
Lombard, John	WM	1	Patient
Loney, Michael	WM	150d	Patient
Long, Mary	WF	176d	Patient
Longmotti, Rose	WF	7	Patient
Longmotti, Virginia	WF	7	Patient
Lupine, Catherine	WF	6	Patient
Lynch, Adelaide	WF	15d	Patient
Lynch, Adelaide	WF	20	Patient
Lyons, Anthony	WM	129d	Patient
Lyons, Catherine	WF	57	Sister of Charity

Mackey, Charles E.	WM	4	Patient
Maher, Lillian	WF	31	Patient
Mahoney, Dennis	WM	3	Patient
Malin, Elizabeth	WF	340d	Patient
Malone, Edward	WM	4	Patient
Mancerdo, Mary	WF	3	Patient
Manelsi, Fanny	WF	1	Patient
Manly, James	WM	160d	Patient
Manning, Mary	WF	76	Sister of Charity
Mantesi, Angeline	WF	98d	Patient
Marcy, Mark	WM	47d	Patient
Marcy, Mary	WF	21	Patient
Marks, Mildred	WF	40d	Patient
Marriman, Margaret	WF	23	Nurse
Marshall, Alice	WF	22	Patient
Martin, Ethel	WF	34d	Patient
Martin, Helen	WF	19	Patient
Martin, John	WM	192d	Patient
Matori, Carmelo	WM	6	Patient
Mattesi, Philomena	WF	39d	Patient
McAleer, Jane	WF	48	Sister of Charity
McAlpin, Mary	WF	35	Sister of Charity
McAvoy, Anna	WF	28	Patient
McBanon, Mary	WF	18	Nurse
McCabe, Agnes	WF	28	Patient
McCabe, Joseph	WM	72d	Patient
McCardy, Anna	WF	1	Patient
McCarthy, Agnes	WF	30	Sister of Charity
McCarthy, Mary	WF	28	Sister of Charity
McCloskey, Edward	WM	6	Patient
McClure, Louis J.	WM	4	Patient
McCormack, Christine	WF	135d	Patient
McCormack, Mary	WF	19	Patient
McCormick, Anna	WF	47	Sister of Charity
McCrystal, Jane C.	WF	73	Sister of Charity
McDevitt, Anthony	WM	1	Patient
McDevitt, Susan	WF	36	Patient
McDonald, Mary	WF	4	Patient
McDonald, Mary	WF	41	Patient
McEnney, Florence	WF	18	Nurse
McGam, Robert	WM	122d	Patient
McGarr, Clara	WF	50	Sister of Charity

McGarr, Mary	WF	23	Nurse
McGarry, Helen	WF	167d	Patient
McGee, Rose	WF	45	Portress
McGovern, Marie	WM	332d	Patient
McGowan, Delia	WF	40	Patient
McGowan, Herbert	WF*	1	Patient
McGowan, Lillian	WF	2	Patient
McGrath, Alice	WF	20	Patient
McGrath, Joseph	WM	1	Patient
McGrath, Joseph	WM	165d	Patient
McGrath, Teresa	WF	19	Patient
McGuade, Anna	WF	38	Clothes Room Maid
McGuire, Julia	WF	26	Matron of Nursery
McGuire, Phillip	WM	253d	Patient
McGuirk, Joseph	WM	219d	Patient
McKenna, Joseph	WM	3	Patient
McLarney, Catherine	WF	69	Patient
McLaughlin, Antonia	WF	40	Portress
McLawrence, Delia	WF	35	Patient
McLernen, Bridget	WF	31	Sister of Charity
McMahon, Katherine	WF	5	Patient
McManus, Frank	WM	266d	Patient
McManus, George	WF*	23d	Patient
McManus, Mary	WF	24	Patient
McManus, Thomas	WM	5	Patient
McMirth, Margaret	WF	54	Sister of Charity
McMullen, Mary	WF	42	Matron of Nursery
McNamara, Bridget	WF	36	Patient
McNicholl, Elizabeth	WF	22	Patient
McNulty, Anna	WF	23	Patient
Meckey, Margaret	WF	78	Sister of Charity
Merok, Mary	WF	24	Patient
Merrion, Richard	WM	5	Patient
Mersevoich, Mary	WF	5	Patient
Messler, Vincent	WM	105d	Patient
Meyer, Sylvester	WM	5	Patient
Meyers, Josephine	WF	116d	Patient
Michaels, Frank	WM	3	Patient
Michaelson, Anna	WF	7	Patient
Middleton, Grace	WF	5	Patient
Miellen, Marjorie	WF	19	Patient
Miengola, Michael	WM	5	Patient

Miller, Anna	WF	40d	Patient
Miller, James	WM	3	Patient
Miller, John	WM	3	Patient
Miller, John	WM	3	Patient
Miller, Theresa	WF	18	Seamstress
Mirok, Eurana	WF	80d	Patient
Mirr, Louis	WM	211d	Patient
Mitten, Florence	WF	16	Patient
M'Kenee, Mary	WF	39	Sister of Charity
Mohl, Joseph	WM	2	Patient
Monahan, Catherine	WF	29	Patient
Monahan, John	WM	129d	Patient
Mongano, Teresa	WF	282d	Patient
Montako, Bianca	WF	17	Seamstress
Montelone, Joseph	WM	3	Patient
Moon, Edward	WM	10d	Patient
Moon, Margaret	WF	32	Patient
Moore, Evelyn	WF	5	Patient
Moore, Rose	WF	4	Patient
Moran, Anna E.	WF	51	Sister of Charity
Moran, John	WM	25d	Patient
Moran, Mary	WF	20	Patient
Moran, Theodore	WM	82d	Patient
Morgan, Emily	WF	22	Patient
Morgan, Raymond	WM	3	Patient
Morley, Ella	WF	20	Patient
Morley, James	WM	8d	Patient
Morley, Lillian	WF	22	Patient
Morris, Lena	WF	22	Patient
Morris, Paul	WM	22d	Patient
Morrissey, Mary	WF	3	Patient
Morton, Isabella	WF	259d	Patient
Mouisier, Marie	WF	94d	Patient
Moyles, Ernestine	WF	128d	Patient
Moyles, Sabina	WF	18	Patient
Muhan, Joseph	WM	3	Patient
Mulholland, Susanna	WF	50	Sister of Charity
Mulligan, Nellie	WF	35	Patient
Mullin, Sarah J.	WF	37	Bottle Washer
Mulrooney, Isabella	WF	23	Nurse
Murphy, Helen	WF	23	Patient
Murphy, James	WM	170d	Patient

Murphy, Mary J.	WF	51	Sister of Charity
Murray, Albertine	WF	251d	Patient
Murray, Angeline	WF	251d	Patient
Murray, Dorothy	WF	5	Patient
Murray, Mary	WF	22	Nurse
Murry, Mary	WF	22	Patient
Nacy, Loretta	WF	50	Nurse
Napolitano, Leon	WM	134d	Patient
Nappo, Viola	WF	121d	Patient
Nolan, Anna	WF	7	Patient
Nolan, Michael	WM	4	Patient
Nolan, Walter	WM	7	Patient
Nondisi, Mary	WF	18	Patient
Noonan, Annie	WF	29	Sister of Charity
Noonan, Margaret	WF	22	Patient
Novack, Katherine	WF	30	Patient
Novak, John	WM	140d	Patient
Novick, Lydia	WF	77d	Patient
Noyes, Mary	WF	59	Sister of Charity
Nugent, Thomas	WM	43	Elevator Man
Nuizzio, Fannie	WF	1	Patient
Nuizzio, Teresa	WF	20	Patient
O'Brien, George	WF*	7	Patient
O'Brien, Marie	WF	50	Sister of Charity
O'Brien, Sophia	WF	58	Patient
O'Connor, Anna	WF	21	Nurse
O'Connor, Francis	WM	3	Patient
O'Connor, Vincent	WM	4	Patient
O'Connor, William	WM	2	Patient
O'Hara, Alice	WF	59	Sister of Charity
O'Hare, Michael	WM	4	Patient
Olchoura, Julia	WF	3	Patient
Olynik, John	WM	103d	Patient
Oreilli, Ewina	WF	19	Patient
Oreilli, Maria	WF	157d	Patient
O'Rourke, Stella	WF	23	Patient
Orr, Josephine	WF	28	Waitress
Ortlieb, Roy	WM	3	Patient
O'Shea, Mary	WF	279d	Patient
Ouozro, Rose T.	WM*	85d	Patient
Paglia, Irene	WF	22	Patient
Palmer, Norman	WM	4	Patient

Pandolfi, James	WM	4	Patient
Patia, Mabel	WF	49d	Patient
Patrick, Julia	WF	18	Patient
Paul, Peter	WM	7	Patient
Paxton, James	WM	4	Patient
Payn, Victor	WM	48d	Patient
Payton, Beatrice	WF	241d	Patient
Peach, Mary	WF	21	Patient
Peltier, Eugene	WM	26d	Patient
Perro, Laura	WF	3	Patient
Pery, Marguerite	WF	182d	Patient
Peure, Sylvia	WF	32	Patient
Phelps, Caroline	WF	7	Patient
Phillips, Paul	WF	161	Patient
Picciona, Helen	WF	22	Patient
Picciona, Joseph	WM	77d	Patient
Pignole, Rosina	WF	210d	Patient
Platthy, Ella	WF	22	Patient
Platthy, Ernest	WM	203d	Patient
Plunkett, Maud	WF	46	Sister of Charity
Poland, Joseph	WM	3	Patient
Polite, Arnold	WM	4	Patient
Pollard, Albert	WM	6	Patient
Poney, Anna	WF	33	Patient
Porazzo, Dora	WF	5	Patient
Porter, Joseph	WM	175d	Patient
Potts, Janette	WF	24d	Patient
Powers, Earl	WM	5	Patient
Powers, Eudora	WF	75d	Patient
Prescourt, Walter	WM	3	Patient
Prosek, Andrew	WM	159d	Patient
Prosek, Eva	WF	30	Patient
Pune, Catherine	WF	118d	Patient
Puponeck, John	WM	4	Patient
Quigley, Teresa	WF	16	Waitress
Quinn, Daniel	WM	230d	Patient
Quinn, Mary J.	WF	231d	Patient
Quinn, Mary	WF	20	Patient
Quinn, William	WM	3	Patient
Radia, Josephine	WF	3	Patient
Rants, Lempi	WM	110d	Patient
Reardon, Elizabeth	WF	22	Patient

Reardon, Elizabeth	WF	109d	Patient
Reardon, Margaret	WF	109d	Patient
Redden, Elizabeth	WF	36	Patient
Reiber, John	WM	3	Patient
Reilly, Irene	WF	20	Nurse
Reilly, Joseph	WM	6	Patient
Reilly, Mary	WF	4	Patient
Reino, Julia	WF	3	Patient
Rennelles, Virginia	WF	19	Patient
Reynolds, Lillian	WF	20	Nurse
Reynolds, Mary	WF	47	Matron in Nursery
Rice, Elizabeth	WF	25	Nurse
Richy, Bridget	WF	70	Sister of Charity
Rini, Vito	WM	4	Patient
Roberts, Grace	WF	17	Patient
Roberts, John	WM	97d	Patient
Rockfort, Anna	WF	21	Sister of Charity
Roesch, Joseph	WM	53d	Patient
Roesch, Susan	WF	20	Patient
Rokas, Julia	WF	3	Patient
Rooney, Anna	WF	3	Patient
Ross, John	WM	4	Patient
Rothacker, Frances	WF	23	Patient
Rowe, Florence	WF	315d	Patient
Royce, Catherine	WF	4	Patient
Ruddy, Anna	WF	55	Sister of Charity
Rumpt, George	WM	4	Patient
Runcke, Florence	WF	69d	Patient
Rush, Sarah	WF	44	Sister of Charity
Russel, Mary	WF	41	Seamstress
Russell, Marie	WF	17	Patient
Russo, James	WM	160d	Patient
Russo, Mary	WF	18	Patient
Rutledge, Helen	WF	30	Patient
Ruyescka, George	WM	165d	Patient
Ryan, Charles	WM	165d	Patient
Ryan, Elizabeth	WF	15	Patient
Ryan, James	WM	3	Patient
Saari, Helen	WF	47d	Patient
Sabbatino, Joseph	WM	1	Patient
Sacco, Peter	WM	3	Patient
Saemain, Estelle	WF	18	Seamstress

Sagmeister, Alice	WF	6	Patient
Samezyk, John	WM	263d	Patient
Santorelli, Angelo	WM	3	Patient
Saroceno, Angelo	WM	5	Patient
Scarono, Michael	WM	4	Patient
Schimler, Mary	WF	15d	Patient
Schneider, Anna	WF	1	Patient
Schoken, Clara	WF	3	Patient
Schonbom, Lucille	WF	250d	Patient
Schonborn, Anna	WF	18	Seamstress
Schultz, James V.	WM	1, 6m	Patient
Schultz, Robert	WM	64d	Patient
Schumsky, Mary	WF	3	Patient
Schwartz, Sophie	WF	100d	Patient
Scully, Margaret	WF	2	Patient
Scuppa, Teresa	WF	4	Patient
Seaman, Agnes	WF	22d	Patient
Sears, Adrian	WM	165d	Patient
Sege, Jane	WF	273d	Patient
Seigel, Eva	WF	4	Patient
Sever, Charles	WM	3	Patient
Shalitt, Leon	WM	5	Patient
Shanahan, Carmine	WF	1	Patient
Shankey, Mary	WF	52	Sister of Charity
Shano, Carmela	WF	330d	Patient
Sharkey, Margaret	WF	28	Patient
Sharkey, Mary J.	WF	20d	Patient
Shea, Daniel	WM	70d	Patient
Shenker, Lillian	WF	60d	Patient
Shephard, Anna	WF	21	Nurse
Sheridan, Anna	WF	30	Patient
Sheridan, Catherine	WF	202d	Patient
Shields, Edward	WM	230d	Patient
Shimoler, Elizabeth	WF	25	Patient
Simmons, Edward	WM	311d	Patient
Simmons, Mary	WF	35	Patient
Slansky, Hanry	WM	18d	Patient
Slater, Alice	WF	19	Nurse
Smith, Catherine	WF	193d	Patient
Smith, Charles	WM	38d	Patient
Smith, George	WM	29d	Patient
Smith, Joseph	WM	122d	Patient

Smith, Joseph	WM	5	Patient
Smith, Margaret	WF	317d	Patient
Smith, Rose	WF	25	Nurse
Smith, Theresa	WF	22	Patient
Smith, William	WM	37d	Patient
Smith, William	WM	261d	Patient
Snyder, John	WM	5	Patient
Snyder, Stella	WF	2	Patient
Solavi, Paul	WM	3	Patient
Spacione, Marie	WF	3	Patient
Speer, Mabel	WF	28	Patient
Spintler, Gertrude	WF	18	Patient
Spirer, Clara	WF	14	Patient
Spitzer, Henry	WM	182	Patient
Spytcua, Rose	WF	19d	Patient
Spytman, Anna	WF	23	Patient
Stack, Eugene	WM	94d	Patient
Stark, Virginia	WF	17	Patient
Starks, Emma	WF	1	Patient
Starks, Gastio	WM	3	Patient
Steiner, Henry	WM	72d	Patient
Sterling, Cecilia	WF	17	Patient
Stewart, Rosallie	WF	28	Patient
Stokes, Charles	WM	114d	Patient
Stone, Elizabeth	WF	18	Patient
Strassberg, Thuna	WF	159d	Patient
Strauss, Emma	WF	29	Patient
Sullivan, Agnes	WF	43	Patient
Sullivan, Anna	WF	20	Patient
Sullivan, Arthur	WM	185d	Patient
Sullivan, Mary	WF	51	Sister of Charity
Swanclish, Charollett	WF	22	Patient
Sweeney, Albert	WM	68d	Patient
Sweeney, Winifred	WF	1	Patient
Szabados, John	WM	152d	Patient
Szymonska, Martha	WF	202d	Patient
Szymoska, Martha	WF	30	Patient
Tackel, George	WM	176d	Patient
Target, Arthur	WM	145d	Patient
Target, Jane	WF	21	Patient
Tarpey, Margaret	WF	4	Patient
Tasscuro, Joseph	WM	17	Carpenter

Taylor, Agnes	WF	16	Nurse
Taylor, Florence	WF	30	Patient
Taylor, Harriett	WF	116d	Patient
Tellick, Rebecca	WF	183d	Patient
Teokler, Anna	WF	37d	Patient
Tereseck, Julia	WF	28	Patient
Tereseck, Miriam	WF	252d	Patient
Thompon, Elizabeth	WF	27	Patient
Thompson, Frank	WM	138d	Patient
Thorne, Claudine	WF	5	Patient
Thornton, Carrie	WF	16	Patient
Thornton, Elizabeth	WF	50	Patient
Thornton, William	WM	63d	Patient
Tighe, Raymond	WM	4	Patient
Timms, Robert	WM	2d	Patient
Tioce, Andrew	WM	4	Patient
Tobin, Mary	WF	6	Patient
Toker, Elizabeth	WF	20	Patient
Tomney, Elizabeth	WF	61	Sister of Charity
Tontana, Florence	WF	24	Nurse
Toomey, Peter	WM	32d	Patient
Torenda, Mary	WF	42	Nurse
Trumpower, Anna	WF	4	Patient
Trumpower, Susan	WF	23	Nursery Maid
Tulby, Anna	WF	70	Sister of Charity
Tuma, William	WM	5	Patient
Tumoi, Thomas	WM	2	Patient
Tunins, Elizabeth	WF	40	Patient
Turano, Carmella	WF	1, 6m	Patient
Turey, Jane	WF	196d	Patient
Tuscell, Anna	WF	76	Sister of Charity
Udianiska, Rose	WF	5	Patient
Valentine, William	WM	3	Patient
Vandemark, Nellie	WF	9d	Patient
Vandemark, Nellie	WF	26	Patient
Vanderman, Lucille	WF	22	Nursery Maid
Vedracci, Rita	WF	1, 6m	Patient
Vernas, Teresa	WF	6	Patient
Viso, Carmelo	WF	30	Patient
Visosky, Bernard	WM	6	Patient
Vuillemenot, Mary	WF	18	Patient
Wack, Annie	WF	28	Domestic Servant

Wale, Nellie	WF	29	Nurse
Walsh, Anna	WF	19	Nurse
Walsh, Harry	WM	3	Patient
Walsh, Helen	WF	3	Patient
Walsh, Margaret	WF	5	Patient
Walsh, Nellie	WF	20	Patient
Wanes, Allen	WM	57d	Patient
Ward, Edith	WF	49d	Patient
Ward, Hannah	WF	22	Patient
Wardell, Edward	WM	113d	Patient
Wardell, Elsie	WF	113d	Patient
Wardell, Milton	WM	5	Patient
Warner, Edwad	WM	119d	Patient
Warner, Fannie	WF	19	Patient
Warner, Mary	WF	23	Patient
Washington, Catherine	WF	1	Patient
Watline, Alfred	WM	3	Patient
Waylett, George	WM	41d	Patient
Wazennauses, Anthony	WM	77d	Patient
Weiman, John	WM	4	Patient
Weininger, Nathan	WM	3	Patient
Weisburg, Charles	WM	181d	Patient
Weiss, Anthony	WM	4	Patient
Welsh, Geraldine	WF	255d	Patient
Wertenstein, Pelina	WM	193d	Patient
Willem, Mary	WF	16	Patient
William, Inez	WF	254d	Patient
Wilson, Agnes	WF	21	Patient
Wilson, William	WM	1	Patient
Wiseman, Edward	WM	5	Patient
Witney, Cahterine	WF	2	Patient
Wolfert, Julia	WF	5	Patient
Woods, Mary	WF	60	Patient
Yanack, Bertha	WF	24	Patient
Yanack, Catherine	WF	242d	Patient
Yates, Joseph	WM	333d	Patient
Young, Elizabeth	WF	69d	Patient
Young, Florence	WF	3	Patient
Zablewoska, John	WM	205d	Patient
Zacchardi, Bernardo	WM	5	Patient
Zender, Ignatius	WM	6	Patient
Zenosky, Sophia	WF	20	Patient
Zimmer, Alma	WF	110d	Patient

Index to the
Federal Enumeration of the Inhabitants of

The New York Foundling Hospital

175 East 68th Street
New York, New York

January 1, 1920

Supervisor's District No. 1
Assembly District No. 15
Election District No. 1074
Pages 1A - 20A

Joseph P. Murphy, Enumerator

Guide to Column Headings

in the

1920 Federal Enumeration

Name   Name of each person whose usual place of abode was in the institution on January 1, 1920. The census includes the name of every person living on January 1, 1920. Children born since January 1, 1920 were omitted. The surname is listed first, then the given name and middle initial.

R-G   Race and gender. White is designated by the letter "W", black by the letter "B", and Mulatto by the letters "Mu". Males are designated by the letter "M" and females are designated by the letter "F".

*   Notes that the enumerator may have reported the name or gender incorrectly.

A   Age at last birthday. Designated in years, unless otherwise noted with an "m" for "months". Generally, children who were less than four years old were described in terms of months or in terms of years and months.

Relation   Relationship of each person to the institution.

Note   Although the birthplace of each child was always listed as "New York", the Nativity of his mother and father was sometimes listed. The enumerator also noted whether or not the child had attended school any time since September 1, 1919. Refer to the original census for this information. Also, refer to the orginal census for the Nativity of each adult occupant and her parents, as well as her Mother Tongue, Citizenship, Education and Marital Status.

Name	R-G	A	Relation
Abatangolis, Mary	WF	1, 11m	Inmate
Abbozzi, John	WM	7m	Inmate
Abruzzi, Joseph	WM	4	Inmate
Adams, Amelia	WF	6	Inmate
Adams, Raymond	WM	5m	Inmate
Ademio, Paul	WM	2, 10m	Inmate
Adochi, Florence	WF	9m	Inmate
Adochis, Helena Amelia	WF	16	Nurse
Agostina, Louis	WM	2, 6m	Inmate
Ahearn, Joseph	WM	4	Inmate
Aiella, James	WM	4	Inmate
Alamo, Rosario	WM	6	Inmate
Alanoi, James	WM	7	Inmate
Albino, John	WM	2, 7m	Inmate
Albino, Theresa	WF	2, 3m	Inmate
Allen, Bernard	WM	3, 2m	Inmate
Allen, John	WM	8	Inmate
Allen, Margaret	WF	1	Inmate
Allen, Paul	WM	2	Inmate
Allesancho, Mary	WF	1, 7m	Inmate
Allison, Agnes Vincent	WF	20	Trained Nurse
Almese, John	WM	2, 9m	Inmate
Alonci, Fortunata	WF	2	Inmate
Altieri, Peter	WM	1, 6m	Inmate
Alvich, Annie	WF	5	Inmate
Alvischi, Joseph	WM	6	Inmate
Amato, Antonio	WM	4	Inmate
Ambosina, Pasquale	WM	2, 5m	Inmate
Ambrose, John	WM	2, 6m	Inmate
Ambrosia, Joseph	WM	2, 4m	Inmate
Amendola, Charles	WM	2, 6m	Inmate
Amos, Florence P.	WF	21	Nurse
Amos, George	WM	1, 8m	Inmate
Anderson, Charles	WM	4	Inmate
Anderson, John	WM	7	Inmate
Anderson, Mary Agnes	WF	23	Boarder, Clerk
Anderson, Paul	WM	5	Inmate
Anderson, Raymond	WM	5	Inmate
Andrew, Grace	WF	24	Nurse
Andrewcetti, Pietro	WM	5	Inmate

Andrews, Agnes	WF	1, 11m	Inmate
Angela, Helen	WF	2, 3m	Inmate
Angin, Salvatrise	WF	2, 6m	Inmate
Angotti, Salvatore	WM	5	Inmate
Anzalone, Rose	WF	3, 3m	Inmate
Apostolio, Mary	WF	1, 4m	Inmate
Appleton, Aloysious V.	WM	29	Bookkeeper
Aquaviva, Catherine	WF	2, 11m	Inmate
Arcangel, Benedict	WM	2, 4m	Inmate
Arico, Sara	WF	4	Inmate
Arnold, Jennone	WM	6	Inmate
Arnold, John	WM	5	Inmate
Arnold, Terence	BM	3, 9m	Inmate
Aschen, Edward	WM	7	Inmate
August, Joseph	WM	1, 3m	Inmate
August, Walter	WM	2, 1m	Inmate
Austin, Isabella	BF	1, 9m	Inmate
Avello, Anthony	WM	4, 3m	Inmate
Bacigalispo, John	WM	7m	Inmate
Bailey, David	WM	0m	Inmate
Baker, Joseph	WM	5	Inmate
Bakosk, George	WM	6	Inmate
Balantonio, Victoria	WM	3, 11m	Inmate
Balinska, Mary	WF	1, 11m	Inmate
Balkash, Annie	WF	2, 10m	Inmate
Balkash, Joseph	WM	5	Inmate
Bambino, Antoinette	WF	6	Inmate
Bambino, Francesco	WM	5	Inmate
Bambino, Michael	WM	1, 11m	Inmate
Banett, Joseph	WM	7m	Inmate
Baney, William	WM	1, 11m	Inmate
Baniszeroski, Vincent	WM	3, 4m	Inmate
Bank, Albert	WM	5	Inmate
Baptisata, Valentine	WM	2, 3m	Inmate
Barba, John	WM	3, 4m	Inmate
Barnes, John	WM	2	Inmate
Barnes, Joseph	WM	2, 11m	Inmate
Barnett, Frank	WM	7	Inmate
Bates, Matthew	WM	3, 6m	Inmate
Battaglia, Rose	WF	6	Inmate
Battaglis, Lola	WF	23	Nurse
Battogabsi, John	WM	6m	Inmate

Baubo, Edward	WM	2, 6m	Inmate
Beatty, Walter	WM	7	Inmate
Becker, Hubert	WM	9	Inmate
Bell, John	WM	2, 3m	Inmate
Bellefiore, Thomas	WM	1, 7m	Inmate
Bellisimo, Josephine	WF	7	Inmate
Bellisimo, Katie	WF	5	Inmate
Bellisimo, Rose	WF	5	Inmate
Bend, Mary Frances	WF	13	Ward
Benvattia, Anthony	WM	2, 3m	Inmate
Beramoko, John	WM	2, 7m	Inmate
Bergmowski, Eva	WF	2m	Inmate
Berman, Frances	WF	6	Inmate
Bernassen, Celilia	WF	7	Inmate
Best, Henry	WM	5	Inmate
Betram, Anna	WF	3, 9m	Inmate
Bianchi, Esther	WF	4	Inmate
Biebel, Peter	WM	1, 11m	Inmate
Bielick, Stanislaus	WM	6	Inmate
Bifunso, Florenza	WF	3, 4m	Inmate
Biggin, John	WM	11m	Inmate
Bila, Frank	WM	4	Inmate
Billis, Caroline	WF	18	Nurse
Binno, Mary	WF	1, 10m	Inmate
Biro, Elizabeth	WF	2, 5m	Inmate
Bisberi, Charles	WM	5	Inmate
Bisclay, Francis	WM	1, 5m	Inmate
Biscoglio, Joseph	BM	8	Inmate
Bishop, Mary	WF	4m	Inmate
Bishop, Mary	WF	1, 9m	Inmate
Bisuso, Rose	WF	2, 11m	Inmate
Blackstock, Lena	WF	4	Inmate
Blaskowitz, Jacob	WM	2m	Inmate
Blaskowitz, Pauline	WF	25	Nurse
Blaskowitz, William	WM	1, 3m	Inmate
Blaubelt, Margaret	WF	12	Inmate
Bliss, Jenette	MuF	3, 8m	Inmate
Blon, Mary	WF	1, 9m	Inmate
Bloom, Emil	WM	1, 5m	Inmate
Bloyney, John	WM	4	Inmate
Bobacik, Joseph	WM	2, 11m	Inmate
Boccanifuso, Dennis	WM	4	Inmate

Boketska, Julia	WF	7m	Inmate
Bolin, Josephine	WF	42	Sister of Charity
Bologneso, Frank	WM	3, 7m	Inmate
Bologneso, Louis	WM	1, 6m	Inmate
Bonando, Helen	WF	2, 4m	Inmate
Bonell, Peter	WM	2, 9m	Inmate
Bookiman, Rose	WF	6	Inmate
Boroski, Ruth	WF	1m	Inmate
Boss, Bernard	WM	5	Inmate
Bostivich, Mary	WF	0m	Inmate
Bottari, Joseph	WM	3	Inmate
Bouksdale, Christmas	MuF	5	Inmate
Bourne, Joseph	WM	2	Inmate
Bowen, Catherine Irene	WF	56	Sister Superior
Bowen, Mary	WF	53	Nurse
Boyle, Irene	WF	0m	Inmate
Boyle, Johanna	WF	22	Nurse
Boynon, Sarah	WF	32	Servant
Bozler, Casimir	WF*	6	Inmate
Bradford, Sextus	WM	0m	Inmate
Brady, Bridget	WF	29	Nurse
Brady, John E.	WM	4	Inmate
Brady, Patrick	WM	0m	Inmate
Brannigan, John	WM	1m	Inmate
Brannigan, Mary	WF	19	Nurse
Bremer, Charles	WM	2, 11m	Inmate
Brennan, Stephen	WM	3, 7m	Inmate
Brennen, Mary C.	WF	52	Sister of Charity
Breslin, Nellie Evelyn	WF	25	Nurse
Bressler, Mary	WF	7	Inmate
Bretagni, Josephine	WF	75	Servant
Brett, Veronica	WF	41	Servant
Brickman, Agnes	WF	3, 10m	Inmate
Brodko, William	WM	2, 10m	Inmate
Brodnisk, Thomas	WM	3, 10m	Inmate
Broff, Marie	WF	7m	Inmate
Bronn, Mary Margaret	WF	21	Nurse
Bronnackant, Anna	WF	3, 2m	Inmate
Brook, Frank	WM	3, 5m	Inmate
Brookes, Philip	WM	2, 10m	Inmate
Brooks, Donald	WM	2, 2m	Inmate
Brooks, Dorothy	WF	4	Inmate

Brotsky, Stella	WF	21	Nurse
Browell, Josephine	WF	7	Inmate
Brown, Arthur	WM	2, 5m	Inmate
Brown, Dorothy	WM	3, 6m	Inmate
Brown, Edward	BM	7	Inmate
Brown, Gerald	WM	3, 11m	Inmate
Brown, Harold	WM	8	Inmate
Brown, James	WM	6m	Inmate
Brown, Julia	WF	5	Inmate
Brown, Mary Agnes	WF	24	Chambermaid
Brown, Mildred	WF	7	Inmate
Brown, Rose	WF	7m	Inmate
Bruno, Arthur	WM	2, 5m	Inmate
Bruzese, Carmine	WF	2, 6m	Inmate
Brynes, Miskeal	WM	3	Inmate
Bunett, Edith	WF	4	Inmate
Buoncore, James	WM	6	Inmate
Burger, Henry	WM	4	Inmate
Burke, George	WM	2, 6m	Inmate
Burke, Henry	WM	5	Inmate
Burke, Louis	WM	3, 4m	Inmate
Burke, Marion	WF	6	Inmate
Burke, Thomas	WM	2	Inmate
Burke, Walter	WM	4	Inmate
Burnes, Joseph	WM	1, 2m	Inmate
Burnett, Joseph	WM	6	Inmate
Burns, Fanny	WF	40	Nurse
Burns, Frances	WF	5	Inmate
Burns, Margaret	WF	4	Inmate
Burns, Margaret M.	WF	34	Sister of Charity
Burton, Julia	WF	5	Inmate
Bush, Mary	WF	5	Inmate
Busheville, Willie	BM	8	Inmate
Buskey, Henry	WM	2, 3m	Inmate
Buskley, Elizabeth	WF	22	Kitchen Girl
Bussi, Peter	WM	3, 11m	Inmate
Butler, Agnes	WF	0m	Inmate
Butler, Agnes	WF	2, 4m	Inmate
Butler, John	BM	7	Inmate
Butler, Leroy J.	WM	29	Medical Doctor
Butler, Nellie	WF	20	Nurse
Butoro, Angelo	WM	2, 5m	Inmate

Butrisa, Tony	WM	10m	Inmate
Bychkovaska, Felix	WM	3, 3m	Inmate
Cabatt, William	WM	5m	Inmate
Cafarelle, Anna	WF	1, 7m	Inmate
Caggirano, Constantine	WF	2, 8m	Inmate
Caggirano, Delmena	WF	2, 8m	Inmate
Caines, Charles	WM	4	Inmate
Calcian, Joseph	WM	6	Inmate
Calcian, Oneretto	WM	4	Inmate
Calindo, Margaret	WF	3, 7m	Inmate
Calislo, Andrew	WM	2, 1m	Inmate
Callahan, Eugene	WM	7	Inmate
Callery, Julia	WF	5	Inmate
Callon, Joseph	WM	1, 1m	Inmate
Camarda, Tony	WM	4	Inmate
Cammirutti, Concetti	WF	3, 11m	Inmate
Campbell, Eileen	WF	2, 10m	Inmate
Campbell, Joseph	WM	8	Inmate
Cannon, Agnes	WF	1, 10m	Inmate
Cannry, Thomas	WM	2, 4m	Inmate
Capaldo, Frederick	WM	2, 4m	Inmate
Cappola, Louisa	WF	3, 7m	Inmate
Capullo, Millie	WF	1, 10m	Inmate
Caputo, Virginia	WF	9m	Inmate
Carano, Micheal	WM	1, 7m	Inmate
Caravane, Francis	WM	2, 3m	Inmate
Cardinele, Victor	WM	3, 1m	Inmate
Carley, Francis	WM	6	Inmate
Carlotti, Charles	WM	3, 1m	Inmate
Carlson, James	WM	1, 5m	Inmate
Carlson, Victor	WM	6	Inmate
Carlson, William	WM	4, 6m	Inmate
Carlyle, Henry	WM	3, 7m	Inmate
Carmy, Leo	WM	1m	Inmate
Carpa, Eshra	WF	3, 5m	Inmate
Carroll, Damino	WM	2, 5m	Inmate
Carroll, Dorothy	WF	2, 5m	Inmate
Carroll, Elizabeth	WF	4m	Inmate
Carroll, Elizabeth	WF	1, 3m	Inmate
Carroll, Elizabeth M.	WF	35	Servant
Carroll, Gerald	WM	4m	Inmate
Carroll, Isabel	WF	26	Nurse

Carroll, Mary	WF	3, 3m	Inmate
Carson, Justin	WM	1, 4m	Inmate
Carty, Thomas	WM	2, 1m	Inmate
Carvidi, Angelo	WM	5	Inmate
Cary, Rosina	WF	2, 1m	Inmate
Casale, Edward	WM	8	Inmate
Cascioli, Leonara	WF	3, 3m	Inmate
Cascioli, Madeline	WF	4, 7m	Inmate
Casey, Fransis	WM	1m	Inmate
Casista, Angleinia	WF	3, 4m	Inmate
Casobano, Grace	WF	2, 9m	Inmate
Cassa, Thomas	WM	2, 11m	Inmate
Cassidy, Edward	WM	6	Inmate
Cassidy, Frank	WM	6m	Inmate
Castagusio, Concetta	WF	5	Inmate
Caswell, Willis	WM	5	Inmate
Cavaznie, Frank	WM	2, 6m	Inmate
Ceder, Joseph	WM	6	Inmate
Cerasi, Salvatore	WM	5	Inmate
Cerrito, Rosario	WM	1, ?m	Inmate
Cervello, Antonio	WM	1, 11m	Inmate
Chapman, Henry	WM	1, 11m	Inmate
Charles, Sarah Ann	WF	48	Sister of Charity
Chescku, John	WM	7	Inmate
Chissholme, William	WM	11m	Inmate
Chuesano, Michael	WM	2, 11m	Inmate
Chusta, Daniel	WM	4	Inmate
Cianciolo, Josephine	WF	7	Inmate
Cichon, Jerome	WM	3, 3m	Inmate
Cicicco, Rose	WF	5m	Inmate
Ciesbask, Stanley	WM	5	Inmate
Cimano, Stefano	WF*	3, 1m	Inmate
Ciminelle, Nicolo	WM	9m	Inmate
Cincinotta, Mary	WF	5	Inmate
Cincinotta, Mary	WF	31	Nurse
Cinciotta, Katie	WF	6	Inmate
Cirlinione, Placido	WM	5	Inmate
Ciromouti, Cecilia	WF	7	Inmate
Cischetti, Florinda	WF	6	Inmate
Cischetti, Liscettie	WF	5	Inmate
Clark, Edna	WF	1, 3m	Inmate
Clark, James	WM	1, 3m	Inmate

Clark, Mary	BF	9	Inmate
Clarke, Bridget Anna	WF	62	Sister of Charity
Cleffard, Ralph	WM	3, 6m	Inmate
Cloos, Annie	WF	23	Servant
Cloos, Gustave	WF	1, 3m	Inmate
Cody, Agnes	WF	4	Inmate
Cody, Isabella	WF	1, 6m	Inmate
Cody, Marguerite	WF	26	Nurse
Coffey, Adelaide	WF	1, 8m	Inmate
Cohen, Charles	WM	6	Inmate
Cohen, George	WM	4	Inmate
Cohen, Ruth	WF	3, 1m	Inmate
Cole, Edwin	WM	3, 11m	Inmate
Cole, Felix	WM	7	Inmate
Cole, Margaret	WF	18	Nurse
Coleman, Elizabeth	WF	8	Inmate
Coleman, Gerald	WM	6	Inmate
Coleman, Viola	BF	8	Inmate
Colley, Adelaide C.	WF	37	Nurse
Collins, Grace	WF	21	Nurse
Colofretti, Umberto	WM	4	Inmate
Comes, Walter	WM	3, 3m	Inmate
Conen, Henry	WM	8	Inmate
Conesmeous, John	WM	1, 3m	Inmate
Conley, Catherine	WF	3, 4m	Inmate
Conlon, Peter	WM	4	Inmate
Connelly, David	WM	1, 9m	Inmate
Connelly, Eleanor T.	WF	50	Sister of Charity
Connelly, Joseph	WM	3, 7m	Inmate
Connolly, Leo	WM	6	Inmate
Connolly, Mary Agnes	WF	22	Nurse
Connolly, Mary Louis	WF	35	Nurse
Conroy, Francis	WM	2, 8m	Inmate
Conroy, Henry	WM	7	Inmate
Consolla, Annie	WF	6	Inmate
Consolla, Concetta	WF	7	Inmate
Conway, Elizabeth Mary	WF	19	Nurse
Conway, Joseph	WM	11m	Inmate
Cooney, Annie Cecilia	WF	28	Nurse
Corcoran, Helen	WF	2, 11m	Inmate
Corcoran, Helen	WF	5	Inmate
Coriadi, Louise	WF	3, 10m	Inmate

Corin, Anna	WF	24	Nurse
Cornell, Harry	WM	2, 6m	Inmate
Costa, Rita	WF	3, 3m	Inmate
Costibile, Paolo	WM	1, 6m	Inmate
Cote, Alice	WF	7m	Inmate
Cote, Pauline	WF	22	Nurse
Coughin, Ellen	WF	2	Inmate
Couppe, Henry	WM	4	Inmate
Cox, Daisey	BF	2, 7m	Inmate
Cozzi, Antonio	WM	6	Inmate
Cozzi, Doloreta	WF	7	Inmate
Craimpo, Anthony	WM	2, 3m	Inmate
Cromie, Mary E.	WF	26	Laundress
Cronin, John	WM	5	Inmate
Cronin, Mary	WF	6	Inmate
Cronin, Thomas	WM	4	Inmate
Crosby, Edward	WM	2	Inmate
Crosby, Harold	WM	4	Inmate
Crowley, Joseph	WM	1, 9m	Inmate
Cucetro, Louis	WM	3, 1m	Inmate
Cucetro, Robert	WM	4	Inmate
Cufiano, Rocco	WM	5	Inmate
Cullen, Rose Lillie	WF	26	Trained Nurse
Cullin, Thomas	WM	3, 3m	Inmate
Cunningham, Edwin	WM	1, 7m	Inmate
Cunningham, Helen	WF	1, 10m	Inmate
Cunningham, James	WM	2, 3m	Inmate
Cuomo, Rafaello	WM	7	Inmate
Cupryk, Michael	WM	5	Inmate
Curan, Mary	WF	34	Nurse
Curcio, Thomas	WM	6	Inmate
Curnney, Anna	WF	3m	Inmate
Currie, Annie	WF	35	Sister of Charity
Cusick, Joseph	WM	4	Inmate
Cusick, Thomas	WM	4	Inmate
Custic, John	WM	5	Inmate
Cvitkuvico, William	WM	7	Inmate
Czentocky, Paul	WM	2, 11m	Inmate
Dady, Irene	WF	1, 1m	Inmate
Dady, Irene	WF	17	Nurse
Daley, David	WM	6	Inmate
Daley, Stephen	WM	3, 2m	Inmate

Dalton, Ann	WF	26	Nurse
Dalton, James	WM	3, 3m	Inmate
Daly, Rita	WF	3, 6m	Inmate
Daniels, George	WM	1, 1m	Inmate
D'Anna, Salvatore	WM	5	Inmate
Danshea, Arthur	WM	5	Inmate
Darcey, Matthew	WM	0m	Inmate
Darnn, Edward	WM	2, 5m	Inmate
Darzi, Dominick	WM	2, 11m	Inmate
D'Augustino, Marie	WF	1, 5m	Inmate
D'Aurio, Antoinette	WF	2, 5m	Inmate
Davino, Tessie	WF	1, 5m	Inmate
Davis, Charles	WM	4	Inmate
Davis, Emma	WF	6	Inmate
Davis, John	WM	8m	Inmate
Davis, Lucy	WF	21	Nurse
Day, Francis	WM	5	Inmate
D'Carlo, Rose	WF	1, 4m	Inmate
Deak, George	WM	6	Inmate
DeAngelis, Angelo	WM	3, 3m	Inmate
December, Peter	WM	4	Inmate
DeCicco, Dominick	WM	2, 5m	Inmate
DeCicco, Felix	WM	4	Inmate
DeCisso, Rose	WF	5	Inmate
Decker, Charles	WM	3, 5m	Inmate
DeFrania, Louis	WM	2, 5m	Inmate
Degan, Bernard	WM	4	Inmate
DeLalla, Antonio	WM	3, 3m	Inmate
DeLalla, Marie	WF	3, 3m	Inmate
Delaney, John	WM	5	Inmate
Delaney, Joseph	WM	4	Inmate
DeLea, Bertha	WF	1, 2m	Inmate
Dellacambria, Tony	WM	6	Inmate
Dellacona, Jennie	WF	2, 11m	Inmate
Dellastein, Madeline	WF	2, 10m	Inmate
Delledansko, Gactano	WM	2, 4m	Inmate
Delors, Sophia	WF	5m	Inmate
Delsomo, Lawrence	WM	3, 3m	Inmate
DeLusia, Helen	WF	2, 10m	Inmate
Delvey, Carrie	WF	3	Inmate
DeMarino, Catherine	WF	6	Inmate
DeMarso, Catherine	WF	1, 3m	Inmate

DeMartina, Elsie	WF	2, 11m	Inmate
DeMartuso, Carlo	WM	4	Inmate
DeMarzo, Dorothy	WF	2, 7m	Inmate
Demetto, Juliette	WF	4	Inmate
Demits, Hattie	WF	24	Cook
Dempsy, Loretta T.	WF	23	Laundress
Derbyshire, Gertrude	WF	2, 11m	Inmate
Dernny, George	WM	4	Inmate
DeSantis, Ida	WF	3, 4m	Inmate
DeSanto, Franceso	WM	2, 1m	Inmate
Deschulka, Victoria	WF	5	Inmate
DeStephano, John	WM	2, 5m	Inmate
Detville, Rodolpho	WM	1, 5m	Inmate
Devanney, Annie	WF	4	Inmate
Devine, Frank	WM	7	Inmate
Devlin, Mary Josephine	WF	20	Bookkeeper
Diaz, Elise	WF	21	Nurse
Diaz, Paul	WM	4	Inmate
Diconza, Giulomica	WF	1, 4m	Inmate
DiCristina, Rocco	WM	2, 7m	Inmate
DiDomino, Tony	WM	2, 6m	Inmate
DiDonato, John	WM	1, 11m	Inmate
Dietrich, Harry	WM	2, 8m	Inmate
DiGennaro, Frank	WM	1, 6m	Inmate
Diguiseppi, Mary	WF	4, 4m	Inmate
DiMarino, Nunziata	WM	5	Inmate
DiMartin, Phillip	WM	3, 1m	Inmate
Diovanni, Alfred	WM	6	Inmate
Dismond, Thomas	WM	6	Inmate
Dixon, Emily Frances Ann	WF	19	Stenographer
Dixon, Emma	WF	46	Boarder
Dmytrysozn, Michael	WM	1, 3m	Inmate
Dobrowlska, Dorothy	WF	5	Inmate
Dolan, Mary	WF	4m	Inmate
Dominico, Guiseppe	WM	5	Inmate
Donahue, Edward	WM	3, 2m	Inmate
Donahue, Emmit	WM	4	Inmate
Donaldson, Joseph	WM	4	Inmate
Donavan, Margaret	WF	11m	Inmate
Donavan, William J.	WM	3m	Inmate
Donegan, John J.	WM	32	Steam Engineer
Donilock, John	WM	2, 1m	Inmate

Donnellan, Edward	WM	2, 8m	Inmate
Donnelly, James	WM	5	Inmate
Dooley, Thomas F.	WM	49	Porter
Doran, Vincent	WM	11m	Inmate
Doreshen, William	WM	3	Inmate
Dorne, Frank	WM	2, 2m	Inmate
Dorrity, Mary	WF	3, 3m	Inmate
Dorsett, Germain	BF	10	Inmate
Dousy, James	WM	3, 3m	Inmate
Dowling, Helen	WF	4	Inmate
Down, Gabriel	WM	8	Inmate
Downey, Robert	WM	1, 5m	Inmate
Doyle, Augusta F.	WF	33	Sister of Charity
Doyle, Catherine	WF	42	Trained Nurse
Doyle, Charles	WM	3, 7m	Inmate
Doyle, Mary	WF	2, 3m	Inmate
Doyle, Thomas	WM	2, 6m	Inmate
Drake, John	WM	3, 3m	Inmate
Drfay, Elizabeth	WF	40	Laundress
D'Sonato, Angeline	WF	2, 8m	Inmate
Duane, Thomas	WM	3, 8m	Inmate
Dubry, Alexander	WM	6	Inmate
Duffy, Marie	WF	9m	Inmate
Duffy, Paul	WM	4, 10m	Inmate
Duffy, Sabina	WF	39	Teacher
Dugan, Frank	WM	4	Inmate
Dugan, John	WM	5	Inmate
Dugan, Thelma	WF	5m	Inmate
Duggan, Edward	WM	4	Inmate
Dujick, Julius	WM	3, 11m	Inmate
Dulla, John	WM	5	Inmate
Dum, John	WM	7m	Inmate
Duma, Anna	WF	48	Laundress
Dunfry, Agnes	WF	4	Inmate
Dunleavy, Thomas	WM	1, 11m	Inmate
Dunn, Albert	WM	10	Ward
Dunn, Ellen	WF	61	Sister of Charity
Dunne, George	WM	3, 1m	Inmate
Dunne, James	WM	4	Inmate
Dunninghan, Margaret	WF	54	Trained Nurse
Durant, John	WM	3, 10m	Inmate
Dursey, Walter	WM	10	Inmate

Dwyer, John	WM	6	Inmate
Dwyer, P. Harold	WM	5	Inmate
Dxehold, Jenni	WF	30	Kitchen Girl
Dziengielewski, John	WM	2, 4m	Inmate
Early, Barbara	WF	1m	Inmate
Early, Clara	WF	5	Inmate
Edgerton, Elizabeth	WM*	5	Inmate
Edwards, Gladys	BF	8	Inmate
Edwards, Harold	WM	6	Inmate
Edwards, Joseph	WM	5	Inmate
Edwards, William	WM	8m	Inmate
Egan, Catherine	WF	37	Sister of Charity
Ehlern, Rose	WF	6m	Inmate
Ehlern, Rose	WF	26	Nurse
Elconta, Rose	WF	2, 4m	Inmate
Elizabeth, Christie	WF	7	Inmate
Elliot, John	WM	9	Inmate
Ennis, John	WM	4	Inmate
Ershoff, Leon	WM	4	Inmate
Eskhart, John	WM	5	Inmate
Esposito, Armiello	WM	2, 3m	Inmate
Esposito, Ralph	WM	2, 9m	Inmate
Esposito, Rose	WF	2, 11m	Inmate
Evans, Elizabeth	WF	1, 5m	Inmate
Evans, Joseph	BM	8	Inmate
Evans, Maud	WF	4	Inmate
Everett, Margaret	WF	3m	Inmate
Everett, Paul	WM	0m	Inmate
Ewing, Francis	BM	8	Inmate
Exlen, Mary	WF	3, 5m	Inmate
Facome, Dominick	WM	2, 4m	Inmate
Fainia, Lillie	WF	2, 11m	Inmate
Fairfield, Julia Mary	WF	34	Sister of Charity
Falsini, Jennie	WF	7	Inmate
Fanen, Veronica	WF	4	Inmate
Fanote, Lilian	WF	1, 7m	Inmate
Farley, Edward	WM	1, 9m	Inmate
Farley, Eugene	WM	2, 6m	Inmate
Farley, Joseph	WM	6	Inmate
Farley, Josephine	WF	33	Nurse
Farmar, Mary Josephine	WF	10	Ward
Farrell, Harold	WM	5	Inmate

Farrell, James	WM	3	Inmate
Fasanelli, Katie	WF	5	Inmate
Fasanelli, Marie	WF	4	Inmate
Fay, Joseph	WM	2, 11m	Inmate
Fazzino, Joseph	WM	4	Inmate
Feaser, William	WM	6	Inmate
Feeley, Eugene	WM	2, 5m	Inmate
Feeney, Augustine	WM	3, 4m	Inmate
Feeney, Rose Veronica	WF	40	Laundress
Feiger, Helen	WF	2, 3m	Inmate
Feiger, Henrietta	WF	3, 10m	Inmate
Feininski, John	WM	4	Inmate
Feldman, Albert	WM	2, 5m	Inmate
Fenari, Vincenzo	WM	3, 3m	Inmate
Fenaso, John	WM	2, 3m	Inmate
Fenatta, Dominick	WM	3, 2m	Inmate
Fenatta, Frances	WF	3, 2m	Inmate
Fencole, Joseph	WM	5	Inmate
Ferguson, Margaret	WF	5m	Inmate
Ferguson, Olive E.	WF	24	Nurse
Ferretto, Edith	WF	4	Inmate
Fersht, Rosine	WF	1, 4m	Inmate
Fiancione, Frank	WM	3, 1m	Inmate
Fiaron, Sarah, E.	WF	54	Sister of Charity
Fiattolilio, Joseph	WM	3, 5m	Inmate
Fiby, Francis	WM	3, 7m	Inmate
Figuirno, Mary	WF	7	Inmate
Filoso, Ellen	WF	2, 1m	Inmate
Fimal, Michael	WM	7	Inmate
Finan, Helen	WF	3, 8m	Inmate
Fink, Edward	WM	3, 4m	Inmate
Fink, William	WM	3, 4m	Inmate
Finnegan, Catherine	WF	5	Inmate
Finnegan, Edward	WM	2, 7m	Inmate
Finnegan, Rita	WF	5	Inmate
Finnernan, Rose	WF	3, 1m	Foundling
Fiorentino, Maurice	WM	5	Inmate
Fischu, Margaret	WF	6	Inmate
Fisher, Anna	WF	1, 4m	Inmate
Fisher, Beatrice	WF	3	Inmate
Fisher, Florence	WF	2, 2m	Inmate
Fisher, Florence	WF	6	Inmate

Fiszia, Josephine	WF	1, 9m	Inmate
Fitzgerald, Anna	WF	7m	Inmate
Fitzgerald, Helen	WF	2, 7m	Inmate
Fitzgerald, Mary	WF	32	Nurse
Fitzpatrick, Thomas	WM	4	Inmate
Fitzsimmons, Alfred	WM	3, 1m	Inmate
Flanagan, Ella	WF	3, 6m	Inmate
Flanigan, Charles	WM	4	Inmate
Flanigan, Dorothy	WM	4	Inmate
Flaskner, Marion	WF	6	Inmate
Foley, Edward	WM	1, 7m	Inmate
Fontana, Florence	WF	28	Nurse
Forbes, Katherine H.	WF	27	Trained Nurse
Ford, Albert	WM	3, 4m	Inmate
Ford, Alphonse	BM	2, 11m	Inmate
Ford, Bryon	BM	4	Inmate
Fortmasi, Alfred	WM	7	Inmate
Fost, Doris	WF	1, 11m	Inmate
Francio, Cohen	WM	5	Inmate
Franko, Arthur	WM	6m	Inmate
Franko, Mary	WF	20	Nurse
Franks, Maria	WF	33	Nurse
Frauso, John	WM	1, 9m	Inmate
Freidenbery, Almeta	WF	3m	Inmate
Freiling, Anna	WF	3, 4m	Inmate
Freitz, George	WM	3, 11m	Inmate
French, Louis	WM	3, 7m	Inmate
Fribert, Catherine	WF	13	Nurse
Fridowitz, Helen	WF	4	Inmate
Friedenbrug, Lillian	WF	21	Domestic
Fry, Mary	WF	5	Inmate
Funicelli, Philomena	WF	1, 7m	Inmate
Fusaro, Eugene	WM	9m	Inmate
Gabbamoni, Antonio	WM	3, 8m	Inmate
Gabelatto, Louis	WM	3, 7m	Inmate
Gaffney, Julia	WF	5	Inmate
Gaglimo, Girolamo	WM	2, 10m	Inmate
Gaigerslaw, Christina	WF	47	Trained Nurse
Gaines, Joseph	WM	3m	Inmate
Gale, Clement	BM	10	Inmate
Galis, Bridget	WF	3, 7m	Inmate
Gallager, Anna	WF	6	Inmate

Gallager, Helen	WF	4	Inmate
Gallager, John	WM	2, 5m	Inmate
Gallagher, Henry	WM	5	Inmate
Gallagher, John	WM	1, 4m	Inmate
Gallagher, Marie	WF	1m	Inmate
Gandetta, Joseph	WM	2	Inmate
Gannucci, Aberto	WM	6	Inmate
Gardella, Rita	WF	1, 6m	Inmate
Garguillo, Antoinette	WF	2, 11m	Inmate
Garrity, Gregory	WM	3	Inmate
Garry, Rita	WF	4	Inmate
Gattio, Guido	WM	2, 7m	Inmate
Gatto, Peter	WM	9m	Inmate
Geilock, Bronstoff	WM	5	Inmate
Geimusa, Carmelo	WM	1, 5m	Inmate
Gemiliaro, Frances	WF	1, 3m	Inmate
Gennuso, Mary	WF	7	Inmate
George, Eleanor	WF	1, 5m	Inmate
George, Mary	WF	6	Inmate
Gerlando, Caliguo	WM	11m	Inmate
Gerome, Julia	WF	3, 5m	Inmate
Gerome, Mary	WF	1, 6m	Inmate
Gerus, Olga	WF	11m	Inmate
Gessler, Marie	WF	1, 9m	Inmate
Giacomazzo, Katie	WF	1, 9m	Inmate
Giacomo, Mary	WF	1, 1m	Inmate
Giambolo, Domino	WM	4	Inmate
Gibbins, Dorothy	WF	20	Nurse
Gibbins, Joseph	WM	2, 5m	Inmate
Giglia, Nicholas	WM	2, 11m	Inmate
Giglor, Dominic	WM	2, 3m	Inmate
Giliberti, Franceso	WM	2, 11m	Inmate
Gill, Bernard	WM	7	Inmate
Gillen, Gertrude	WM	3, 5m	Inmate
Gillen, James	WM	3, 10m	Inmate
Gillespie, Joseph	WM	4	Inmate
Gillespie, Peter	WM	1, 7m	Inmate
Gilligan, Joseph	WM	2, 8m	Inmate
Gimby, Frederick	WM	1, 11m	Inmate
Ginglino, Gino	WM	4, 1m	Inmate
Ginsbery, Morris	WM	4	Inmate
Giordano, Rose	WF	1, 11m	Inmate

Giroux, Anna C.	WF	59	Sister of Charity
Glass, Bernard	WM	1m	Inmate
Gleason, Joseph	WM	4	Inmate
Glicto, Rose	WF	1, 4m	Inmate
Godet, Helen	WF	5	Inmate
Goff, Peter	WM	3	Inmate
Goggin, James	WM	2, 9m	Inmate
Gold, David	WM	7	Inmate
Gold, Pauline	WF	5	Inmate
Goldberg, Ray	WF	2, 7m	Inmate
Golden, Bert	WM	7	Inmate
Goldenbury, Frederick	WM	5	Inmate
Golis, Anna	WF	1, 3m	Inmate
Gonescue, Charles	WM	5	Inmate
Gonzales, Mario	WM	5m	Inmate
Gonzales, Rita	WF	25	Nurse
Goodbroad, John	WM	7	Inmate
Goodcraft, Mary	WF	5	Inmate
Gordon, Phillip	WM	4, 1m	Inmate
Gorgodinsky, Louisa	WF	1, 7m	Inmate
Gotti, Catherine	WF	17	Nurse
Gracey, Loretta	WF	54	Nurse
Grady, Edward	WM	5	Inmate
Grady, Ena	WF	3, 3m	Inmate
Graf, Anna	WF	9m	Inmate
Graf, Ruth	WF	3	Inmate
Graff, Anne	WF	2, 3m	Inmate
Graff, Caroline	WF	3, 5m	Inmate
Granger, Helen	WF	19	Nurse
Grant, Catherine E.	WF	65	Sister of Charity
Grant, James	WM	3, 10m	Inmate
Gravine, Elizabeth	WF	3, 1m	Inmate
Gray, Alfred	BM	8	Inmate
Gray, Margaret	WF	1, 11m	Inmate
Gray, Nicholas	WM	3m	Inmate
Graysore, Walter	WM	6	Inmate
Graziaso, George	WM	2, 11m	Inmate
Green, Edward	WM	4	Inmate
Green, Fredrick	WM	3, 9m	Inmate
Green, Isaac	WM	5	Inmate
Green, Maurice	WM	5	Inmate
Green, Ralph	WM	6m	Inmate

Green, Vernon	BM	1, 8m	Inmate
Greene, Viola	WF	17	Nurse
Grego, Josephine	WF	3, 2m	Inmate
Griffen, George	WM	2, 3m	Inmate
Griffin, Delia	WF	28	Servant
Griffin, Helen	WF	5	Inmate
Griffin, William	WF	3, 11m	Inmate
Griffiths, Mary	WF	32	Nurse
Grimes, Gerald	WM	3, 1m	Inmate
Grisalti, Vincenza	WF	2, 5m	Inmate
Gronchiska, Charles	WM	11m	Inmate
Gross, Nettie	WF	5	Inmate
Gruttadami, Mary	WF	4, 7m	Inmate
Guaino, Vincent	WM	4, 7m	Inmate
Guianto, Assunta	WF	2, 7m	Inmate
Guilford, Eleanor McBride	WF	29	Trained Nurse
Guirno, Anthony	WM	6m	Inmate
Gunn, Joseph	WM	3m	Inmate
Gursh, Louis	MuM	7	Inmate
Haas, Henry	WM	3, 7m	Inmate
Haberi, John	WM	1, 5m	Inmate
Habichd, Frank	WM	5	Inmate
Hadley, Geroge	WM	2, 2m	Inmate
Haffner, Wendell	WM	2, 11m	Inmate
Hage, Sara	WF	6m	Inmate
Halden, Catherine	WF	3, 7m	Inmate
Halden, James	WM	6	Inmate
Haldner, Henry	WM	4	Inmate
Haleman, Edward	WM	2, 1m	Inmate
Hall, Francis	WM	2, 10m	Inmate
Hall, Harold	WM	1, 11m	Inmate
Hall, James	WM	4m	Inmate
Hallenbeck, Mabel	WF	5	Inmate
Hallic, Edwin	WM	7	Inmate
Halvel, Helen	WF	5	Inmate
Hamagan, Mary	WF	3, 2m	Inmate
Hamilton, Eveyn	WF	17	Nurse
Hamilton, Ralph	WM	1m	Inmate
Hamion, John	WM	2, 11m	Inmate
Haney, Genevieve	WF	3, 6m	Inmate
Haney, Mary	WF	1, 6m	Inmate
Hanifin, Loretto	WF	33	Chambermaid

Hanington, James	WM	2, 3m	Inmate
Hanley, Richard	WM	6	Inmate
Hannigan, Annie	WF	48	Waitress
Hannington, Louis	WM	3, 7m	Inmate
Hanson, Anthony	WM	4	Inmate
Hanson, Fransis	WM	9m	Inmate
Hansotty, Jerome	WM	1, 1m	Inmate
Hardy, Theresa	WF	7m	Inmate
Hare, Elizabeth	WF	20	Nurse
Hare, William	WM	2, 5m	Inmate
Harper, Anna Marie	WF	23	Nurse
Harper, Charles	WM	1, 11m	Inmate
Harper, Gladys	WF	3	Inmate
Harrifen, Francis	WM	9m	Inmate
Harrington, Cecilia	WF	2m	Inmate
Harris, Ernest	WM	1, 11m	Inmate
Harris, Helene	WF	5	Inmate
Harris, John	WM	4	Inmate
Harris, John	WM	6	Inmate
Harris, Randoph	BM	5	Inmate
Harrison, Pauline	WF	23	Student, Boarder
Hart, Delia	WF	47	Kitchen
Hart, Mary	WF	2, 1m	Inmate
Hart, Nora	WF	27	Servant
Harth, Clara Agnes	WF	20	Nurse
Harth, Joseph	WM	2, 2m	Inmate
Harting, Paul	WM	4	Inmate
Harvey, Marie	WF	3, 6m	Inmate
Havens, Rudoph	WM	3, 4m	Inmate
Haviland, Louis	WM	4	Inmate
Hawkins, Alice	WF	1, 5m	Inmate
Hayes, Michael	WM	7m	Inmate
Hayes, Vincent	WM	3, 8m	Inmate
Hayman, Henry	WM	5	Inmate
Hayman, Stephen	WM	4	Inmate
Haynes, Reginald	WM	3, 2m	Inmate
Haynor, Joseph	WM	3, 10m	Inmate
Hayward, Malcolm	WM	7	Inmate
Healey, Joseph	WM	7	Inmate
Healy, Anna	WF	11m	Inmate
Healy, Rita	WM	4	Inmate
Heaney, Thomas	WM	2, 1m	Inmate

Hefferman, Joseph	WM	?m	Inmate
Hefferman, Josephine	WF	5	Inmate
Heil, George	WM	5	Inmate
Heinn, Alfreda	WF	1, 10m	Inmate
Heins, Anna	WF	32	Kitchen
Heins, Otto	WM	4	Inmate
Henk, Sophie	WF	4	Inmate
Henning, Charles	WM	4	Inmate
Henry, Bernard	WM	1, 11m	Inmate
Heny, Marjorie	WF	2, 7m	Inmate
Hertel, Henry	WM	11m	Inmate
Hescka, John	WM	2	Inmate
Hess, Joseph	WM	2	Inmate
Hessler, Nicholas	WM	2m	Inmate
Higby, Mary	WF	20	Trained Nurse
Higgin, Marie	WF	4	Inmate
Higgins, Joseph	WM	6m	Inmate
Higgins, Mary	WF	29	Nurse
Hill, David	WM	4	Inmate
Hill, Harry	WM	1, 7m	Inmate
Hill, Lillian	BF	9	Inmate
Hill, Marion	WF	1, 7m	Inmate
Hines, Jennie	WF	27	Servant
Hitchellen, Rita	WF	4m	Inmate
Hoar, Martin	WM	3, 2m	Foundling
Hoey, Joseph	WM	2	Inmate
Hoffler, Albertina	WF	26	Trained Nurse
Hoffman, Louise	WF	3, 4m	Inmate
Hoffman, Rudoph	WM	6	Inmate
Holland, Gabriella	WF	4	Inmate
Holman, Wilfred	BM	8	Inmate
Holmes, Robert	BM	6	Inmate
Holske, Mary	BF	8	Inmate
Hoodley, Walter	WM	3, 10m	Inmate
Hook, William	WM	3, 11m	Inmate
Hoolahan, William	WM	6	Inmate
Horan, Ethel	WF	1, 6m	Inmate
Horrigan, Lawrence	WM	3, 4m	Inmate
Howard, Walter	WM	1, 5m	Inmate
Howards, Margaret	WM	1, 8m	Inmate
Howe, Francis	WM	5	Inmate
Hughes, William	WM	4	Inmate

Hunt, Helen	WF	0m	Inmate
Hunt, John	WM	3	Inmate
Hunt, Valentine	WM	3, 8m	Inmate
Hunter, Arthur	WM	1, 11m	Inmate
Hurley, Anna Francis	WF	58	Sister of Charity
Hurley, Edward	WM	2, 2m	Inmate
Hurley, Edward M.	WM	8	Inmate
Iaconne, Mario	WF*	6m	Inmate
Iko, Providence	WF	5	Inmate
Impastato, Gasparo	WM	3, 1m	Inmate
Ingraffa, Lucille	WF	2, 5m	Inmate
Inoheran, John	BM	8	Inmate
Irvolino, Jerry	WM	1, 10m	Inmate
Isaac, Henry	WM	5	Inmate
Isaac, William	WM	3	Inmate
Jackson, Eleanora	WF	3, 7m	Inmate
Jackson, Vincent	WM	2, 1m	Inmate
Jacob, Joseph	WM	7	Inmate
Jakinowitz, Agnes	WF	2, 6m	Inmate
Jakminowitz, Helen	WF	7	Inmate
Jakminowitz, Jennie	WF	5	Inmate
Jakymyio, Johanna	WF	5	Inmate
James, Horace	WM	8	Inmate
Janask, Dorothy	WF	5	Inmate
Jardener, Marie	WF	10m	Inmate
Jaropky, Steven	WM	4, 3m	Inmate
Jogminas, Joseph	WM	6	Inmate
Johnmychalf, Joseph	WM	8	Inmate
Johnson, Beatrice	BF	5	Inmate
Johnson, Carrie	BF	8	Inmate
Johnson, Charles	BM	9	Inmate
Johnson, Christina	WF	11m	Inmate
Johnson, Francis	WM	6	Inmate
Johnson, Joseph	MuM	7	Inmate
Johnson, Mary	WF	7m	Inmate
Johnson, Theophilio	WM	8	Inmate
Johnston, John	WM	2, 4m	Inmate
Johnston, Mary Agnes	WF	33	Nurse
Jordan, Angela	WF	1, 11m	Inmate
Jordan, Julius	WM	8	Inmate
Joyce, Irene	WF	7	Inmate
Juliano, Millie	WF	2, 9m	Inmate

Julik, Frank	WM	4	Inmate
Juliven, Henry	WM	3, 9m	Inmate
Kane, Francis	WM	3m	Inmate
Kane, John	WM	3	Inmate
Kane, Mary	WF	35	Housework
Kane, Thomas	WM	4	Inmate
Kann, Gordan	WM	6	Inmate
Karitzka, Victoria	WF	28	Nurse
Karo, Mary	WF	2, 6m	Inmate
Katavotas, Amelia	WF	2, 11m	Inmate
Katshisk, Edward	WM	2, 8m	Inmate
Katz, Edward	WM	3, 4m	Inmate
Kavanagh, James	WM	3, 5m	Inmate
Kavanagh, John	WM	6	Inmate
Kavanaugh, George	WM	7m	Inmate
Keal, John	WM	2, 5m	Inmate
Keane, Mary	WF	0m	Inmate
Kearney, Margaret	WF	1, 7m	Inmate
Kearney, Margaret M.	WF	36	Sister of Charity
Kearns, John	WM	6	Inmate
Keatos, Felix	WM	5	Inmate
Keefer, Henry	WM	6	Inmate
Keenan, Margaret	WF	2, 1m	Inmate
Kelen, Woodrow	WM	11m	Inmate
Keller, Joseph	WM	3, 8m	Inmate
Kelly, Adrice	WF	3, 1m	Inmate
Kennedy, Catherine	WF	18	Nurse
Kennedy, Henry	WM	1, 4m	Inmate
Kennedy, James	WM	11m	Inmate
Kennedy, Johanna	WF	23	Domestic
Kennedy, Ralph	WM	5	Inmate
Kenny, Joseph	WM	1, 9m	Inmate
Kent, John	WM	2, 1m	Inmate
Kienzle, Alfred	WM	4	Inmate
Kilchik, John	WM	1, 7m	Inmate
Kilcullen, James	WM	4	Inmate
Killard, William	WM	8	Inmate
King, Audrey	BM*	4	Inmate
King, Dorothy	BF	10	Inmate
King, John	WM	1, 11m	Inmate
King, Mary	WF	1, 10m	Inmate
King, Mary Agnonas	WF	23	Nurse

King, Thomas	WM	2, 1m	Inmate
Kinters, George	WM	1, 11m	Inmate
Kirby, Maurice	WM	3, 7m	Inmate
Kireholski, Barbara	WF	21	Nurse
Klal, Bertha	WF	26	Laundress
Klatt, Louis	WM	5	Inmate
Klayne, George	WM	4	Inmate
Kleim, Mark	WM	8	Inmate
Klein, Mary	WF	1, 3m	Inmate
Klein, Micheal	WM	2, 1m	Inmate
Klem, Julia	WF	25	Nurse
Klien, William	WM	4	Inmate
Kodis, Lillian	WF	4	Inmate
Kohovick, Mary	WF	23	Nurse
Kopezor, John	WM	1m	Inmate
Kornborosisk, Wadisloba	WF	1, 11m	Inmate
Kosky, Anna	WF	7	Inmate
Krawl, Charles	WF	3, 3m	Inmate
Krispky, Stephen	WM	2, 11m	Inmate
Krusku, Thomas	WM	4	Inmate
Kubis, Frank	BM	5	Inmate
Kumisky, Stephen	WM	2, 6m	Inmate
Kumpter, Ida	WF	3, 11m	Inmate
Kunseath, George	WM	5	Inmate
Kuring, William	WM	6	Inmate
Kurkchi, John	WM	2, 1m	Inmate
Kusera, Carmela	WF	1, 5m	Inmate
Kuss, Ruth	WF	1, 1m	Inmate
Kutnosyki, John	WM	3, 10m	Inmate
Kwelty, Joseph	WM	5	Inmate
Kyle, Arthur	WM	3, 7m	Inmate
Labato, Concetta	WF	1, 2m	Inmate
Lacrusa, Anna	WF	3, 6m	Inmate
Ladduck, Mary	WF	4	Inmate
LaForte, Katie	WF	3, 7m	Inmate
LaGahon, Olga	WF	3, 5m	Inmate
Laggamana, Kate	WF	4, 11m	Inmate
Laggamana, William	WM	2, 6m	Inmate
Laiken, Mary	WF	2, 2m	Inmate
Lakashovitz, Frank	WM	2, 11m	Inmate
Lallo, Elsie	WF	2, 3m	Inmate
Lamberton, Joseph	WM	9m	Inmate

Lambertson, Anna Agnes	WF	27	Nurse
Lanzelti, Ralph	WM	2, 7m	Inmate
LaPianed, Anthony	WM	4	Inmate
Lapina, Mary	WF	46	Servant
Lappin, Bernard	WM	7	Inmate
Lappin, Ellen	WF	1, 8m	Inmate
Lappin, William	WM	6	Inmate
Larkin, Marion	WF	5	Inmate
Larney, Francis	WM	2, 11m	Inmate
LaRocca, Joseph	WM	7	Inmate
LaRusso, Rosie	WF	4	Inmate
Latuska, Edward	WM	1, 8m	Inmate
Laufe, Eva	WF	1, 8m	Inmate
Laughlin, Joseph F.	WM	61	Elevator Operator
Lavin, Richard	WM	2, 2m	Inmate
Lawler, Mary Anna	WF	21	Trained Nurse
Lawrence, Henrietta	BF	8	Inmate
Leary, Mary E.	WF	32	Nurse
Leary, William	WM	5	Inmate
Leavy, George	WM	3, 2m	Inmate
LeBana, Dolores	WF	9	Inmate
Lee, Alice Josephine	WF	20	Nurse
Lee, Eileen	WF	1m	Inmate
LeGakou, Anna	WF	1, 11m	Inmate
Lehra, William	WM	5m	Inmate
Lehris, Sarah Carrie	WF	22	Nurse
Lenahan, George	WM	7	Foundling
Lenihan, Mary Jane	WF	74	Sister of Charity
Lennonn, Louise Frances	WF	38	Sister of Charity
Lennon, George	WM	3, 4m	Inmate
Lennon, Margaret	WF	3, 5m	Inmate
Leonad, Mary	WF	1, 1m	Inmate
Leonadson, John	WM	4	Inmate
Leonard, Catherine	WF	2	Inmate
Leonardo, Jennie	WF	2, 4m	Inmate
Leone, Adeline	WF	6	Inmate
Lepro, Louis	WM	3, 3m	Inmate
Lesofska, Katie	WF	3, 10m	Inmate
Levine, Adoph	WM	3, 2m	Inmate
Levy, James	WM	5	Inmate
Lewis, Anna	WF	5m	Inmate
Lewis, Euard	WM	4	Inmate

Licata, Charles	WM	1, 11m	Inmate
Lichel, Carl	WM	3	Inmate
Ligscore, Leopold	WM	1, 5m	Inmate
Lind, Andrew	WM	1, 4m	Inmate
Linda, John	WM	2, 5m	Inmate
Linguadvea, Nattine	WF	16	Nurse
Linkovoitch, Thomas	WM	11	Inmate
Lipusky, Helen	WF	5	Inmate
Lisani, Leonard	WM	3	Inmate
Livingston, Edwin	WM	2m	Inmate
Lockett, Katie	WF	23	Nurse
LoGrassa, Ignatz	WM	1, 5m	Inmate
Loney, Michael	WM	4	Inmate
Longstano, Carmela	WF	6	Inmate
Lorance, Theodore	WM	6	Inmate
Loretta, Mary	WF	3, 10m	Inmate
Lorinez, Irene	WF	1, 6m	Inmate
Losi, Mario	WM	5	Inmate
Loughin, Ellen	WF	47	Portess
Louparian, Raymond	WM	1, 7m	Inmate
Lovallo, Joseph	WM	1, 1m	Inmate
Loytey, Eva	WF	1, 3m	Inmate
Lucia, Charles	WM	1, 4m	Inmate
Lucia, Robert	WM	3, 7m	Inmate
Lucy, Raymond	WM	6	Inmate
Ludwig, Frank	WM	4	Inmate
Luigiodoca, Marie	WF	11m	Inmate
Lulli, Augustine	WF	2, 4m	Inmate
Lune, Miriam F.	WF	25	Sister of Charity
Lunny, Ernest	WM	1, 11m	Inmate
Lurosky, Edward	WM	5	Inmate
Lussi, Vito	WM	9m	Inmate
Lynch, Frances	WM	1, 11m	Inmate
Lyons, Catherine Mary	WF	61	Sister of Charity
Macamana, Delia	WF	36	Maid
Mackey, Isabella F.	WF	71	Boarder
Mackey, Mary J.	WF	80	Boarder
Madden, Joseph	WM	2, 4m	Inmate
Madden, Thomas	WM	4	Inmate
Madelina, Benedict	WM	2, 7m	Inmate
Madia, Jennie	WF	2, 9m	Inmate
Madia, Tony	WM	1, 7m	Inmate

Madlima, Rose	WF	1, 1m	Inmate
Maffia, Antonio	WM	1, 11m	Inmate
Mafftone, Rapheal	WF*	2, 7m	Inmate
Mahady, Francis	WM	1, 1m	Inmate
Mahady, William	WM	2, 3m	Inmate
Maher, Elizabeth	WF	5	Inmate
Mahoney, Edward	WM	2, 3m	Inmate
Maiello, Patsy	WM	2, 9m	Inmate
Maimo, Margaret	WF	1, 10m	Inmate
Maivini, James	WM	4	Inmate
Malink, Wysal	WM	6	Inmate
Malinowski, Alexander	WM	7	Inmate
Malkus, Mary	WF	1, 7m	Inmate
Mallete, Angelina	WF	1, 9m	Inmate
Mallory, Thersa	WF	58	Laundress
Malone, Francis	WF	4	Inmate
Maloney, John	WM	5	Inmate
Mamny, John	WM	1, 5m	Inmate
Mancalo, Guiseppe	WM	1, 10m	Inmate
Mancer, Lillian	WF	6	Inmate
Manciartodo, Lolitia	WF	6	Inmate
Manley, James	WM	5	Inmate
Mann, August	WM	4	Inmate
Manning, Mary F.	WF	72	Sister of Charity
Mannis, Clare	WF	3	Inmate
Mannix, Raymond	WM	2, 11m	Inmate
Manolia, Ernest	WM	2m	Inmate
Marcowitz, Jennie	WF	5	Inmate
Marcurio, Peter	WM	3, 3m	Inmate
Maresoco, Joseph	WM	6	Inmate
Mario, Sadie	WF	3, 3m	Inmate
Marion, Francis	WM	6	Inmate
Markiesh, Salvatore	WM	4	Inmate
Marmorale, Mary	WF	2	Inmate
Marone, James	WM	1, 7m	Inmate
Marshese, John	WM	2, 11m	Inmate
Martin, Catherine Frances	WF	17	Nurse
Martin, Joseph	WM	3, 10m	Inmate
Martin, Mary	WF	15	Ward
Martin, Pauline	WM*	2, 10m	Inmate
Martino, Carlo	WM	4	Inmate
Martino, Giovanni	WM	6	Inmate

Marzigliano, Madeline	WF	4	Inmate
Marzigliano, Marguerite	WF	6	Inmate
Marzigliano, Rosie	WF	5	Inmate
Marzigliano, Vito	WM	7	Inmate
Mascirelli, Gertrude	WF	4, 3m	Inmate
Maskie, John	WM	4	Inmate
Masoia, Anna	WF	2, 5m	Inmate
Massasa, John	WM	2, 1m	Inmate
Maston, Carrillia	WF	2, 9m	Inmate
Masy, Mark	WM	4	Inmate
Mateo, George	WM	1, 4m	Inmate
Matthews, Harry	WM	4	Inmate
Mauceri, Joseph	WM	4	Inmate
Maund, Alfred	WM	7	Inmate
Maxcuto, Frank	WM	4	Inmate
Mazzia, Carmelia	WF	1, 10m	Inmate
McAide, John	WM	2	Inmate
McAlar, Jane T.	WF	52	Sister of Charity
McBride, Katie	WF	5	Inmate
McCabe, Julia	WF	29	Nurse
McCabe, Mary	WF	5	Inmate
McCarmody, Helen	WF	11m	Inmate
McCarthy, Elizabeth	WF	2m	Inmate
McCarthy, Frances	WF	17	Nurse
McCarthy, Kathleen	WF	1, 11m	Inmate
McCarthy, Mary	WF	7m	Inmate
McCarthy, Mary Louise	WF	35	Sister of Charity
McCarthy, Thomas	WM	4	Inmate
McClure, Frederick	WM	7	Inmate
McCluskey, Joseph	WM	5	Inmate
McColliers, Joseph	WM	8	Inmate
McConnell, Margaret	WF	6m	Inmate
McCormack, Leo	WM	4	Inmate
McCormack, Marguerite C.	WF	23	Trained Nurse
McCormick, John	WM	5	Inmate
McCormody, Helen	WF	24	Nurse
McDonald, Joseph	WM	4	Inmate
McDonald, Marion	WF	11	Ward
McDonald, Richard	WM	2, 8m	Inmate
McDonald, Sarah	WF	22	Nurse
McDonald, Vincent J.	WM	7	Inmate
McDonough, Margaret	WF	6	Inmate

McFadden, Beatrice Teresa	WF	30	Chambermaid
McFarland, Mark	WM	5	Inmate
McGahran, Mary	WF	7m	Inmate
McGanigle, Anna	WF	3, 3m	Inmate
McGee [Blank]	WM	1m	Inmate
McGee, Helen	WF	18	Chambermaid
McGee, James	WM	1, 10m	Inmate
McGee, John J.	WM	45	Coal Passer
McGee, Rose Frances	WF	40	Servant
McGloria, Joseph	WM	1, 7m	Inmate
McGonery, William	WM	6	Inmate
McGowan, Alice	WF	16	Nurse
McGowan, Robert	WM	0m	Inmate
McGowan, Walter	WM	3, 5m	Inmate
McGrath, Mary	WF	3m	Inmate
McGraw, Russell J.	WM	25	Medical Doctor
McGrorey, John	WM	4	Inmate
McGuiness, John	WM	3, 11m	Inmate
McGuire, Agnes	WF	1, 9m	Inmate
McGuire, Arthur	WM	2, 4m	Inmate
McGuire, Ceclilia	WF	2, 1m	Inmate
McGuire, Julia	WF	33	Nurse
McGuire, Mary	WF	25	Servant
McGuirk, Joseph	WM	8	Inmate
McGurk, Catherine	WF	3, 4m	Inmate
McHale, John	WM	3, 7m	Inmate
McHugh, Joseph	WM	6m	Inmate
McHugh, Rudoph	WM	5	Inmate
McIneenay, Francis	WM	1, 4m	Inmate
McKenna, Clara C.	WF	61	Sister of Charity
McKenna, Teresa	WF	1, 3m	Inmate
McKneally, Mary Agnes	WF	42	Sister of Charity
McLain, Elizabeth	BM	8	Inmate
McLaughlin, Antoina	WF	40	Servant
McLaughlin, Lena	WF	45	Servant
McLean, Paretta	WF	6	Inmate
McMahon, [Blank]	WF	4	Inmate
McManns, Helen	WF	22	Nurse
McManus, Francis	WM	1, 4m	Inmate
McMilty, James J.	WM	7	Inmate
McMonon, Charles	WM	4	Inmate
McMullen, John	WM	1, 1m	Inmate

McMunay, Michael	WM	5, 1m	Inmate
McNeal, Minnie	WF	2, 2m	Inmate
McNeil, Bertrand	WM	3, 6m	Inmate
McNeil, Rita	WF	3, 1m	Inmate
McNight, Dorothy	WM*	6m	Inmate
McNulty, Annie Agnes	WF	30	Nurse
McQuay, Ernestine	BF	6	Inmate
McQueeny, Margaret	WF	1m	Inmate
McQueeny, Margaret	WF	32	Nurse
McShelty, Marjorie	WF	60	Sister of Charity
McSherry, Francis	WM	4	Inmate
Mead, Elizabeth	WF	28	Servant
Mead, Walter	WM	2, 11m	Inmate
Meade, Louis	BM	3, 11m	Inmate
Meany, John	WM	1, 11m	Inmate
Meany, Nellie	WF	1, 10m	Inmate
Meany, Thomas	WM	3, 7m	Inmate
Meeshan, Loretta	WF	5m	Inmate
Meesinshu, Edward	WM	3, 2m	Inmate
Meraski, Stephen	WM	2, 8m	Inmate
Merchant, Carl	WM	2, 11m	Inmate
Merolu, Alfred	WM	4	Inmate
Merpes, Gussie	WM	5	Inmate
Meskrim, Francis	MuM	2, 4m	Inmate
Michaels, Frank	WM	7	Inmate
Miched, Serg	WM	3, 7m	Inmate
Middleton, Winifred	BF	9	Inmate
Mile, Alfred	WM	5	Inmate
Mile, Nicholas	WM	6	Inmate
Miller, Elizabeth	WF	2, 4m	Inmate
Miller, Howard	WM	2m	Inmate
Miller, Peter	WM	3, 5m	Inmate
Miller, Raymond	WM	3, 11m	Inmate
Milo, Michael	WM	4	Inmate
Mincovi, Joseph	WM	6	Inmate
Mingeni, Tomina	WF	2, 6m	Inmate
Miotte, Louise	WF	2, 10m	Inmate
Mirabella, Nicolo	WM	2, 11m	Inmate
Mirone, Alessio	WM	2, 3m	Inmate
Mischant, Susan	WF	40	Nurse
Miseta, Tomasina	WF	3, 10m	Inmate
Mitchell, Edward	WM	6	Inmate

Mohler, Marie	WF	0m	Inmate
Moldawn, Steve	WM	2, 11m	Inmate
Moldowan, Annie	WF	4, 3m	Inmate
Mole, Mary	WF	3, 7m	Inmate
Monahan, William	WM	2, 1m	Inmate
Mondello, Frederick	WM	3, 4m	Inmate
Mone, Amelia	WF	5	Inmate
Monnelly, Elizabeth	WF	23	Trained Nurse
Montagna, Vincent	WM	3	Inmate
Montalbano, Joseph	WM	3, 1m	Inmate
Moon, Edward	WM	4	Inmate
Moonial, Mary	WF	1, 5m	Inmate
Moore, Catherine	WF	23	Nurse
Moore, Charles	WM	1, 1m	Inmate
Moore, Grace	WF	1, 4m	Inmate
Moore, Margaret	WF	1, 6m	Inmate
Moore, Thomas	WM	3, 7m	Inmate
Moran, Ann Agnes	WF	54	Sister of Charity
Moran, Anna	WF	2, 3m	Inmate
Moran, Arthur	WM	5	Inmate
Moran, Edward	WM	4	Inmate
Moran, Francis	WM	7	Inmate
Moran, John	WM	5	Inmate
Moran, Monica	WF	18	Trained Nurse
Moravec, Albert	WM	4	Inmate
Morganelli, Rose	WF	2, 11m	Inmate
Morie, Gorki	WM	2, 3m	Inmate
Morissey, Michael	WM	5	Inmate
Morley, Eleanor	WF	1, 8m	Inmate
Morris, Edith	WF	6	Inmate
Morris, John	WM	4	Inmate
Morrisey, Margaret	WF	2, 11m	Inmate
Morrisey, Mary	WF	1, 5m	Inmate
Morry, Rose	WF	7	Inmate
Morten, John	WM	1, 9m	Inmate
Morton, John	WM	3, 2m	Inmate
Morton, John J.	WM	22	Asst. Engineer
Morwin, Victor	WM	4m	Inmate
Moscowitz, Reuben	WM	7	Inmate
Moser, Francis	WM	3, 5m	Inmate
Mott, Julia	WF	1, 4m	Inmate
Motta, Dominick	WM	3	Inmate

Motta, Julius	WM	3, 7m	Inmate
Mottley, Mabel	WF	27	Domestic
Muhoy, Helen	WF	2, 2m	Inmate
Mulholland, Susanna M.	WF	54	Sister of Charity
Mulhull, Edward	WM	4	Inmate
Mulin, Josephine	WF	3, 10m	Inmate
Mullane, Mary	WF	86	Boarder
Mullany, Walter	WM	6m	Inmate
Mullen, Mary	WF	1, 10m	Inmate
Muller, Helen	WF	2, 1m	Inmate
Muller, John	WM	7	Inmate
Muller, Marjorie	WF	24	Nurse
Mulligan, Arthur	WM	4	Inmate
Mulligan, John	WM	1, 8m	Inmate
Mulligan, Katie	WF	29	Nurse
Mulligan, Nellie	WF	30	Nurse
Mupent, Francis	WM	2	Inmate
Murphy, Bernard	WM	6	Inmate
Murphy, Cecilia	WF	1, 9m	Inmate
Murphy, Della	WF	3, 5m	Inmate
Murphy, Dennis	WM	4	Inmate
Murphy, Edward	BM	9	Inmate
Murphy, Elizabeth	WF	2, 11m	Inmate
Murphy, Elizabeth	WF	3, 3m	Inmate
Murphy, Ellen	WF	2, 7m	Inmate
Murphy, Florence	WF	5	Inmate
Murphy, Margaret	WF	1, 7m	Inmate
Murphy, Thomas	WM	8	Inmate
Murtell, Anita	WF	4, 4m	Inmate
Murucho, Mary	WM	7	Inmate
Musamacci, Marie	WF	2, 3m	Inmate
Muziak, Helen	WF	2	Inmate
Muzzio, Augustine	WF	3, 4m	Inmate
Myrtle, Robert D.	WM	6	Inmate
Naducci, Halrina	WF	3, 3m	Inmate
Nallase, Geraldine	WF	24	Nurse
Napolitano, Lisandio	WM	5	Inmate
Nargi, Julia	WF	3, 2m	Inmate
Nargi, William	WM	5	Inmate
Natale, Pasquale	WM	2, 4m	Inmate
Naton, Emilie R.	WF	52	Nurse
Naughton, John	WM	1, 10m	Inmate

Nealony, Francis	WM	2, 6m	Inmate
Neuman, Mark	WM	3, 6m	Inmate
Newell, Joseph	BM	6	Inmate
Newman, Walter	WM	4	Inmate
Nezulka, Joseph	WM	2, 1m	Inmate
Nishobo, Joseph	WM	5	Inmate
Nolan, Helen	WF	41	Ward
Nolan, Joseph	WM	4	Inmate
Nolasco, Mark	WM	14	Inmate
Nondello, Anthony	WM	1, 8m	Inmate
Noonan, Conrnelius	WM	5	Inmate
Nordt, William	WM	8	Inmate
Norton, Dorothy	WF	1, 3m	Inmate
Norton, Maria Regina	WF	46	Servant
Nottuno, Consetinn	WF	6	Inmate
Novak, John	WM	4	Inmate
Novelino, Margaret	WF	6	Inmate
Noyes, Mary Elizabeth	WF	63	Sister of Charity
Nuso, Madeline	WF	6	Inmate
Oaring, James	WM	3, 4m	Inmate
O'Brien, Albert	WM	4	Inmate
O'Brien, Catherine C.	WF	3	Inmate
O'Brien, Joseph	WM	0m	Inmate
O'Brien, Maria Ann	WF	49	Sister of Charity
O'Brien, Patrick	WM	4	Inmate
O'Brien, Raymond	WM	6	Inmate
O'Brien, Sophia Mary	WF	63	Cook
O'Conner, Winifred	WF	2, 10m	Inmate
O'Connor, George	WM	6	Inmate
O'Connor, Mildred	WF	1, 4m	Inmate
O'Connor, Rita	WF	4m	Inmate
O'Donnell, James	WM	1, 1m	Inmate
O'Hagan, George	WM	1, 10m	Inmate
Ohal, Mary	WF	1, 6m	Inmate
O'Hara, Anna	WF	23	Nurse
O'Hare, Bessie	WF	1, 7m	Inmate
OHare, Clement	WM	2, 4m	Inmate
Ohue, Christopher	WM	3, 5m	Inmate
Olgie, Rose	WF	1, 7m	Inmate
Oliver, Anthony	WM	4	Inmate
Olroad, Elizabeth	WF	43	Nurse
O'Mara, Winifred	WF	4	Inmate

O'Neil, Helen	WF	1, 5m	Inmate
O'Neil, William	WM	6m	Inmate
O'Reilly, James	WM	3m	Inmate
O'Rourke [Blank]	WM	4	Inmate
O'Rourke, Mary	WF	3, 4m	Inmate
O'Rourke, William	WM	2, 4m	Inmate
Orresto, Raphael	WM	3, 5m	Inmate
O'Shea, Irne	WF	3, 1m	Inmate
Ozynnyi, Barbara	WF	5	Inmate
Paduna, Alenandre	WM	1, 3m	Inmate
Pagano, Margaret	WF	1, 11m	Inmate
Paglice, Irene	WF	4	Inmate
Paiks, John	WM	5m	Inmate
Palazzo, Carmela	WF	3, 11m	Inmate
Palimbo, Joseph H.	WM	2, 4m	Inmate
Palmedo, Harold	WM	4	Inmate
Palmer, Eddie	WM	5	Inmate
Palmer, Norman	WM	8	Inmate
Palmeri, Marie	WF	3, 3m	Inmate
Palmnitesta, Vincenzo	WM	3, 6m	Inmate
Palo, Adeline	WF	6	Inmate
Papassio, Florence	WF	4	Inmate
Pardiso, Alphonse	WM	2, 3m	Inmate
Pardo, Marie	WF	3, 8m	Inmate
Pardovani, Carmina	WF	6	Inmate
Parisi, Tessie	WF	1, 7m	Inmate
Parona, Anna	WF	2, 5m	Inmate
Parsacetti, Nickolas	WM	10m	Inmate
Parson, Donald	WM	2, 3m	Inmate
Pata, Dominca	WF	2, 11m	Inmate
Paul, Charles	WM	3, 9m	Inmate
Paul, Veronica	WF	5m	Inmate
Pavomia, Anna	WF	6	Inmate
Paybold, Joseph	WM	1, 5m	Inmate
Payn, Victor	WM	4	Inmate
Pearson, Virginia	WF	1, 6m	Inmate
Peccetti, Mary	WF	2, 11m	Inmate
Pecciatore, Carmine	WM	3, 11m	Inmate
Pecciatore, Joseph	WM	5	Inmate
Pedro, Alto	WM	6m	Inmate
Peltier, Euguene	WM	4	Inmate
Pena, John	WM	4	Inmate

Pendergrast, Louisa Lynch	WF	82	Boarder
Penna, Anna	WF	2, 11m	Inmate
Penrose, Richard	WM	2m	Inmate
Perla, Josephine	WF	2, 1m	Inmate
Perlonsky, Walter	WM	3, 6m	Inmate
Perroni, Giovanni	WM	2, 6m	Inmate
Persy, John	WM	2, 5m	Inmate
Pfausch, Beatrice	BF	8	Inmate
Pfeister, Margaret	WF	1, 1m	Inmate
Phillips, Frances Dorothy	WF	17	Ward
Phillips, James	WM	4	Inmate
Picone, Italia	WF	3, 11m	Inmate
Pieno, Antoinette	WF	4	Inmate
Pierce, Philomena	WF	5m	Inmate
Pilaitano, John	WM	3, 1m	Inmate
Pilius, John	WM	5	Inmate
Pinko, Adolph	WM	1, 11m	Inmate
Pinko, Marie	WF	6m	Inmate
Pinnell, Charles	WM	6	Inmate
Pirotta, Cosmos	WM	3	Inmate
Pirotta, Dominick	WF	1, 11m	Inmate
Piscitello, Josephine	WF	2, 7m	Inmate
Pitonzo, Carmello	WM	4m	Inmate
Pitonzo, Vito	WM	4m	Inmate
Plant, Genevieve	WF	6m	Inmate
Playford, Ruth	WF	2	Inmate
Plisak, Annie	WF	2, 3m	Inmate
Pochuckowski, Casimer	WM	4	Inmate
Poggi, Antonio	WM	4	Inmate
Pohpnerio, James	WM	6	Inmate
Polacshini, Louis	WM	3	Inmate
Poligestro, Antionette	WF	1, 7m	Inmate
Polkola, Mary	WF	4	Inmate
Pollack, John	WM	1, 11m	Inmate
Polzello, Concetta	WF	5, 5m	Inmate
Polzello, Peter	WM	3, 6m	Inmate
Popetto, Nicholas	WM	1, 11m	Inmate
Popovish, Michael	WM	3, 4m	Inmate
Porter, Joseph	WM	5	Inmate
PoseKavo, Olga	WF	1, 11m	Inmate
Potter, Francis	WM	5	Inmate
Pouser, Catherine	WF	1, 11m	Inmate

Powers, David	WM	8m	Inmate
Powers, Mary	WF	0m	Inmate
Prendergast, Arthur	WM	4	Inmate
Prestieri, Alfonso	WM	3, 5m	Inmate
Price, Eugene	WM	3, 6m	Inmate
Price, Rudoph	WM	2, 3m	Inmate
Prico, Edward	WM	3, 3m	Inmate
Privatello, Ernesto	WM	5	Inmate
Probac, Gerard	WM	2, 6m	Inmate
Pronasky, Bertand	WM	3, 4m	Inmate
Provetera, Salvadore	WM	11m	Inmate
Pulco, Josephine	WF	2, 4m	Inmate
Pusanzano, James	WM	6	Inmate
Putraglia, Paul	WM	2, 4m	Inmate
Quiezzice, Mario	WM	3, 10m	Inmate
Quiezzice, Nicholas	WM	5	Inmate
Quigley, Edward	WM	4	Inmate
Quigley, Teresa	WF	21	Servant
Quigly, Loretto	WF	1, 9m	Inmate
Quilan, Winifred	WF	2m	Inmate
Quinlan, Winifred	WF	26	Nurse
Quinn, Bertram	WM	2, 9m	Inmate
Quinn, Elizabeth C.	WF	33	Trained Nurse
Racoppi, Catherine	WF	2, 6m	Inmate
Racoppi, Peter	WM	1, 4m	Inmate
Raffi, Michael	WM	3, 3m	Inmate
Raho, Judith	WM	6	Inmate
Raia, Anne	WF	2, 10m	Inmate
Railing, Clarence	WM	5	Inmate
Randino, Nuszosta	WF	2, 11m	Inmate
Randino, Sebastian	WM	4, 11m	Inmate
Ranklin, Elizabeth	WF	3, 4m	Inmate
Ranno, Carlo	WM	6	Inmate
Ranno, Philip	WM	4	Inmate
Rappaport, Sylvia	WF	3, 4m	Inmate
Ratshipp, Joseph	WM	7	Inmate
Raup, Anthony	WM	1, 11m	Inmate
Rautchie, Vincent	WM	3, 10m	Inmate
Ray, Joseph	WM	5	Inmate
Rea, Oreste	WM	4	Inmate
Readdy, Annie K.	WF	59	Sister of Charity
Reccobeni, Alfred	WM	1, 1m	Inmate

Reddick, John	BM	6	Inmate
Reddin, Elizabeth Mary	WF	45	Cook
Reddy, Alice	WF	1, 9m	Inmate
Reder, Matilda	WF	5	Inmate
Redner, Katherine	WF	2m	Inmate
Redner, Rebecca	WF	16	Nurse
Reed, Ethel	WF	2, 3m	Inmate
Reed, Harold	WM	1, 3m	Inmate
Reeves, Julius	WM	4	Inmate
Reeves, Winifred	WF	9m	Inmate
Refan, Thomas	WM	3, 10m	Inmate
Regan, Joseph	WM	1m	Inmate
Regan, Mary Veronica	WF	18	Chambermaid
Regent, George	WM	6	Inmate
Rehman, Joseph	WM	5	Inmate
Reiber, John	WM	9	Inmate
Reilly, Alice	WF	11m	Inmate
Reilly, Anni Elizabeth Mary	WF	21	Nurse
Reilly, George	WF	3, 4m	Inmate
Reilly, Jean	WF	11m	Inmate
Reilly, Joseph	WM	3, 3m	Inmate
Reilly, Margaret	WF	2, 11m	Inmate
Reilly, Thomas	WM	3, 4m	Inmate
Reizi, Linda	WF	2, 11m	Inmate
Rejesca, George	WM	5	Inmate
Remsen, Marie	WF	9m	Inmate
Renalde, Vito	WM	6	Inmate
Renaldi, Guitana	WF	5	Inmate
Renzly, Rosina	WF	49	Boarder
Reynold, Joseph	WM	3, 6m	Inmate
Reynold, Mary	WF	58	Nurse
Reynolds, Marion	WF	1, 7m	Inmate
Reynolds, Mary	WF	1, 3m	Inmate
Reynolds, Mary	WF	23	Nurse
Rhors, Sarah	WM	4	Inmate
Riedy, Elizabeth	WF	50	Servant
Riley, Cecilia	WF	5	Inmate
Ringo, Irene	WF	3	Inmate
Riordan, Anna	WF	17	Domestic
Riordan, Edward	WM	9m	Inmate
Rippert, John	WM	3, 6m	Inmate
Rise, John	WM	5	Inmate

Rispolis, Jennie	WF	1, 11m	Inmate
Ritchel, Julia	WF	20	Nurse
Ritschel, John	WM	1, 11m	Inmate
Rlosty, Helen	WF	2, 11m	Inmate
Robinson, Robert	MuM	7	Inmate
Robusta, Marion	WF	2, 7m	Inmate
Rocco, Helena	WF	6	Inmate
Rocco, Salvatore	WM	5	Inmate
Rock, Bruno	WM	1	Inmate
Rocoke, George	WM	6	Inmate
Roeder, Joseph	WM	2, 6m	Inmate
Rokitska, Rosalia	WF	27	Nurse
Romali, Vincinzo	WM	6	Inmate
Roman, Albert	WM	3, 10m	Inmate
Roman, Rose	WF	11m	Inmate
Romano, Josephine	WF	4	Inmate
Romano, Michael	WM	1, 11m	Inmate
Romeo, Catherine	WF	5	Inmate
Romerie, Angelo	WM	1	Inmate
Romes, Nunziata	WF	2, 9m	Inmate
Rononger, Elsie	WF	1, 4m	Inmate
Rooney, Walter	WM	2, 8m	Inmate
Rootza, Herbert	WM	8	Inmate
Ropalko, Sadie Cecilia	WF	17	Nurse
Rose, Angleina	WF	6	Inmate
Rose, Grace	WF	6	Inmate
Rose, John	WM	4	Inmate
Rosen, Joseph	WM	4	Inmate
Rosen, Robert	WM	7	Inmate
Rosenbery, Edward	WM	4	Inmate
Ross, Dorothy	WF	2, 7m	Inmate
Rossi, Anthony	WM	4	Inmate
Rossi, Gerald	WM	4m	Inmate
Rossi, Louise	WF	2, 7m	Inmate
Rovins, Bertha	WF	1, 5m	Inmate
Rowley, Leslie L.	MuM	7	Inmate
Rubin, Lucille M.	WF	40	Sister of Charity
Rudolph, Herbert	WM	5m	Inmate
Rudut, Francies	WF	2, 1m	Inmate
Ruffals, Anna	WF	2, 1m	Inmate
Rusashek, John	WM	4	Inmate
Rusca, Anasta	WF	2, 3m	Inmate

Rush, Vincent	WM	6	Inmate
Rusiecker, Michael	WM	1, 3m	Inmate
Russell, Dundon	WM	3, 7m	Inmate
Russell, Joseph	WM	5	Inmate
Russell, Mary R.	WF	58	Seamstress
Russo, Mary	WF	4	Inmate
Russo, Rose	WF	3	Inmate
Rusta, Angelina	WF	4	Inmate
Rutledge, Helen M.	WF	29	Chambermaid
Ruziku, Keopold	WM	1, 10m	Inmate
Ryan, Catherine	WF	3, 11m	Inmate
Ryan, Francis J.	WM	4m	Inmate
Ryan, John	WM	1, 3m	Inmate
Ryan, John	WM	3, 9m	Inmate
Ryan, Joseph	WM	3, 7m	Inmate
Ryan, Joseph	WM	5	Inmate
Ryan, Mary	WF	2, 1m	Inmate
Ryan, Robert "Besty"	WM	1, 6m	Inmate
Ryan, William	WM	3, 7m	Inmate
Sabata, Mildred	WF	17	Chambermaid
Saboto, Mary	WF	6m	Inmate
Saddidy, Edward	WM	6	Inmate
Saguino, Nina	WF	2	Inmate
St. John, William	WM	4	Inmate
Sala, Andrea	WM	4	Inmate
Salak, Alexander	WM	6	Inmate
Salardi, Carmella	WF	4	Inmate
Salerno, Alphonso	WM	3m	Inmate
Salerno, Mary	WF	18	Nurse
Sallino, Louis	WM	4, 1m	Inmate
Salvatore, Anna	WF	4	Inmate
Salvatti, Salvatore	WM	3, 1m	Inmate
Saminto, Dominic	WM	1, 3m	Inmate
Samios, Ralph	WM	2, 6m	Inmate
Samtora, Angelo	WM	2, 5m	Inmate
Samuel, Patrick	WM	2, 9m	Inmate
Sanci, "Sarret" Joseph	WM	10m	Inmate
Sandford, Inez	WF	5	Inmate
Sanford, Catherine	WF	20	Nurse
Sanford, Margaret	WF	3, 8m	Inmate
Santora, Margaret	WF	1, 3m	Inmate
Santorelli, Rose	WF	6	Inmate

Santors, Mary	WF	3, 7m	Inmate
Sarjus, John	WM	4	Inmate
Sarkinson, Helen Maria	WF	24	Boarder, Clerk
Saroccio, James	WM	5	Inmate
Savage, Joseph	WM	6	Inmate
Scafide, Alonzo	WM	6	Inmate
Scalata, Joseph	WM	1, 4m	Inmate
Scanlon, Daniel	WM	2m	Inmate
Scanlon, Harold	WM	2, 6m	Inmate
Scanlon, Mary Margaret	WF	21	Nurse
Scanlon, Rose	WF	1	Inmate
Scarola, Lucy	WF	1, 10m	Inmate
Schaefer, Joseph	WM	2, 7m	Inmate
Schaeffer, Charles	WM	1, 11m	Inmate
Schask, Anna	WF	5	Inmate
Schennan, Irene	WF	2	Inmate
Schiefele, Francis	WM	1, 5m	Inmate
Schinkey, Edward	WM	1, 7m	Inmate
Schleffler, Henry	WM	2, 5m	Inmate
Schleffler, Nellie	WF	4m	Inmate
Schmidt, John	WM	4	Inmate
Schneider, Joseph	WM	5m	Inmate
Schneider, Mary	WF	1, 11m	Inmate
Schnitz, John	WM	4	Inmate
Schohn, Alfred	WM	12	Foundling
Schultz, Frederick	WM	3, 4m	Inmate
Schultz, James	WM	6	Inmate
Schultz, Paul	WM	2, 11m	Inmate
Schuyler, Vivian	BF	3, 1m	Inmate
Schwartz, Rose	WF	2, 11m	Inmate
Scicili, Catherine	WF	1, 4m	Inmate
Scott, George	WM	4	Inmate
Scott, Mary	MuF	7	Inmate
Seaman, Francis	WM	2, 1m	Inmate
Seaman, Helen	WF	2, 1m	Inmate
Seary, Edward	WM	5	Inmate
Seigal, Minnie	WF	7	Inmate
Seigel, Jane	WM*	5	Inmate
Selter, Elizabeth	WF	1m	Inmate
Semkovitz, Sadie	WF	6	Inmate
Seonie, Philip	WM	1, 10m	Inmate
Sepulvae, Fiovarile	WM	2, 4m	Inmate

Sepwartz, Clara Teresa	WF	14	Ward
Seris, Salvatore	WM	4	Inmate
Sexton, Catherine	WF	1, 7m	Inmate
Sexton, Thomas	WM	2, 6m	Inmate
Seymonska, Martha	WF	4	Inmate
Shafin, Jennie	WF	1, 11m	Inmate
Shamekian, Mary	WF	1, 11m	Inmate
Shanahan, Josephine	WF	40	Laundress
Shankey, Mary G.	WF	65	Sister of Charity
Shapiro, Leonora	WF	1m	Inmate
Sharkoff, Frank	WM	4	Inmate
Shea, Augustine	WM	4	Inmate
Shea, William	WM	5	Inmate
Shepard, Julia	WF	25	Trained Nurse
Sheridan, Philip	WM	1, 5m	Inmate
Shiaro, Anthony	WM	7m	Inmate
Shields, Edward	WM	3, 1m	Inmate
Shira, Charles	WM	2, 3m	Inmate
Signorellie, Anala	WF	2, 11m	Inmate
Simien, Mark	WF*	6	Inmate
Simmon, Adolphus	WM	5	Inmate
Simms, Julia	WF	3, 4m	Inmate
Simon, Louis	WM	3, 7m	Inmate
Simpkins, Dorothy	BF	7	Inmate
Sirmott, Rita	WF	4	Inmate
Sisari, Joseph	WM	2, 5m	Inmate
Sispeck, Henry	WF*	4m	Inmate
Sisson, Edith	WF	7m	Inmate
Skuza, John	WM	4m	Inmate
Smart, Albert	WM	1, 4m	Inmate
Smith, Anna	WF	5m	Inmate
Smith, Arnold	WM	6	Inmate
Smith, Catherine	WF	5	Inmate
Smith, Dolley	WF	21	Trained Nurse
Smith, Elizabeth	WF	5m	Inmate
Smith, Florence	WF	2, 1m	Inmate
Smith, Germain	WF	35	Trained Nurse
Smith, Gertrude	WF	9	Inmate
Smith, James	WM	4	Inmate
Smith, Joseph	WM	1, 7m	Inmate
Smith, Joseph	WM	2, 10m	Inmate
Smith, Joseph	WM	4	Inmate

Smith, Lillian	WF	3, 2m	Inmate
Smith, Margaret	WF	36	Nurse
Smith, Margaret M.	WF	24	Nurse
Smith, Mary	WF	21	Servant
Smith, Mary J.	WF	42	Laundress
Smith, Steadman	BM	8	Inmate
Smith, Thomas	WM	4	Inmate
Snow, Margorie	WF	0m	Inmate
Snyder, Henry	WM	2, 3m	Inmate
Soccia, Mary	WF	7	Inmate
Sonn, Charles	WM	2, 2m	Inmate
Soprick, Eleanor	WF	1, 9m	Inmate
Soryne, Edward	WM	2, 5m	Inmate
Souter, Frederick	WM	7	Inmate
Southern, Elizabeth	WF	2, 6m	Inmate
Sowincki, Erminia	WF	1, 7m	Inmate
Sozepanisk, Stephen	WM	3, 3m	Inmate
Spagnolia, Muched	WM	2, 1m	Inmate
Speares, Clara	WF	18	Ward
Sperry, Ella Agnes	WF	27	Nurse
Sperry, Margaret	WF	3, 5m	Inmate
Spiole, Joseph	WM	4	Inmate
Springer, Mary	WF	2, 1m	Inmate
Spuma, Robert	BM	8	Inmate
Sputook, William	WM	4	Inmate
Squillasiote, Silvio	WM	1, 7m	Inmate
Stacey, Josephine	WF	1, 11m	Inmate
Stack, Gertrude	WF	1, 7m	Inmate
Stankecnicz, Stanislaus	WF	2, 1m	Inmate
Stanley, Elizabeth	WF	21	Nurse
Stanley, Frederick	WM	5m	Inmate
Stanley, Raymond	WM	12	Inmate
Stark, Edith	WF	4	Inmate
Starpoli, Cecilia	WF	7	Inmate
Starr, Vincent	WF*	5	Inmate
Starzo, Rachel	WF	1, 5m	Inmate
Statuo, Dominck	WM	1, 1m	Inmate
Statuto, David	WM	3, 1m	Inmate
Steele, Florence	WF	2, 11m	Inmate
Steffins, Anna	WF	1, 3m	Inmate
Stein, Edward Anthony	WM	11	Ward
Stein, Mary	WF	3, 7m	Inmate

Stephen, Raymond	BM	3, 10m	Inmate
Stepsinczyk, Michael	WM	6	Inmate
Stevens, Clarence	WM	4	Inmate
Stevens, Emily	WF	5	Inmate
Steward, Charles	WM	2, 10m	Inmate
Steward, George	WM	2	Inmate
Stone, Eleanor	WF	3, 11m	Inmate
Stophas, Joseph	WM	3, 11m	Inmate
Storkie, Anthony	WM	6	Inmate
Strong, Raymond	WM	5, 3m	Inmate
Struck, Charles	WM	1, 10m	Inmate
Stubeds, William	WM	1m	Inmate
Stubenrauch, Eva	WF	16	Ward
Stubenrauch, John	WM	13	Ward
Sullivan, Cornelius	WM	4	Inmate
Sullivan, Florence	WF	7m	Inmate
Sullivan, Frances	WF	4	Inmate
Sullivan, James	WM	3, 10m	Inmate
Sullivan, John	WM	2, 6m	Inmate
Sullivan, Joseph	WM	2, 3m	Inmate
Sullivan, Margaret	WF	6	Inmate
Sullivan, Mary	WF	1, 6m	Inmate
Sullivan, Mary	WF	48	Sister of Charity
Sullivan, Nellie	WF	3, 7m	Inmate
Sullivan, Patrick	WM	4	Inmate
Sullivan, William	WM	4	Inmate
Sunitz, Harold	WM	7	Inmate
Suschetti, Mary	WF	2, 2m	Inmate
Suschetti, Peter	WM	3, 9m	Inmate
Susykiewiso, Helen	WF	2, 4m	Inmate
Sutton, Henry	WM	2, 6m	Inmate
Swan, William	WM	5	Inmate
Sweeney, Mary	WF	0m	Inmate
Sweeney, Michael J.	WM	26	Medical Doctor
Sweeny, John	WM	2, 7m	Inmate
Sweeny, Joseph	WM	9m	Inmate
Swinton, Veronica	WF	6m	Inmate
Szkolnki, Mary	WF	1, 10m	Inmate
Tabaca, Stephen	WM	2, 6m	Inmate
Taino, Seconda	WF	1, 3m	Inmate
Talionni, Thomas	WM	2, 11m	Inmate
Taures, Frank	WM	3, 6m	Inmate

Tauschner, Boleslavo	WM	7	Inmate
Tavano, Joseph	WM	5	Inmate
Tavish, Joseph	WM	5	Inmate
Taylor, Catherine	WF	1, 9m	Inmate
Taylor, Marion	WF	44	Trained Nurse
Taylor, Robert	WM	2	Inmate
Teater, Walter	WM	3, 10m	Inmate
Teffard, Mary	WF	25	Servant
Teninous, Ruth	WF	1m	Inmate
Tenonava, Mary	WF	3	Inmate
Tenonava, Pasquale	WM	4	Inmate
Thomas, Cecilia	WF	2, 6m	Inmate
Thomas, John	WM	5	Inmate
Thompson, Mary	WF	3, 5m	Inmate
Thorton, Elizabeth A.	WF	54	Matron
Thropo, Ernest	WM	6m	Inmate
Tiffany, Lawrence	WM	3, 10m	Inmate
Timbo, Felix	WM	5	Inmate
Timlin, Catherine	WF	2, 1m	Inmate
Todeca, Salvatore	WM	1, 3m	Inmate
Tonal, Anna	WF	25	Trained Nurse
Tonessi, Salvatore	WM	2, 3m	Inmate
Tonkins, Florence	WF	4	Inmate
Totti, Anthony	WM	5	Inmate
Towell, John	WM	1, 9m	Inmate
Trenillian, Louis	WM	4	Inmate
Trimie, Louise	WF	16	Servant
Trimie, Michael	WF*	2, 8m	Inmate
Truatt, Joseph	BM	3, 8m	Inmate
Trumpover, Susan	WF	35	Waitress
Tucke, Wallace	WM	11m	Inmate
Tucker, Herbert	WM	4	Inmate
Tula, Joseph	WM	2, 10m	Inmate
Tulimello, Benedetta	WF	5	Inmate
Tully, Annie	WF	65	Sister of Charity
Tully, Stephen	WM	2, 3m	Inmate
Turano, Carmella	WF	5	Inmate
Tussell, Annie	WF	70	Sister of Charity
Tux, Paul	WM	3, 5m	Inmate
Tyson, George	WM	2, 7m	Inmate
Underhill, Raymond	WM	8m	Inmate
Vacca, Salvatore	WM	3	Inmate

Valentine, Charles	WM	8	Inmate
Valentine, Joseph	WM	7	Inmate
Valone, Angleina	WF	1, 5m	Inmate
VanKruven, Kenneth	WM	2, 6m	Inmate
VanNess, Joseph	WM	5	Inmate
Vassallo, Damiano	WM	4	Inmate
Vecchio, Luke	WM	3, 5m	Inmate
Vegas, John	WM	4	Inmate
Velezza, Dora	WF	1, 2m	Inmate
Venable, Virginia	BF	4	Inmate
Verde, Frances	WF	1, 9m	Inmate
Versi, Maris	WF	5	Inmate
Vilbert, Joseph	WM	1, 4m	Inmate
Villanos, Rose	WF	3, 3m	Inmate
Vincosta, Armizio	WM	1, 11m	Inmate
Visi, Frederic	WM	6	Inmate
Viterelli, Charles	WM	2, 3m	Inmate
Viterellie, Anthony	WM	2, 8m	Inmate
Vivone, Antoinette	WF	3, 2m	Inmate
Vizari, Amanda	WF	5	Inmate
Vlasak, Ladislav	WM	4	Inmate
Volo, Antoinnette	WF	1, 4m	Inmate
Wachtler, Elizabeth	WF	24	Nurse
Wachtler, James	WM	1m	Inmate
Wack, George	WM	6	Inmate
Wagerantz, Marion	WF	2, 5m	Inmate
Wagner, Isable	BF	1, 11m	Inmate
Wahl, Mary Agnes	WF	20	Trained Nurse
Waldron, Arthur	WM	1, 3m	Inmate
Walsh, Bridget M.	WF	68	Sister of Charity
Walsh, Catherine	WF	2, 6m	Inmate
Walsh, Ethel	WF	3, 6m	Inmate
Walter, Madeline	WF	2, 11m	Inmate
Walters, Henrietta	WF	3, 11m	Inmate
Walters, Mary	WF	4m	Inmate
Waltine, Alfred	WM	8	Inmate
Wanamaker, Marie	WF	1, 9m	Inmate
Ward, Mary Frances	WF	27	Nurse
Warner, Arthur	WM	4	Inmate
Warner, Cecelia	MuF	3, 5m	Inmate
Warnock, William	WM	7m	Inmate
Watson, Helen	WF	3, 2m	Inmate

Weber, Jack	WM	1, 3m	Inmate
Weinaiga, Catherine	WF	1, 8m	Inmate
Weinash, Daniel	WM	6	Inmate
Weinstein, Samuel	WM	9m	Inmate
Weiss, John	WM	3, 7m	Inmate
Welku, Agnes	WF	7	Inmate
Wendtlanott, Grace	WF	2, 10m	Inmate
West, Helen Elizabeth	WF	21	Nurse
West, Margaret	WF	2m	Inmate
West, Rose	WF	4m	Inmate
Whalen, Emma	WF	2m	Inmate
Whetton, Helen	WF	3, 4m	Inmate
Whidbee, Charles	WM	6	Inmate
While, Edward	WM	5	Inmate
White, George	WM	4	Inmate
White, Lucille	WF	14	Ward
Whiting, Clarence	WM	4m	Inmate
Whiting, Hilda	WF	28	Nurse
Whiting, John	WM	5	Inmate
Whiting, Weston	WM	4m	Inmate
Whittook, Mary	WF	3, 5m	Inmate
Wichelna, Rose	WF	21	Nurse
Wilczyki, Catherine	WF	2, 11m	Inmate
Wilete, James	WM	9m	Inmate
William, Elizabeth	BF	8	Inmate
William, Helen	BF	10	Inmate
William, John	WM	4	Inmate
Williams, Edith	WF	6	Inmate
Williams, Francis	WM	7	Inmate
Williams, Rita	WF	1, 6m	Inmate
Wilson, Arthur	WM	1, 3m	Inmate
Wilson, George	BM	10	Inmate
Wilson, Harriett	WF	2, 9m	Inmate
Wilson, Martin	WM	4	Inmate
Windrof, Rudoph	WM	6	Inmate
Wiseman, P. Henry	WM	5	Inmate
Wocinick, Frank	WM	7m	Inmate
Wolentinsky, Sophie	WF	7	Inmate
Wolfe, Arthur	BM	4	Inmate
Wolk, Catherine	WF	1, 3m	Inmate
Wolk, Joseph	WM	2, 6m	Inmate
Wolusty, Anna	WF	2	Inmate

Wonty, Walter	WM	2, 11m	Inmate
Wontz, Anna	WF	1, 3m	Inmate
Wood, Anna	WF	5m	Inmate
Wood, Paul	WM	4	Inmate
Woodis, Teresa	WF	1, 11m	Inmate
Woodrow, Alice	WF	9	Ward
Woods, John	WM	0m	Inmate
Wrieth, Lillian	WF	30	Nurse
Wrieth, Thomas	WM	9m	Inmate
Wright, Eno	WM	6m	Inmate
Wright, James	WM	4	Inmate
Yost, Carl	WM	6	Inmate
Young, Catherine	WF	42	Trained Nurse
Young, Howard	WM	3, 7m	Inmate
Zaccarelli, Lusuino	WM	3	Inmate
Zaccaro, Frank	WM	3, 5m	Inmate
Zane, Helen Mary	WF	23	Nurse
Zanella, Vincent	WM	11m	Inmate
Zanes, George	WM	1m	Inmate
Zanowitch, Tony	WM	2, 1m	Inmate
Zarisky, Wanda	WF	6	Inmate
Zeinart, Eleanor	WF	3, 9m	Inmate
Zeltman, Robert	WM	2	Inmate
Zimianary, Catherine	WF	12	Inmate
Zipf, Andrew	WM	5	Inmate
Zito, Joseph	WM	2, 11m	Inmate
Zwan, Agustof	WM	1, 5m	Inmate

Index to the
New York State Enumeration of the Inhabitants of

The New York Foundling Hospital

175 East 68th Street
New York, New York

June 1, 1925

Assembly District No. 15
Election District No. 22
Pages 7 - 32

Joseph Neumann, Enumerator

Guide to Column Headings

in the

1925 New York State Enumeration

Name
Name of each person whose usual place of abode was in the institution on June 1, 1925. The census includes the name of every person living on June 1, 1925. Children born since June 1, 1925 were omitted. The surname is listed first, then the given name and middle initial.

R-G
Race and gender. White is designated by the letter "W", black by the letter "B" and Mulatto by the letters "Mu". Males are designated by the letter "M" and females are designated by the letter "F".

*
Notes that the enumerator may have reported the name or gender incorrectly.

A
Age at last birthday. Designated in years, unless otherwise noted with an "m" for "months" or "d" for "days". Generally, children who were less than one year old were described in terms of days. Some of the older children were described in terms of years and months.

Relation
Relationship of each adult to the institution. The relationship of each child to the institution was not included.

Continued...

Note

The Nativity and Citizenship of each child was listed! Refer to the orginal census for this information. Also refer to the original census for the Nativity, Citizenship, and Occupation of adult occupants. This enumeration appears to be incomplete: the names of the Sisters of Charity and their employees were not included.

Abatangolis, Mary	WF	8	-
Abbott, Eileen B.	WF	-	-
Abramowski, Stanley	WM	5	-
Accornero, Marie	WF	1	-
Acquavia, Catherine	WF	7	-
Affinette, Anna	WF	1	-
Affinette, Ralph	WM	2	-
Ahearn, Agnes	WF	3	-
Ahearn, Daniel	WM	3	-
Ahearn, John	BM	14	-
Ahearn, Margaret	WF	88d	-
Ahearn, Winnie	WF	18	Nurse
Ainsworth, Fred	WM	1	-
Albino, Louis	WM	7	-
Alexander, Thomas	WM	2	-
Allen, Edward	WM	4	-
Alyward, Catherine	WF	1	-
Amato, Antonio	WM	9	-
Amend, Loretta	WF	2, 6m	-
Amico, Teresa	WF	6	-
Amster, Helen	WF	6	-
Anderson, Paul	WM	10	-
Anderson, Raymond	BM	11	-
Angotte, Salvatore	WM	11	-
Aquanna, Anna	WF	5	-
Armendola, Charles	WM	9	-
Ascatigno, Mary	WF	1	-
Asciutto, Mary	WF	6	-
Austin, Mary	WF	3	-
Aylward, Frances	WF	4	-
Aylward, Harry	WM	5	-
Bakanbowitz, Alv.	WF	7	-
Balkash, Charles	WM	5	-
Ballasedes, Paul	WM	3	-
Ballely, Theresa	WF	3	-
Banks, Albert	BM	10	-
Bannon, Dewey	WM	1	-
Barba, John	WM	9	-
Barberi, Andrew	WM	1	-
Barberi, Antonio	WM	1	-
Barkwill, James	WM	2	-
Barlow, Robert	WM	4	

Barnes, Joseph	WM	9	-
Barry, Anthony	WM	56d	-
Barry, George T.	WM	5	-
Barry, Grace I.	WF	4	-
Bartosh, Henry	WM	3	-
Bartosh, Peter	WM	1	-
Bartosh, Stella	WF	1	-
Bartosh, Stephen	WM	1	-
Bary, Rosemond	WF	2, 6m	-
Baskerville, Wm.	BM	14	-
Battema, Marie	WF	4	-
Bauer, Charles	WM	1	-
Bauer, Clifford	WM	3	-
Bauerschmidt, Fred.	WM	1	-
Baun, Ellan	BM	6	-
Bavich, Julius	WM	5	-
Beacher, Frank	WM	4	-
Beauliew, Genevieve	WF	3	-
Beggins, Frances	WF	2	-
Behensky, Arthur	WM	1	-
Behensky, Elva	WF	3	-
Behensky, George	WM	2	
Bellefiore, Thomas	WM	7	-
Belligan, Helen	WF	1	-
Bellone, Wm.	WM	5	-
Belmont, Vincent	WM	1	-
Bender, Rose	WF	3	-
Bennett, John	WM	2	-
Benson, Ralph G.	WM	1, 6m	-
Bergo, Charles	WM	1	-
Bess, Wendell	BM	5	-
Bidnarski, Joseph	WM	3	-
Bila, Frank	WM	9	-
Birbieri, Charles	WM	11	-
Bisceglio, Joseph	BM	14	-
Bishop, George	WM	3	-
Bishop, Lester	WM	3	-
Bishop, Wm.	WM	2	-
Black, Geo.	WM	1	-
Black, Gerald	WM	1	-
Blair, Genevieve	WF	1	-
Blair, Isabel	WF	1	-

Blatko, Theodore	WM	4	-
Bliss, Jeanette	BF	9	-
Blitz, Gerald	WM	1	-
Bolan, Catherine	WF	5	-
Bonini, Colombia	WF	18	Nurse
Bonini, Raymond	WM	1	-
Booker, Eleanor	BF	85d	-
Bowman, Anastasia	WF	1	-
Boyle, Henry	WM	7	-
Bradley, James	WM	1	-
Brady, John E.	WM	10	-
Brand, Joseph	WM	3	-
Brannigan, John	WM	2	-
Bremer, Charles	WM	9	-
Brendell, Wm.	WM	1	-
Brennen, Elizabeth	WF	2	-
Brennen, Wm.	WM	4	-
Brooks, John	WM	3	-
Brooks, Ruth	WF	2, 6m	-
Browell, Josephine	BF	13	-
Brown, Charles	WM	3	-
Brown, James	WM	2	-
Brown, Julian	BM	10	-
Brown, Robt.	WM	2	-
Brunoski, Michael	WM	6	-
Bruzese, Carmine	WM	9	-
Bruziere, Mary	WF	6	-
Brynes, Michal	WM	8	-
Bucho, Dorothy	WF	1	-
Buckley, Joseph	WM	2, 6m	-
Budnick, Edward	WM	127d	-
Bunda, Anna	WF	1	-
Buoncose, James	WM	11	-
Burger, Henry	WM	10	-
Burke, Eugene	WM	107d	-
Burke, Helen	WF	16	Nurse
Burke, Henry	WM	11	-
Burke, Lillian	WF	5	-
Burke, Walter	WM	10	-
Burnett, Joseph	BM	11	-
Burns, Elizabeth	WF	1	-
Bush, Mary	WF	10	-

Butler, Joseph	BM	13	-
Cabatt, Wm.	WM	11	-
Cafarelle, Anna	WM*	6	-
Cafariello, Dorothy	WF	2	-
Cagney, Rita	WF	1	-
Cagney, Robert	WM	1	-
Cahill, Rita	WF	1	-
Caines, Charles	BM	9	-
Calarino, Margaret	WF	2	-
Calbro, Bambina	WF	2	-
Campbell, Walter	BM	5	-
Candelino, Anna	WF	17	Nurse
Candelino, Carmelia	WF	1	-
Cannone, Pauline	WF	5	-
Cannone, Thom.	WM	2, 6m	-
Cantrella, Vila	WF	1	-
Caperson, Catherine	WF	3	-
Caperson, James	WM	1	-
Capozzi, Antoinette	WF	1	-
Carey, Naomi	BM*	1	-
Carlson, James	WM	7	-
Carlyle, Henry	WM	9	-
Carr, Margaret	WF	3	-
Carroll, Edward	WM	3	-
Carso, Josephine	WF	3	-
Caryk, Marie	WF	2	-
Casciale, Madeline	WF	10	-
Casey, William	WM	3	-
Cashin, Joseph	WM	2	-
Casicole, Leanora	WF	9	-
Cassidy, Thomas	WM	6	-
Casso, William	WM	1	-
Castelli, Henry	WM	5	-
Caswell, Wm.	WM	11	-
Catanuto, Nicholas	WM	1	-
Catiello, Marino	WM	5	-
Catrone, Felicia	WF	2	-
Cavazini, Frank	WM	9	-
Centcheck, John	WM	2, 6m	-
Christina, Elizabeth	WF	1	-
Christina, Mary	WF	1	-
Christina, Pauline	WF	20	Nurse

Christopher, Ernest	WM	5	-
Cichetta, Lisetta	WF	10	-
Cichetti, Florence	WF	11	-
Clark, Mary	BF	14	-
Cloos, Gustave	WM	9	-
Clzewski, Beatrice	WF	4	-
Cocoran, Helen	WF	10	-
Cody, Isabelle	WF	8	-
Cody, Mary	WF	20	Nurse
Cody, Wm.	WM	1	-
Coffey, Joseph	WM	1	-
Coletti, John	WM	3, 6m	-
Colman, Viola	BF	14	-
Colon, Mary	BF	2, 6m	-
Combs, Dominic	WM	116d	-
Comerford, Anna	WF	20	Nurse
Comerford, John	WM	1	-
Compitello, Rose	WF	4	-
Conley, Catherine	WF	9	-
Conlin, Peter	WM	10	-
Conlon, Catherine	WF	3	-
Conlon, Catherine	WF	19	Nurse
Conlon, James	WM	41d	-
Connelly, David	WM	6	-
Connolly, Leo.	BM	11	-
Connors, Geo.	WM	3	-
Conppe, Henry	WM	10	-
Cook, Francis	WM	2, 6m	-
Correale, Nicholas	WM	1	-
Costa, Joseph	WM	3	-
Costa, Leonard	WM	1	-
Costello, Gerard	WM	1	-
Costello, Josephine	WF	17	Nurse
Coster, Grace	WF	3	-
Coster, Joseph	WM	4	-
Costo, Vito	WM	9	-
Cowan, Robt. J.	WM	2	-
Cowers, Teresa	WF	1	-
Crane, Delia	WF	3	-
Cronin, Mary	WF	11	-
Cronin, Thomas	WM	9	-
Crosby, Harold	WM	9	-

Crowley, Edward	WM	6	-
Crowley, Joseph	WM	3	-
Cullen, Patrick	WM	2, 6m	-
Cullen, Thomas	WM	9	-
Cummings, Anna	WF	6	-
Cunningham, Edward	WM	8	-
Cunningham, Theodore	WM	5	-
Curley, Margaret	WF	3	-
Curriel, Albert	WM	1	-
Cusack, Joseph	WM	9	-
Cusick, Edward	WM	2	-
Cusimona, Josephine	WF	4	-
Czarnecki, Anna	WF	4	-
Czupas, Wm.	WM	2	-
Daddy, Keneth J.	WM	1	-
Dady, Irene	WF	18	Nurse
Dahl, George	WM	1	-
Dalton, James	WM	9	-
David, Frederick	WM	1	-
Davis, Edna	WF	21	Nurse
Davis, Margaret	WF	1	-
Day, Catherine	WF	18	Nurse
Day, Thomas	WM	1	-
DeCicco, Dominick	WM	9	-
Defrietos, Manuel	WM	7	-
Deghnee, Roberta	WF	1	-
DeGraw, Catherine	WF	2	-
DeGregario, Joseph	WM	6	-
DeLaurentis, Marie	WF	4	-
Dellario, Rose	WF	1	-
Demit, Juliette	WF	10	-
Dempsey, Catherine	WF	17	Nurse
Dempsey, John	WM	1	-
DeSerio, Joseph	WM	3	-
DeSimone, Fred	WM	6	-
Destro, Joseph	WM	1	-
DeVito, Anna	WF	6	-
DeVito, Josephine	WF	4	-
Diaz, Manuela	WF	2	-
DiBernardo, Mary	WF	2	-
Dicenza, Guelomo	WM	7	-
DiCinio, Daniel	WM	3	-

Dickson, Jack	WM	3	-
Dietrick, Harry	WM	9	-
DiGianni, Anthony	WM	1	-
DiGianni, Mary	WF	4	-
DiGiuseppe, Mary	WF	9	-
Dillon, Rose	WF	133d	-
DiMarino, Nunziata	WM	10	-
Diovaimini, Alfred	WM	11	-
DiSimons, Julia R.	WF	113d	-
Dixon, Mabel	WF	1	-
Dobler, Raymond	WM	2	-
Dockery, Elinor	WM	6	-
Dockery, James	WM	7	-
Doherty, Ernest	WM	3	-
Dolan, Gilbert	BM	2	-
Dombussi, Madeline	WF	20	Nurse
Dombussi, Rose	BF	27d	-
Dominco, Giuseppe	WM	11	-
Donilook, John	WM	9	-
Donnigan, Henrietta	WF	1	-
Donohue, Mary	WF	5	-
Donohue, Rose	WF	1	-
Donohue, Walter	WM	5	-
Dorn, Frank	WM	9	-
Dorsett, Germain	BM	15	-
Douney, Agnes	WF	3	-
Downing, Robert	WM	7	-
Doyle, Wm.	WM	2	-
Drake, Herbert	WM	1	-
Dufenek, Stasi	WM	8	-
Duffy, Patrick	WM	1	-
Dugan, Arthur	WM	3	-
Duggan, Edward	WM	10	-
Duggan, John	WM	11	-
Duggan, Margaret	WF	6	-
Duke, Anna T.	WF	3	-
Duke, Tereasa	WF	5	-
Dunleavy, Joseph	WM	7	-
Dunne, Joseph	WM	9	-
Durgson, Maria	WF	37d	-
Dusold, Harry	WM	6	-
Dwyer, Evelyn	WF	2	-

Dwyer, George	WM	1	-
Dzrengielewski, John	WM	9	-
Earle, Ellen	BF	1	-
Early, Clara	WF	11	-
Echart, John	WM	10	-
Edison, Clarance	BM	4	-
Edward, Louis	BM	11	-
Edwards, Edward	BM	11	-
Eerguson, Alphonsus	BM	3	-
Eftera, Louise	WF	3	-
Egan, Charles	WM	134d	-
Egan, Gladys	WF	18	Nurse
Elliott, George	WM	1	-
Emelano, Rose	WF	3	-
Ervert, Irene	WF	1	-
Espinosa, Charles	WM	5	-
Esposito, Armellio	WF	6	-
Esposito, Joseph	WM	7	-
Esposito, Ralph	WM	9	-
Estrada, Arnold M.	WM	2, 6m	-
Eustic, John	WM	10	-
Evans, Cryil	WF	1	-
Evans, Joseph	BM	14	-
Ewing, Francis	BM	13	-
Exlen, Mary	WF	9	-
Faba, Clementine	WF	17	Nurse
Faba, Mary	WF	1	-
Faber, Henry	BM	1	-
Falcone, Dominick	WM	9	-
Fanez, Joseph	WM	11	-
Farley, Edward	WM	8	-
Farmer, Helen	WF	17	Nurse
Farmer, Robert	WM	2	-
Farrell, Helen	WF	1	-
Farren, Veronica	WF	10	-
Farsetta, Vincent	WM	3	-
Fay, Iris	WF	1	-
Felicia, Catrone	WM	2	-
Ferdinski, John	WM	10	-
Ferger, Henrietta	WF	9	-
Ferreri, John	WM	3	-
Ferriole, Joseph	WM	10	-

Ferro, Jennie	WF	1	-
Ferro, Mary	WF	7	-
Ferro, Rosina	WF	1	-
Filardi, Leonard	WM	1	-
Filardo, Lucy	WF	18	Nurse
Finch, Wm.	WM	3	-
Finn, Dorothy E.	WF	133d	-
Finn, Ella	WF	19	Nurse
Finnegan, Catherine	WF	10	-
Finnerman, Rose	WF	9	-
Fiore, Concetta	WF	5	-
Fiore, Joseph	WM	4	-
Fitzpatrick, Joseph	WM	1	-
Fitzpatrick, Thomas	WM	4	-
Fitzsimmons, Edna	WF	2	-
Flaherty, Edward	WM	2	-
Flannery, Dorothy	WF	4	-
Fletcher, Edmond	WM	1	-
Flynn, Bartholomew	WM	5	-
Flynn, Francis	WM	9	-
Flynn, John	WM	1	-
Forde, Veronica	WF	4	-
Francheski, Frank	WM	1	-
Francheski, Henry	WM	3	-
Frankowksy, James	BM	3	-
Fraser, James	WM	1	-
Fratolello, Antonio	WM	8	-
Frink, Francis	WM	3	-
Fulton, Genevieve	WF	1, 6m	-
Gafoni, Concetta	WF	1	-
Galante, Rtia	WF	1	-
Galasso, Anthony	WM	8	-
Galasso, John	WM	6	-
Gale, Clement	BM	15	-
Galetta, Daniel	WM	128d	-
Galetta, Grace	WF	17	Nurse
Galetto, Harry	WM	1	-
Gallager, Anna	WF	17	Nurse
Gallager, Elizabeth	WF	1	-
Gallager, Francis	WF	2, 6m	-
Gallager, John	WM	9	-
Gallager, Mary	WF	1	-

Gallagher, Gene	WF	4	-
Gamatasio, Madeline	WF	1	-
Ganci, Antoinette	WF	3	-
Gantin, William	BM	2	-
Gargowski, Francis	WM	140d	-
Garrett, Ralph	WM	1	-
Gatello, Arthur	WM	3	-
Gatello, Orlando	WM	4	-
Gavin, Angela	WF	1	-
Gavin, Martin	WM	1	-
Geraldine, Gerolomo	WM	4	-
Gerard, Blackly	BM	1	-
Gerelardo, Casagera	WF	8	-
Gernon, George	WM	9	-
Gibba, Vincent	WM	6	-
Gibbons, Joseph	WM	1	-
Gibson, James	BM	3	-
Gill, Margaret	WF	3	-
Gill, Mary	WF	6	-
Gill, William	WM	4	-
Gilligan, Raymond	WM	1	-
Gipolla, Alfred	WM	6	-
Givins, Jessie	BM	1	-
Glynn, Charles	BM	2, 6m	-
Gordon, Anthony	WM	3	-
Gordon, Sylvia	WF	3	-
Gorr, Peter	WM	9	-
Goulette, Marie	WF	4	-
Grabeck, Vincent	WM	5	-
Grabeline, Ronald	WM	1	-
Grady, Edna	WF	9	-
Graf, Ruth	WF	9	-
Grant, Frederick	WM	1	-
Grant, James	WM	9	-
Graveline, Alice	WF	19	Nurse
Gray, Gertrude	WF	3	-
Grazinso, George	WM	9	-
Grecco, Millie	WF	5	-
Grecco, Nicholas	WM	1	-
Green, Edward	WM	10	-
Greer, William	WM	1	-
Grey, Alfred	BM	13	-

Griffin, Helen	WF	11	-
Griffin, Wm.	WM	9	-
Gross, Alice	WF	1	-
Gross, Charles	WM	3	-
Gross, John	WM	3	-
Gross, Patricia	WF	302d	-
Guarnino, Vincent	WM	9	-
Gubas, Frank	WM	1	-
Gueriero, Antonette	WF	1	-
Gundersen, Dennis	WM	1	-
Gurrt, Louis	BM	13	-
Haban, Catherine	WF	4	-
Hackenbrock, Caroline	WF	4	-
Hackenbrock, Catherine	WF	6	-
Hackenbrock, Charles	WM	8	-
Hackenbrock, Ernest	WM	1	-
Haffner, Wendell	WM	9	-
Haggerty, Gertrude	WF	17	Nurse
Haggerty, Joseph	WM	1	-
Haldner, Henry	WM	9	-
Hall, Loretta	WF	1	-
Hall, Rita	WF	3	-
Hand, Walter	WM	6	-
Hanley, Mary	WF	4	-
Hanlon, Dorothy	WF	6	-
Hanlon, Helen	WF	3	-
Hanlon, Lillian	WF	2, 6m	-
Hannon, Joseph	BM	2	-
Harrington, Leo	WM	9	-
Harris, Randolph	BM	10	-
Harrison, Kathleen	WF	91d	-
Harrison, Rose	WF	16	Nurse
Hart, Mary	WF	7	-
Hartley, Bernadine	WF	1	-
Hartman, Shirley	WF	1	-
Harvey, Wm.	WM	2, 6m	-
Hawkins, Mary	WF	2, 6m	-
Hayard, Malcolm	BM	11	-
Hayard, Malcolm E.	BM	13	-
Hayes, Vincent	WM	9	-
Healey, Rita	WF	9	-
Hendy, George	WM	7	-

Hennekeus, Aloysius	WM	4	-
Henning, Chas.	BM	10	-
Henrich, Margaret	WF	1	-
Herms, Raynord	WM	2	-
Herrold, John	WM	1	-
Hess, Dorothy	WF	2	-
Hess, Joseph	WM	7	-
Hickey, John	WM	60d	-
Higgins, Catherine	WF	1	-
Hill, Lillian	BF	14	-
Hillis, Eileen	WF	92d	-
Hillis, Leona	WF	17	Nurse
Hintele, Edward	WM	1	-
Hlavka, Mary	BF	14	-
Hodyno, Josephine	WF	5	-
Hoehn, John	WM	2	-
Hogan, Virginia	WF	3	-
Holiman, Wilfred	BM	14	-
Hollosi, Albert	WM	3	-
Holmes, Robert	BM	11	-
Hopkins, John	WM	3	-
Howard, Walter	WM	7	-
Howe, Francis V.	WM	11	-
Hughes, Joseph	WM	1	-
Hunt, Mary A.	WF	1	-
Hunter, Reuben	WM	1	-
Hyland, Maurice	WM	1	-
Iko, Andrew	WM	11	-
Isaac, Henry	WM	10	-
Jacobson, John	WM	1	-
Janaschick, John	WM	3	-
Janek, Frances	WF	5	-
Jarofsky, Steve	WM	9	-
Jennings, Walter	WM	2	-
Jerome, Julia	WF	9	-
Jerome, Mary	WF	7	-
Jewels, Thomas	WM	1	-
Jewels, Veronica	WF	3	-
Jewels, Wm.	WM	5	-
Johnson, Beatrice	BF	11	-
Johnson, Carrie	BF	14	-
Johnson, Elmer	BM	1	-

Johnson, Joseph	BM	13	-
Johnson, Theophlio	BM	13	-
Joseph, Lillian R.	WF	5	-
Joy, Francis	WM	6	-
Joy, Helen	WF	1	-
Judge, Michael	WM	2	-
Kachanoroski, Ignatz	WM	2	-
Kachanoroski, Stanley	WM	4	-
Kapton, Mary	WF	4	-
Karayan, Anna	WF	3	-
Karayan, Edward	WM	2	-
Kasputys, Mary	WF	4	-
Kealos, Felix	WM	11	-
Keane, Jacqueline	WM*	2	-
Kearns, John	WM	11	-
Keeler, Catherine	WF	18	Nurse
Keldy, Joseph	WM	1	-
Keller, Robert	WM	1	-
Kelly, Adria	WF	9	-
Kelly, Catherine	WF	17	Nurse
Kelly, Dorothy	WF	1	-
Kelly, Josephine	WF	1	-
Kelly, Kathleen	WF	3	-
Kelly, Margaret	WF	107d	-
Kelly, Margaret	WF	123d	-
Kelly, Michael	WM	1	-
Kelly, Patrick	WM	2	-
Kellyman, Lillian	BF	1, 6m	-
Kellyman, Louisa	BF	4	-
Kennedy, Edmund	WM	1	-
Kennedy, John	WM	3	-
Kennedy, John	WM	4	-
Kenny, Adele	WF	1	-
Kenny, Joseph	WM	117d	-
Kerrigan, Cecelia	WF	1	-
Kerrigan, Margaret	WF	2, 6m	-
Kessler, Dorothy	WF	3	-
Ketchell, George	WM	5	-
Kienz, William	WM	10	-
Kiernan, Bertha	WF	1	-
Kilchick, John	WM	8	-
Kilcullen, James	WM	10	-

King, Audrey	WF	9	-
King, Dorothy	BF	15	-
King, Helen	WF	1	-
King, Margaret	WF	1	-
Kingman, John	WM	2	-
Kingsley, Arthur	WM	2	-
Kingsley, George	WM	3	-
Kirby, Maurice	WM	9	-
Kirwin, James	WM	6	-
Kisch, Edward	WM	3	-
Kivanzinyci, Hanry	WM	2	-
Klatt, Louis	WM	10	-
Knauss, Homan	WM	2	-
Knowles, Vincent	WM	2	-
Knox, Dorothy	WM	6	-
Kornycheck, Julia	WF	1	-
Kramersey, Wm.	WM	114d	-
Krane, Margaret	WF	1	-
Krane, Margaret	WF	17	Nurse
Kresky, Evelyn	WF	4	-
Kroeschel, James	WM	2	-
Kryci, John	WM	4	-
Kubie, Frank	BM	11	-
Kuchman, Wm.	WM	7	-
Kulick, Agnes	WF	5	-
Kulick, Andrew	WM	3	-
Kulman, John	WM	4	-
Kulty, Joseph	WM	10	-
Kurkchi, John	WM	9	-
LaForgia, Eugene	WM	2, 6m	-
Lagahan, Anna	WF	8	-
Lagamma, Katie	WF	10	-
Lagamma, Wm.	WM	9	-
Lagrande, Joseph	WM	4	-
LaMonte, Marion	WF	1, 6m	-
Lancelletto, Rachel	WF	17	Nurse
Lancellotto, Jos.	WM	1	-
Lando, Paul	WM	111d	-
Lando, Sadie	WF	18	Nurse
Landy, Anna	WF	2	-
Lang, Angela	WF	1	-
Lang, Frances	WF	17	Nurse

Lannon, Charlotte	WF	1	-
Lappas, Earle	WM	4	-
Lappas, Thomas	WM	5	-
Larney, Francis	WM	7	-
Lasalata, Frank	WM	3	-
Lasalata, Tony	WM	1	-
Lashway, Matthew	WM	75d	-
Lashway, Veronica	WF	19	Nurse
Latanzio, John	WM	1	-
Lawrence, Henrietta	BF	14	-
Lawrence, John	WM	131d	-
Leary, Wm.	WM	4	-
Lee, Joseph	BM	1	-
Lee, Margaret	WF	5	-
Lennon, Wm.	WM	3	-
Leo, Mary	WF	1	-
Lesaco, Alec	WM	4	-
Leslie, Anna	WF	73d	-
Lewis, Frank	WM	3	-
Lewis, Wm.	WM	159d	-
Licattlessie, Joseph	WM	5	-
Licattlessie, Mary	WF	7	-
Licthfield, Loretta	WF	1	-
Lindsey, Milton	BM	6	-
Lingg, Edward	WM	78d	-
Lingg, Elizabeth	WF	19	Nurse
Lippiello, Antoinette	WF	160d	-
Lombardo, Frank	WM	3	-
Lombardo, Jennie	WF	9	-
Loneghan, Raymond	WM	7	-
Long, Viola	WF	95d	-
Longos, Frank	WM	4	-
Lopez, Joseph	WM	1	-
Lorance, Theodore	BM	12	-
Lorshback, Robt.	WM	5	-
Lott, Joseph V.	WM	2, 6m	-
Loughlin, Marie	WF	1	-
Loughlin, Veronica	WF	68d	-
Ludwig, Elizabeth	WF	2	-
Lukas, Anna	WF	8	-
Lynch, Anna	WF	1	-
Lynch, Joseph	WM	3	-

Lynch, Stanford	WM	1	-
Lyons, Robert	WM	152d	-
Lyons, Terance	WM	2	-
Lyons, Thomas	WM	2	-
Lyons, Wm.	WM	4	-
Macchia, Arthur	WM	3	-
Machio, Marino	WM	1	-
Machio, Pietro	WM	1	-
Mackaron, Michael	WM	1	-
Mackey, Jennie	WF	4	-
Maculuso, Rosario	WF	5	-
Magaldeno, Mary	WF	7	-
Mahady, Francis	WM	7	-
Maher, Elizabeth	WF	10	-
Mahoney, Anna	WF	1	-
Mahoney, Joseph	WM	4	-
Maiello, Patsy	WM	9	-
Maisto, Louis	WM	3	-
Makason, Julia	WF	4	-
Malley, Charles	WM	4	-
Maloney, John	WM	11	-
Manley, James	WM	10	-
Manzella, Joseph	WM	2	-
Manzella, Pasqualina	WF	17	Nurse
Manzi, Frances	WF	1	-
Marazzio, Rose	WF	6	-
Marchese, John	WM	9	-
Marcigliani, Nicolo	WM	4	-
Marcigliani, Vincezo	WM	3	-
Marciniszen, John	WM	2	-
Marconier, Wm.	WM	3	-
Marino, Gussie	WM	137d	-
Marino, Lillie	WF	3	-
Marion, Frances	BF	11	-
Markey, Earle	WM	1	-
Marsh, Gabriel	WM	1	-
Marshak, Dominick	WM	3	-
Marshall, Amelia	WF	18	Nurse
Marshall, Henry	WM	1	-
Marshall, James	WM	1	-
Marshall, Mary	WF	1	-
Marsighano, Michael	WM	1	-

Marsto, Carmello	WM	1	-
Martin, Charles	WM	1	-
Martin, Pauline	BF	9	-
Martino, John	WM	1	-
Martino, Samuel	WM	1	-
Martucci, Anna	WF	1	-
Mascia, Annie	WF	9	-
Masella, Raymond	WM	5	-
Masterson, Mary	WF	3	-
Matthews, Harry	WM	10	-
Mattis, Margaret	WM	139d	-
Maund, Alfred	BM	12	-
Mauro, Geo.	WM	4	-
Mauro, Jane	WF	2	-
Maxwell, Elinor	WF	8	-
Maynard, Elizabeth	WF	1	-
Maynard, Wm.	BM	7	-
Mazone, Mary	WF	1, 6m	-
Mazzone, Frank	WM	4	-
McArdle, John	BM	7	-
McBride, Mary	WM	2	-
McCaffrey, Michael	WM	5	-
McCann, Eileen	WF	2	-
McCloskey, Irene	WF	2	-
McCluskey, Harold	WM	1	-
McCluskey, Joseph	WM	10	-
McCormach, Donald	WM	1	-
McCormach, Ruth	WF	1	-
McCormack, John	WM	11	-
McDermott, Cornelius	WM	10	-
McDonald, Dorothy	WF	2	-
McDonald, Edwin	WM	1	-
McEnroe, Harold	WM	3	-
McGarry, James	WM	67d	-
McGarry, Mary	WF	18	Nurse
McGinnis, Alice	WF	3	-
McGovern, James	WF*	4	-
McGovern, Patricia	WF	1	-
McGowan, Lawrence	WM	1	-
McGrory, Agatha	WF	17	Nurse
McGrory, Wm.	WM	1	-
McGuire, Cecilia	WF	9	-

McHugh, Rudolph	BM	11	-
McIver, Laurence	WM	4	-
McKee, John	WM	9	-
McKenna, Robt.	WM	2	-
McKiernan, Phylis	WF	1	-
McLaughlin, Thom.	WM	5	-
McMahon, Joseph	WM	2	-
McMahon, Thomas	WM	2	-
McMarrow, Chas.	WM	10	-
McNeil, Bertrand	BM	8	-
McNulty, James	WM	12	-
Meade, Louis	WM	9	-
Meade, Walter	WM	9	-
Meegan, Charles	WM	5	-
Melican, Anna	WF	122d	-
Melican, Birdie	WF	17	Nurse
Mellen, Mary	WF	125d	-
Melville, Hurley	WM	1	-
Merolle, Claudia	WF	3	-
Messana, Joseph	WM	4	-
Metta, Vincent	WM	3	-
Meyers, James	WM	1	-
Meyers, Joseph	WM	2	-
Meyers, Margaret	WF	16	Nurse
Michael, Joseph	WM	39d	-
Michaeler, Agnes	WF	2	-
Middleton, Winifred	BF	15	-
Miller, Grace	WF	1	-
Miller, Jane	WF	3	-
Miller, Joseph	WM	3	-
Miller, Mary	WF	2	-
Miller, Raymond	WM	9	-
Mills, Pearl	WF	3	-
Minnick, Frank	WM	2	-
Minnick, Mary E.	WF	5	-
Minnis, Elizabeth	WF	1	-
Miraglia, Anna	WF	2	-
Misch, Frances	WF	5	-
Modica, Jerry	WM	1	-
Monahan, Loretto	WF	7	-
Mondello, Chas.	WM	6	-
Montemagno, Rose	WF	7	-

Moon, Edward	WM	10	-
Mooney, Alice	WF	1	-
Mooney, Harry	WM	2, 6m	-
Moran, Eugene	WM	110d	-
Moran, Frank	WM	2	-
Moran, Margaret	WF	7	-
Moran, Mary	WF	17	Nurse
Moran, Rita	WF	1	-
Morella, Mary	WF	5	-
Morgan, Gloria	WF	2	-
Morris, Edith	BF	12	-
Mortinich, Anna	WF	1	-
Mortley, Eleanor	WF	7	-
Morton, James	WM	1	-
Morton, John	WM	9	-
Mosco, Josephine	WF	7	-
Moses, Anna	WF	3	-
Mott, Julia	WF	8	-
Muhlon, James	WM	4	-
Mukarr, Dorothy	WF	47d	-
Mulhall, Edward	WM	10	-
Mulharr, Helen	WF	19	Nurse
Mullen, Walter	WM	4	-
Mullen, Wm.	WM	1	-
Muller, Edward	BM	4	-
Muller, Helen	WF	7	-
Muller, John	WM	15	-
Mullin, John	WM	2, 6m	-
Mulvihill, Charles	WM	1	-
Munch, Caroline	WF	2, 6m	-
Mundus, Alfred	WM	4	-
Mundus, Anthony	WM	4	-
Murphy, Delia	WF	9	-
Murphy, Edward	BM	14	-
Murphy, Edward	BM	15	-
Murphy, Edward	WM	1	-
Murphy, Elizabeth	WF	9	-
Murphy, Ellen	WF	8	-
Murphy, Joseph F.	WM	1	-
Murriska, Edward	WM	9	-
Musche, Maggie	WF	1	-
Nabel, Evelyn	WF	1	-

Nagel, Dorothy	WF	1	-
Naideck, Dorothy	WF	107d	-
Napoli, Frank	WM	1	-
Napolitano, Lisandro	WM	11	-
Nase, Teresa	WF	94d	-
Nash, Stephen	WM	2	-
Nero, Madeline	WF	2	-
Nestor, Thomas	WM	3	-
Neustadt, James	WM	5	-
Nevins, Charles	WM	4	-
Newman, Walter	WM	10	-
Nichols, Joseph	WM	10	-
Nicolosi, Mary	WF	5	-
Nolan, Joseph	WM	9	-
Norton, Robt.	WM	3	-
Novak, John J.	BM	10	-
Nugent, Francis	WM	9	-
O'Brien, Albert	WM	10	-
O'Brien, Beatrice	WF	11	-
O'Brien, Patrick	WM	1	-
O'Connell, James	WM	3	-
O'Connell, Mary	WF	7	-
O'Connor, Francis	WM	1	-
O'Connor, Frederick	WM	1	-
O'Connor, Geraldine	WM*	3	-
O'Day, Michael	WM	2	-
O'Dea, William	WM	4	-
O'Gara, Mary	WF	1	-
O'Hara, Francis M.	WM	2	-
O'Hare, Bessie	WM*	7	-
Olivia, Mary	WF	1	-
Olwell, Helen R.	WF	4	-
Olwell, Rose M.	WF	4	-
Olzewski, Edward	WM	7	-
O'Malley, Margaret	WF	5	-
O'Neil, Raymond	WM	2	-
O'Neill, Robt.	WM	5	-
Onesta, Loretta	WF	7	-
Onesto, Arma	WF	3	-
Opperman, Muriel	WF	1	-
O'Rourke, Catherine	WF	17	Nurse
O'Rourke, Joseph	WM	1	-

O'Rourke, Robt. E.	WM	4	-
Otto, Bertha	WF	1	-
Otto, Henry	WM	2	-
Otto, Richard	WM	5	-
Packenham, Wm.	WM	4	-
Paczkowski, Helen	WF	19	Nurse
Palermo, Mario	WM	3	-
Palmedo, Harold	WM	10	-
Palmer, Dorothy	WF	83d	-
Palmer, Eddie	WM	10	-
Palumbo, Bernard	WM	5	-
Parksdale, Christina	BF	12	-
Parmarici, Elizabeth	WF	4	-
Pascal, Catherine	WF	1	-
Paszklowski, Bronslava	WF	1	-
Pata, Dominick	WM	9	-
Patti, Nicholas	WM	1	-
Paulo, Catherine	WF	5	-
Pavelka, John	WM	7	-
Payne, Victor	WM	10	-
Pears, Clara	WF	2	-
Peccitti, Mary J.	WF	9	-
Pedrazzano, Leo	WM	3	-
Pedruzzi, Anna	WF	1	-
Pegorske, Francis	WM	3	-
Pepe, Donald	WM	3	-
Perrino, Emanuel	WM	5	-
Perrino, Francessa	WM	7	-
Perritti, Dorothy	WF	5	-
Perry, Catherine	WF	3	-
Perry, Loretta	WF	3	-
Peterson, Arnold	BM	1	-
Petrelli, John	WM	1	-
Petrocelli, John	WM	3	-
Petrocelli, Nicholas	WM	3	-
Petrone, Jeanne	WF	5	-
Pfansch, Beatrice	BF	13	-
Pfeiffer, Irene	WF	2, 6m	-
Phelan, Catherine	WF	5	-
Phillips, James	WM	9	-
Picone, Vincent	WM	7	-
Pigliese, Concetta	WF	1	-

Pigliese, Mary	WF	4	-
Pinko, Adolph	WM	8	-
Pirano, Stephen	WM	6	-
Pisani, Catherine	WF	1	-
Piso, Yolanda	WF	2	-
Pitonzo, Carmello	WM	7	-
Pleva, Fannie	WF	1	-
Plukofsky, Alexandra	WF	1	-
Pochucouski, Casimar	WM	10	-
Poggi, Antonio	WM	9	-
Polaccini, Louis	WM	9	-
Poliato, Kate	WF	5	-
Pollard, John	WM	2	-
Pollichetti, Eugene	WM	5	-
Porromo, Pauline	WF	1	-
Postiglione, Marie	WF	2	-
Potter, Francis	WM	11	-
Pratt, Alfred	WM	2	-
Pravata, Thomas	WM	1	-
Prendergast, Mary F.	WF	1	-
Prisco, George	WM	2	-
Procopio, Clara	WF	1	-
Procopio, Clement	WM	2	-
Prusko, Josephine	WF	4	-
Putralga, Paul	WM	9	-
Quartucci, Frank	WM	1, 6m	-
Quast, Joseph L.	WM	1	-
Quigley, Eugene	WM	3	-
Quinlan, Winifred	WM	6	-
Quinn, James	WM	1	-
Quinn, John	WM	1	-
Rabanick, John	WM	2	-
Radowitch, Mollie	WF	4	-
Ragusa, Joseph	WM	2	-
Railing, Clarence	WM	11	-
Ramero, Andrew	WM	2	-
Ramero, John	WM	5	-
Randino, Nunziata	WM	9	-
Rango, Anthony	WM	8	-
Ranieri, Josephine	WF	5	-
Ranovitch, Ester	WM*	2, 6m	-
Raphael, Unesto	WF	9	-

Rautchie, Vincent	WM	9	-
Ravizza, David	WM	1	-
Reccobene, Alfred	WM	7	-
Reddy, Joan	WM	2	-
Redict, John	BM	12	-
Reeves, Madeline	WF	1	-
Reid, John E.	WM	1	-
Reynolds, Joseph	WM	49d	-
Rheinhardt, Eliza	WF	19	Nurse
Rheinhardt, Mary	WF	1	-
Rice, Joseph	WM	10	-
Ried, Harry	WM	8	-
Riley, Cecilia	WF	11	-
Riley, Rita	WF	4	-
Rinaldi, Vito	WM	12	-
Rinoldo, Adolfa	WM	3	-
Riordan, Anna	WF	1	-
Ripperty, John	WM	9	-
Robinson, Frances	WF	2	-
Robinson, Robert	WM	3	-
Robinson, Walter	BM	13	-
Rocco, Jerry	WM	4	-
Rocco, Lillian	WF	1	-
Roche, Robert	WM	2, 6m	-
Rock, Bruno	WM	6	-
Rodesky, Theodore	WM	4	-
Rodriguez, Lydia	WF	2	-
Rodriguez, Raymond	WM	4	-
Roeder, Joseph	WM	9	-
Rohrs, Sarah	WM	9	-
Rokitzka, Stanislaus	WM	1	-
Rootze, Herbert	BM	14	-
Rorodko, Wm.	WM	9	-
Rosen, Joseph	WM	10	-
Rosky, Anna	WF	14	-
Rosseau, Agnes	WF	1	-
Rowan, Alma	WF	7	-
Rowley, Leslie	BM	13	-
Rubicco, Geo.	WM	166d	-
Ruckert, Leonard	WM	2	-
Ruffano, Philomena	WF	1	-
Ruffer, Arthur	WM	1	-

Ruffrano, Anna	WF	3	-
Rummingham, James	WM	9	-
Rush, Charles	WM	1	-
Russell, Florence	WF	1	-
Russell, Lillian	WF	5	-
Russell, Ruth	WF	4	-
Russo, Carlo	WM	1	-
Rutigliano, Alfred	WM	1	-
Ryan, Catherine	WF	4	-
Ryan, Geraldine	WF	1	-
Ryan, Helen	WF	20	Nurse
Ryan, Joseph	WM	10	-
Ryan, Robert B.	WM	7	-
Sabato, Mary	WF	6	-
Sabella, Katie	WF	7	-
Salvatoro, Anna	WF	9	-
Sammis, Ralph	WM	9	-
Sandford, Margaret	WF	9	-
Sands, Anna	WF	3	-
Sanford, Inez	WF	11	-
Sansone, Dominic	WM	4	-
Sansone, Joseph	WM	6	-
Santoro, Angelo	WM	9	-
Santoro, Mary	WF	9	-
Santucci, Rosario	WF	1	-
Sapienzo, Agnes	WF	1	-
Saraceno, Josephine	WF	5	-
Sassa, Antoinette	WF	20	Nurse
Sassa, Ernest	WM	67d	-
Sayers, John	WM	10	-
Scamponi, Raphael	WM	6	-
Scarano, Joseph	WM	6	-
Scarano, Josephine	WF	2, 6m	-
Scarano, Millie	WF	5	-
Scelsi, Irene	WF	3	-
Schaffler, Charles	WM	9	-
Scheaffler, Joseph	WM	8	-
Schiefele, Francis	WM	7	-
Schoonmaker, Morgan	BM	2	-
Schultz, Dorothy	WF	4	-
Schwartz, Rose	WF	9	-
Scolaro, Joseph	WM	7	-

Scott, George	WM	10	-
Scott, Helen	WF	1	-
Scott, Walter	WM	4	-
Scura, Martina	WF	4	-
Serw, Annie	WF	6	-
Sharpley, Dorothy	WF	8	-
Shaw, Edward	WM	3	-
Shea, Gloria	WF	1	-
Shearer, Anna	WF	2	-
Sheridan, Mary	WF	2, 6m	-
Sheridan, Philip	WM	7	-
Sheridan, Thomas	WM	1	-
Shermi, Lucy	WF	5	-
Shiaro, Anthony	WM	7	-
Shields, Edward	WM	9	-
Shiro, Mary	WF	7	-
Shopmyer, Ethel	WF	1	-
Sica, Joseph	WM	2	-
Siegel, Jane	WF	10	-
Sienkiewics, Edna	WF	7	-
Signorella, Anala	WF	9	-
Simien, Mark	WM	11	-
Simino, Rinaldo	WM	5	-
Simmons, Adolphus	BM	11	-
Simone, Mary	WF	7	-
Simpson, Dorothy	BF	13	-
Simpson, Edward	WM	2	-
Sirle, Victor	WM	1	-
Sivenson, Dorothy	WF	5	-
Smith, Agnes	WF	72d	-
Smith, Albert	WM	1	-
Smith, Bernard	WM	4	-
Smith, Catherine	WF	1	-
Smith, Catherine	WF	10	-
Smith, Charles	WM	3	-
Smith, Daniel	WM	2	-
Smith, Elizabeth	WF	5	-
Smith, Frank	BM	7	-
Smith, Gerald	WM	5	-
Smith, Gertrude	BF	13	-
Smith, Helen	BF	59d	-
Smith, Helen	WF	4	-

Smith, Helen	BF	5	-
Smith, James	WM	4	-
Smith, John	WM	3	-
Smith, John	BM	6	-
Smith, Joseph	WM	1	-
Smith, Joseph	BM	8	-
Smith, Joseph	WM	10	-
Smith, Lillian	WF	9	-
Smith, Lloyd	BM	5	-
Smith, Margaret	WF	1	-
Smith, Margaret M.	WF	2	-
Smith, Michael	WM	1	-
Smith, Steadman	BM	14	-
Smith, Thomas	WM	10	-
Smith, Timothy	WM	4	-
Snozzo, Josephine	WF	6	-
Sonn, Charles	WM	9	-
Sopko, Helen	WF	1	-
Sopko, Joseph	WM	3	-
Sorley, Edward	WM	3	-
Sorriero, Josephine	WF	1	-
Spann, Robert	BM	14	-
Stark, Eugene	WM	10	-
Stein, Mary	WF	9	-
Stevens, Clarence	WM	9	-
Stevens, Emily	WF	10	-
Stevens, Mary	WF	6	-
Stevenson, Joseph	WM	86d	-
Stevenson, Josephine	BF	19	Nurse
Stewart, Charles	WM	9	-
Steyne, Robert. G.	WM	3	-
Stone, Florence	WF	19	Nurse
Stone, Raymond	WM	62d	-
Straub, Elizabeth	WF	5	-
Strong, Raymond	WM	10	-
Suachick, John	WM	5	-
Sulivan, Henry	WM	9	-
Suliveres, Letitia	WF	1	-
Suliveres, Louis	WM	4	-
Suliveres, Octavius	WF*	3	-
Sullivan, Cornelius	WM	9	-
Sullivan, Frances	WF	5	-

Sullivan, John	WM	5	-
Sullivan, Mortimer	WM	7	-
Sullivan, Nellie	WF	9	-
Sullivan, Patrick	WM	9	-
Sullivan, Rita	WF	176d	-
Sullivan, Rita	WF	2	-
Sullivan, Wm.	BM	10	-
Suozzo, Dominick	WM	1	-
Supko, Louis	WM	1	-
Sutton, John	BM	3	-
Swan, Wm.	WM	10	-
Sweeney, John	WM	9	-
Sweet, Natalie	WF	114d	-
Tackel, George	WM	10	-
Takmyro, Johanna	WF	10	-
Tanzi, Antoinetta	WF	2	-
Tardebono, Catherine	WF	4	-
Tatum, Robert	WM	1	-
Teague, John	WM	1	-
Terella, Jennie	WF	3	-
Testone, Domonic	WM	6	-
Thesere, Catherine	WF	2	-
Thomas, Evelyn	WF	1	-
Thomas, Geo.	WM	3	-
Thomas, Philip	WM	3	-
Thornton, Margaret	WF	4	-
Timbo, Felix	WM	11	-
Timms, John	WM	5	-
Tinnerillo, Dominick	WM	5	-
Tinnerillo, James	WM	1	-
Tobin, Alice	WF	3	-
Tofty, Alma Helen	WF	6	-
Tofty, Kenneth	WM	3	-
Tracy, Joseph	WM	2	-
Treglio, Anna	WF	3	-
Trezza, Lillian	WF	1	-
Truatt, Jos.	BM	9	-
Tucker, Herbert	WM	10	-
Turgeon, Mary	WF	19	Nurse
Turner, Catherine	WF	1	-
Tyler, Rose	WF	176d	-
Tyson, George	BM	8	-

Ulland, Robert	WM	1, 9m	-
Unietis, John	WM	1	-
Vacchio, Luke	WM	9	-
Vagnini, Joseph	WM	1	-
Valdes, Aurelio	WM	1	-
Valdes, Valma	WF	1	-
Valenzo, Antonio	WM	1	-
Varcarielli, Joseph	WM	2	-
Vasta, Carmela	WF	4	-
Vasta, Joseph	WM	4	-
Venable, Virginia	WF	9	-
Venezia, Nicholas	WM	10	-
Venezzia, Mario	WM	9	-
Verdicchio, Joseph	WM	1	-
Vincent, Thomas	WM	120d	-
Visconti, Gennaro	WM	6	-
Vitale, Josephine	WF	6	-
Vlordt, Wm.	BM	13	-
VonBatenburg, Geo.	WM	1	-
Vrgosh, Mary	WF	5	-
Vzsea, Anthony	WM	11	-
Wagner, Isabel	BF	9	-
Wallace, Kenneth	WM	3	-
Walsh, Alice	WF	5	-
Walsh, Catherine	WF	3	-
Walsh, Catherine	WF	9	-
Walsh, Edward	WM	3	-
Walsh, Jane	WF	177d	-
Walsh, Mary	WF	1	-
Walter, Madeline	WF	9	-
Warner, Cecelia	WF	9	-
Warren, Charles	WM	1	-
Watkins, Robert	WM	2	-
Weatherbee, Raymond	WM	2	-
Weber, Joseph	WM	7	-
Weber, Loretta	WF	7	-
Weck, John	WM	137d	-
Weck, Marie	WF	17	Nurse
Weeks, Alice	WF	20	Nurse
Weeks, Thomas	WM	1	-
Weiss, John	WM	9	-
Weisse, Philip	WM	2, 6m	-

Wenck, Florence	WF	4	-
Wenger, Theodore	WM	3	-
Weninger, Catherine	WF	8	-
Werner, Elfreda	WF	8	-
Wetzel, Elsie	WF	1	-
Whidbee, Charles	BM	12	-
White, Joseph	WM	198d	-
White, Josephine	WF	3	-
White, Margaret	WF	5	-
White, Mary	WF	2	-
Wicknar, Elizabeth	WF	2	-
Wiles, Herbert	WM	7	-
Willett, Afred	WM	5	-
Willett, Arthur	WM	3	-
Williams, Caroline	WF	18	Nurse
Williams, Edith	BF	11	-
Williams, Elizabeth	BF	14	-
Williams, Florence	BF	2	-
Williams, Francis	WM	113d	-
Williams, Helen	BF	15	-
Williams, John	WM	10	-
Williams, Loraine	BF	2	-
Wilson, George	BM	15	-
Winters, Gregory	BM	42d	-
Wolfe, Arthur	BM	10	-
Wolk, Joseph	WM	9	-
Wood, Paul	WM	9	-
Woodley, Arthur	BM	9	-
Woodley, Walter	BM	9	-
Woods, Alexander	WM	2	-
Young, Mary	WF	131d	-
Zabro, Adeline	WF	4	-
Zaccaro, Frank	WM	9	-
Zeehandelsar, Agnes	WF	2	-
Zeigler, Richard	WM	1	-
Zeltman, Robert	WM	9	-
Ziegler, Josephine	WF	18	Nurse
Zientara, Elizabeth	WF	1	-
Zinna, Florence	WF	3	-
Zipp, Andrew	WM	9	-

9 780806 345901